The Artistic Censoring of Sexuality

The Artistic Censoring of Sexuality

FANTASY AND
JUDGMENT IN THE
TWENTIETH-CENTURY
NOVEL

Susan Mooney

THE OHIO STATE UNIVERSITY PRESS
Columbus

Copyright © 2008 by The Ohio State University.
All rights reserved.

Library of Congress Cataloging-in-Publication Data
Mooney, Susan.
　The artistic censoring of sexuality : fantasy and judgment in the twentieth century novel / Susan Mooney.
　　　p. cm.
　Includes bibliographical references (p.　) and index.
　ISBN-13: 978-0-8142-1082-6 (alk. paper)
　1. Fiction—20th century—History and criticism. 2. Sex in literature. 3. Censorship—History—20th century. I. Title.
　PN3352.S48M66 2008
　809.3'93538—dc22

　　　　　　　　　　　　　　　　　　　　　　2007032766

This volume is available in the following editions:
Cloth (ISBN 978-0-8142-1082-6)
CD-ROM (ISBN 978-0-8142-9161-0)
Paper (ISBN: 978-0-8142-5741-8)
Cover design by Dan O'Dair
Text design and typesetting by Jennifer Shoffey Forsythe
Type set in Adobe Bembo

For Kees

Contents

PREFACE
Sexuality in Literature: Toward an Ethics · *ix*

ACKNOWLEDGMENTS · *xvii*

INTRODUCTION
The Sense of Censoring · *1*

CHAPTER 1
Censorship: Political and Theoretical Structures · *23*

CHAPTER 2
Circean Censoring: Joyce's Theater of Judgment in *Ulysses* · *39*

CHAPTER 3
Lolita: American Mimetic Fantasy, Ethical Reading, and Censoring Narrative · *112*

CHAPTER 4
The Masochistic Pleasure of Censoring Modes of Fantasy: Alienation, Cancer, and Judgment in *Tiempo de silencio* · *161*

CHAPTER 5
Apocalyptic Beauty, Russian Sublimity: Viktor Erofeev's *Russkaia krasavitsa* · *215*

CONCLUSION
Comparative Reflections · *268*

APPENDIX
Summaries of Novels' Historical Censorship · *277*

WORKS CITED · *279*

INDEX · *309*

Preface

SEXUALITY IN LITERATURE: TOWARD AN ETHICS

*Sex*uality has often had an uneasy relationship to art. Art aspires to beauty, sublimity, and eros, and surveys a shifting border of acceptability of sexual expression. Today, as through the twentieth century, sex in art can potentially degrade the form to mere pornography. Yet sexuality is close to the core of understanding ourselves and our social life, so omitting it from artistic discourse altogether is nowadays seen as prudish or repressive. This perception is the result of a twentieth-century historical trajectory when, in Europe and North America, the modern novel became increasingly the site for creative exploration of sexual themes and references. To include sexuality became a mark of social progressiveness and artistic innovation, dual aims evident in modernist and postmodernist novels of leading innovators such as James Joyce, Vladimir Nabokov, Luis Martín-Santos, and Viktor Erofeev.

In fact, despite these authors' and novels' very different chronological, cultural, and political contexts, they all seek to make sexuality a central social issue, a key to understanding our weaknesses and inequalities. While sexuality in literature can offer eroticized aesthetic pleasure, it is also problematized critically by the inclusion of social considerations of the status of women, pornography, prostitution, marriage and interpersonal relationships, reproduction and fertility, and of the status of men as purveyors, consumers, fantasists, and masters of sexuality. The contemplation of sexuality has the human subject reflect back on himself or herself, as is the case with the three male protagonists of the first three novels, and with Irina, the female protagonist of the fourth novel. Thus narrative avenues of masculinity and femininity are explored, often revealing the modern human subject in deep conflict. Sexuality is also politicized in these novels because their national social settings (British colonial 1904 Dublin in *Ulysses;* pre-WWII France and democratic 1944–1952 America in *Lolita;* 1949 Madrid and Spain under Franco in *Tiempo de silencio;* the Soviet Union of the late 1970s in *Russkaia krasavitsa*). We are prompted to reflect critically on the actual performance of the respective countries and their governments and social institutions.

Censoring sexuality is an artistic act. These novels' treatment of sexuality emphasizes how language is regulated. To express the condition of sexuality, these novels present it as something that needs to be both confronted and censored artistically—that is, judged, negated, elided, screened over, or transformed. Censoring is part of the writing process, creating choices that negotiate the degree of explicitness. Sexuality seems to contain knowledge, power, and freedom. Yet these novels use it to reveal social problems and degradation of ethical values; thus, they suggest alternative ways of knowing, beyond dominant discourses and national master narratives. To achieve a critical investigation, raise questions, and solicit readerly judgment, the authors do not elevate the protagonists in their explorations of sexuality to heroic status, but rather, situate them, at best, in critical frameworks.

By selecting these four novels that all experienced some degree of censorship in their early publication years, I have aimed to gain a view of their differences and similarities in relation to their cultural and sociopolitical contexts as well as explore each novel's project with sexuality. Why include sexuality in a narrative? What kind of meaning and complications does sexuality add to characterization, plot, and themes?

The aim to censor or control sexuality in literature has similar motivations and origins across the decades and political and legal systems. If we agree with Michel Foucault that the twentieth century became a confessional society, then we may propose that sexuality divulged in literature is offered for analysis and judgment, as well as for potential pleasure. The countries involved in these novels' censorship—England, Ireland, the United States, France, Spain, and (Soviet) Russia—provide a twentieth-century sampling of different cultures' and societies' persistent, common need to censor the disseminated expression of sexuality in literature. This question of the need to censor is further complicated by the twentieth century's

marked liberalization of the freedom to express sexuality in an increasingly diverse range of media.[1]

In the context of the twentieth-century novel in Europe and North America, I suggest that there are two basic artistic approaches to the treatment of sex in fiction. These two approaches share an interest in sexuality as both a source for critical social commentary and an artistic innovation. However, their paths diverge in terms of how that commentary and innovation should be carried out. The four novels chosen for this study share the first approach, which includes irony, intertextuality, self-reflectiveness, and suggestion. Meanwhile, the second approach finds examples in the novels by D. H. Lawrence and Henry Miller. Novels of this latter group tend toward a remarkable expressive explicitness in portraying sexuality and a strong sense of didacticism or militancy; they also tend to avoid intertextuality, allusion, substitution, irony, and other modes of complicating or diversifying interpretation. At times, the didactic tone or message counterbalances to some degree the explicitness.[2]

In the four novels of this study, sexual portrayals can be seen in the following ways: (1) as artistic negotiations with ethical values vis-à-vis sexuality and the censorial forces of both the human subject and society; (2) as representations of, or references to, what cannot or should not be known (*das Ding*) (thus these particular novels do not strive toward full explicitness; they employ a good deal of allusion and substitution, avoid didacticism, use intertextuality and irony as subterfuges and enrichment of the discourse); (3) as attempts to create contemporary narratives of ethics for the individual (his negotiation between the good and the pleasurable) by integrating sexuality into a value system to be judged; (4) as problematic scenarios in which man questions his relations with women (especially prostitution, pornography, marriage and other relationships, reproduction) and his set of values for them (e.g., fantasy, beauty, sublimity, disease, death, seduction, creation).

---

1. For studies on the liberalization of censorship laws (and the problems with these), see Beardsmore; Burt, Introduction, *The Administration of Aesthetics;* Butler; Califa; *Censorship and Freedom of Expression; Censorship and Obscenity; The Censorship of Books; Communications Control;* Craig, *Banned Books* and *Suppressed Books;* Daily; Day; De Grazia; Dollimore; Ernst; Gaskins; Geller; Goodrich, *Languages of Law;* Jonathon Green; Leslie Green; Harrison; Jansen; Langton; Lewis; MacKinnon; McKee; Miller; *Pornography and Censorship;* Post; *Press and Speech Freedoms in the World;* Randall; Robbins; Robins; Schauer; Tribe; *Versions of Censorship.*

2. For critical and historical perspectives on Lawrence in particular, see Goodheart, "Censorship and Self-Censorship" and *Desire and Its Discontents;* Grant; H. Montgomery Hyde. For commentary on Miller, see Bécourt; *La censure en France;* Pauvert. Couturier's *Roman et censure* and De Grazia discuss both authors. De Grazia offers a survey of twentieth-century American censorship of literature, and thus discusses a wide range of authors, legal problems, and changes in laws affecting publishing.

Thus, these novels do not provide clear-cut moral premises or resolutions, but rather offer possibilities of complicated interpretation which would require the reader to take on a provisional judgmental role. The reader's role is challenged by the novels' features relating to sexuality because such passages are designed to delight, shock, disgust, enlighten, offend, and intrigue (and thus can complicate interpretation or judgment).

My inquiry is informed, in part, by Roland Barthes's and Pierre Bourdieu's recognition of the potential power of censorship in our discourse, literary and otherwise. Barthes observes that French literary history can be constituted by a counterhistory of censorship. He catalogues four basics "acts" of censorship: the censorship of social class; of sexuality; of the concept of literature; of language ("Reflections," 73). He reveals an underside of literature, the unwritten history of the conditions that determine the literary text. Barthes's determining "acts" of censorship can be related to Pierre Bourdieu's concept of censorship as an imposition of form. Bourdieu maintains that censorship imposes form on all our communications:

> This structural censorship is exercised through the medium of sanctions of the field, functioning as a market on which the prices of different kinds of expression are formed; it is imposed on all producers of symbolic goods, including the authorized spokesperson, [. . .] and it condemns the occupants of dominated positions either to silence or to shocking outspokenness. (138)

Censorship connects the individual artist (and reader) to institution. The institution's discourse insists on being recognized in some way. The point is that one makes a basic disavowal, conscious or unconscious, in order to "accept" the importance, relevance, or power of the institution: "I know that it is just an arbitrary construction but even so I will go through the motions of its discursive practice. . . ." Bourdieu explains that the ability to impose form can be found in both society and the individual; censorship should not be seen as limited to one particular linguistic, legal, or political mode, although these are significant areas of its manifestations.

In my study, thematic censoring practices belong not only to a variety of institutions (e.g., in *Tiempo de silencio,* these include the Catholic Church, medicine, and Franco's regime) but also to various groups and individuals, especially the protagonists and supporting characters. The censoring practices are played out in dialogues, narration, plot developments, characterizations, metaphor, and other poetic devices.

The treatment of sexuality in these novels has often suggested to readers that there is a way to achieve a certain truth or liberation through revealing sexual knowledge. Through censorship trials and difficulties with publishing certain works, *causes célèbres* were produced. The reader reception of such celebrated works has involved an expectation of heroic and rebellious revelation. In such novels, the sexual can acquire the cachet of some kind of progressive respectability or aesthetic superiority versus a sanitized, innocent, or austere art as supported by puritans and moralist censors.

My study partly responds to Foucault's suggestions that our supposedly "open" society has its own repressive practices; that the manipulation of sexuality in discourse is a method of control, and not one of liberation. In the twentieth century, sexuality has entered public discourses to an unprecedented degree—be they medical, psychoanalytic, legal, philosophical, political, aesthetic, or religious. Sexuality's ample commoditization has become commonplace in the world market. By contrast, in the narrative worlds of these novels, sexuality is integrated into the thematic and aesthetic signifying structures, while in the corresponding contemporary actuality of those novels' settings (be it 1904 Dublin, 1940s and 1950s America, 1949 Madrid, or 1980 Moscow) sexuality was kept marginalized, silenced, or screened in discourses and public communications. In these societies, sexuality, if it actually was named, was subversive and it had the potential to signify pleasure, transgression, danger, and lawlessness.

Foucault's theory of the confessional society relies on tenets of psychoanalysis. Yet he also criticizes its supposedly altruistic therapeutic aim which belies an alliance of power. For example, he sees the endless reworking of the "transcultural theory of the incest taboo" as a way of governing sexuality; and he consequently views this "deployment" of sexuality as one of power or alliance (*The History of Sexuality: An Introduction,* 109–10). He overlooks, however, Freud's and Lacan's repeated criticism of altruism.

Foucault's pessimistic view of power and alliances should be balanced by the observation that we as human subjects seek to have signifying structures to make our lives livable. If we did not have an incest taboo or other features of the Symbolic that provide differentiation (language, law, etc.), how would we have any way of creating signification?[3] Meaning and value are determined through exchange, negotiation, commonly shared usage, disavowals, and also through transgression or abuse. In Wolfgang Iser's terms, a message cannot be communicated unless the sender and receiver share or understand linguistic and cultural codes. In turn, these verbal and interpersonal exchanges necessarily involve issues of power and alliances.

In this book, it is understood that communication involving sexuality also involves power relations. The novels explored do not posit sexuality

---

3. My position is grounded, in part, in Freud's "Civilization and Its Discontents," "Three Essays on Sexuality," *The Interpretation of Dreams,* and *Beyond the Pleasure Principle.*

as some innocent Eden for revelry, but rather as a complicated field of potential pleasure (especially pertaining to men) that also can encroach dangerously, even fatally, on others (especially women). The Iserian implied readers of Joyce, Nabokov, Martín-Santos, and Erofeev are thus not only called upon to engage in the decoding of the complex messages of the aesthetic texts but also to weigh or judge the power relations described in the novels' forays into sexuality.

While we may be concerned by the application of publication censorship and by the potential threat of diminishing our freedom of expression, we should recall that censorship and censoring emphasize important values in civilization. As part of the Law, it functions to regulate and determine acceptable standards for the social group at stake.[4] It also confirms our need to have language maintain its signifying value.

If language did not mean anything, there would be no need or desire to communicate and likewise no need to censor. The combative element of censorship, while admittedly at times unbearably and unnecessarily brutal or didactic in certain societies, is essential to the (re)creation of signification, the exchange of value, and, in particular, the erotically charged conflicts inherent in human sexuality.

The power struggle in censorship is between the Law and subject. While art tries to achieve something more than pure mimesis of life (which in any event would be impossible to achieve), the Law is concerned that glamorous, beautiful, or desirable sexual transgression will inspire readers to change their values and to imitate that art (and perhaps not serve the social good). If lawlessness and sexual transgression are assigned an aesthetic component, then the right of the Law has been challenged, and formally agreed-upon (or presupposed) social values have been questioned.

We could consider a pivotal modern novel's collision with censorship. The *Madame Bovary* trial (1857) exemplified the state's fear that other women readers might copy the protagonist's sexual transgressions and suicide. Ironically, Flaubert had been inspired by some real-life stories of adultery and bankruptcy in the newspapers. Further, his novel appeared

---

4. I use the Lacanian terms the Symbolic, Imaginary, Real, and Law here and throughout my discussion. For Lacan, our existence is divided into three orders or registers. The Symbolic represents language and all our civilization practices and relationships within the codified system. The Symbolic is the determining order of the subject. The Imaginary is the subject's psychic perception (conscious and unconscious) of relations, experiences, and phenomena; the Real is actual reality which, although tangible, can never be directly known (i.e., outside the Symbolic and Imaginary; it is the residue or foreclosed element). The Law refers to laws written and unwritten that regulate our social and civil relations. The Law both signifies the Symbolic Father and is authored by him. See Lacan's *Fundamental Concepts of Psychoanalysis* and Ragland-Sullivan's excellent exploration of these terms.

shortly after a string of French novels highlighting adultery had been published. *Madame Bovary* could thus provide a critical reflection on this special genre. Meanwhile, within his text, Flaubert shows us a young woman who is partly motivated to commit adultery after reading too many romantic novels. Thus he complicated issues of influences and authorial intent.[5]

Like the authors of this study, Flaubert challenged the Law with his artistic inclusion of sexuality. As the novels in this study demonstrate, sexuality challenges not only the Law, but also us in our relation to the Law, our social institutions, our appreciation of art, and our ethics.

---

5. The state's censorial reaction to the potential power of the word was perhaps not as unreasonable as we might think it today when we remember that half a century earlier in Europe there had been many actual emulators of the fictional young Werther: the obsessive wearing of a blue coat and yellow vest as well as the act of suicide.

Acknowledgments

For this book and its earlier embodiments as conference papers and dissertation, I must recognize the generosity and enrichment extended to me by several people and organizations: Mario Valdés, as teacher and illuminator of hermeneutics; Jean-Michel Rabaté for his inspirational teaching of modernism and psychoanalytic theory; the members of my dissertation defense committee—Roland Le Huenen, Garry Leonard, Christopher Barnes, Edward Chamberlin, and Jorg Bochow—for their encouragement and critiques; Linda Hutcheon for invaluable guidance in my education and the profession, the early planning of this study, and more recently for her wise counsel; the University of Toronto for doctoral grants and especially the travel grants that allowed me to conduct research in Moscow, Barcelona, and Madrid; Manuel Abellán for sharing his experience of investigating Spanish censorship and urging me to consult the Archivo General de la Administración in Alcalá de Henares; Marianna Tax Choldin and Paul Goldschmidt for their support in dialogue with my explorations of the Russian and Soviet histories of censorship; Ekaterina Genieva, Director General, Library of Foreign Literature in Moscow, and the staff in the library's International Relations Department for their organization of my stay in Moscow.

Aspects of this study were presented in the following conference papers:

"Joyce's Theatre of Judgment: The Scene of 'Circe'" (The Twelfth Annual Comparative Literature Colloquium, Centre for Comparative Literature, University of Toronto, April 19, 2001); "Sexuality Framed by Censoring: Soviet Censorship and Viktor Erofeev's *Russkaia krasavitsa*" (American Association for the Advancement of Slavic Studies 31st National Convention, St. Louis, Missouri, November 19, 1999); "Behind the Scene of Publishing Nabokov's *Lolita*: Post-Publication Censorship of the Sexually Obscene in Britain, France, and the U.S. in the 1950s" (Seventh Annual SHARP Conference [Society for the History of Authorship, Reading, and Publishing], Madison, Wisconsin, July 16, 1999).

I thank the organizers and discussants in these sessions.

Herman Ermolaev and Edward DeGrazia offered helpful commentary and encouragement.

In recent months, several special individuals deserve my sincere gratitude: Hunt Hawkins and James Phelan for their encouragement and guidance; the manuscript's anonymous external reviewers, whose insights helped the rigor of discussion; Sandy Crooms, senior editor at OSUP, for her grace and savvy professionalism. All the OSUP staff involved in producing this book are offered particular thanks, including Eugene O'Connor, managing editor, and Mary Read, copyeditor.

Finally, and most especially, I'm indebted to Kees Boterbloem, steadfast reader, resourceful respondent, and historian extraordinaire.

Introduction

THE SENSE OF CENSORING

This book explores four novels written under historical censorship conditions in their respective places of composition and publication: Great Britain, Ireland, France, the United States, Spain, and Soviet Russia. Owing to their controversially artistic treatment of sexuality, James Joyce's *Ulysses* (1922), Vladimir Nabokov's *Lolita* (1955), Luis Martín-Santos's *Tiempo de silencio* (1961; *Time of Silence*), and Viktor Erofeev's *Russkaia krasavitsa* (1990; *Russian Beauty*) became landmark cases of historical censorship.[1] Each novel, in its early publication history, was the object of court trials, bannings, rejection by publishers, and prepublication censors' cuts. The conservative sensibility and criteria for these forms of censorship were remarkably similar, despite differences in time, region, and obvious cultural and political features. The United States and Great Britain of the 1920s through 1960s did not essentially differ in their resistance to

---

1. While I have consulted a variety of editions of these novels, I use the following editions for direct quotations. For *Ulysses,* I cite the Gabler edition; Jeri Johnson's edition of the 1922 text is helpful for some notes to the text. For *Lolita* discussions, I make use of Appel's *The Annotated Lolita* (which keeps the pagination of many Vintage editions). For *Tiempo de silencio,* I use the definitive edition of 1980, supplemented by comparisons with other editions. See the introductory note in chapter 4 for more details. For *Russkaia krasavitsa,* I quote from the uncensored Russian version of 1994; I have compared the censored edition (1990) and subsequent uncensored Russian editions of the novel. Andrew Reynolds's English translation, *Russian Beauty* (1992), is generally satisfactory for direct quotations (although I have occasionally pointed out some nuances in the Russian original for non-Russian readers).

publishing certain sexual expressions from the censors of the Soviet Union (1917–1990) and Franco's Spain (1939–1975).

Censorship signifies on textual and extratextual levels, in literature and life, and no civilization is without some taboos that help to set parameters and transform human life and creative production. Twentieth-century novelists in Europe and America sought to make the sexual subject critical in literature by integrating motifs and stratagems of censoring. This book investigates how censorship themes and techniques have shaped the meaning of the sexuality in the twentieth-century novel, thus requiring the reader's critical judgment. This invocation complicates possible explicit claims to truth. Censoring acts as a creative form of writing that both veils the sexual subject and implicates themes of judgment, condemnation, and negation.

In the selected novels for this study, the reader's role as judge (through interpretative activity) implicitly confirms a commonly felt but often tacit need (or desire) to evaluate sexuality, especially our ethical involvement in it. With modernism's and postmodernism's foregrounding of textual self-consciousness, literary sexuality has posed a puzzle.

I have selected these four novels because they were considered particularly provocative in their day for their representation of sexuality. I wanted to determine how they integrated sexuality in the novel and which sexual features prompted censors to respond. As we shall see, the novelists integrated actual motifs of censoring in their deployment of sexuality so that censoring became paradoxically a productive, generative set of practices. In terms of thematic integration of sexuality, the writers tend to embed it in the modernist domains of the mind—such as fantasy—and the modernist and postmodernist registers of the existential—namely, judgment. These authors offer sexuality as fantasy at a price: it must be evaluated by powers of judgment, thus pushing the boundaries of artistic expression of their time.

In this book, my special use of the term "censoring" intends to demarcate it from the connotations of historical pre- and postpublication censorship and the psychoanalytic censorship. "Censoring" of course derives some signification and strategies from these censorships. But as a hybrid term, it particularly connotes the activity and artistic production of censorship in a literary text.

Let us first then consider how forms of publication censorship originate in modern European languages and become a varied practice in our production and circulation of written discourse. I will then turn to the operations of psychic censorship, and finally the artistic censoring of sexuality in literature, in order to set the parameters of the literary analysis of the four novels.

1. CENSORSHIP: ETYMOLOGY AND HISTORICAL PRACTICES

"*Censor*"'s Latin origins involve an essential duality that is never lost through the centuries. *Censor* and its adjuncts in most Romance, Germanic, and Slavic languages derive from the Latin noun *censor*, from the verb *censere*, "to give as one's opinion, recommend, assess" (*Oxford English Dictionary*). In the ancient Roman republic, there were two official censors: one who kept the register or census of citizens and one who supervised manners and morals. In late antiquity, with the institutionalization of censorship, these two responsibilities became combined and were related to the powers of the church or state. With Pope Innocent I (r. 401–17) and his list of forbidden books, books were submitted to postpublication censorship by the church, a formal process. A millennium later, the effort to exercise control over the written word became far more complicated, as a result of the invention of book printing in the West. As Norman Davies explains, after Gutenberg's invention around 1450 in Mainz, "presses spread quickly to Basle (1466), Rome (1467), Pilzno in Bohemia (1468), Paris (1470), Buda (1473), Cracow (1474), Westminster (1476), and Cetinje in Montenegro (1493). Printing reache d Moscow in 1555" (*Europe*, 445). We can see that in a mere hundred years the press became distributed through Europe, simultaneously accompanied by practices of official censorship.

Printing developed at various rates and was controlled diversely in Europe, and then, with European expansion, in the New World. Despite the accelerated pace of new printing technology, the production of printed matter did not bypass regulated application of criteria designated by religious or political authority. To consider one example of real practice, we could take Russia. It was one of the last countries in Europe to acquire the press, and then its presses were extremely limited in number (no more than three) and under the tsars' direct control. Russia thus developed a deeply ingrained tradition of rigorous censorship of literature from the press's inception through to the period of 1905–1917, when censorship was briefly relaxed. Prior censorship resumed its hold through the entire Soviet period, with only some marked relaxation of practices in the final years of the regime under glasnost' (1986–1991).

Overall, in each country, writing and censorship go hand in hand; one is not produced without the other. Writing is conditioned by writers' awareness of, and sensitivity to, contemporary and prior publication and censorship standards and criteria. The stricter the censorship conditions, the more attuned good writers need to be to subtle (and not so subtle) signs of what is permissible by judging contemporary publications, both of books and periodicals, the latter providing a more immediate sense of political and moral criteria.

Censorship had an early symbiotic relationship with printing, arbitrating the growth and development of print culture. Davies reminds us of how power worked both ways in this relationship:

> The power of the printed word inevitably aroused the fears of the religious authorities. Hence Mainz, the cradle of the press, also became the cradle of censorship. In 1485, the local ruler, the Archbishop-Elector, asked the city council of nearby Frankfurt-am-Main to examine books to be exhibited at the Lenten Fair, and to help in the suppression of dangerous publications. (445)

These early European beginnings set up a continuous and conditioning relationship between censorship and subsequent writing practices over the ages. The legal offices of censorship have followed and adjusted to changing forms of state power and authority, as well as to the status of the writer. With the rise in constitutional monarchies, liberal democracies, and modern market economies, writers moved away from patronage to self-employment. The advent of copyright laws further determined an individual and responsible role of the artist.

The slackening of censorship does not eliminate it. In a liberal democracy, in general, the activity of censorship is widely dispersed through the law and society, whereas in repressive regimes it is usually concentrated as a designated office.

The development of institutionalized censorship practices in Europe over the centuries varied according to factors of religion, government, economy, literate population, and cultural values and interests. The nineteenth century witnessed the steady and rapid growth of literacy and printed materials. With these, we note a paternalistic concern for the effects of these materials on a growing reading public, especially on women and children.[2] Governments, educators, collective groups, and private individuals contributed to this conservative, at times reactionary, regulating trend. By the late nineteenth century, copyright redefined the concept of authors as individuals owning a creative product. Copyright as a contract connotes responsibil-

---

2. This movement derives from state initiatives in legislation or law enforcement and from individuals who took a passionate interest in censorship. Perrin describes Dr. Bowdler and his legacy. Sharing Bowdler's concern for sanitary reading conditions for the people were the various self-appointed societies for the suppression of vice which emerged in Great Britain and the United States during the nineteenth century. De Grazia and others have researched the contributions to American censorship made by Anthony Comstock. The Anglo-American tradition particularly includes a citizen-based participation in control (which demonstrates the communal, social needs, and dynamics of censorship and the danger of simplifying criteria to one basic readership).

ity and a degree of poetic license.³ In the emerging liberal democracies of western Europe in the 1800s, prepublication censorship offices were replaced by various legislative measures to effect a postpublication censorship of offensive materials.⁴ As a result, in such states, the Catholic Church's index of prohibited books came to represent one opinion among many in terms of general censorship and publication practices.

Generally, the nineteenth and twentieth centuries have witnessed fluctuating censorship offensives depending on various arbitrary factors, such as whether a potentially offensive work had a large print run and distribution, its author was well known, or its text well written. In liberal democracies, the onus of the publishing decision fell usually upon the writer along with his editor or publisher (and at times on printers or book dealers). Using his discretion and knowledge of what was currently acceptable in society, an author decided on the text's form and message. If the risk of prosecution seemed too great, he would probably revise or not publish, although the history of censorship shows that some significant writers have dared to overstep the contemporary demarcations of morality or decency. That kind of daring could have painful personal consequences, experienced by such different writers as Gustave Flaubert, Thomas Hardy, Radclyffe Hall, Mikhail Bulgakov, and Juan Goytisolo, as well as the writers focused on in this study.

In the twentieth century, one can recognize two fundamental ways for a state or society to apply publication censorship to an author's artistic expression. Here Bourdieu's concept of the "imposition of form" finds expression in law. First, in liberal democracies, censorship is applied through the judiciary system. A work must first be published and then, if it gives offense in some way, it may be suppressed through legal action or through the postal or customs office, public libraries, or schools. Twentieth-century liberal democracies have seen the laws and procedures that impose forms of censorship change dramatically toward a liberal ideal of freedom of expression. Definitions of "obscene" and "immoral," which have traditionally relied on some tautology and the assumption that the "obscene" corrupts youthful or easily influenced readers, have been replaced by measurement of standards according to contemporary trends and local community or zoning needs (e.g., regulated placement, number, and management of adult venues [bookshops, video stores, etc.] in a municipality).

Most liberal democracies have been obliged to reassess the balance between freedoms and rights of writing and reading at various junctures

3. See Birrell; Lyman Ray Patterson.
4. See Hudon; LaCapra; Levine; Joss Marsh, *Word Crimes;* Née; Perrin; Walsh; Weeks, *Sex, Politics, and Society.*

throughout the twentieth century. What has been a continuous trend is the fact that there has generally not been a *prior censorship* (or prepublication censorship) of literary works in most liberal democracies in the twentieth century.[5] This trend reflects the democratic judiciary principles of being innocent until proven guilty and the need to show a burden of proof. In print culture and regulation, these legal tenets have contributed to a general liberal-democratic movement toward an ideal of "flexible legality."[6]

By contrast, in dictatorial regimes, such as Franco's Spain or the Soviet Union, preemptive censorship takes on hardened forms, offices, and bureaucratic and punitive procedures. Simply put, nondemocratic regimes assume a writer's lack of innocence; the burden of proof lies in the manuscript which must be submitted for review and permission before publication.[7] Unlike the democratic ideal of flexible legality, the nondemocratic ideal would appear to be an immutable legality. Moreover, these regimes tend to bind together state leadership with the law. Many repressive regimes install and maintain a prepublication censorship bureaucracy on the pretext that it is a temporary, military action to deal with a national state of emergency.

5. By contrast, plays and films have fallen into a different category and have undergone censorship assessment prior to performance or screening. Great Britain's prior censorship of theater lasted until the 1960s; the Licencing Act (1737), which allowed for the Lord Chamberlain's prior review and approval prior to performance, was repealed only in 1968. Another form of censorship has been an attack on the author himself: witness the intriguing phenomenon that was the trial of Oscar Wilde of 1895, potentially setting subsequent twentieth-century authors on the defensive. E. M. Forster, to mention one prominent modernist, did not publish in his lifetime works referring to homosexuality (e.g., *Maurice;* "The Other Boat"). While an analysis of these issues is beyond the aim of this book, they remind us that twentieth-century liberal democracies have resorted to what today we generally consider unjust or overly paternalistic control of artistic production. In the first case, the communal experience of theater and explosive consequences of a scandalous work have been deemed reasons for prior censorship. Theater in such cases is considered a powerful, political, and public medium; this medium's effect must therefore be anticipated and possibly curtailed by the censor in order to avoid public disorder. In the second case, a writer's fictional texts (especially drama) are used as evidence to condemn him in court for his private relationships. Wilde's trial curiously reversed the elements of a traditional censor's ad hominem attack on a writer's text; in some ways, Wilde's trial realized many authors' private censorship fears. Also compare Wilde's trial with Flaubert's (see LaCapra's Madame Bovary *on Trial* and Née's "1857: Le double procès de Madame Bovary et des *Fleurs du mal*").

6. For more on this concept, see my chapter 1 and Gaskins, 8–9.

7. Our assessments are complicated by many censorship-related issues that can arise with prior censorship. Authors' reputations, connections, and nonliterary activities can influence whether they will be permitted to publish. Furthermore, published authors and their works may suffer from post-censorship strategies (conducted by various authorities in a repressive regime) such as restricting print runs, distribution, promotion, engineering negative reviews in well-known publications, fines, jailing, prosecuting and sentencing under criminal codes, punishing by camp detention, hard labor, psychiatric rehabilitation, or execution.

These repressive strategies all convey the state's perception of the individual writer as a potentially dangerous individual, and not as an individual with rights to freedom of expression and equality.

Francoist Spain and the Soviet Union demonstrated two basic ideological approaches to prepublication censorship. In Spain, authoritarian rule sought to preserve a certain illusory view of the country's glorious past and an ideal of Catholic nationalism, and its censorship focused on eliminating anything overtly anti-Catholic, anti-Franco, or obscene. Thus Francoist censorship was characterized by its proscriptive paternalism.[8]

Meanwhile, the Soviet Union's censorship functioned as both a proscriptive *and* prescriptive organ. It could suppress or cut offensive material, but it also aimed to promote an ideological program through literature.[9] Soviet censorship displayed the panoptic and paternalistic tendencies of the totalitarian state. It stressed the state's forceful application of the Law, which in turn revealed the state's reliance on secrecy, surveillance, and didactic forms in education or indoctrination.

In the twentieth century in Europe and North America, the censorship of sexuality in literature for decades affected the oeuvre of writers on the cutting edge. Joyce had to publish *Ulysses* outside of his native Ireland, where neither the local Irish nor the imperial English would have permitted publication. The cessation of its serialization in the *Little Review* due to censorship action by trial blocked further U.S. publication. Only through the dedication of Sylvia Beach and her Paris bookstore Shakespeare and Company could Joyce bring his novel fully into print in 1922. And only after 1933, and a new U.S. trial, could his book be circulated legally for sale in the United States and other countries that had followed the U.S. example of a ban.

Under the censorious market conditions of the 1950s, Nabokov's manuscript was rejected by a series of overly cautious U.S. publishers and would only be initiated into print through a small English-language press in Paris, Olympia Press, in 1955. As we shall see, *Lolita* challenged legal and state censorship practices in both France and Great Britain, as well as influencing cultural reception in the United States and elsewhere.

While by the late 1960s sexuality in literature was becoming more acceptable in liberal democracies, in dictatorial regimes such as Franco's Spain and the USSR censorship of sexuality was integral to the maintenance of a sanitized public national image. I have selected two pivotal moments in both countries when the censorship started to give way to liberalization, for it could only be in such relatively relaxed phases of censorship that a literary treatment of sexuality might be granted permission. In Spain, the early 1960s was a time of gradual increased permissiveness,

---

8. For the concept of "Eternal Spain" in Francoist censorship, see Neuschäfer.
9. For more on the prescriptive element of Soviet censorship, see Lenin; James.

with a new liberalizing censorship law being under review. Martín-Santos's manuscript underwent heavy excisions with the Spanish censor's blue pen prior to first publication in late 1961. The last fifteen years of Francoist censorship, from roughly 1960 through 1975, experienced various challenges of the status quo in literary publications, with contemporary Spanish authors often citing *Tiempo de silencio* as a benchmark for change. Meanwhile, in the case of the Soviet Union, it is only in the final years of glasnost' or "openness" that the official prior censorship started to relax its standards. After more than ten years of searching for a willing editor, Erofeev could publish his *Russkaia krasavitsa* in 1990, initially with some words censored (words considered obscene or pornographic). In 1994, with his first fully uncensored edition of the novel, Erofeev still had to negotiate carefully with resistant typesetters to set the previously excised words in print, so ingrained were censorship practices and prudish morality in Russia.

2. CENSORSHIP IN MENTAL LIFE AND SOCIETY

The Artistic Censoring of Sexuality draws on an understanding of censorship as a determining, normative function in the individual's mental life just as it has been in our collective social existence.[10] The novels in this study emphasize how the protagonists' mental life is in conflict with their society, and how much of this perspective involves sexuality as potentially problematic and in need of censoring. In this sense, the artistic censoring inscribed in the text resembles psychic censorship in dreaming.

In Freudian psychoanalysis, the psyche's censorship is a kind of agency which particularly regulates the *way* we dream. In dreams, thoughts and wishes normally repressed in waking hours are given some form of expression, but usually in a mediated manner. Desires and fantasies are altered or distorted in some way in order to pass the mind's censorship, often resulting in a dream difficult to interpret. But giving usually forbidden thoughts some form of expression provides mental satisfaction and relief. In fact, the subject's inability to grasp consciously the full significance of what he has dreamt may be an additional protection from unsettling emotions and desires. Repressed wishes and fantasies are often irrational, unreasonable, or unattainable, so knowing them can cause feelings of guilt or worry.

---

10. The following account of psychoanalytic censorship derives from my understanding of Freud, "The Censorship of Dreams"; "Civilization and Its Discontents"; *The Interpretation of Dreams; Jokes and Their Relation to the Unconscious;* "Leonardo da Vinci"; "A Note upon the 'Mystic Writing-Pad'"; "Repression." Also informative are Lacan and Laplanche and Pontalis *(The Language of Psychoanalysis)*.

Meanwhile, dreaming can provide pleasure, as it is inventive and creative, with witty and ingenious subterfuges for evading the censorship (e.g., screening, transformations, distortions, displacements, digressions, negating or oppositional replacements). Freud's *Interpretation of Dreams* identifies some of these strategies, such as condensation and displacement (which can be related in poetic terms to metaphor and metonym). The creative, transformational qualities of dreaming allow the subject to work through unpleasant or unsavory aspects of his unconscious desires.

Sexuality figures as one of the most censored elements in a subject's life precisely because, as an infant, the subject has had to organize his unruly "polymorphously perverse" sexuality to agree with the predetermined, ritualized role he will assume in the family and social life. In order to relate to his fellow subjects, the infant subject must renounce powerful attachments he has developed to his caregivers and replace them with socially acceptable aims and objects. He is persuaded to negotiate these renunciations in his efforts to retain the love and approval of his caregivers, and later those of his friends, teachers, and others in his society. The subject's development includes the formation of the superego which incorporates moral, regulatory values. The superego may undergo further changes throughout life as the subject may call into question or discard some of these values, but it will continue to exert its influence on the subject's mental life.

This structuring of the subject's psychic apparatus depends on the participation of social elements (starting usually with the parents). While every subject is born with innate propensities, gifts, and characteristics which may or may not come to light during his development, he must try to find acceptable ways to behave sexually and ethically in social life. This transformation particularly becomes manifest when the subject enters the Symbolic register, that is, when he acquires language (and by extension other cultural codes of exchange), which will shape the way he thinks and acts and interacts with others. Indeed, the Symbolic involves the powerful language of the Law which allows the development of the superego. We can consider the early intimate entwining of the Law with language. Language as a system of signs adheres to values codified and maintained by society; by learning a language, one enters into relations with others who all use agreed-upon, often tacit, collective rules. Language depends on mental censorship, both in waking hours and in dreams, to regulate human integration in civilization.

As long as we live with others there has been a constitutive need for us to regulate and control our behavior. In any society, there are therefore at least a few regulative taboos and customs which may not always have a rational purpose but which provide some structural boundaries for civilization.¹¹ A cluster of conventional sexual practices guides us in ethical approaches to sexuality. Our perceptions of right and wrong are strongly related to (if not produced by) both our sexual formation and social institutions that govern sexuality and gender (e.g., the church or temple, the law, the market, the school).

Writers' desire in creating potentially offensive material may be to challenge readers' values. Writing that gives offense has been often considered subversive, containing the potential to overthrow authority or contradict dogma.¹² In a parallel sense, a person's internal, psychic censorship is essential to his ability to live in society and to arbitrate his communications and actions. Lacan explains that this relationship between the individual and his surroundings "places man in the mediating function between the real and the signifier [involves the Thing] . . . , all forms of which created by man belong to the sphere of sublimation" (*Ethics,* 129). The act of writing, as with any creative act, any sublimation, is a mediation which employs consciously and unconsciously overvaluation and disavowal, transformation and interpretation, inclusion and omission, suggestion and negation.

The subject's aim to censor himself or others and his conflicting aim to express himself or act transgressively constitute a basic common dilemma. By our resolutions to this conflict, we exercise judgment. So, too, in the novels of this study the same dilemma is played out, based on diverse cultural and historical contexts. In each novel, when sexuality is evoked, the motifs and dynamics of censorship, fantasy, and judgment are deployed. The trials and stresses of historical and cultural censorship are embedded in the novels' themes and aesthetics.

In the European and North American cultural contexts of our inquiry, institutionalized Christianity constitutes a decisive and crystallizing factor in the development of sexual morality and of social censorship. Sacred texts such as the Bible, as well as church law and local policies, have served as sources of prohibitions and prescriptions which determined how people regulated their lives. Christianity emphatically prefers chastity, often limiting sexuality to a reprehensible practice necessary for procreation. Even with increased secularization of legal and moral codes during and after the Enlightenment, much of our ethics and laws continue to derive in some

---

11. See Claude Lévi-Strauss for an elaboration of these studies. Lévi-Strauss's structuralist approach is influential in the Lacanian theory from which much of my discussion derives.

12. Our lasting belief in the power of the word is implied in laws regarding slander, libel, sedition, blasphemy, and treason. With the increased number of writers and readers (and consequently increased plurality of perspectives and contexts), liberal democracies have had to relax their interpretation and enforcement of these laws. That relaxation should not be mistaken for relinquishment in belief (or susceptibility to be offended). For just a short sample of the past decade's explosion of publications about the censorship issues involving new electronic media, see Bozonnet.

way from church doctrine.

This institutionalized, restrictive attitude toward sexuality is reflected clearly in publication censorship.[13] The textual explosion that came with the advent of the printing press in Europe made the church's censoring interests more frantic. The church aimed to maintain authorization over all printed matter. It sought to prohibit blasphemy and obscenity in print. Furthermore, not long after the advent of the press in the 1450s and the coinciding establishment of a coordinated regulating ecclesiastic censorship, there followed university and governmental censorship offices to control the publication of scholarly and lay texts.[14] Whether religious or lay, the three institutionalized censorships all presupposed the incredible power of the written word. Temporally and spatially, however, the severity of European censorship varied greatly (e.g., the Roman and Spanish Inquisitions, the *Indices librorum prohibitorum,* Calvin's repressive policies in Geneva, the licensing act in England).

Since Gutenberg, what the church might gradually relinquish in censorship control, the state or its representative branches usually gained, and with it, the obligation to apply moral standards to censoring practices. In Europe and North America, as literacy and print culture have grown over the years, the perceived need to regulate and supervise both education and publications has not slackened, but rather has been modified. An institution's actual enforced authority over the production of the printed text have enhanced the sense of that institution's general power to rule, and its loss of or diminished censorship authority might indicate its own decline and not censorship's.

3. OBSCENITY AND WRITING

The modern novel has its origins in the Italian *novella* and the French *roman* or romance, both of which involved tales of love and adventure, often accompanied by veiled or overt expressions of sexuality. Boccaccio's *Decameron* and Rabelais's *Gargantua and Pantagruel* are early examples of the emerging modern novel's interest in sex, and encountered censorship

---

13. For histories of censorship, see Legendre; *Censorship and Obscenity; Censorship and Silencing: Practices of Cultural Regulation; Censorship and the Control of Print in England and France, 1600–1910; The Censorship of Books; La censure en France à l'ère démocratique (1848– . . .);* De Grazia; Dollimore; Dury, *La censure: La prédication silencieuse;* Patterson, "Censorship"; *Censures: De la Bible aux larmes d'Eros; Istoriia sovetskoi politicheskoi tsenzury;* Minois; Negroni; Oboler; Shackleton; Strauss.

14. Censoring practices could be in competition with one another in some circumstances (e.g., Dury; Legendre; Harrison; Hiley; Hunter et al.; Jansen; Walsh; *Patterns of Censorship around the World*).

repeatedly. In their wake, many novels representing sexuality in some form were determined indecent, immoral, obscene, or pornographic.

These censorious labels deserve some attention, especially because they have been used interchangeably by censors and legislation over the centuries to describe works of very different content and intent. "Indecent" and "immoral" describe by negative inference—what is not decent, not moral, what is adverse or offensive to morality (Christian morality), in particular to the proscriptions of sexual conduct. These proscriptions could involve anything which threatens chastity, inspires lust, or suggests adultery, fornication, or any "unnatural" sexual act. This range seems to cover a lot of territory, but censorship often exceeded even these prohibitions to include sensual, lurid, crude, or straightforward descriptions of bodily parts or functions, as well as descriptions of food, clothing, surroundings, nature, and so on.

"Indecent" and "immoral" became outmoded in the twentieth-century censorship, replaced by "pornographic" and "obscene." These terms form part of the inner dynamics of the novels of this study. "Pornographic" derives from the Greek *porne* (harlot) and *graphos* (writing, writer). The term only emerged in mainstream European usage in the eighteenth century (in English by the nineteenth century), perhaps coinciding with the increased appearance and circulation of writing about prostitution and the secularization of the Enlightenment.[15] Of uncertain origin, "obscene" possibly came from the Latin *ob* and *scena,* can mean "off scene," that is what is not to be shown, what takes place off scene.[16] In its etymological entry "obscene," the *Oxford English Dictionary* notes the classical Latin *partes obscenae* that denote the genitals; the classical *obscenus* or *obscaenus* "has been variously associated, by scholars ancient and modern, with *scaevus* left-sided, inauspicious [. . .] and with *caenum* mud, filth."

Legally, "obscene" came to mean "tending to deprave and corrupt." Appearing in English as early as 1593, the term later became codified and aligned with censorship in Great Britain in 1858 and 1859, with the Obscene Publications Act. With the first case and appeal (*Regina v. Hicklin* 1858) under this new law, the Queen's Bench produced an obscenity test. As Richard Randall explains, this test would determine whether

---

15. See, for example, Hunter et al.'s *On Pornography: Literature, Sexuality and Obscenity Law; The Invention of Pornography: Obscenity and the Origins of Modernity, 1500–1800; Perspectives on Pornography: Sexuality in Film and Literature; Pornography and Censorship.*

16. The etymology of "obscene" is complicated and somewhat obscure. See Havelock Ellis's essays "The Function of Taboos" and "The Revaluation of Obscenity," and, for example, Butler; *Censorship and Freedom; Censorship and Obscenity;* Craig; Daily; Davies; De Grazia; Ernst; Freud, *Jokes* and "Repression"; Gordon; Hunter et al.; *The Invention of Pornography;* Kaite; Kaplan; Levine; Lewis; Oboler; Perrin; *Pornography and Censorship;* Randall; *"To Deprave and Corrupt. . . ."*

the material tended to "deprave and corrupt those whose minds were open to such immoral influences and into whose hands a publication of this sort may fall." Perhaps without intending to, the *Hicklin* rule, as it came to be known, recognized the personal and idiosyncratic character of the pornographic. "Whose minds are open to such influences" effectively institutionalized the variability of obscenity, while at the same time failing to provide triers of fact with guidelines to relieve their own subjectivity. (50)

In the twentieth century, lawmakers were obliged eventually to move away from *Hicklin* rules, for obscenity eludes clear, quantifiable identification and puts judge and jurors in the awkward position of having to identify and then deny or admit apparent obscenity's effects.

Roland Barthes notices how obscenity does not have to apply to sex, depending on historical context. In his fragment "Love's Obscenity" in *A Lover's Discourse,* he suggests that the "moral tax levied by society on all transgressions affects passion still more than sex today. Everyone will understand that X has 'huge problems' with his sexuality; but no one will be interested in those Y may have with his sentimentality: love is obscene precisely in that it puts the sentimental in place of the sexual" (178). Barthes indicates how the sexual became part of everyday discourse in 1970s France, while the sentimental realm of love had become rarefied enough to seem outlandish or obscene, an affront to modern human relations invested in an openness about sex (perhaps to the detriment of love relations). Discourse finds ways to regulate itself through social appraisal, codification, and difference.

Writing is at once a part of regulated behavior and a commentary on it from the margins. It offers a contextualized web of perceptions, thoughts, and emotions which can then be recognized, appraised, misinterpreted, tolerated, celebrated, rejected, or disregarded by others.[17] Writing embraces both *poesis* and *ethos,* despite their conflicting aims. In the history of writing, the author emerges as an individual who can be held accountable for his work; the law potentially concentrates its focus on the responsibility of the legal person. With the shift of emphasis on the creative individual (signaled, for example, by Enlightenment thinkers), and with the dramatic increase in general literacy and amplification of print culture in the eighteenth and nineteenth centuries, the writer gained greater legal and moral responsibilities as well as a greater sense of independence and individuality than before (e.g., the establishment of copyright which emphasizes the substance of writing as "legal property"; the instances of writers in self-exile

---

17. See Holquist on some of the paradoxical features of censorship.

or imposed exile, who suffer incarceration, or who are denied travel visas at home or abroad through the twentieth century).

The concerns of censorship and writing are intricately related, whether censorship is an external, administered office, a self-administered selection process, or usually a combination of both. Writers' inspiration competes with their inhibition: their own values and sense of prohibition may differ from those of external authority and of substantial social groups. In executing their profession, writers clearly risk giving offense to certain readers.

4. CENSORSHIP, THE LAW, AND THE PRODUCTION OF SIGNIFICATION

The complex function of censorship manifests itself in many ways in order to regulate, control, transform, or repress any kind of expression or behavior that can have meaning in a given society and for a given subject. Censoring practices are observable in all societies through their deployment of the law, religion, and other customs; individuals take on personal censoring practices by being raised by others (parents) in a society with certain laws and values. Certainly censorship practices can vary widely in terms of degree, emphasis, system of values, and other cultural and historical contexts, but the basic practice appears to be a common regulatory feature to all societies.

Presumption of guilt or innocence may simply be two sides to the same law. While liberal democracies and nondemocratic states differ in their approaches to the freedom of expression, they share some underlying assumptions. First, they believe in the power of the word to influence. Second, they believe that the state has a responsibility to protect the average citizen from harm or wrongdoing. Third, they share a faith in the Law despite their differences in wielding it. Fourth, they believe that sexuality needs to be regulated through law and custom.

Sexuality in literature has proven to be a thorny issue for legislators and censors because of the ambiguous questions of harmful influence and intent. It cannot be consistently proven that reading literature does or does not influence its readers in some way. An author's intention to create a certain effect on a reader cannot be readily determined either. Even if an author attempts to clarify the purpose or meaning of his work, he cannot ultimately control or determine the possible variety of readers' responses to it (one reader alone can have more than one response to a given work, whether rereading it the same day or revisiting it after twenty years).

Influence and intent are terms used readily in the law (crimes or acts committed without intent are considered less reprehensible than premeditated ones), but these terms are used differently in literary interpretation, often in the form of suggestion. It is probably impossible to resolve the conflict between the legal context of a person's intent, act, and consequences of the act and the literary context of writing, text, and interpretation, although both liberal democracies and nondemocratic regimes have sought to do so through their varying approaches to censorship. In Foucault's thought, the dispersed power that keeps watch over and controls modern society shows us that we are not really ever "free." Nor in our confessions, including literary revelations of sexuality, do we obtain freedom. However, I suggest that novelists have been historically interested in this paradox, questioning the limitations that we impose upon ourselves. By comparing censorship under very different political and legal conditions, we discover that sexuality becomes deeply politicized and that the law is inscribed in artistic and contemplative ways in the literary text.

The conflict of legal and aesthetic approaches to literature—what the text claims to be—can be, however, a tantalizing issue to pursue and dramatize in literature itself.[18] My study shows how the law's interest in regulating sexuality is what often becomes reenacted and reinterpreted in literary fiction involving sexual portrayal. In the novels of this study, sexuality is especially explored as sexual transgression: prostitution, pornography, obscenity in literature, problems with reproduction and fertility, the fallen woman, pedophilia, and incest. All of the selected novels consider the power relations between men and women, with men generally positioned as the desiring subject and women as the elusive, sexual other. All of the novels emphasize motifs of judgment, including narratives of court trials, fatal and punishing sentences, martyrdoms, and the apocalypse.

5. ARTISTIC CENSORING THROUGH FANTASY AND THE LAW

Much like publication censorship, psychic censorship evaluates and conditions words or signifiers; it changes signification in order to avoid expressing anything that comes too close to being explicit about (forbidden) desires or objects. It does this in order to disavow a lack that is at the center of the desired other, to prevent the subject from realizing fully his

18. François Ost has recently contemplated the deployment of the law in literature, one that "poses the most fundamental questions about justice, the law and power" (4). Sharing one of the aims of my inquiry, Ost proposes a study of the law in literature that asks the question, "What can literature gain by the understanding of the presence of the law in its works?"

desire. Desire and fantasy have important relations to censorship, and owe their intriguing, circulating, and at times antithetical forms to censorship's regulatory function. We only consciously perceive desire and fantasy once they have passed through censorship. They rely on the prohibitionary force of the superego, as played out in censorship, in order to create meaning by contrast. Thus, censorship functions to help transform meaning. In this way, it can be seen as aligned with the function of sublimation, which also works to transform and elevate the erotic drive to some nonsexual but creative activity.

There is a basic ethical presupposition involved with legal, social, and psychic censorships, and artistically portrayed censorship and sexuality; that is, our need to censor implies that there is a good that can be achieved, usually through some correction or regulation. This ethical drive can become entangled with the possibility of deriving pleasure from regulating oneself or others. Pleasure may also be derived from sublimating our sexuality through the creative processes of writing and reading. At bottom, the problem of ethics can be said to be found in our lack of ability to resolve the difference between what is supposed to be good (as opposed to bad) and what is pleasurable (as opposed to unpleasurable). On an irrational, libidinal plane, the subject equates what is pleasurable with what is good. Meanwhile, through the series of renunciations of erotically charged objects and activities that the subject has had to make throughout childhood and afterwards, the subject has a competing set of criteria about what constitutes the good for others (and therefore for himself, too). In the intersection of these two planes, there is an area of negotiation in which pleasure and signification can still be procured through censorship.

In our mental life, censorship might be seen as a function that makes these signifying negotiations possible. The sense of censorship relates in part to a psychoanalytic concept of a system of checks and balances. Our psychic economy helps to produce our conscious awareness of values and ethics. In his *Ethics of Psychoanalysis,* Lacan discusses our tendency toward rectification, the reality principle and its fundamentally conflicting character. He stresses the importance of our sense of a lived experience and that that experience have a moral foundation.

This need to have a sense of a lived experience relates to censorship, literature, and sexuality in crucial ways. First, the general need to censor literature in some way or form is a way to determine meaning. The need to censor sexuality in literature is one aspect of how sexuality is controlled and regulated in society. Both expressing and censoring sexuality endow it with meaning. In the novels selected for this inquiry, the "need to censor" gets transformed into creative literary strategies and themes of judgment and transgression. Accompanying the need to censor are the epistemic drive and the ethical drive: in the texts, there is often a presupposition that there is some kind of (special) knowledge to be attained through sexuality.[19] Competing with this drive toward determining some knowledge is the urge to evaluate what is right and wrong (versus what is pleasurable and unpleasurable). Sexuality becomes a value factor for both the ethical drive and the epistemic drive.

In the novels chosen for this study, sexuality is often represented as fantasy and desire. Artistic censoring helps to fashion fantasy into its unusual, dynamic forms and enactments of transgression, subjection to pain, or judgment. Slavoj Žižek's definition of fantasy clarifies what is at stake in my claim:

> [I]n the fantasy-scene the desire is not fulfilled, 'satisfied,' but constituted (given its objects, and so on)—*through fantasy, we learn 'how to desire.'* In this intermediate position lies the paradox of fantasy: it is the frame co-ordinating our desire, but at the same time a defence against '*Che vuoi?*,' a screen concealing the gap, the abyss of the desire of the Other. Sharpening the paradox to its utmost—to tautology—we could say that *desire itself is a defence against desire*: the desire structured through fantasy is a defence against the desire of the Other, against this 'pure,' trans-phantasmic desire (i.e. the 'death drive' in its pure form). (*Sublime*, 118; emphasis in original)

This definition of fantasy supports an understanding of the subject's need to censor. What Žižek describes as a "defence against '*Che vuoi?*'" and a defense against the desire of the Other approximates what I describe as part of psychic censorship and part of the artistic censoring of sexuality in the selected novels. This defensive function has its parallels in artistic, social, and political censorship. Sexuality is censored in various ways at all levels, which is how it is endowed with conflicting signification.

In *Ulysses*, *Lolita*, *Tiempo de silencio*, and *Russkaia krasavitsa*, sexual acts viewed as crimes or transgressions, such as adultery, voyeurism, prostitution, masturbation, pedophilia, necrophilia, and pornography, are dramatized and submitted to forms of judgment. These forms of judgment often depict or allude to the erotic desire or fantasies of the subject, usually the masculine

---

19. What I have called "epistemic drive" or drive toward knowledge, Brooks, after Freud and Irigaray, calls "epistemophilia" (*Wisstrieb*), or the "epistemophilic urge," "which we find repeatedly conjoined in presentations of the body" (Brooks, *Body Work*, 9, 11).

subject. The enactment of censorship moments provides values for sexuality. By applying values, decisions can be made about good and bad, right and wrong, and not just desirable and undesirable. The dramatization of censoring maneuvers in fantasy provides complex, often difficult combinations of ethics and eroticism.

These novels bring to the fore the problems in ethics by using sexuality as the hotly contentious value; that value can then serve as a problematic issue or action to be judged. Sexuality is a useful motif of conflict in narrative art, especially in the modern novel, because sexuality's values are not clear and undisputed. Because these novels rely in part on a very active reader response, particularly a contemporary readership cognizant of the social, cultural, and political values in the novel's local setting, they tend to activate judgment. The necessary tension at stake in the ethical premise of these novels can be outlined by Lacan's general explanation of the dynamics of an ethics: "an ethics essentially consists in a judgment of our action, with the proviso that it is only significant if the action implied by it also contains within it, or is supposed to contain, a judgment [. . .]. The presence of judgment on both sides is essential to the structure" (311).

Joyce, Nabokov, Martín-Santos, and Erofeev establish in their novels the sense of a two-sided process of judgment producing an ethics. In the theater of judgment of *Ulysses*'s midnight chapter "Circe," Bloom and Stephen, along with their sexual fantasies, face judges in themselves as well as in various censorious parental and social figures and institutions. In *Lolita,* Humbert the character-narrator presents himself for judgment to the reader-jurors and submits himself and his sexual desires and transgressions to his own forms of creative judgment. *Tiempo de silencio* sets up several trials for the protagonist Pedro to fail and to be judged by the authorities, the director of his institute, and himself. All of these male protagonists seem to derive a degree of masochistic pleasure through their sufferings. Finally, in *Russkaia krasavitsa,* Irina as another character-narrator constructs a confessional text in which she relates her experiences as a sexual being who is harshly judged by others in power. She uses the text as a form of self-judgment as well, ultimately ending her life with the end of the text. While some of the characters inspire a modicum of sympathy, they are generally offered to us as flawed beings whose sexuality, or their approach to others' sexuality, merits critical and often negative judgment. In each of these texts, I examine censoring as a productive function, even though it is often a negating force.

6. CENSORING'S ARTISTIC AFFIRMATION AND NEGATION

Censoring in artistic production, such as in the narrative, is potentially creative as well as destructive. Artistic censoring uses strategies and motifs similar to those of psychic censorship. Both aim to transform or sublimate (forbidden) wishes and to exercise judgment that will produce signifying value. Our need to represent wish fulfillments for ourselves (as we do in dreams) coincides with, and may be dependent upon, a need or drive to be judged (and thus create values).

The selected novels dramatize themes and metanarratives of judgment and oblige the reader to adopt a judge's role. First, these novels manifest an awareness of and opinions about the law, religion, education, science and medicine, and other regulating forces. Second, through allusion, parody, intertextuality, and other means, they make references to other works of art, especially controversial ones which had at some time been judged harshly. In this way, they appeal to a kind of artistic canon and a continuum across time. Third, these novels tend to highlight the arbitrariness of judgment, its inability to account for everything all of the time. Finally, the narratives reflect aspects of a superego, expressing at times harsh and irrational forms of parental and other laws.

Put broadly, the demanding parental superego motivates the subject to achieve approval and love *or* rebellion and enjoyment of forbidden sexuality (e.g., the conflicts in the Oedipal and pre-Oedipal stages). Censorship as a psychic function must negotiate meaning with the rule-bound superego. On an artistic plane, a similar negotiation (conscious or unconscious) helps to transform the raw material of artistic work into a signifying creation. This transformational aspect of artistic censoring uses digression, oscillation, screens to conceal or transform, allusion, intertexts, disavowal, metonymy, metaphor, and irony in combination with motifs of judgment and sexuality. All of these techniques allow for the coexistence or suggestion of two or more meanings, often in conflict.

The novels' strong emphasis on sexual pleasure and knowledge gained through negative or negating means poses a potential double criticism. The protagonists, along with their freedom or aim to serve the good, may suffer under an abusive or unjust society or regime. Or, the society suffers the transgressions of the individual that do harm to the other and betray the good. Sexuality serves as a source of a new realism in the modern novel, a metaphor for possible concealed truth and pleasure, and a screen for the subject's struggle with the Law and judgment. In this way, while Foucault's concept of a confessional and regulating society may remain valid, it does not consider, as I do, the dynamic ethical potential of literary sexuality and its relation to twentieth-century political contexts.

Finally, we should allow for the occurrence of artistic transnational cross-fertilization, in spite of national censorship practices and attempts to banish provocative foreign works by dictatorial regimes. For Joyce, incorporating sex into his novel was part of a modernist reevaluation of art and a call to include the body and desires explicitly and innovatively in novelistic discourse. For twentieth-century modernists and postmodernists, *Ulysses* became a touchstone for possibilities in literature, including original explorations of sexuality. Nabokov, Martín-Santos, and Erofeev all acknowledge *Ulysses* as formational in their own development, particularly in relation to the novels selected for this study. Erofeev additionally salutes Nabokov and *Lolita*. In such cases as *Ulysses,* we can see how twentieth-century novelists, in pushing literature's margins of acceptability of sexual expression, looked beyond national borders for aesthetic trends and practices, while maintaining a critical focus on a specific national context.

Concomitantly, Joyce, Nabokov, Martín Santos, and Erofeev draw from the very particular social and historical contexts of 1904 colonial Ireland, post–World War II America, Spain under Franco in 1949, and Soviet Russia around the late 1970s for the treatment of the settings in their novels. These historically grounded contexts lend additional politicized force to the daring sexual expression integrated in the novels. While the years of first publication of the novels are somewhat distanced from the time periods of the fictional settings, a national critique of censorship standards is implied. The authors all experienced, firsthand, difficulties with getting these novels into print, facing as they did conservative laws, whether in liberal democracies, dictatorship, or totalitarian regime. The legal forms of censorship are intimately related to power and authority.

Chapter 1 compares the selected novels' historical encounters with actual censorship and the legal and political theories underpinning these moments. Both *Ulysses* and *Lolita* challenged the contemporary limits of acceptability of modes of sexual expression in literature and served as landmark works that influenced legal decisions of subsequent cases regarding other works. These novels obliged the judicial sphere to adopt new ways of regulating and judging literature.[20] The chapter proceeds with a

---

20. This literary history is the topic of my forthcoming article *"Lolita*'s Foundations in Censorship."

comparative publication history of *Tiempo de silencio* and *Russkaia krasavitsa* in countries with state-operated censorship bureaucracies. The permission to publish came at a cost to the works' initial integrity. For both novels, the first publications in 1961 and 1990, respectively, involved suppression of parts of the texts.

After the comparative chapter 1, the subsequent chapters (chapters 2 through 5) focus on *how* the artistic censoring of sexuality is developed as a theme and creative strategy in each of the selected novels. These chapters are sequenced according to the chronology of the novels' publication. This book's study spans from early in the century (*Ulysses*, 1919–1922) to late (*Russkaia krasavitsa*, 1990–1994): while occurring in different decades through the century, the novels each transpire at crucial points in the changing of the law, acting at the very least as signs of change (e.g., *Russkaia krasavitsa*) and at best as actual catalysts (e.g., *Ulysses* and *Tiempo de silencio*). In my conclusion, I offer some further comparisons of the chapters' interpretative findings.

Censorship

POLITICAL AND THEORETICAL STRUCTURES

In interpreting sexuality in literature, we could recall a premise at the heart of psychoanalysis: there is no sexual relationship. This absence is at the core of fantasy; it is why fantasy is always about the sexual relationship, a staging of it (Žižek, *Sublime Object,* 126). In mental life, the processes of censorship help to create the illusion of the existence of the sexual relationship. A parallel dynamic is at work in many literary representations of sexuality.

We create and portray meaningful relationships in order to disavow a lack of connection and coherence. Žižek illuminates this basic state of affairs with some analogies. In ideology, there is no class relationship; in law, there is no justice, no freedom. "Society as a corporate Body" is the fundamental ideological fantasy versus the impossibility of the social relationship ("Society doesn't exist") (126).

Literature insists upon finding meaning and form in the world, especially in human relationships. By involving sexual contexts or expressions in an aesthetic text like a novel, a writer seeks to discover meaning and value (despite the absences and fantasy relations Žižek identifies). Because sexuality is so highly regulated in any given society (whether politically liberal or repressive), it has the power to offend, to attract, to promise or withhold knowledge, to activate judgmental forces. The sexual relationship in literature solicits our judgment, thus indicating that we have posited some meaning or value in that relationship. Sexuality in literature can tie together fantasy and actuality. In the twentieth century, such writing represented to many readers an act of defiance toward society. The conflicting perceptions of the use and meaning of sexuality in literature can be seen in the vicissitudes of legal methods of pre- and postpublication censorship.

The legal and literary worlds view literary fiction in different but inter-referential ways. Literature as a legal thing (*res*) differs from literature as an aesthetic object (*poesis*). That intersection of values—legal and literary—serves as a point of reference for writers. The four novels discussed in this book dramatize how sexuality is received by conflicting, judgmental forces of society (1904 colonial Dublin; postwar America; 1949 Francoist Madrid; the USSR of the late 1970s to 1980). These societies can be grouped into two generalized spheres: the liberal-democratic (*Ulysses* and *Lolita*) and the repressive (authoritarian or totalitarian; *Tiempo de silencio* and *Russkaia krasavitsa*). In this comparative study, these differences are important to writers' production and sense of censorship. However, the premises of censorship are rather similar across these societies, and some of the censoring practices and their impact do not suggest enormous differences in theory.

1. LIBERAL-DEMOCRATIC CENSORING AND THE WILL TO JUDGMENT

Over the course of the twentieth century, liberal democracies have increasingly liberalized their regulatory practices for literary (and nonliterary) works with sexual content. The changes made in the law transpired in part because writers like Joyce and Nabokov produced highly artistic, controversial novels. Moreover, the twentieth century witnessed a dramatic increase (and diversity) in general publishing and specifically in works with sexual content. Legal transitions occurred also because new judges with fresh, less conservative values and modes of perception started to replace the old. For example, the Warren Court era of the mid-twentieth century (1953–1969) profoundly changed how law has been practiced in the United States and in other English-language countries using common law. Similar liberalization occurred around the same time in many liberal democracies beyond the Anglophone sphere.

One of the main ideals of law in liberal democracies is the maintenance of a "flexible legality." The arbitration of twentieth-century issues of the freedom of expression depends upon this methodology. Liberal-democratic law tends to demonstrate its fairness by its sensitivity to context and detail.

A second fundamental ideal in liberal-democratic law is the presumption of innocence until guilt is proven. This ideal has organized the legal reception and censorship of books and authors. In twentieth-century liberal democracies, a novel was published without undergoing prior censorship; the assessment of the book made prior to publication took place at the publishing house with editors (in that in-house assessment, discussions might include concerns regarding legal action after publication). After publication, if a work offended someone or group, or was claimed to be harmful (or obscene, pornographic, immoral), then accusations or seizures were made and a legal process could begin. In legal cases, the possibly offending text or the author is examined for harmful intent or effect. By the mid-twentieth century, and especially since the late 1960s and early 1970s, the law has relinquished its pretense of being able to determine harmful intention or effect in literature, but it nonetheless has sought through "flexible legality" to regulate the reception of possibly sensitive material through other modes of limitation of dissemination (e.g., zoning, age restrictions, etc.). "Flexible legality" was also exemplified in the century's shifting legal approach to assessing obscene effects in literature: the trials of *Ulysses* and *Lady Chatterley's Lover* dramatized in the courtroom the transition in emphasis from a censorious reading of potentially offensive passages out of context to the judging of a literary work as a whole (with an understanding of how potentially offensive portions or words contribute to the total work and its meaning).[1]

These two ideals in democratic law—presumption of innocence and flexible legality—can be seen as carried over into the premises of reading fiction. In the history of print culture, the book can have a long or short period of recognition, a far-reaching or limited impact on readerships, and a benefit (or not) for various parties including the writers, readers, publishers, and other producers and facilitators in the publication process. The book has been seen as a complex sign of communication (e.g., a legal thing [*res*], or a poetic or discursive thing related to *poesis* or *logos*) and product of exchange (e.g., an item marked for monetary exchange and profit). The book is interpreted and used differently, according to its context and position in, for example, the law, the market, and artistic or

---

1. See De Grazia; Ernst; Cowan. For *Ulysses* cases and censorship, see especially Vanderham; Parkes; Bryer; Culleton; Herr; Law; Leckie; Loss; Mahaffey; McCleery; Thomas; *The United States of America v. One Book Entitled* Ulysses *by James Joyce*. For *Lady Chatterley's Lover*, see Goodheart; Grant; Hyde; Thody.

scholarly discourses.[2] Censorship issues arise often because a text offends individual or social rights or values. A text tends to provoke a conflict because it is markedly different from the existing literature that is accepted and exchanged in the contemporary market. Such conflicts demonstrate the potential resonance of writing and reading. Novels and other artistic discourses tend to complicate language; readers may not all read an avant-garde or high-literary text in a comprehensive way because they may not share or cannot appreciate the set of codes and points of reference that the writer has developed. Thus, censorship generally entails a situation of conflicting receptions of texts.

In the twentieth-century novels chosen for this study, the novelists use sexual themes and representations to highlight these conflicts of interpretation and judgment. Joyce's "Circe" and Nabokov's *Lolita*, in their metanarrative and narrative forms, explore the human subject's encounter with Law. In these texts, sexual transgressions and desires are developed critically and aesthetically in themes such as adultery, prostitution, and pedophilia. Legal and religious regulative discourses (trials, confessions, judgment) respond to the instances of sexuality.

The narrative forms of writing encourage readers' active, flexible response to judging the sexual thing. Modernism's interest in revealing the inner movements of the mind through literature makes the revelation of sexual thoughts and fantasies almost inevitable. Joyce and Nabokov choose narrative forms that emphasize the mind's lines of thought and imagination, with special attention to the gendered and sexual aspects of subjectivity. For Joyce and Nabokov, the exposition of the human mind involves depicting discursively how the subject artistically censors his thoughts, fantasies, and perceptions. The narrativized drama organizes the topsy-turvy action and characters of "Circe." "Circe" is emblematic of artistic censoring of sexuality, for it depicts the subject's (or artist's) psychic struggle with repression, judgment, sexual transgression, and artistic expression. Meanwhile, the first-person narration that comprises most of *Lolita* is another way to expose mental life. The concept of a posthumously published confession of a criminal supplies *Lolita*'s signifying framework.

Joyce's and Nabokov's novels deploy censoring methods that are commensurate with both psychic censorship and, to some degree, social, political, and publication censorship. The artistic modes of censoring in the literary

2. For example, see Burt; Butler; *Censorship and Silencing;* Derrida, "Before the Law"; Dollimore; Flieder; Freccero; Gaskins; Geller; Geng; Goodrich; Gordon; Leslie Green; Harrison; Hiley; Hudon; Jansen; Frances M. Jones; LaCapra; Ladenson; Langton; Legendre; Levine; Lewis; MacKinnon; Joss Marsh, *Word Crimes;* Obeler; Lyman Ray Patterson; Pauvert; Perrin; Post; Randall; Robbins; Robins; Said; Scholes; Shackleton; Strauss; Zaczek.

discourses that relate to psychic censorship include disavowal, digression, ironic devices, negation—competing discourses. The artistic modes related to social, political, and publication censorship include the integration of censorious institutions in the plots, characterization, and various discursive strategies. These institutions include the nuclear middle-class family, the Catholic Church, the British Empire, and the American education and legal systems. The poetic and narrative strategies control and produce meaning about the fantasies of the sexual relationship. They promote ethical interpretations because the male subjects themselves (Bloom, Stephen, Humbert) question their aims and responsibility as they struggle between enjoying sexual pleasure (and transgression) and recognizing the differing needs and status of the other.

Generally, *Ulysses* and *Lolita* may seem to presuppose a sense of "flexible legality." In fact, they dramatize man's literal confrontation with the Law within their texts. In both texts, flexible legality can be seen as the narrative oscillation of highlighting the subject as alternately guilty and innocent. In a reflection of the psyche, with its powerful, censorious superego, the characters Bloom, Stephen, and Humbert posit themselves as already guilty, and the institutions they evoke tend to be strongly censorious of them and their desires. Readers of *Ulysses* may be lenient in their judgment of Bloom and Stephen in Nighttown. These men do more harm to themselves than to others, and their transgressions are largely imagined fantasies. Meanwhile, readers of *Lolita* may be seduced into an overindulgence of Humbert, who makes his guilt evident early in the text and repeatedly, somewhat like the purloined letter in Poe. His transgressions are not limited to private mental fantasies, and turn out to require our harsher judgment. In both novels, the ironic presentation of the texts encourages the implied readers to operate along the lines of flexible legality. However, the readers may or may not presume innocence.

The publishing histories of these two novels show a variety of examples of how flexible legality can come into play in censorship. *Ulysses* first encountered censorship while the novel was being published by serialized chapters in the *Egoist* and the *Little Review* (1919–1921). For modernist writers, the successful dissemination and reception of their groundbreaking work depended on reaching their readers; the "little" magazines helped to promote literature such as Joyce's. At the same time, by using the postal system and subscribers, and in the push for more subscribers, the publications encountered legal trouble, in the form of readers objecting to the mailing of "obscene" or "pornographic" material and the cooperation of the postmaster in the censoring of public mail. While *Ulysses* was eventually published legally in Paris in 1922, the novel's circulation encountered trouble because of the bans of the prior court actions. Finally in New York in 1933, legal action managed to reverse earlier decisions, with Judge Woolsey's insistence that the book was not obscene. While his arguments were not always sound, the general idea promoted in this case was to judge literature as a total work, not by excerpts, and to move away from the idea of influence on readers, as this could not be reasonably measured. The arguments regarding the potential negative influence of "obscenity" and the question of value of literature that included possible obscenity were revisited several times in the twentieth century in the United States and elsewhere.[3] With the U.S. Supreme Court's *Roth* decision in 1957, obscenity was debated in terms of whether a work involving obscenity offered redeeming social value or contributed to knowledge. The conservative side argued that obscene literature had no such values, and the liberal side asserted that it cannot always be immediately apparent whether an obscene expression, especially in literary fiction, might have such values. The liberal side cited several great works of literature, including *Ulysses*, that challenged contemporary norms of decency in literature. Such legal cases show how avant-garde literature can play a political and legal role. *Ulysses* set an early twentieth-century standard for publishing in liberal democracies. The shift between its early trials of 1919–1921 and the later 1933 trial can be attributed in part to changing social values. Also in this interim, *Ulysses* continued to be championed by intellectuals and scholars who added credibility to arguments for the lifting of the ban.

Lolita (1955) was published in the midst of a changing publishing legal stage, which accounted for Nabokov's worries about court actions. By publishing the novel in Paris with Olympia Press, he followed a path similar to that of Joyce. The outcome in terms of censorship, however, was very different. Unlike *Ulysses*'s first publisher (Sylvia Beach's Shakespeare and Company), Olympia Press was notorious (or, for some, revered) for publishing erotica; since Maurice Girodias made profits from the sale of this literature, he could indulge in publishing the occasional avant-garde literature, such as *Lolita* or works by Samuel Beckett.[4] As an English-language publisher

---

3. See the U.S. Supreme Court decisions. These can be conveniently reviewed through that court's historical society's Web page: www.supremecourthistory.org. The midcentury case in question here is *Roth v. the United States* 354 U.S. 476 (1957). Randall provides a list (324–25) and analysis of various U.S. and British legal cases in the nineteenth and twentieth centuries that affected the interpretation of "obscenity" and freedom of expression.

4. For details of this history, see, for example, Boyd (*Vladimir Nabokov: The American Years*); Girodias; and De Grazia. In 1959, Lawrence's novel was finally published in the United States by Grove Press after being championed by U.S. District Court Judge Frederick van Pelt Bryan, who found it to be "an honest and sincere novel of literary merit." At the time, the novel faced opposition in the Postmaster General Arthur E. Summerfield and President Eisenhower. See Evans, 144–46 and Kazin, 34 for details. See Gontarski for a history of Grove Press's championing of censored works.

in Paris, Girodias sold his books largely to British, American, and other English-speaking travelers. The importation of publications deemed obscene by British or U.S. customs could be complicated for travelers and importers, including booksellers and libraries, and consequently for publishers and writers. Although *Lolita* did not end up encountering legal challenges in the United States, it became an item of censorship in British Customs after Graham Greene praised it in a widely read book review. Greene's praise, and subsequent published debates over the potential obscenity of *Lolita,* prompted a strong interest in the novel among English readers. British Customs encountered an overwhelming importation of the book. The British government determined an unusual way to censor *Lolita* by persuading the French Ministry of the Interior to conduct a raid of Olympia Press and ban *Lolita.* The French complied, but their only available censorship law dated from the pre–World War II era. With this law, it could be claimed that the book would damage the "bonnes moeurs" of young readers. This worry was hardly a fair possibility, given that French adolescents were unlikely to have a command of English sophisticated enough to follow Nabokov's language; furthermore, *Lolita* condemns Humbert and his acts. By 1957, Nabokov managed to have his novel published in the United States by a more reputable press, G. P. Putnam's Sons, and thus disengage himself from Olympia. *Lolita* further contributed to censorship law in Great Britain. In the late 1950s, the British updated the old nineteenth-century law for obscenity that had used the *Hicklin* rule. The result was a new Obscene Publications Bill (1958). The British used *Lolita* in its debates of what does and does not constitute obscenity. As an added bonus, with the resulting new law, *Lolita* could be published in England. Further, with the new law, a modernist classic could finally be authorized. Britain's Obscene Publications Bill provided the way for the much belated legal proceedings in 1960 (in England) of D. H. Lawrence's *Lady Chatterley's Lover* (1928) which had been banned in England and in many English-speaking countries since the Italian publication of the novel in the 1920s.[5] The English trial (*Regina v. Penguin Books Limited* 1960) offered a fascinating midcentury application of flexible legality, for it involved having a group of jurors, an array of British citizens, read the novel and then give evidence in court as to the value and potential obscenity of the work. Lawrence's masterpiece, ultimately judged as a whole work of art, was allowed to be published at long last, although arguably, like Judge Woolsey, the English jurors would have had to be disingenuous at times in their responses.

5. For various accounts of the censorship of Lawrence's novel, see Cowan; Goodheart ("Censorship"); Grant; *D. H. Lawrence's "Lady": A New Look at* Lady Chatterley's Lover; Hyde; and *The Lady Chatterley's Lover Trial (Regina v. Penguin Books Limited).*

This new law and trial would not have been possible without *Lolita*, and the British government's involvement in first censoring it through diplomacy with the French, a French obscenity law, and British Customs, and later relying on it as a legal model of art that may suggest obscenity.

In our review of twentieth-century publication censorship, prior to the 1970s, the concept of "flexible legality" in liberal democracies should be modified to recognize real historical conditions. Both *Ulysses* and *Lolita* (and many other literary works) were treated, in various ways, as guilty or non-innocent prior to, and during, legal challenges. Part of this uneven treatment owes to the weight of earlier legal rulings, legal and publication precedents, and social contexts. The continued application of versions of the *Hicklin* rule well into the twentieth century increasingly proved to be out of date and clashed with contemporary social sensibility regarding sexuality. The twentieth century witnessed an increased prioritization of sexuality in an array of discourses. In science, the Kinsey reports of the 1940s and 1950s and Masters and Johnson reports of the 1960s and 1970s,[6] as well as the overall impact of psychoanalysis and branches of psychotherapy and psychology, all studied the role of sex in our lives and made the public aware of this growing body of knowledge. Social, cultural, and political discourses marked gradual changes in gender relations toward an increased emancipation of women and gender equality. Formerly taboo topics for public discourse were aired. The latter half of the century saw an increased openness to discussing in print all manner of references to sexuality, be they feminine hygiene, erectile dysfunction, transmission and prevention of venereal diseases, cancers of organs of sexual reproduction, homosexuality, transvestism, incest, and pedophilia. Flexible legality has allowed for some of these transitions.

Ulysses and *Lolita* are not primarily pornographic or obscene, but they do touch upon some very sensitive sexual matters that invoke pornography and obscenity in ways that their contemporary readership would find provocative and unusual. Furthermore, these works make sexuality fundamental to their thematic explorations; sexuality becomes ethically insistent, impossible to ignore in the consideration of human relations and responsibility.

While flexible legality determines to a large extent liberal-democratic law, the first part of the twentieth century saw that law prejudging sexuality in ways that theoretically resemble those of repressive regimes. Moreover,

---

6. Alfred Kinsey's *Sexual Behavior in the Human Male* (1948) and *Sexual Behavior in the Human Female* (1953); William H. Masters and Virginia Johnson's *Human Sexual Response* (1966), *Human Sexual Inadequacy* (1970), and several more works in the following decades.

in the four novels of this study, the textual settings in terms of censorship and social judgment are very similar.

2. PREPUBLICATION CENSORING AND THE ALWAYS ALREADY GUILTY SUBJECT'S CONTRACT WITH STATE IDEOLOGY

Twentieth-century politically repressive regimes—such as Franco's Spain and the Soviet Union—have provided elaborate examples of prepublication censorship.[7] The state's excessive application and promotion of its ideology necessitate a systematic suppression of dissenting voices and ideas. The Francoist system of censorship, although fairly comprehensive, was not ultimately as all-embracing and smothering as the Soviet censorship, which used several more methods to effectuate a totalitarian control on authors and publications.

The repressive regime shares with the liberal democracy a belief in the power of words to inform and influence. But the repressive regime conceives differently of the Law and the state's role in the Law, including the sphere of communication. Whereas liberal democracies have come to celebrate the concept of flexible legality and presumption of innocence, regimes such as the Soviet Union and Franco's Spain tended to present the Law and the state as interlocking units, insisting on a paternalistic ideology of an "immutable legality" and a presumption of guilt or non-innocence until innocence is proven.[8]

---

7. For historical and analytical accounts of Francoist and Spanish censorship, see Abella; Abellán; *Arte del franquismo;* Beneyto; Bozal; Brea; Carr; Cirici; Cisquella; Delibes; Foster; Godzich; Gubern; Gumbrecht; Herzberger; Jiménez Losantos; Jordan; Linz; Llorens Castillo; Molinero; Pérez; Pérez Rojas; Reig Tapia; Sánchez Reboredo; Sinova; Southworth; "Spain: *Indice:* Twenty Years of Censorship"; Terrón Montero; Wasserman.

For historical and analytical accounts of Soviet and Russian censorship, see Aksenov; Ambler; Barron for KGB-censoring methods of dissident authors; Blium; Brodsky; Chalidze; Choldin; Drugovskaia; Edwards on three prominent, censored writers; Epshtein, "How Society Censors Its Writers"; Ermolaev; Garrard; Goldschmidt; Hosking; *Imperial Russia;* "Interview with Chief Censor"; James; Johnson; Krasnogorov; Lenin; Losev; Markstein; Joss Marsh, *Soviet Marxism;* Rosalind J. Marsh; Medvedev; Monas; Neuschäfer; *Perspectives on Literature and Society in Eastern and Western Europe;* Popovskii; Radley; Reck; *The Red Pencil: Artists, Scholars, and Censors in the USSR;* Ruud; Scotto; Shanor; Shneidman; Slonim; *The Soviet Censorship;* Streliani; Swayze; *Tsenzura v tsarskoi Rossii i Sovetskom Soiuze;* Tsymbal; Twarog; Vladimirov; Wozniuk.

8. In practice this "legality" was subject to all manner of distortions in Francoist Spain and the Soviet Union. What is important is the irrational dependence on the illusion of an immutable legality, as demonstrated in the standard examples of a repressive regime's use of a show trial or its retroactive editing of historical documents.

See also *The Distinctiveness of Soviet Law* for legal analyses of the theory and practice of Soviet law, which underline the gap between Soviet jurists' theory of a supposedly solidified code of law

These two premises directly informed the official censorship practices in these countries. In general, the presupposition of prepublication or prior censorship is that the writer or his work is not-innocent, guilty, or at fault *before* proven otherwise. The prepublication censorship is the stage for assessment. The state, through its censorship offices, approaches the literary text and its writer with profound distrust. But the law is not explicit about what would cause suppression of a text. The writer therefore creates his work from a position of guilt and will be judged by a set of unspecified, harsh rules (the application of which paradoxically may vary widely according to the context). (This oppositional or embattled position is somewhat commensurate with that of writers like Joyce and Nabokov in liberal democracies, who also were unsure of how their work would be judged.)

Despite Francoist Spain's and the Soviet Union's political differences, their ideologies shared several assumptions about writing and sexuality. First, both states valued a limited, ideologically correct version of literary realism. Second, that realist vision was supposed to exclude references to sexual situations or themes. Censors in both countries tended to label almost any sexual representation in literature as pornographic, immoral, obscene, or indecent.[9]

This sensitivity to the expression of sexuality reveals the strong faith of literal association between the signifier and the signified. For the regimes, literature represented the artists' and intellectuals' perceptions and values, yet conversely the regimes wished literature to serve the state and present "positive" works. Francoist and Soviet prepublication censorship aimed to maintain virtues of sanitized realism and prudish morality unsullied by vulgarity, obscenity, and explicit sexual expression and themes. The didacticism inherent in the Francoist and Soviet regimes was played out in their censoring practices. Francoist ideology largely sought to promote a nostal-

---

and their very different practice of it. See Abellán and Román Gubern's *La censura: Función política y ordenamiento jurídico bajo el franquismo (1936–1975)* for further detailed understanding of how censorship was incorporated into legal practice and how Spanish jurists interpreted the law in theory and practice during the Francoist period.

9. Spanish (self) perceptions of sexuality during the Francoist era are explored in the following works: Abella; Abellán, *Censura y creación literaria;* Amezúa; *Arte del franquismo;* Bozal; Brea; Caballero; Carr; Cirici; García Ronda; Hart; Labanyi; Malo de Molina; Ramos Gascón; Sieburth.

Works in philosophy about Russian sexuality include Berdiaev, Rozanov, Popovskii, and Epshtein. Igor Kon is a primary source of information on Russian sexuality, his books extensively examining cultural, medical, psychological, and sociological facets of sexuality. For scholarly studies of aspects of Russian sexuality (pre-Soviet, Soviet, or post-Soviet) see, for example, Attwood; Blium; Edwards; Engelstein; Ermolaev; Etkind; Goscilo; Hubbs; Mamonova; Rosalind J. Marsh; Naiman; *Sexuality and the Body in Russian Culture;* Shneidman; Slonim; *Women in Russia; Women in Russia and Ukraine.*

gic, heroic historical narrative of Spanish plenitude and self-reliance. While there was some promotion of ideology in art, most Francoist censoring of manuscripts worked by negating opposing or offensive expression. Borrowing in part from Spanish Catholic censorship formulae of pre-Francoist eras, the regime used a form with four key criteria to be considered by censor-readers in their evaluation of manuscripts for approval or denial: "Does the work attack Dogma? morality? the Church and its Ministries? the Regime and its Institutions?"[10] Once the censor had assessed the work in question, various methods of censorship could be determined, depending on the acceptability or potential offensiveness of the work. These methods included editing (excising words, phrases, pages, or segments; replacing words with other more benign words or with blanks, asterisks, or ellipses); declining permission to publish; banning if the work was published and then found to be harmful or offensive; or even strategically controlling print runs and distribution (e.g., circulating in secondary towns and in one or no major city; allowing library acquisitions and sales abroad but little or no domestic sales; limiting critical reviews or author interviews in magazines and newspapers, promotions, and other ways of publicizing a publication).

In contrast, Soviet censorship functioned dually by negating counter-ideological expression *and* promoting a writing program of socialist realism. The USSR's utopian aspirations could be expressed in the devotion to Marxist-Leninist ideals, cleanliness, work, and its products (the betterment and advancement of the Soviet project by the people for the people). Soviet ideology was premised on working toward a radiant future of shared abundance and equality. Useful to the prescriptive aims of Soviet censorship was a hallowed, pre-Revolutionary history of approaching Russian literature as a guide to life.[11] This didactic trend in literary culture contributed later to the Soviet project to create a new Soviet man and woman through advances made in the fields of biology, psychology, "pedology," education,

10. This list of Francoist criteria could almost be transcribed to the Soviet context, with the exception of the third concern regarding a work's possible attack on the Church. I quote the list of criteria from the actual censors' reader reports kept in Spain's Archivo General de la Administración in Alcalá de Henares. Unfortunately, in my research of several Soviet archives that had sections pertaining to culture and censorship, I could not find comparable readers' reports, for it appears that these documents are not available or have been destroyed. See Ermolaev and Goriaeva's *Istoriia sovetskoi politicheskoi tsenzury: Dokumenty i kommentarii* (1997) that gathers together many archival sources.

11. Engelstein, among others, points out how pre-Revolutionary Russian readers eagerly read aloud together newly published fiction and nonfiction. In the late nineteenth century and early twentieth century, reading was an intensely signifying event, often involving dramatic comparisons between the fictional situations and one's own life and determining an adjustment in how one lived.

Marxist-Leninist theory, and agitation and propaganda. Thus, the Soviet censorship of literature involved the prescription as well as the more common proscription of writing.

Soviet censors applied the criteria of socialist realism to their reading and criticism of literary texts. Basically, a realistic mode of description was supposed to complement an ideologically correct plot and resolution. Socialist realism in the arts aimed to glorify political and social ideals of communism, building on three areas: the ideological (*ideinost'*), party-line (*partiinost'*), people-oriented (*narodnost'*). In Soviet censorship and mainstream Soviet literary criticism (thus, excluding the Russian Formalists and their successors, i.e., Tartu semioticians, Prague structuralists), many readers esteemed an ideal text as one exhibiting total control and totalized meaning, a kind of wholeness, completeness (*tselostnost'*), whose integrity (*tselnost'*)[12] would be blemished or disturbed by critical inquiry.[13]

While Francoist ideology does not so explicitly codify these terms, wholeness and integrity were equally functional in their censoring program. The concept of a unified Spain covered up regional diversity, class disparities, gender inequality, and, of course, the deep division effectuated by the civil war. For Franco and his ideologues, promotion of unity had a particular heroic, militaristic, and Catholic historical resonance, allusive of the "reunification" of Spain under the Catholic kings, Ferdinand and Isabel, in 1492. Emphatic expressions of unity and homogeneity resulted from a Francoist censorship and its regime, with its aims to present a serene, organized impression of contented order in Spain and to conceal difference and dissent.

In the realm of art and literary fiction, the Francoist and Soviet Russian regimes shared an ideological goal of unity, wholeness, and homogeneity. This goal characterizes the state as a parental force which appeals to its subjects to enter the unifying frame of its Symbolic register. The writer (or other individual) may resist or submit such an interpellation, but his contract with the state is defined by that relationship.

Martín-Santos's *Tiempo de silencio* and Erofeev's *Russkaia krasavitsa* emphasize the individual's confrontation with his or her paternalistic society and its judgmental, regulatory forces. The two novels' treatments of sexuality include topics which were generally taboo (prostitution, venereal disease, disease and mental illness, abortion, incest). The narratives are dynamic, presenting paradoxes and complexities of relationships, voice, and perspec-

---

12. For discussions of the important significance of the concepts *tselostnost'* and *tselnost'* in relation to various streams of Russian thought, see Epshtein, *After the Future*.

13. For example, Dark sees *Russkaia krasavitsa* as working toward an ironized totalizing effect, an "encyclopedia of Russian life" (178), and as an antimemoir and a fable (among other things).

tive (as opposed to presenting order and coherence). The texts' extensive, sophisticated use of intertextuality, irony, and rhetorical play complicate and enrich interpretation, engaging ironically with ideological master narratives. Both novels depart from the respective prevailing contemporary literary aesthetics. Instead of the glassy objectivism of the *novela social*, *Tiempo de silencio* prefers an ironic, modernist style of inner mental perceptions combined with exterior narrative perspectives. *Russkaia krasavitsa* revels in postmodernist parodies and apocalyptic metanarratives and a modernist confessional narrative. Both novels focus on the problems of their respective countries, highlighting their sense of Sartrean *engagement* while preferring sophisticated literary artistry over a plain or middle-brow prose accessible to a wide reading public.

These two novels emphasize the contractual relationship binding the subject-characters (Pedro; Irina) to the Law. Like the protagonists of *Ulysses* and *Lolita*, Pedro and Irina are framed as already guilty before the Law; both find themselves in defensive, oppositional, or embattled positions vis-à-vis the Law. In *Tiempo de silencio*, Pedro, despite some resistance, eventually is interpellated (hailed) through his nation's master narrative.[14] In *Russkaia krasavitsa*, Irina is unable to fulfill the demands of the Soviet contract and ends her existence in an apocalyptic wedding. The value of sex as unlawful or obscene counterbalances the protagonists' desire for knowledge and love.

Tiempo de silencio and *Russkaia krasavitsa* take the functions and aims of Francoist and Soviet censorships for wholeness or unity as a set of regulatory presuppositions. *Tiempo de silencio* fractures the perception of Pedro by dividing his character zone into several narrative perspectives. In *Russkaia krasavitsa*, Irina struggles to make a coherent text of herself and her situation out of many shards of experience, memory, and reflection. Pedro resists and ultimately coheres to his country's ideological narrative, thus ironically completing the desire of the big Other. The character-narrator Irina and her text are negatively defined by their lack of coherence to Soviet literary and censorship ideals; her narrative shows up the irrational, incongruous, and incoherent aspects of Soviet life and ideology. The text and its writer exhibit multiple meanings and a lack of control; while Irina may aspire to achieve a utopian ideal of *tselostnost'* (wholeness, completeness),

14. In his landmark 1968 essay on Ideological State Apparatuses, Althusser explains how the subject is interpellated (or "hailed") by ideology in a reciprocal act of recognition. Interpellation is meant to resonate with notions of legal and bureaucratic subjects and procedures, and to challenge our perception of individuality and personal freedom. While Pedro resists the dominant Spanish ideology in some ways, he also wants to be recognized by it and ultimately submits to its values and codes. We could see the protagonists of each of these four novels involved in interpellation struggles.

her writing and her body are presented in fragments which do not add up to a satisfying wholeness that resists conflicting meaning. Like Nastasya Filippovna, Irina is a study of contrasts that would seem to cancel each other out. Her sublime beauty and genius of love promise salvation, but ultimately cannot fulfill it. *Russkaia krasavitsa*'s partially fulfilled promise of the pornographic fantasy of discovering a sexually desiring woman's voice further complicates and enriches the interpretation of literary sexuality and subject's foundations in lack.[15]

Like *Ulysses* and *Lolita*, these Spanish and Russian novels use the contrast between the role of the individual and his or her sense of alienation from the rest of society. All of the protagonists are portrayed as being at odds with the homogenizing discourses of society. At the same time, because of the contrasts in point of view, the characters' and narrators' perspectives illuminate diverse facets of society, matters which were often censored, overlooked, or blindly accepted. Explorations of sexual themes and situations are counterbalanced with the censorious judgments of society.

The crisis of the individual in literature personalizes the forces of censorship which emphasize, in turn, the importance of authorship, an author's life, political convictions, and individuality. All of the novels in question here focus strongly on character, character development, and the importance and signifying value of inner thoughts and fantasy.

Not unlike some of the pre-1970 legal action against works like *Ulysses* and *Lolita* in liberal democracies, Francoist and Soviet censorships perceived sexuality as dirty, offensive, and unaesthetic. The sexuality presented in *Tiempo de silencio* and *Russkaia krasavitsa* develops from that negative and negating perception. The texts metonymically attach sexuality to disease, doomed sexual reproduction, and death. Naiman notes this trend in Soviet culture:

> [S]ex is so evidently an avenue for contamination that other metonymic categories tend to become equated with it. It may be bound with language as

---

15. Basing himself on Hegel and Freud, Lacan sees the human subject as a site of lack or a cut, in part through castration, centering of drives, and his entry into the Symbolic; the subject attempts to fill this lack with his desires, including his gaze toward the other. The other or *objet petit a* stands in for a lack. The *a* stands for *autre* or the little other. See, for example, *Four Fundamental Concepts*, 103–5; also, Lacan's *Écrits* explores the negative formation of the subject and desire (1–7 and 281–325). Silverman adds gender distinctions to the concept of lack: the male subject views the female subject or *objet petit a* as a place of deficiency and inadequacy; he "disburdens himself of his lack" (*Acoustic Mirror*, 1). Silverman expands on this theory in *Male Subjectivity*. Kaite builds on both Lacan's and Silverman's concepts of lack in order to reveal the functioning of pornography, which is always playing with veiled castration. As I discuss, sexuality in the novel, including allusions to pornography, often develops similar situations of lack in the subject.

equivalent agents of pollution, it may be depicted—by virtue of its role in procreation—as the embodiment of historical and therefore antiutopian forces, and it may combine easily with disease or crime to produce cultural events and themes capable of holding a society spellbound. (15–16)

Both Spain and the USSR imposed idealistically nostalgic or utopian systems of values for their societies, and those values were not to be sullied by the disease or vulgarity of sex. We can note the affinities between the desire to censor sexuality and the utopian impulse. Naiman points out that this impulse "manifests a deep dissatisfaction with prevailing social institutions, values, and modes of thought, although inextricably and agonizingly bound up in all these realia" (16). Likewise, for Francoist ideologues, sexuality can be censored by nostalgia in its selective, sanitizing glorification of the past. Turning the tables on this censorial trend, authors like Martín-Santos and Erofeev reintegrate censored sexuality in their texts to signal their deep dissatisfaction with their societies.

In *Tiempo de silencio* and *Russkaia krasavitsa*, the protagonists' confrontations with their self (including their lacks and faults) might give them cause to desire "the perfect, untainted state of being" (Naiman, 16). But if one aims at the ideological ideals of one's state, one has to repress, eradicate, or loathe the grotesque or repulsive aspects of one's environment (and one's self) that do not cohere with those ideals. In both novels, the aspects of sexuality promising fertility, growth, caring, warmth, happiness, beauty, and love are eventually rendered or perceived as sterile, mismanaged, unproductive, barren, rotten, cancerous, or dead. In both novels, the pregnancies do not come to term, but rather end in grotesque deaths of the mothers; no new Spanish or Soviet child is born.

In the negative resolutions of these novels, sexuality as utopia is clearly denied. The narratives play with the suggestion of sexuality as a potential life force and source of knowledge and creative, aesthetic pleasure, as well as a sensuously enjoyable set of practices, but ultimately do not make sexuality triumphant.

The reality not produced by the state and its ideology (a reality that counters the ideological ideals) is that of disease, corruption, ruin. The novels' protagonists Irina and Pedro attempt to realize the fundamental ideological fantasy ("Society as a corporate Body") as described by Žižek (*Sublime Object,* 126). Yet their desire to signify something special in that corporate Body is not appropriate to the fantasy. "Society as a corporate Body" requires homogeneity, coherence, plenitude, and cooperation; the self submits to the collective whole or dies.

■

In all four novels, sexuality is elaborated on the tension between secrecy and openness. The authors avoid having sexuality signify pure freedom, pleasure, or paradise (although the protagonists may at times harbor such fantasies). Instead, Joyce, Nabokov, Martín-Santos, and Erofeev rigorously question sexuality as a site of possible knowledge about ourselves. As we have seen, despite these authors' differing cultural, geopolitical, and even temporal positions in the twentieth century, their projects, based in and conditioned by censorship, all lead us to an investigation of the artistic censoring of sexuality.

2

Circean Censoring

JOYCE'S THEATER OF JUDGMENT IN *ULYSSES*

At the climactic midnight center of *Ulysses* we find a narrativized drama that emphasizes the fantastic, unruly, and dangerous aspects of sexuality: the pleasures of the body (*aphrodisia*), instincts, and desires are held accountable to, and are constructed by, social and moral preoccupations. The Nighttown setting of Monto, Dublin's turn-of-the-century prostitution district, offers a space to explore masculine sexuality, yet it is not a place to escape the Jewish and Catholic and Irish middle-class traditions governing sex and marriage. Self-definition is an unrealized ideal: the boundaries of masculinity and heterosexuality are blurred; the seeking of the self through the other suggests a mutable, flexible sexual desire that oscillates between masculine and feminine allures and that is propelled by drives to know and not know.

"Circe," the central whorl of narrativized drama in *Ulysses,* draws from a wide-ranging European and Irish heteroglossia, and incorporates other dramatic works and structures while serving novelistic discourse. This narrativized drama develops censoring motifs, which include substitution or oscillation, omission, suppression, desire, alternation, metamorphosis or transformation, and repeated, reimagined fantasies of judgment. These motifs are elaborated through metaphor, metonymy, narrative fragments from other episodes, dramatic dialogue, the nightmarish and comic effects of farce, and intertextual allusions to other literary works. The narrative design of the text recalls the movement of a dreamlike state, in which there are formed and articulated images and words of desire and then the censoring of these in some creative fashion. Given that the "Circe" narrative privileges the movement of censoring, a dramatic form is never fully realized. Rather, the various acts and scenes have indistinct borders. A classical dramatic action is lessened by the dual interest in the leading characters Bloom and Stephen and their lack of traditional heroic qualities and emphasis of masochistic qualities of the new man.

Joyce's *Ulysses* is a novel about censoring that happened to become a target for publication censorship, in both its serial magazine form and its 1922 unification as a book.[1] His works consecutively challenged existing censorship standards in literature, and *Ulysses* represents a landmark case in twentieth-century legal history of literature and art.[2] Joyce's novel expands

---

1. Joyce knew he was being provocative with his work, but in literary publication history, we discover that some events do "happen" while others don't, sometimes intentionally, sometimes not. Some works slip past below the radar. Nabokov and publishers agonized that *Lolita* would encounter court action in the United States, and it never did; it did encounter significant censorship in France and England. *Ulysses* was interrupted and banned in serial form when a sixteen-year-old girl in Connecticut happened to read an installment of "Nausicaa" in the *Little Review*. Her father happened to be a lawyer. If this girl had not been such a good reader and her father a prurient lawyer, then *Ulysses* might have continued serial publication in the 1920s. When in the early 1930s, Joyce's lawyer Morris Ernst was planning to bring about the case of the *United States of America v. One Book Entitled* Ulysses, he had *Ulysses* imported from abroad, aiming to have Customs seize it. But by this time, Customs had become blasé about the importation of this novel, so Ernst had to send someone to Customs in person to point out that the novel was still officially banned and by law should be seized. See Ernst and De Grazia, for example, on these actions prompting the trial. It should be noted that Joyce was aiming to publish his work, not to have it remain unpublished. So although censors gave him problems and vice versa, he did not expressly aim to write in order for his work to go unpublished and thus unread.

2. Many scholars have examined the influence of *Ulysses* on modern publishing and law. For a legal perspective, see, for example, Morris Ernst and Alan U. Schwartz, *Censorship: The Search for the Obscene;* Edward De Grazia, *Girls Lean Back Everywhere: The Law of Obscenity and the Assault on Genius;* Paul Vanderham, *James Joyce and Censorship: The Trials of* Ulysses; Adam Parkes, *Modernism and the Theatre of Censorship.* Several recent works consider how the mutually influential rhetoric of legal debates and the discourse of *Ulysses;* see, for example, Michael Groden, Ulysses *in Progress;* Rosa Eberly, *Citizen Critics;* Katherine Mullin, *James Joyce, Sexuality and Social Purity;* Allison Pease, *Modernism, Mass Culture and the Aesthetics of Obscenity;* Marisa Anne Pagnattaro, "Carving a Literary Exception: The Obscenity Standard and *Ulysses*"; Carmelo Medina Casado, "Sifting through Censorship: The British Home Office *Ulysses* Files (1922–1936)"; Brook Thomas, "*Ulysses* on Trial: Some Supplementary Reading"; *The United States of America v. One Book Entitled* Ulysses *by James Joyce: Documents and Commentary; a 50-Year Retrospective;* David Weir, "What Did He Know, and When Did He Know It: The *Little Review,* Joyce, and *Ulysses*"; William S. Brockman, "American Librarians and Early Censorship of *Ulysses:* 'Aiding the Cause of Free Expression'?"; Alistair McCleery, "A Curious History: United Kingdom Government Reaction to *Ulysses*"; Claire Culleton, "Joyce and the G-Men"; Cheryl Herr, "Irish Censorship and 'The Pleasure of the Text':

the parameters of what is acceptable as art (as opposed to pornography or obscenity), not withstanding the fact that Joyce and others have acknowledged that the novel is obscene in places.³ The novel manages to represent censoring techniques and standards, both those of the publishing and legal worlds as well as the artistic world. "Circe" internalizes dialogically a series of discourses related to art, the unconscious and social taboos, pornography and prostitution, institutions regulating sexuality including the Catholic Church, the Dublin police, the English military and generally English colonial rule, the social purity movements, and the economy.⁴

The 'Aeolus' Episode of Joyce's *Ulysses*"; Archie Loss, "The Censor Swings: Joyce's Work and the New Censorship"; Walter Kendrick, "The Corruption of Gerty MacDowell"; Morris L. Ernst, "Reflections on the *Ulysses* Trial and Censorship"; Jackson R. Bryer, "Joyce, *Ulysses,* and the *Little Review.*"

Editors, too, have been involved in censoring Joyce. See, for example: Ezra Pound's aversion to the jakes scene at the end of "Calypso" in Paul Vanderham's "Ezra Pound's Censorship of *Ulysses*"; the odyssey of the Gabler edition is surveyed critically in Vicki Mahaffey's "Intentional Error: The Paradox of Editing Joyce's *Ulysses.*" In relation to excremental language and insinuations, such as those in "Calypso" that bothered Pound, see Vincent Cheng's "'Goddinpotty': James Joyce and the Language of Excrement."

3. Judge Woolsey's famous published ruling on the nonobscene quality of *Ulysses* should be taken as a well-intentioned lie. Vanderham devotes an entire chapter to the issue of Woolsey's "well-intentioned lie," explaining its significance in the law and why we must be cautious in our own interpretations of such rulings. To accept Woolsey's judgment is to assert that there is nothing offensive, obscene, or pornographic in *Ulysses*. Both Vanderham and Parkes offer excellent, detailed discussions of the *Ulysses* trials and publication censorship. Jules David Law develops a sound argument for Woolsey's traditional masculine response to pornography, and for the "Nausicaa" episode's displacement of the masculine, patriarchal subject.

4. For Richard Brown, commercialism is the "sordid reality" to which things return in "Circe." He appraises the 1904 scene: "Dublin was a city where prostitution was rife, largely because of the presence of a garrison of English soldiers. 'Monto' was arguably one of the clearest indications of Ireland's imperial subordination and that is an aspect that Joyce brings to the surface by staging Stephen's fight with the absurdly patriotic English soldiers in that area in 'Circe,' even bringing Edward VII, in freemasonic trowel and apron, to back his representative up" (*James Joyce and Sexuality,* 121).

Shechner's historical contextualization of "Circe" addresses Joyce's keen awareness of the "sordid reality" described by Brown: in addition to courting censorship, Joyce "was conscious of the partial dependence of sexual and intrapsychic repression upon the political and religious institutions that sponsor it in Ireland. Seeing sexual repression primarily as a function of cultural oppression, he undertook a regime of personal desublimation as an act of cultural radicalism" (Shechner, 105).

Peter Hitchcock's article on Bakhtin, answerability, and Joyce points out the prevailing anti-Joycean response of English and Marxist readers in the 1920s, conflicted between balancing the values of social historical content and aesthetic forms. The larger problem is Marxism's difficulty with modernism (66). Hitchcock cites Vincent Cheng's *Joyce, Race and Empire*, which "shows that part at least of the modernist dilemma is an aesthetic confrontation between the promise of more fluid conceptions of subjectivity that modernity makes available and the inhibiting binary logic that inheres in the racial and colonial discourses of Joyce's time" (67).

1. CRITICAL SYNOPSIS

"Circe" occurs from roughly midnight through one o'clock in the morning in Dublin's Monto or redlight district, June 17, 1904. In the previous chapter, "Oxen of the Sun," Leopold Bloom and Stephen Dedalus have been at the hospital, and then drinking at a pub with friends. Upon leaving the pub, the group separates. Stephen and his friend Lynch depart for Nighttown, and Bloom, under the pretext of protecting the drunk young Stephen, follows them there. At the outset of the chapter, we see the arrival of Stephen and Lynch in Monto, and then the separate gasping arrival of Bloom. The men only later encounter each other at Bella Cohen's brothel. Like much of *Ulysses,* there is little plot: in the chapter's "climax" of sorts, Stephen breaks a lamp at Cohen's and later, at the chapter's end, he is knocked unconscious. Bloom protectively shadows Stephen once he has found him at Cohen's; at the end of the chapter Bloom leans over the slowly reviving, murmuring Stephen and sees a vision of his dead son Rudy. Most of the text is consumed with Stephen's and Bloom's fantasies, presented in a loosely associated series of vignettes, often not linked by logical causation, and transposed atop the dark, lurid setting. Bloom has scenes with his father, mother, Molly, grandfather, various Dubliners, imaginary and real, from his present and past. Stephen is accompanied by his friend Lynch as they first stroll the streets of Nighttown and later are revealed idling in Cohen's parlor with several prostitutes. He has fewer fantasy scenes than Bloom, and these include scenes with former teachers, his father, mother, Buck Mulligan, Haines, and various Dubliners. "Circe" is the novel's longest chapter (some 170 pages), but not the densest, formatted as a play rather than a novel. There are no demarcated acts or scenes, as in a conventional play. The action that can be considered "actual" is the men's arrival in Nighttown; Bloom finding Stephen at Cohen's and taking care of his money and stick; some of the conversation and dance at the brothel, ending with Stephen's smashing of the lamp and Cohen's attempt to haggle for the money; Bloom's attempt to move Stephen away from the altercation with Private Carr in the street; Carr's and Stephen's verbal exchange ending with Carr's physical blow to Stephen's head; and Stephen's state of unconsciousness and recovery under Bloom's care.

2. DRAMATIC DISCOURSE IN THE NOVEL

Critics have remarked on the indebtedness of "Circe" to drama. Hugh Kenner notes Shakespeare (especially *Hamlet, Othello*), Ibsen (especially *Ghosts,*

When We Are Dead, Rosmersholm which treats father-daughter incest),[5] and Goethe (*Faust*, especially the *Walpurgisnacht* scenes), as well as the relative contemporary coincidence of the Celtic Renaissance's theater (e.g., Synge's *Playboy of the Western World* and the Abbey Theatre) and the 1904 setting of *Ulysses* (the Abbey's inaugural year), and the Dublin Christmas pantomime. Cheryl Herr develops an in-depth exploration of "Circe"'s investment in pantomime.[6] Pantomime was highly popular in nineteenth-century Ireland, and it has a long tradition as a genre of silent, gestural storytelling. Kathryn Wylie points out that pantomime originates with classical Greek dance, and is especially distinct as a "genre in the Greco-Roman pantomimes [narration of heroic myth and legend] and the nineteenth century *pantomime blanche*" (1). For Aristotle (and for Stephen) mime is linked to the low arts. Commedia dell'arte—with its masks, grotesqueries, satires, parodies, and Bakhtinian carnivalesque reversals of identity and release from cultural restraints—can also be related to features in "Circe."

Margot Norris remarks on the influence of German Expressionist theater on Joyce (in 1901 he translated two plays by Gerhart Hauptmann, *Sunrise* and *Michael Kramer*, and generally took a keen interest in continental drama).[7] Hauptmann's play *Hanneles Himmelfahrt* (*The Ascension of Joan*) offers hallucinations of an abused girl. Norris discusses the parallels in such expressionistic plays and "Circe": the "collapse of boundaries between mind and world in order to create an extremely subjectivized space, a universe that is an externalized expression of the most extreme feelings and experiences of the mind [. . .]"; "a mystical 'dark night of the soul' [or] *Seelendrama*" ("Theater," 80).[8]

I shall return to some of these discussions, including the history context of Irish theater and Joyce's Dublin of 1904 in "Circe," the importance of costumes and the flexible representation of gender (Herr's identification

---

5. In her exploration of triangles of sin in *Ulysses*, especially incest, adultery, and suicide, Jane Ford notes Ibsen's influence on Joyce "in this recurrent preoccupation with sexual frustration, the power of the dead over the living, man's relentless need to cope with his guilt, and possibly also, *kindermord*" (124).

6. See Cheryl Herr's *Joyce's Anatomy of Culture*.

7. See Norris's "Disenchanting Enchantment: The Theatrical Brothel of 'Circe'" and "Theater of the Mind: 'Circe' and Avant-Garde Form." In "Disenchanting Enchantment," Norris identifies Joyce's highly critical use of pornography as a discourse in the "enchantment" of 'Circe': "By pretexting the pornographic episodes of "Circe" with other pornography—for example, citing *Venus in Furs* as the incitement for mimicking its language ("He addressed me in several handwritings with fulsome compliments as a Venus in furs and alleged profound pity for my frost-bound coachman Palmer" [15:1045–47])—Joyce doubles the transgressive position of pornography by allowing it to mock, exploit, and resexualize its own censorships and suppressions" (232). In "Theater of the Mind," Norris highlights Joyce's indebtedness to German expressionism.

8. The German *Seelendrama* translates literally as "soul drama."

of pantomime features in "Circe"), and the aesthetic influences from other dramatic genres.

The discourse of "Circe" does not constitute a play; rather, the language of theater is subordinated to the overall novelistic system of discourse that is *Ulysses*. "Circe," presented as a "piece of theater," masquerades as such. It remains a chapter in a novel, and continues to deploy primary and secondary features of the novel, particularly by its referential system to other parts of the novel, be these dialogues, character development, description of action or setting, and so on.[9] The language of "Circe" configures the novelistic language of *Ulysses* into both the direct discourse of speaking characters and things (mimesis) and into stage directions and indications (diegesis).

Both mimetic and diegetic elements of "Circe" employ poetic and realistic expressions. Mimesis in "Circe" does not limit itself to realistically conveying actual speech. In many mimetic discourses of characters and things in "Circe" emerge words and phrases expressed elsewhere in the novel by the narrator or other characters. Much of the language of "Circe" is focalized by the dialogic capacities (speaking, listening, responding capacities) of Bloom and Stephen from other areas and dimensions of the novel (including their history prior to June 16 and 17, 1904). For example, cigarette smoke wreaths say to Bloom: "Sweet are the sweets. Sweets of sin" (429): a transposition of the title of a novel bought by Bloom for Molly (227) and creative variations of the title, a topic and wordplay revisited many times throughout the day and night, starting from Bloom's postprandial book shopping in "Wandering Rocks."

The mimetic dramatic form of "Circe" does not cohere to dramatic standards.[10] Well beyond a theater of the absurd, "Circe" would be virtu-

---

9. In *Joyce's Anatomy of Culture,* Cheryl Herr examines theatrical elements in "Circe" such as its use of dramatic techniques, dramatic genres such as melodrama and pantomime, and transvestism on the stage. My interpretation of the episode's dramatic content differs from Herr's in that it seems to me that that content is always determined by greater narrative structures and elements of the novel. Perhaps in a mimetically theatrical way, the episode masquerades as drama while remaining essentially a part of the narrative discourse. There is no reason, however, not to include dramatic discourse and structures into the novelistic one. In keeping with Bakhtin's heteroglossia that defines the modern novel, *Ulysses* incorporates dramatic discourse and references into its great swath of heteroglossia. In contrast to the hybrid dialogic dramatic-narrative that is "Circe," a conventional play does not feature dialogism. Sue Vice explains that, for Bakhtin, "[d]rama cannot be dialogic [...] because it possesses no scope for the fictional narrator—'a unity that encompasses and stands above'" (*Introducing Bakhtin,* 187). In a discussion on dialogism, Vice acknowledges *Ulysses* as a successful "'novelization' of epic" (82), by novelization meaning dialogic on Bakhtin's terms.

10. Marilyn French warns readers not to be lured by the naturalistic promise of the stage (186–87), especially with regard to the "hallucinations" of Bloom and Stephen; she goes on to explain that "[t]he dramatic form of the chapter is appropriate to a technique in which details of the imagination are projected as realities. The form not only permits the hypostatization of

ally impossible to produce on stage; its literary foundation is the novel, not theater. Nonetheless, discursively, the chapter relies on heteroglot narrative that incorporates dramatic features and themes, particularly the theme of judgment. Circe's frequent character transformations do reflect the tradition of farce, in particular the British extravaganza, burlesque, and pantomime, with their heavy reliance on the lively, grotesque, and absurd. Further over-the-top theatricality is seen in the numerous striking visual and acoustic changes of costume and scene.

Joyce's lengthy, detailed stage directions are similar to the equally intricate stage directions of Regency pantomimes (such as *Aladdin* by Edward Litt Leman Blanchard). Moreover, as Michael R. Booth points out, in his history of nineteenth-century British theater, "[i]n the Regency harlequinade man's plight is often created by transformation, misbehaviour, and relentless hostility of objects and mechanical devices" (7), and that pantomime combined "fantasy and comic nightmare" (21). Pantomime became a favorite of the Victorian and Edwardian public, thus forming part of the historical context of *Ulysses*. Joyce uses it further to provide a popular and aesthetic structural context for some dramatic action of "Circe." The actions of Stephen and Bloom in Nighttown—some actual and much imagined—reflect an alternating sense of comedy and nightmare, in keeping with the overall censoring movement of the chapter. Booth points out that in farce, danger and despair, while presented or threatened, are also ultimately invalidated (23). Likewise, for Stephen and Bloom, whatever danger or despair confront them in "Circe" (and these are impressive in number and fantastic form), the two men are ultimately spared lasting noxious consequences.

Meanwhile, some other dramatic influences of "Circe" are vague and impressionistic. Although Ibsen is one of Joyce's favorite playwrights, Ibsen's *Ghosts* and *When We Are Dead* are relatively weak intertexts for this chapter, evocative thematically of death, doomed social progress, and ghostliness, but showing no strong parallels of character, action, setting, or crisis. Joyce's own play *Exiles* (1918), with its critique of the double standard and the

---

thoughts and feelings but give the illusion of objectivity. Narrator comment seems to be lacking. However, a glance at any of the 'stage directions' should dispel that illusion. [. . .] The point of view of Circe, like that of its predecessors, is from far above the scene. What is being examined is the irrational world, which is defined as the world of feelings, and the subject matter is thus connected with that of Sirens, Cyclops, and Nausikaa. The particular feelings being examined are secret and hidden ones, primarily sexual" (195–96).

Hélène Cixous reflects on the psychodramatic features: "schizotext [. . .]. He who enters here casts aside the interiority of the body and of thought, the self's unity and integrity in space, continuity in time, to be pushed to the limit of suffering. [. . .] Here things are other things. Everything is endlessly transformed. [. . .] The self is without a core of identity. [. . .] Are you sure of not being what you are not?" (388).

stifling moralistic provincialism of Dublin, shows more effort to follow Ibsen, while "Circe" does not aim to produce primarily a social thesis nor an Edwardian problem play.

Kenner emphasizes Joyce's development of a Shakespearean dialogism and concerns of the aforementioned farce (rejection of normativity):

> [. . .] Shakespeare, all of whose faults, as noted by all of his critics, he [Joyce] seems to have heaped together for imitation: the word-play, the cavalier disregard of unities, the motivation turning on trivia, the tickles for the groundlings, the offhand mechanics ("Exit, pursued by a bear"), the topicalities, the flagrant mixing of genres, the bawdry. How better to epitomize the essential Shakespeare than by seizing on all that distinguishes him from normative dramatists? He made the play illustrate Stephen's Shakespearean discourse, too—"We walk through ourselves, meeting robbers, ghosts, giants, old men, young men, wives, widows, brothers-in-love. But always meeting ourselves." (119)

In my analysis, the dramatic structure and discourse of "Circe" are subservient to the overall dialogism of the novel *Ulysses*. While the episode could be read alone, its full potential is realized in its relation to the rest of the text. I will presently discuss the features of the dramatic discourse, but for now I wish to address how I diverge partially from Bakhtinian narrative theory; some of my terminology draws from Bakhtin, Genette, and Barthes. The narrator in "Circe" is largely a zero-degree focalizer, that is, he/it/she surveys omnisciently the scene, directing through the utterances, actions, and other aspects of the mise-en-scène. The narrator's tone varies from terse simplicity ("*He is howled down*" [15:965]) to ironic or poetic elaborations ("*He lifts his mutilated ashen face moonwards and bays lugubriously*" [15:1213–14]). In general, the stage directions are excessive in their precise and abundant detail, tending to reflect a novelist's rather than a dramatist's sensibility.

The characters' speeches often reflect discourse stated elsewhere in the novel, sometimes words belonging to others previously, what Bakhtin calls an intrusion of "concealed form." This technique can be noted in other episodes, such as "Nausicaa": the "concealed form" "designates the introduction of the speech of another into the author's discourse without any of the formal markers," an utterance itself "other to the author as well" (36). In considering how the dramatic form of "Circe" serves the novel, we might well turn to Wallace Martin's account of how conventional drama, even modern drama, cannot be equated with narrative:

> While drama can present scenes and actions economically, it cannot summarize

and thus blend in stretches of time not worth enacting; hence its choppy structure. Unlike a book, a play or film can't be picked up and set down at will. The pauses for intermission are imposed on us, and the span of human attention is such that performances seldom entertain us for more than three hours. The distinguishing feature of narrative—access to the thoughts and feelings of the characters, as Blanckenburg noted in 1774—is simply missing in drama, unless it is clumsily introduced. [. . .] [Immediacy of drama] is small compensation for what is lost in a medium that can show us everything but tell us nothing. The dramatist is absent, leaving us to infer meaning from an illusion; the narrator, on the other hand, can take the responsible choice of speaking to us directly. (109–10)

If we judge by Martin's list of features, "Circe" is joined more closely to narrative traditions than the conventions of drama. It is true, however, that Joyce makes great strategic use of drama by making exterior (seen and spoken) the "thoughts and feelings of the characters." The wily, knowing narrator is not absent when we encounter lines like, "*The car jingles tooraloom round the corner of the tooraloom lane. Corny Kelleher again reassuralooms with his hand. Bloom with his hand assuralooms Corny Kelleher that he is reassuraloomtay*" (15:4916–19). It is also true that the text in dramatic form can *seem* to distance itself from the narrator's control. For example, Stephen, as he is recovering consciousness, murmurs fragments of Yeats's "Who Goes with Fergus": STEPHEN [. . .]: . . . shadows . . . the woods / . . . white breast . . . dim sea. / (*He stretches out his arms, sighs again and curls his body. Bloom, holding the hat and ashplant, stands erect.* [. . .].) BLOOM (*communes with the night*): Face reminds me of his poor mother. In the shady wood. The deep white breast. Ferguson, I think I caught. A girl. Some girl. Best thing could happen him" (15:4940–50). While this passage could be related in a narrative rather than a play, the dramatic discourse emphasizes the incongruity of the two men's speeches. Bloom "answers" Stephen's words without fully understanding them, and to a large degree in fact, misapprehending them.[11] The narrator masquerades as dramatist.

3. JUDGMENT IN MASOCHISM: GENDER PERFORMANCE

In "Circe," the theater of judgment is developed often through masculine masochistic constructions. It might be recalled that Leopold Sacher-Masoch's

---

11. I will return to comment on this part of the episode later in this chapter.

Venus in Furs (1870), a narrative intertext for "Circe" and ur-text for masochist theory, and other narratives with masochist story lines involve a contract between the masochist and his designated dominatrix. This contract results in stylized, dramatic (role-playing, fantasizing, aggressive) players within a circumscribed stage and costumes designed to aestheticize further the erotic events. In "Circe," masochistic role-playing, as well as the frequent changing of costumes and roles, is a central feature and signals judgment on two levels. First, the masochist gains pleasure and drama in being judged harshly by his dominatrix; his drama is based on being found guilty, condemned, and punished. Second, the masochistic fantasy develops a larger critique of staid social and aesthetic standards. The various martyrdoms that Bloom and Stephen endure dramatize social intolerance of transgressive, alternative, or progressive sexuality, art, and politics.

Suzanne Stewart notices a change in gendered norms by the mid-nineteenth century in Europe. Her discussions of Heine, Freud, Wagner, and Sacher-Masoch can be related to the masochistic men of "Circe" in the sense that the masochistic man expresses a reordering of values of power and preference in modern society. She argues that

> [...] masochism establishes a new normativity in the name of anti-normativity, and that this new normativity has questionable political effects. The masochistic claims of male renunciation as staged, as rhetorical, must be taken at their word, even though this rhetoric has had real social and political effects: masochism, as it was formulated both as a medical diagnosis of the age and as an aesthetic concept that ordered a new relationship to the culture at large, contributed significantly to the rearticulation of male subjectivity. In the name of marginalization, a new norm was constituted: men were viewed and viewed themselves as always already wounded or fragmented, subjected and enslaved to modern civilization by their own desires, which, of necessity, remained unfulfilled. Masochism expressed both a crisis of male subjectivity and the positive valorization of that crisis whereby crisis itself became a constitutive feature of that same masculinity. (13)

Within this system of gendered values, the Cruel Woman—as the dominatrix and aesthetic object—complements the inadequate but persistent male body. Stewart describes the masochistic male body as one that "submits to an aestheticized and eroticized gaze and voice, thus conceiving of man as deeply penetrated by relations of political and sexual power" (14). We can compare this evaluation with Gilles Deleuze's assessment of masochism's symbolism: "The masochist feels guilty, he asks to be beaten, he expatiates, but why and for what crime? Is it not precisely the father-image in him that is thus miniaturized, beaten, ridiculed and humiliated? What the subject atones for is his resemblance to the father and the father's likeness in him: *the formula of masochism is the humiliated father.* Hence the father is not so much the beater as the beaten" (60–61).

In "Circe," the male body, through its series of diverse sufferings, reaffirms masculine control and authority. The control is portrayed in the elaborate stagings, deferrals, contracts; the primary setting is the site of prostitution, a place for the exchange and circulation of male bodies, masculine subjectivities (transformation, deferral of satisfaction, expressions of unconscious wishes), and their return intact. The aestheticized women in the chapter support the men's drama. The women's roles as prostitutes set up a critical condemnation of contemporary values of Irish identity as related to the economy founded in colonial subjugation and poverty. The reward for the men's sufferings is the ghostlet Rudy in his Eton attire, and not Molly nor May Dedalus, nor the various prostitutes.

Bloom's masochistic role-playing of womanliness can be seen as negating a standard Irish colonial masculinity.[12] In a 1929 article, Joan Riviere examines three cases of women attempting to masquerade as a more womanly woman. She argues that "women who wish for masculinity may put on a mask of womanliness to avert anxiety and the retribution feared from men" (210). One of the women studied tended to perform for men, particularly "unmistakable father-figures," whose "judgment [. . .] would in reality [not] carry much weight" (211). In her article "Castration and Its Discontents," Kimberly Devlin relates Riviere's early contribution to gender performance (especially the concept of masks and the masquerade) to Lacanian theory. With Lacan, gender is developed making up for the lack of the phallus; this is the case for both men and women (hetero- and homosexual). Symbolically, women can "be" the phallus, while men can "have" the phallus (*Écrits*, 289). Lacan explains how these sexed relations,

---

12. We could compare Bloom's masquerade of femininity with Mrs. Kearney's performance of masculinity in Joyce's "Ivy Day in the Committee Room"; see Garry Leonard's Lacanian discussion of a woman's doubly ironic masquerade ("The Masquerade of Gender," esp. 144). Kimberly J. Devlin explores Joyce's "self-conscious anatomy of feminine as well as masculine roles" in "Penelope" ("Pretending in 'Penelope': Masquerade, Mimicry, and Molly Bloom," 77). Sue Vice builds on Devlin's discussion by suggesting how a Bakhtinian double-voicedness could be recognized in Penelope's discourse ("The Construction of Femininity"). It would be interesting to compare the phallic order underpinning these performances of gender. Martha Black surveys *Ulysses* for negotiations of gender, arguing that Bloom "is, indeed, a test case and sometime parody of an androgyne. In him Joyce composed qualities that have been scripted as stereotypically feminine [e.g., intuition, tenderness, domesticity, etc.]" ("S/he-Male Voices in *Ulysses*," 71).

In a shift to masks, narrators, and dialogism, we could also recall that *Ulysses*'s narrators are generally masked. See Brandon Kershner's *Joyce, Bakhtin, and Popular Literature* and "Teaching" (esp. 163).

"by referring to a signifier, the phallus, have the opposed effect, on the one hand, of giving reality to the subject in this signifier, and, on the other, of derealizing the relations to be signified." Lacan continues:

> This is brought about by the intervention of a "to seem" that replaces the "to have," in order to protect it on the one side, and to mask its lack in the other, and which has the effect of projecting in their entirety the ideal of typical manifestations of the behaviour of each sex, including the act of copulation itself, into the comedy. These ideals take on a new vigour from the demand that they are capable of satisfying, which is always a demand for love, with its complement of the reduction of desire to demand. [. . .] [I]n order to be the phallus [. . .], the signifier of the desire of the Other, [. . .] a woman will reject an essential part of femininity, namely, all her attributes in the masquerade. (289–90)

In Lacan's view, love and desire are at odds; the woman in a love relationship ends up offering love, and not the phallus, while the phallus can in turn be sought by the man in the "other" woman, such as a prostitute or virgin. Lacan observes how the feminine draws on masculine qualities for its maintenance: "The fact that femininity finds its refuge in this mask, by virtue of the fact of the *Verdrängung* [repression] inherent in the phallic mark of desire, has the curious consequence of making virile display in the human being itself seem feminine" (291). In Devlin's application of the Lacanian masking and "seeming" the phallus, she notes how some men in *Ulysses* (Bloom, Stephen, Simon) are often contemplating dispossession and loss; she quotes Restuccia's argument that "Joyce shows that the Dublin male's preoccupation with phallic power is a sign of its lack" (125).

I would add that the Irish masculinity largely on display in *Ulysses* is the Catholic one. Although Catholics formed a majority, they were generally unable to attain positions of power or wealth, in part owing to the barring of Catholic men from influential posts. Devlin points out Lacan's term for the male masquerade, *parade virile,* translated as "virile display." She goes on to explain: "He [Lacan] establishes this term [. . .] to delineate a different enunciation ("I am the ideal of manliness"), an enunciation similar in kind to the masquerade of womanliness in its essential fraudulence. Lacan explicitly links the two gender acts when he notes that 'virile display in the human being itself seem[s] feminine,' presumably because the exaggeration of the pose betrays it *as* pose" ("Castration," 132; emphasis in original). Devlin explores the tenuous masculine parades of Mulligan and Boylan.

Riviere's examination and Lacan's further theorization reveal two important elements about gender performance that can be related back to

Bloom,[13] and perhaps to Stephen.

First, behaving in a womanly way is something that can be done by women or men. In Bloom's case, his womanly act as brothel novice or expectant mother takes the masochistic masculine role into a feminine, aestheticized domain. Another of his fantasies casts him as a female impersonator in a play *Vice-Versa: A Farcical Fantastic Play* (1882) by F. Anstey.[14] As if to complement Bloom's performance as woman, the dominatrix Bella masquerades as masculine (Bello), and while clearly maintaining the role of phallic sadistic dominator (the farting, the cigar, the rough treatment), Bello also aids in revealing Bloom's fears, anxieties, and desires, as well as providing a heteroglot critique of the traffic in women at the fin de siècle.[15]

---

13. I agree with Joseph Allen Boone that the positive features of Bloom's womanliness are often overlooked. Boone explains how Joyce, "[c]apitalizing on Otto Weininger's notion of Jewish 'effeminacy,' [...] attributes these submissive tendencies to Bloom in order to suggest his desire to experience a wider spectrum of sexual behavior than is traditionally acceptable, one that includes both active and passive principles" ("A New Approach to Bloom as 'Womanly Man,'" 71). While Joyce may have borrowed some notions from Weininger's *Sex and Character* [1903], the treatment in *Ulysses* is alternately critical and ironic. The jury still seems to be out on Weininger's possible misogyny and anti-Semitism; Daniel Steuer's introduction ("A Book That Won't Go Away") to the new translation of *Sex and Character* contextualizes Weininger's Jewish identity and contemporary attitudes toward Jews and Jewishness.

14. In "Theater of the Mind," Norris explains that this play, "a story about a father and son whose minds are switched into each other's bodies, is discussed by Bloom as though it were about homosexual transvestism in order to explain his donning of female clothing in his fantasy with Bello ('It was Gerald converted me to be a true corsetlover when I was female impersonator in the High School play *Vice Versa*' [15.30009])" (89–90). Norris notes that Bloom invents this fantasy, as he would have graduated from high school before the play's publication, and that Stephen has performed in this play at Belvedere in *Portrait* (and that one boy, little Bertie Tallon, had to play a girl's part) (94 n.10).

At schools of all boys or all girls, male and female roles in theater productions generally have to be shared. The female roles in earlier English drama such as Shakespeare were played by boys or men. The title of this particular play provides a double entendre for Bloom's fantasy transvestism: the vice is on the versa side (on the homosexual side or side of the other sex), plus the reversible connotation of the Latin *vice versa*. In addition, the exchange of the father and son of minds/bodies suggests a transcendent yet eroticized signification, perhaps more at play in Stephen's awkward relation to his father than Bloom's to Rudolph. See Kershner's *Joyce* (180–85) for a reading of Stephen and Simon via *Vice-Versa*. Kershner also explains how *Vice-Versa, or a Lesson to Fathers* was first published as a novel in 1882. Its unexpected success led to nineteen reprints in 1882 and to a dramatic version in 1883, and a later expanded version in 1910. Joyce performed in this Whitsuntide play, probably in 1898 (Kershner, 180).

15. Katherine Mullin's excellent *James Joyce, Sexuality and Social Purity* makes clear that "Circe" draws on rhetoric and motifs of brothel policing, pornography, reformist literature. In her discussion, of the Bloom-Bello exchange, Mullin notes how "Bloom's surrender of the supposedly 'masculine' power of spectatorship is integral to his transformation as prostitute woman. Joyce here emphasises the extent to which the prostitute was culturally produced as spectacle, as Bloom's sex change transforms him into the kind of abject sight he has previously attempted to regulate" (193). Mullin goes on to notice how the "Circe" prostitute motif reflects the language and structure of the social purity movement's literature of fallen women through a "Gothic exploitation" of coerced innocent girls.

Second, the "masquerade" of womanliness belies a hidden, repressed phallic and sadistic characteristic in the woman's psyche. There is an anxiety on the part of the woman to hide aesthetically her masculinity by using a veil of physical and behavioral feminine qualities, as if to be seen as masculine would be wrong and might elicit retribution from men. The complex is indicative of the conflict some modern women have experienced in trying to balance oppositional gendered roles of worker and domestic goddess, or the sexually liberated woman versus the meek, submissive, or repressed woman. Bloom's womanly masquerades find resonance in Aubrey Beardsley's turn-of-the-century gender-bending images that can be seen as threatening to dominant culture. Allison Pease explains how Bloom's submission to Bella/Bello involves both a transformation from man to woman and from woman to prostitute. Like Mullin, Pease finds that this masochistic parody "makes obvious the hegemonic cultural association between the working classes and the sexual body. The prostitute is the sexualized, working-class body. What's more, her body becomes the object of capitalist penetration: whoever will pay may subject it to his will" (116).

While I fully agree with these social readings of "Circe," ultimately Bloom functions as the center or focalizer of the prostitution-class fantasy and other fantasies of subjugation and oppression. Bloom's explorations through gender and sexual fantasy produce potentially pleasurable scenes which are counterbalanced by the social condemnation inherent in the use of heteroglot discourse, that is, to involve the discourses of pornography and erotica,[16] social purity reformist literature, idealized sexuality of romance literature, and public debates of institutionalized flagellation and other practices in girls' schools and reformatories (as a sign of bourgeois concern with regulation of the unruly body of the underclasses). What pleasures Bloom derives from his various fantasies are negated or censored by the social concerns constructing them. And if the social concerns are constructed from his knowledge of this repertoire of social and cultural discourses, the censoring is creatively enacted by him, first and foremost.

The masquerade case discussed by Riviere can be related to Bloom in subversive ways that go beyond the approach to gendered performativity as outlined by Judith Butler (*Bodies That Matter*). Bloom averts the anxiety of proving to be a man by approximating women's experience; he thus avoids

---

16. For a review or overview of this literature, both historical and invented (e.g., *Ruby, the Pride of the Ring*), see, for example, Leslie A. Fiedler's "To Whom Does Joyce Belong? *Ulysses* as Parody, Pop and Porn." While Ruby is taken for (red-herring) erotica in *Ulysses,* Mary Power found its prototype, *Ruby: A Novel: Founded on the Life of a Circus Girl* (1889) by Amye Reade. See Power's "The Discovery of Ruby."

being a male sadist and receiving an awful retribution by men. When he does suffer, he suffers as a woman, and experiences pleasurable masochism that has been organized on his terms. The essence of the woman's fantasy in the Riviere case is the woman's supremacy over her parents.

Riviere contemplates the possible meaning of womanliness as masquerade:

> The acceptance of "castration," the humility, the admiration of men, come partly from the over-estimation of the object on the oral-sucking plane; but chiefly from the renunciation (lesser intensity) of sadistic castration-wishes deriving from the later oral-biting level. "I must not take, I must not even ask; it must be *given* me." The capacity for self-sacrifice, devotion, self-abnegation expresses efforts to restore and make good, whether to mother or to father-figures, what has been taken from them. It is also what Radó has called a 'narcissistic insurance' of the highest level. (220; emphasis in original)

In the masquerades enacted by Bloom (and Stephen) in "Circe," the men's narcissism, sadistic-castration wishes, and self-abnegation can be related to a desire to don a type of womanliness in defense of a rejected masculinity. The masochistic scenes effectuate a kind of censoring of the manly self, as well as the censure of the colonial scenes of gendered subjugation (e.g., Irish Catholic men's lack of social mobility and political influence; impoverished Irish women's reliance on prostitution funded in good part by the English).

In the emerging modern society of turn-of-the-century Europe, the traditional emulation of fathers is being replaced by a resistance of refusal *not* to take the father's place in order to become a man. Stewart argues that in the late nineteenth and early twentieth centuries one can observe the obliteration of the traditional father's role (and the son's taking of the father's place) "in order to generate the new man" (3). This revalorized masochistic fantasy opposes the sadistic institutionalized superego of the father. Instead, the "contract" is made with the pre-Oedipal, oral mother. In Stewart's argument, the masochist shows the crisis of the failed paternal system and symbolization, demonstrating that it takes trauma to be a "real man" (5). In the new contract, the impossible object (such as the Lady) is transformed into a prohibition. The masochist stages his transformation through a "process of unending postponement" (6). Bloom and Stephen, in different ways, seem locked into a performance of their masochistic stance toward the world: Bloom in his postponed sexual consummation that actually has come to be his primary mode of erotic pleasure; Stephen in his ever-delayed blossoming as an artist.

The masochistic stances of Bloom and Stephen should not be regarded as resulting in failure. Instead, these stances indicate a redefinition of masochism in terms of power. For Victor Smirnoff, the actualization of a contract must regulate the relationship in the masochistic performance ("Masochistic Contract"). He explains that "[t]he symbiotic relation, as found in masochism, makes use of suffering, pain and humiliation, not in order to obtain pleasure, but as a symbolic representative of both the unattainable fusion with, and the impossible separation from, the primary sexual object" (72).

Smirnoff's examination of the masochistic contract is particularly interesting when compared with the masochistic men of "Circe" because he underlines the powerful role of the masochist, who in fact organizes every aspect of the scene as would a director of a play. Smirnoff sees this role of director as homologous to that of a teacher:

> To institute and enact the endless repetition of this denial, masochism can only be based on a contract that is also an alliance. By instituting such a ritual, with all the compulsive elements included, the executioner must be part of the masochistic position, not an outside figure. Sacher-Masoch does not use the vocabulary of a victim, but that of the director of this play. Thus the masochist does not appear as the victimized accomplice to a sadistic executioner, but as his educator—just as the sadist is the pedagogue of his reluctant victim. (72)

If such an assessment of the masochistic contract holds true, then we should regard the masochist as a powerful agent, capable of changing others. Is it possible to consider Bloom and Stephen as possible educators in "Circe"? These characters seem to elide the role of educator in this scene, perhaps because their dominatrices/dominators are largely fantasmatic.

It is perhaps more pertinent, then, to consult Jean Laplanche's consideration of a nuanced masochism, what he calls "reflexive masochism"

> or the middle voice, a fantasy which, however, has a properly masochistic content in the 'passive' sense: I am being beaten by my father. [. . .] To fantasize aggression is to turn it around upon oneself, to aggress oneself: such is the moment of autoerotism, in which the dissoluble bond between fantasy as such, sexuality, and the unconscious is confirmed. ("Aggressiveness and Sadomasochism," 122)

Laplanche sees this reflexive masochism as part of a more generalized self-reflexive, anaclitic eroticism. After all, the turning around upon oneself is a general movement in sexuality. To a certain degree, in combination with the oscillating narrative technique of "Circe," we could consider the subject's turning of things like aggression around upon itself as reflected in the narrative structure or movement of the episode. The aggression in "Circe" is turned around back on Bloom and Stephen, alternately, in varying and transformative ways. Surely, this is a kind of mastery that upends traditional paternal power.

4. NARRATIVE OSCILLATIONS AND DRAMATIC DISCOURSES

In order to observe how an artistic or creative censoring is carried out in the language of "Circe," we can consider the concept of oscillation as narrative technique. Oscillation in narrative reflects the movement of the mind when approaching sensitive or taboo subjects. In dreaming, the mind's censorship could be said to use a pattern of oscillation at times, shifting from one subject to another to avoid direct or lengthy contemplation. Although he does not connect the concept of oscillation to censoring, John Paul Riquelme sees "Circe" as "the Play of Consciousness."[17]

Riquelme notices, in "Circe" and "Penelope," "oscillating styles" in "wide frames of reference. Those contexts include literary genres and the status of fictional language as mimetic or self-referential. The two episodes provide the most intense version in *Ulysses* [. . .] of the dramatic and the lyrical within the epical. By placement, function, and implication, [. . .] they act as a climax and a post scriptum for the narration" (136).

Riquelme links his idea of oscillating styles to the concept of the mirror: "In the reflective and self-reflective styles of Joyce's late texts, the writer inscribes and the reader recognizes their composite image in the looking glass of art. That looking glass is always visible because cracked" (136). He particularly insists that "Circe" "is not a window but a mirror. We see it as a mirror because of the oddities in the episode's form."

I can agree with Riquelme that interpretations of "Circe" explaining language as "a mimesis of action fail to deal convincingly with the episode's implications" (137). But I would add that the concept of the narrative as a mirror can only be noticed in particular instances of repetition and variation. Drama usually offers many instances of mimesis (as opposed to diegesis which tends to be more prominent in narrative discourse), especially because drama usually stages spoken dialogue. As we know from the pantomime discussion, the drama of "Circe" is not developed on the idea

---

17. See especially 135–53 of his *Teller and Tale in Joyce's Fiction: Oscillating Perspectives*.

of re-represented speech alone.[18] Of course, "Circe" repeats and repositions many narrative fragments from the novel's previous episodes and hours of the day and night (the accretive composition of "Circe"), in this way offering instances of reflection and preoccupation on the parts of Stephen and Bloom.

For Riquelme, "Circe"'s digressions work as a prominent discursive strategy, and even "the core of the work itself" (139). In my view, digression and oscillation are two of several strategies of the censoring movements of "Circe," but not constitutive of a "core." If anything, "Circe" seems to operate around lack and absence. In order to avoid an overly sensitive topic, the narrative digresses to another topic, substituting or transforming. Censoring offers an organizational structure and theme, for it involves judgment, masochism, desire, and the struggle for artistic and personal liberation.

Counter to Riquelme's argument, we can see narrativized drama forming the dynamic center of "Circe." The episode brings together in destabilizing and unfamiliar ways various strands, allusions, and inferences from the other chapters. The two main characters, in narrative style, provide further dramatic focus in this indeterminate setting. Drama further reverberates through the episode's reference to theater and performances in other episodes: for example, the novel's Shakespearean episode "Scylla and Charybdis";[19] Molly as a performer, in concert and out; opera references and intertextuality.[20]

---

18. The play's dialogue, the novel's dialogue, and dialogism need to be distinguished. Jola Škulj notes that dialogism, for Bakhtin (*Dialogic Imagination*), implies another logic (e.g., that of the narrator): "The logic of dialogue in the novel, is «a *dramatic* <banter>,» and this is 0–2 poetic logic, which is, in fact, aporetic. But dialogue is the novelistic *morfè*, and dialogism might be explained as «the characteristic epistemological mode of a world dominated by heteroglossia.» Dialogue in the novel is, Bakhtin asserts, a dialogue of a special sort and it should be considered its minimal constitutive artistic feature" (47). Relating Austin's and Searle's linguistic interchange of speech, and Bakhtin's point that in dialogue "speaking «persons would not confront each other as sovereign egos»," Škulj shows how the "relational character and non-sovereignty" are emphasized (47). The absorption and transformation of another's voice: this is the result of dialogue.

19. "Scylla and Charybdis" offers a brief play's formatted dialogue embedded in the novelistic discourse; Stephen's focalization allows for this dramatization of the speakers' dialogue.

In his "Polyphony and the Carnivalesque in Shakespeare and Joyce," Willi Erzgräber-Freiburg makes a strong case for considering drama's discourse in *Hamlet* as open and polyphonic, refuting Bakhtin's exclusion of drama in his scheme of polyphony. Meanwhile, with "Circe," Erzgräber maintains that the "principle of transcending the limits, which is typical of carnival, is expressed clearly in this chapter, [. . .] set in Bella Cohen's brothel, in that individual realistic passages are combined with surreal passages, for which the concept of 'hallucinations' was sometimes used" (274). He notes the grotesque and the "obscene emphasis on the physical" to disparage "the religious and spiritual domain" (274–75).

20. Ultimately, Riquelme seems to work against his own argument: his overemphasis of mimesis and narrative does not allow him to study the drama and dramatic speech as serving novelistic discourse.

The "play" of "Circe" does not parody any particular play, but it touches on a variety of theatrical motifs and discourses in direct or tangential ways, including references to deceit, adultery, *Hamlet,* and the historical Shakespeare. Shakespeare's *Hamlet* combines the betrayals of the parents and son (the filial crisis) and the adultery crisis. *Hamlet*'s integration in "Circe" (and *Ulysses*) joins Stephen (filial narrative) and Bloom (adultery and filial narratives) on a higher dialogic level.[21] *Hamlet* also offers two pantomime or "dumb shows," both of which become thematically linked to paternal-filial codes of *Ulysses:* the ghost of Act I who gestures (and speaks) to Hamlet (I.iv–v); the myse-en-abîme of the dumb show preceding "The Murder of Gonzago, or The Mousetrap" (III.ii). These plays within the play highlight adulterous deception and the hidden primal scene, signaling sexuality as dangerous, amoral, and destructive.

Joyce taps into the novelistic attraction to the theme of adultery. In the nineteenth century, adultery dominates the plot of several landmark works, especially novels (in which theater and themes of forbidden love are embedded); sexuality becomes linked to both freedom and transgression, to love and unethical conduct such as deceit. Wayward wives like Emma Bovary and Ana Ozores[22] experience the harsh judgment of society, a reaction related to Friedrich Nietzsche's theory of *"ressentiment* ethics" or "slave morality," the bourgeois societal response to return matters to a state of mediocrity.[23]

The adulterous heroine in the nineteenth-century novel poses as the heroic modern individualist who attempts a virile masquerade in search for love. Modernist works like *Ulysses* critically reframe the adultery motif by using it to question marriage, societal morality, and the premises of eroticism. Although Bloom suffers from Molly's adultery with Boylan, he also derives erotic pleasure from the triangle and the accoutrements of transgression. Perhaps in accepting his own deficiencies and preferring a status quo over rupture, he prefers to tolerate Molly's infidelity. In this way,

---

21. Stephen and Bloom are joined dialogically in other ways. See, for example, John Rickard's in-depth exploration of the cock, fox, and bell riddles and allusions that entwine the co-heroes in mourning and guilt in "Circe" (esp. 145–66); Andras Ungar's exploration of Irish and Hungarian historical, nationalist, and aesthetic elements that join father and "son."

22. Of Leo Tolstoy's *Anna Karenina* (1877), Gustave Flaubert's *Madame Bovary* (1856), and Leopoldo Alas "Clarín"'s *La Regenta* (1884), respectively.

23. See Nietzsche, *On the Genealogy of Morals;* for studies of adultery in novels, see, for example, Tony Tanner, *Adultery in the Novel;* Maria Rippon, *Judgment and Justification in the Nineteenth-Century Novel of Adultery,* especially for discussions of varied use of narrative voice, distance, and focalization, as well as *ressentiment* ethics (xii–xiii) (Nietzsche, Max Scheler, Svend Ranulf, and Maria Ossowska); Barbara Leckie, *Culture and Adultery;* Bill Overton, *The Novel of Female Adultery.* For more on the bourgeoisie, see Peter Gay, *The Bourgeois Experience.*

Bloom and Molly are not exactly a bourgeois couple in a Nietzschean sense, although the adulterous pleasure for both of them derives to some extent from the transgressiveness of the situation, particularly in a setting like stolid Catholic 1904 Dublin.

Ulysses makes use of the general centralizing agent of Shakespeare, whose comedies and dramas frequently exploit the dramatic action and climactic revelation and ensuing judgment, such as noted in themes of mistaken identity, including gender (e.g., *Twelfth Night, A Winter's Tale*), and the actions of the fates (e.g., *Lear*) or magic and metamorphoses (e.g., *A Midsummer Night's Dream*). The historical Shakespeare also serves as a personal touchstone for both Bloom and Stephen in Nighttown, particularly when they simultaneously look in the brothel mirror and see their reflection as Shakespeare.[24] In the pattern of oscillating digression to replace an unbearable, unconscious wish (Bloom's excited viewing of Boylan and Marion's adulterous coupling [15:3756–3816]), Lynch interrupts the whores' laughter with his own:

> LYNCH (*points*) The mirror up to nature. (*he laughs*) Hu hu hu hu hu!
> (*Stephen and Bloom gaze in the mirror. The face of William Shakespeare, beardless, appears there, rigid in facial paralysis, crowned by the reflection of the reindeer antlered hatrack in the hall.*) (15:3819–24)

For Stephen, the apparition implies a comparison between the young aspiring Irish writer whose artistic language is English, and Shakespeare, master of English and genius creator. Stephen's Shakespeare is also a reminder of Stephen's far-fetched biography-based explanation of Shakespeare's unhappy marriage to Anne Hathaway, argued ostentatiously in the library earlier that day.[25] "A father," asserts Stephen in his discussion of *Hamlet* in that library scene, "is a necessary evil. [. . .] *Amor matris* [. . .] may be the only true thing in life. Paternity may be a legal fiction. Who is the father of any son that any son should love him or he any son? What the hell are

---

24. The framing of Shakespeare locks identity to image and parole, all show, framed within a frame. Stephen's and Bloom's quest for self-identity or self-knowledge leads them to the crossroads of a Shakespearean mirror which offers them a homosocial disclosure of alternative identities and alternative desires. Cf. Kimberly Devlin's exploration of phallic variations of Shakespeare in *Ulysses* ("Castration and Its Discontents").

25. Paul Schwaber finds that Stephen's biography argument offers ideas agreeable to Stephen's own mental state and artistic ambition: that the ghost is central to the biographical theory; "that Ann devastated her husband's erotic confidence and thereby captured his imagination; and that Shakespeare's writing was reparative—it recurred to and refashioned a fixed heartache" (51). For Schwaber, these same themes can be related to Stephen's mourning of his mother's death a year ago.

you driving at?" (9:828–46).

Stephen's Shakespeare treatise concludes with a recommendation for masturbation over conjugal sexual satisfaction ("there are no more marriages, glorified man, an androgynous angel, being a wife unto himself" [9:1051–52]). The appearance of Stephen's Shakespeare in the mirror reminds him of this ultimately narcissistic and nonprocreative tendency and of his fear of women (contamination; betrayal) and of men. This argument is connected to fears of male homosexual desire. Buck Mulligan, who haunts Stephen's "Circe" repeatedly, has ridiculed and praised Stephen's thesis, and he has suggested possible homosexual tendencies in Shakespeare (the sonnets; charge of pederasty). Buck has also derided Bloom in Stephen's presence, implying that Bloom's interest in the library statues' buttocks indicates a homosexual tendency and that Bloom has looked at Stephen "to lust after you" (9:1210).[26] Stephen's Shakespeare in the mirror remembers in a concentrated image and discourse Stephen's fear of, and secret wish for, artistic creativity and sexual liberation, his circulating narcissism and self-contemplation, and his preoccupation with fathers and mothers. This mirror scene reassembles Stephen as a mocking conscience: "'Tis the loud laugh bespeaks the vacant mind" (in partial reference to Stephen's nervous laughs at intervals in the library scene).

Stephen's Shakespeare, evoked by his one last friend, Lynch ("the mirror up to nature"), expresses a censoring sign. How can a budding young artist ever hope to overcome or replace the father of English literature?[27] The sign of Shakespeare replaces (or overlays) the sign of Stephen Dedalus, as though Stephen's image should be censored out or replaced. Stephen's

---

26. Joseph Valente notes Stephen's "recognition [. . .] of a romantic/erotic valence in his dealings with Mulligan, and he clarifies this affect, significantly, by reference to Wilde, whose name was synonymous not just with homosexuality but with the homosexual as effeminate, as invert, as 'queer.' Only in 'Scylla and Charybdis,' however, does this interlude finally accrue its full meaning. Stephen no sooner finishes piecing together the feminine 'constellation of his identity—'*Stephanoumenos*. . . . S. D.: *sua donna*' (9.939–40)—than his mind reverts to his borrowed footwear [of Mulligan]: '*Stephanos,* my crown. My sword. His boots are spoiling the shape of my feet' (9.947–48). Not only does Stephen hereby rewrite his part in the Cinderella legend, denying the connubial fit of his foot and Mulligan's boot, his words also glance at the founding pun of another, darker tale of orphanage, resentment, and consummation, the story of Oedipus, a name which translates as 'swollen foot.' In both of these legends, the foot stands forth as both a phallic substitute and the key to the protagonist's secret identity. Accordingly, the convergence of these male and female counterparts in Stephen's struggle for self-definition overdetermines his feet as just this sort of signature fetish, a part object that incorporates desire and identification indirectly" ("The Perils of Masculinity," 129).

27. Valente explains how for Stephen, "Shakespeare's art, like Odysseus's warfare, manifests the sort of phallic overcompensation that the world calls greatness. Instead of a (martial) show of mastery, Shakespeare dissimulates his lack in a mastery of the (dramatic) show" ("Perils," 119).

censoring signifies a wish to discard the remnants of a defunct Stephen, attached to Irish-Catholic identity, familial duty, and doom. We can consider Stephen as daring to desire a masculine ideal in Shakespeare, in keeping with Colleen Lamos's discussion that the mingling of identification with erotic desire ("what a man wants to be and what he wants to have") is "forbidden under the rule of normative heterosexuality" (341). Valente argues that Stephen's identification with Shakespeare positions the two men on the transcendent level of a "hypermasculine sublime" (135).[28] By extension, in my interpretation, the hypermasculine sublime Shakespeare censors or covers up the lacking Stephen (i.e., Stephen as Stephen cannot obtain that sublime state).

For Bloom, the Shakespeare reflection compares Bloom's cuckolded state with that of Shakespeare's (comparative husbands). The mirror Shakespeare's laughing reference to Iago of *Othello* implies an analogy between Bloom and Othello. The *Othello* analogy is not accurate on a literal diegetic level (for Molly does commit adultery, unlike the trustworthy Desdemona), but rather it establishes Bloom's wish for mistaken adultery, thus replacing or censoring the prior enjoyment of debasement and vicarious pleasure of Molly being had by a manly man. The censoring is artistic in its re-centering of the cuckold: the cuckold does not behold his own image in the mirror, but that of Shakespeare framed by reindeer antlers (a playful coincidence, implying the horned husband). The movement of the dramatic discourse and stage directions maintains the primary positions of Bloom and Stephen. The dialogic Shakespeare in the mirror unites and differentiates the two men's fantasies. In both cases, Bloom and Stephen do not see themselves in the mirror, but rather are replaced and apprehended by the Shakespeare-mirror, whose ventriloquy relies on the thoughts of each man to complete the chain of judgmental censoring signification. Shakespeare's cry of "Iago" reinforces Stephen's insistence on theorizing Shakespeare's mind ("His unremitting intellect is the hornmad Iago ceaselessly willing that the moor in him shall suffer" [9.1023–24]). Furthering the dialogic discussion of Stephen, Sheldon Brivic suggests that this character "projects a voice that constantly criticizes him" (e.g., the use of "you" for internal monologue), and that he "thinks of his intelligence in an alien, accusing voice" ("Dialogic, Monologue, or Divided Discourse," 172).

---

28. An idea not far removed from Paul Schwaber's recognition of Stephen's idealization of a "[n]onsexual begetting, male and self-sufficient, requiring only himself and his consciousness, [which] could yield him a world without end, consubstantial with him, where he would have no need of his mother, father, siblings, or anyone else" (75).

5. FANTASY AND MIMESIS

In a hybrid of dramatic and narrative discourses, and through the heteroglot character zones (*zony geroev*)[29] of Bloom and Stephen, "Circe" writes out fantasy, making objects of desire visible, making hallucinations readable, casting dreams into the externalized diegetic and dialogized form of a tragicomedic play. Casting psychic fantasy into artistic writing requires censoring expressions along with ones to make obscene and explicit, censoring maneuvers which counteract the unruly drive to represent (forbidden) desires and their objects.[30] The text of "Circe" as dramatic narrative draws on a metatextual mindlike consciousness of the whole narrative that is *Ulysses*. In this way, various memories, experiences, thoughts, feelings, and desires of Bloom and Stephen emerge and present themselves to these characters. By imposing dramatic discourse and structure on the novel's narrative discourse and structure, Joyce conveys a sense of involuntary and unconscious aspects of mental life.

In contrast to the initial six episodes of the novel which highlight these two characters' simultaneous inner and outer experiences in their waking contact with the world, the Nighttown episode lightens the prior emphasis on phenomenological experience of character. But mimesis of the unspeakable is developed in other ways. "Circe" deploys some sexually obscene language and erotic or pornographic imagery, much of which had not been part of high modernist literature. The lurid, impoverished, bawdy setting is an integral part of Dublin's after-hours economy.

This site, where traditionally heteromasculinity can be confirmed and reified, in a shifting of male lack to female subjects,[31] is additionally a location for the ironic deconstruction of that standardized heteromasculine reification. Stephen's and Bloom's fantasies have relatively little to

---

29. In "Discourse in the Novel" in *The Dialogic Imagination,* M. M. Bakhtin describes a character zone as those narrative features (e.g., transmission of a character's speech, thoughts, image, relations, etc.) that contribute to our understanding of a character (voice, point of view, worldview, belief system, emphases, accent, etc.) (316).

30. Colin MacCabe argues that "Circe" "is [*Ulysses*'s] unconscious as the events of the day get reworked in Nighttown" (128). He also suggests that "[i]t is with the reworking of the text in Circe, a reworking which refuses any possibility of an end to the book, that bisexuality undermines any simple phallic position" (124).

31. Berkeley Kaite explains gendered dynamics of pornography of the male reader and female model, in which the "dominant discursive sexual arrangement [. . .] assigns otherness to women" (*Pornography and Difference,* 80–81). A broader survey of the construction of conventional male subjectivity, with its basis in a delusional equation of the phallus and penis, a fundamental *méconnaissance* or misrecognition of the masculine self, is discussed in detail in Kaja Silverman's *Male Subjectivity at the Margins* (especially chapter 1, "The Dominant Fiction").

do with Bella Cohen's scrawny, pitiful prostitutes and cheap heterosexual intercourse. The men's voyeurism, exhibitionism, postponement, narcissism, and masochistic posturing are indicative of complex performative, solitary masculinity, in which the traditional phallic man and dominant discursive sexual arrangement are marginalized. Normative heterosexual relations, especially the pleasures derived from the subjugation of impoverished women, are signaled as socially problematic and not erotic for the liberated or new man. In this sense, the Monto scene is censored by Bloom's and Stephen's actions, which do not follow a traditional path of heteromasculine indulgence; instead they retain themselves as "other."

These two leading characters nurture desires in a dual set of operations. First, they seek, behold, and enact transgressive sexual fantasies that foreground their masochistic stance. Second, they counteract those transgressively sexual fantasies with censoring acts or thoughts which both confirm and negate their desires. The hybrid dramatic-narrative form of the episode de-emphasizes their autonomy in decision making in the events, thus opening the discourse of fantasy. In an inversion of conventional pornography, the subject in "Circe" remains male. We as readers are positioned at times as viewers of a pornographic scene that deconstructs and criticizes itself by maintaining a focus on male lack.[32]

Taken altogether, this series of operations can be seen as a way of grappling with the Thing (the Thing in itself): an attempt to master one's desires and surrounding environment through action, or imitation of action.[33]

---

32. By writing about prostitutes, Joyce follows a nineteenth-century trend of French realist writing (e.g., Balzac; Zola). See, for example, Peter Brooks's *Reading for the Plot,* especially chapter 6, "The Mark of the Beast: Prostitution, Serialization, and Narrative"; he examines the erotic, commercial, and social aspects of this prostitution/pornography trend in nineteenth-century French literature. In *James Joyce and Sexuality,* Richard Brown reminds us that pornography (Greek for "writing about prostitutes") became a term applied to such literature. He examines Stephen's "thoroughly heterodox intellectual position" as seen in chapter 5 of *Portrait* (when Stephen and Lynch converse):

> [Stephen] picks out a phrase which most suggests an aestheticist freedom from moral constraints: "*Pulchra sunt quae visa placent.*" Seen in its full context, what Stephen means by "pornography" [...] is not so much the treatment of sexual or erotic objects in art, but the intrusion into art of non-aesthetic considerations, and the threat of intrusion comes more from the censorious than from the libertine party. There is a possibility that Joyce was being consciously ironic in his choice of the term "pornography" for the kinds of art Stephen rejects in *A Portrait* [i.e., the pornographic and didactic arts which are kinetic]. (131–32)

Meanwhile, in "Circe," we find Stephen (and Lynch and Bloom) inserted into the pornographic text of the world of prostitution.

33. The Kantian Thing, Thing in itself, *das Ding-an-sich*. I am also including Lacan's additional theorizing of the Thing. See his *Écrits,* especially 314, and Slavoj Žižek's gloss of Kant and Lacan: "one has to make use of Lacan's formula of fantasy ($\$ \lozenge a$): 'I think' only insofar as I am inac-

Bloom's and Stephen's fantasies mimetically combine the subject's experience of the "real" world and mental world. Lacan explains that "the phantasy is really the 'stuff' of the 'I' that is originally repressed, because it can be indicated only in the 'fading' of the enunciation" (*Écrits*, 314). After listing traits of margins or borders of erogenous zones ("mark of the cut"), objects of analytic theory such as "the mamilla, faeces, the phallus (imaginary object), the urinary flow [. . .], the phoneme, the gaze, the voice—the nothing," Lacan explains the common features of these objects in terms of fantasy stuff:

> they have no specular image, or, in other words, alterity. It is what enables them to be the "stuff," or rather the lining, though not in any sense the reverse, of the very subject that one takes to be the subject of consciousness. For this subject, who thinks he can accede to himself by designating himself in the statement, is no more than such an object. [. . .] It is to this object that cannot be grasped in the mirror that the specular image lends its clothes. (315–16)

This grappling with the Thing can be related to a quest narrative (in which part of the suspense lies in the fact that the subject's intentioned outward quest really brings his focus back to himself as unknown object). It activates a process of judgment by which the subject subjects himself every time he is faced with decisions involving his pleasure or unpleasure. "Circe" ultimately dramatizes the psychic theater of judgment that the subject submits himself to when he seeks (transgressive) pleasure and reduction of unpleasure (such as forgetfulness of painful memories). As we shall see, in this narrative theater, personal judgments dramatize social and national identity, sexuality in society, and literary and artistic freedom.

Artistic censoring in "Circe" takes several forms: in themes, in discourses, in narrative structures and operations, in poetic forms, in setting and plot, and, of course, in dramatic forms. Within the marginalized chronotope of Nighttown, Stephen and Bloom enact fantasies involving judgment which connect them to the dominant ideologies of 1904 Dublin while also criti-

---

cessible to myself qua noumenal Thing which thinks. The Thing is originally lost and the fantasy-object (*a*) fills out its void" (Žižek, *Tarrying*, 14). Christine van Boheemen-Saaf, in consideration of Henry Staten's *Eros in Mourning* and Lacan, explains how Lacan "postulates the presence of the negative drive to destruct in the same place as the locus of jouissance. This apocalyptic or transcendent negativity, which aims at destroying even the cycles of nature, is, via Melanie Klein, in Lacan related to the figure of the mother as the mediator-occupant of the place of 'the Thing'" (185). She quotes Staten: "*Das Ding* itself is absolutely inaccessible, a reminiscence like that of immortality; it is 'the prehistoric other that it is impossible to forget.' The law of the father comes to save us from the 'choking pap' of the mother's love so that the transcendental form of desire may be revealed behind the empirical beings that stand in for it" (185).

cizing and rejecting these. Some motifs suggest freedom and independence, which can be imagined and articulated but not attained. In keeping with Peter Brooks's discussions of desire as the initiator and drive of narrative, the Circean heroes' plots appear to be self-determined; we might consider Bloom's and Stephen's plots as resistances to follow a standardized heroic or normative masculine line of conduct. This does not exclude their interests in ambition (e.g., Bloom as social or political reformer; Stephen as full-fledged artist), somewhat like the nineteenth-century "desiring machines" (heroes of Balzac, Stendhal, etc.) explored by Brooks (*Reading for the Plot*, 39).

One key difference with "Circe" is the lack of traditional plot. The meanderings in Nighttown seem accidental and involuntary, as opposed to intentional, goal-driven, or predetermined. Nevertheless, the overall arc of action gently indicates a quest motif for both heroes. In this way, Joyce subverts traditional plot lines of narratives and plays (in what Brooks calls "a context of radical doubt about the validity of plot" [286]): our Circean protagonists are observed in a kind of free fall of time and space that suggest and offer various situations on which action and fantasy can be developed. The proairetic level of action in "Circe" is fairly limited (Barthes's code of actions).[34] Adjacent to that action flourish fantasy events of excessive diversity and detail. Within each fantasy, however, one can certainly discern a kernel of plot, at times clichéd or stereotyped but refreshed by the involvement of Bloom and Stephen. The tension between the proairetic and the hermeneutic (Barthes's code of enigmas and answers) in "Circe" stands in for a narrative plot. "Circe"'s plot resists particularization, while parading interests in fatherhood and authority, desire and pleasure, and quests of (self) knowledge (motifs developed in part from the Homeric plot underpinning *Ulysses*).

Ulysses's general chronotope of Dublin in June 16 and 17, 1904, is particularized in each chapter, with the "Circe" chronotope being both very particular—midnight in Dublin's prostitution district—and hybridized. The chapter uses mise-en-scène prose and dramatic dialogue to represent the personalized stages of Bloom and Stephen in Nighttown as a crossroads of historical urban site (with its realist fictional-cum-historical correlatives, such as Bella Cohen's brothel) and psychic, imaginary, phantasmatic inner space.[35] Furthermore, the chronotope of Nighttown hybridizes conven-

---

34. Roland Barthes describes the "five major codes under which all the textual signifiers can be grouped": the hermeneutic code (enigmas and answers; Voice of Truth), semic code, symbolic code, proairetic code (code of actions or Voice of the Empirical), and cultural code(s) (*S/Z*, 18–21).

35. My discussion of chronotopes is derived from M. M. Bakhtin's catalogue and explication of chronotopes from the ancient epic to the modern novel ("Forms of Time and Chronotope in

tional novelistic chronotopes: it includes both the chronotope of the road (setting for unexpected encounters and allowing for heteroglossia) and the chronotope of the salon (internal setting highlighting intense dialogic exchanges and further heteroglot permutations). These two chronotopes in Nighttown allow for a heightened development of exchange, often with unexpected interlocutors, and for a broad sampling of European and Dublin heteroglossia (heteroglossia = multilanguagedness) which provides the linguistic form and content for the two protagonists' quests.

The hybridized chronotope of "Circe" also qualifies the heteroglot structure of discourse. "Circe" offers a heightened heteroglot space because dramatic dialogue takes place there among people and things of disparate times and social and cultural contexts. For instance, the conversations in the brothel combine the prostitutes' knowledge with Stephen's and Lynch's knowledge of French when Stephen is encouraged to "speak French" to relate his experience of Paris: "ZOE: O go on! Give us some parleyvoo. [. . .] / STEPHEN: [. . .] All chic womans which arrive full of modesty then disrobe and squeal loud to see vampire man debauch nun very fresh young with *dessous troublants. (he clacks his tongue loudly) Ho, là là! Ce pif qu'il a!* / LYNCH: *Vive le vampire!* / THE WHORES: Bravo! Parleyvoo!" (15:3874–98).

Here and further on, Stephen displays a detailed knowledge of clichéd pornographic and erotic tableaux. It is unclear the degree to which the prostitutes understand him, but some gap in comprehension is likely. Ironically, even if Zoe does not know that the word "*pif*" is a nose (alluding to the penis), she is familiar with the male anatomy. Stephen and Lynch share a secret relish of the vampire's prowess, in a mocking identification with him in this hard-core scenario. The vampire motif is also a condensation of Stephen's earlier poetic musing (in "Proteus") of the vampire kiss ("He comes, pale vampire, through storm his eyes, his bat sails bloodying the sea, mouth to her mouth's kiss. [. . .] His lips lipped and mouthed fleshless lips of air: mouth to her moomb. Oomb, allwombing tomb. His mouth moulded issuing breath, unspeeched" [3:397–403]). Here the poet considers the generative potential of the sea ("blood not mine, *oinopa ponton,* a winedark sea" [3:394]) and her various guises as feminine-inflected place (i.e., womb–"Bridebed, childbed, bed of death, ghostcandled. *Omnis caro ad te veniet*" [3:396]).[36] Stephen's imaginary Circean vampire debauches a

---

the Novel").

36. Jeri Johnson points out that Stephen is not creating his own poem with "He comes . . . ," but rather is freely revisiting and adapting a Gaelic poem "My Grief on the Sea" translated by Douglas Hyde in his *Love Songs of Connacht*. His stanza: "And my love came behind me— / He came from the South; / His breast to my bosom, / His mouth to my mouth" (qtd. in Johnson, 791).

nun, an aggressive negation of feminine virginity guarded by the Church; the tableau is performed for the benefit of female clients ("all chic womans [. . .] full of modesty"), apparently sophisticated Continental women. The pornographic vampire tableau recounted by Stephen frames women as desiring subjects and objects, consumers and participants in prostitution. This Circean scene is a violent transition from the poetic deathly male element that kisses the womb/tomb of the sea. The gothic male ("pale vampire") goes to sip blood from mother sea (*mère/mer*) much like an infant to suckle milk from the maternal breast. The hypermasculinity of the vampire in both scenarios, the pornographic rape and the necrophilic kiss (kiss of the "allwombing tomb"), indicates a phallic lack (symbolic) and anxiety of that lack. Stephen's incorporation of Buck Mulligan's Greek quotation from the *Odyssey* signals his ongoing preoccupation with homoeroticism. Here and elsewhere in "Circe" male friendship and homoerotic suggestions coincidentally appear when heterosexual desire is unveiled or contemplated. I will return to the vampire imagery in my discussion of Stephen and the maternal.

The mimetic features of dialogue in "Circe" are connected prominently to the alternating protagonist, Bloom or Stephen. In Susan Lanser's explanation of textual voice, the private narrator or character and focalizer, a "fleshed-out character," carries "considerable mimetic authority" whereas the public narrator is the one most closely attached to narrative authority (142). The character-narrator or focalizer offers the authority of lived experience, while the public narrator suggests the authority of intellection. This schema of diverse narrative authority, when applied to "Circe," suggests an additional plane of authority. First, we could consider the speech of the various characters, especially of the focalizers Bloom and Stephen, as mimetic (almost doubly mimetic, as they recycle fragments of their or others' speech from other episodes or times). These focalizers also strongly convey lived experience, although some of that experience is not always occurring in an actual physical sphere (it is presented as real, thus signaling

---

The vampire motif is Stephen's, as is the evident inversion of poetic voice (Stephen uses a male voice; the original Hyde poem is a woman's account). We can notice, too, that Stephen ascribes a femininity to the sea that the original poem does not (the woman sings of her grief on the sea).

Ewa Ziarek argues that Stephen appropriates the feminine maternal for his creative process: "There is a strange double necessity for the recurrence of maternal images in the process of Stephen's artistic self-definition—they are simultaneously evoked and expelled as if the artist could know himself only by differentiating himself from a maternal nonself. Yet, the artist's confrontation with the pregnant goddess [Mina Purefoy of the Circean black mass], who not only delays but denies parturition, who does not release the "content" of her womb, no longer works in the economy of self-knowledge or self-definition" (154). This reading excludes sociohistorical considerations of the crippling condition of constant pregnancy experienced by Stephen's mother, Mina Purefoy, and other Irish Catholic women that Stephen deplores.

the presence of another mental experience beyond the usually visible one). Meanwhile, the elaborate stage directions indicate a public narrator who normally appeals to our intellect: a way to make sense of the dialogue by grounding it in the mise-en-scène.

Given the juxtaposition of intelligible and fantastic (or uncanny) elements, the unseen, zero-degree narrator provides a sense of orchestrating the characters and events through a kind of alternative authority. This special authority might be found in between the authorities of intellection and experience:that is, in the sphere of the desire and judgment. The invisible hetero-diegetic narrator as organizer of the dramatic-narrative elements maintains character zones in which a character's elements are not always literally connected to him but are within his sphere of action or apprehension (e.g., the mutable "sweets of sin" and the Shakespeare in the mirror).

6. "CIRCE"'S FUNCTION IN *ULYSSES*

It is possible to discern discursive, poetic, and thematic features of the censoring of sexuality throughout *Ulysses*. The novel conceives of censoring as both an integral part of life and of art and thus sees it as a worthy domain to treat in art. Joyce's incorporation of sexuality raises questions about the limitations of what has been considered acceptable artistic expression. In general, his works trace his multistranded inquiries into the vicissitudes of morals in art and life. The theme of the individual's struggle with the rules of society, church, law, family is an identifiable thread running throughout his opus.

A cursory review can show how other episodes of *Ulysses* treat censoring. For example, the initial six episodes' narrative transmission of interior monologues of Stephen and Bloom and the final episode of Molly all represent a character's flickering stream of inner thoughts and sensations. This stream emerges as semicensored, in the way that thinking subjects monitor and adjust thoughts, memories, and feelings when these come into consciousness. The interior monologues in such episodes as "Proteus" and "Penelope" are mimetic of our concept of how we think, perceive, remember, and feel in language.

These chapters' style and frank subject matter represent an inner consciousness that occasionally resorts to sexual or erotic echoes, allusions, or recesses. The mode of narrative attempts to achieve a sort of hyperrealism or mimesis: the accurate reproduction of a person's thoughts and patterns of thinking.[37] After the sixth episode, "Hades," the novel's composition and

---

37. Budgen is one of the earliest readers of *Ulysses* to make this observation.

styles of subsequent episodes diverge increasingly. Parody, orchestration, multiple focalization, editorial and aurteurial[38] strategies all complicate point of view, representation, access to stable reference points of reality and the world of the novel.

Meanwhile, motifs of censored sexuality continue to thread through the novel's fabric, generated by the juxtaposition of the private and public worlds of Dublin, particularly through the collision of personal mental worlds of Bloom and Stephen (who each suggests alternative modern values) with the societal, cultural, and political limitations of the public world of Dublin in 1904. Barbara Leckie makes a compelling argument for a discourse of censorship in "Nausicaa," the episode that ended the serialization of the novel. She considers how "Nausicaa" (along the lines of sensation novels and novels like *Madame Bovary*) "dramatizes the gendered reading body, or the young female reader of the sensation novel debate," in the sense that Gerty's weak, sexual body "registers sexual knowledge; in parallel with her status as young reader runs a practice of blushing censorship" (71).[39]

Joyce styled and structured less mimetic concluding chapters of *Ulysses*, in part owing to worries of the *Little Review* trial (that focused weighty judgment on "Nausicaa"). The chapter variety and chapter evolution into ostensibly more difficult narrative forms could be seen as writing strategies to elude the censorship actions of the American courts, libraries, and leagues against vice. But Joyce's hybridized writing strategies did not automatically garner publication freedom, and in many ways they confront head-on the restrictions regarding sexual explicitness and allusion in literature. Throughout Joyce's years as a writer, he was plagued by censorious reactions to his literary work, reactions which usually had an adverse effect on his prospects for publishing and being read widely.[40] The censors tended to focus on particular passages or words, as opposed to considering the entire work of art and its effects and merits.[41] In *Ulysses*, the accumulative

---

38. See my conception of the "aurteur" of "Sirens."

39. For example, Leckie explains how Gerty's blushes "[signal] a need for censorship in the sensation novel debates" and ironically are also "folded into the erotic moment of the text" (73).

40. See, for example, Sally Dennison's historical survey of Joyce's oeuvre (from *Chamber Music*, *Dubliners*, and *Stephen Hero* to *Portrait*, *Exiles*, and *Ulysses*) in relation to censorship (*[Alternative] Literary Publishing: Five Modern Histories*, 77–114).

Susan Stanford Friedman makes a case for self-censorship as a modernist element in Joyce's *Stephen Hero*. She notices how the character of the Censor is removed in the published *A Portrait of the Artist as a Young Man*. In *Stephen Hero*, Stephen has two separate confrontations with Jesuit "Censors"; Friedman argues that these are "key moments in the production of [Stephen's] alienation as an artist in the making" (55).

41. Here the whole work of art could mean the chapter or the entire novel.

variety of styles, the interrelated content from one episode to another, the coherence of the chronotope, and the referential or interpretative schemas all contribute to the reader's impression that the novel is an integrated work of art whose effect is dependent on the inclusion of all parts, including ostensibly lewd and crude parts.

To appreciate the features of artistic censoring of sexuality in "Circe," we should be aware of the desires and concerns of Stephen and Bloom, as revealed in preceding chapters. The flexible and direct discursive form of theater used in place of conventional narrative discourse allows for a creative (re)assembly that enacts dynamically and critically these desires and concerns. For example, the opening episode "Telemachus" introduces us to Stephen's preoccupation with his mother's death, in his thoughts and through dialogue with Mulligan. Later, in "Aeolus," which takes place at the offices of the *Freeman's Journal,* the typographical and editorial maneuvers in narrative portray the press's manipulation of information and signification. Various individuals' private thoughts—especially those of Stephen and Bloom—advance the narrative in counterpoint to the open conversation and interpolated headlines and develop personal and social portraits of these two characters. Rhetoric, or the artistic manipulation of the word, is the central technique and idea. In "Lestrygonians," Bloom's thoughts jostle among themselves as he ponders food, sex, and sensuality and wards off the subject of Molly's adultery with Blazes Boylan later that day. Bloom's anticipation, imagination, disavowal, and shameful pleasure of this adultery constitute a recurrent and foundational aspect of Bloom's and the novel's censoring treatment. In "Scylla and Charybdis," the topics revolve dialogically in the library around literature, especially Shakespeare, marking Stephen's predilection for relating biographical detail to the interpretation of the text. Stephen argues that Anne Hathaway makes a cuckold of Shakespeare and that *Hamlet* is the product of the playwright's mourning for his son Hamnet. Stephen's apparent preference for Aristotle over Plato suggests that he opposes literary censorship as promoted by Plato. Yet, elsewhere, such as in *Portrait,* Stephen seems to support Plato in a wariness of the arts, proposing that art should not be "kinetic" nor arouse the senses, but rather inspire contemplation. It would seem Stephen wants an unwieldy synthesis of Aristotle and Plato, for he basically distrusts the flesh and the material while believing in art as the imaginative transformation of life.[42]

---

42. Stephen's analysis of literature and art becomes reworked later on in "Circe" as an erotic drive to transform language into reality of forms and gestures; Lynch mocks the effort as a disavowal of why they have come to Nighttown:

STEPHEN (*looks behind*) So that gesture, not music not odour, would be a universal

The novel's episodic sequence sets up "Circe" as a climax to the individual character developments of Stephen and Bloom. "Circe" is the only chapter presented fully in dramatic discursive form.[43] The departure from "regular" narrative and entry into narrativized theater mark a thematic and representational turn: theater—with its forms of direct discourse, dialogue, song, and directed action—is ostensibly more mimetic than narrative discourse. The implication is that, through theater, the truth will out, and that the characters enter a discursive mode of freedom. Ironically, the understanding of truth and freedom is deliberated through the oscillation of desire between the transgressing subject and the subject called into judgment.

7. DIALOGIC ACCRETION IN "CIRCE"

Ulysses was not written entirely in sequence, and it is notable that "Circe" was the last episode composed by Joyce. There are several advantages Joyce gained by writing it last: it serves, perhaps more than any other chapter, as a compendium of the novel's contents. In fact, it seems to serve as the novel's unconscious and conscious memory. In it we find all manner of details related to both Bloom and Stephen, from their childhood to their contemporary life to their fantasy lives. Virtually every character in the book, as well as many notable historical figures and some imaginary ones, appears in or is mentioned in some way in "Circe."

This repository aspect of the episode functions not just to complete, but to add new signification. Groden and other scholars have remarked on Joyce's "accretive" method of creation. He made particular use of the final

---

language, the gift of tongues rendering visible not the lay sense but the first entelechy, the structural rhythm.
LYNCH Pornosophical philotheology. Metaphysics in Mecklenburgh street! (15:104–9)

I see "philology" suggested in "philotheology"—love of learning and literature and theology (or literature/word of God) and Stephen's interest in speaking in tongues; the philotheology could also be shown in Stephen's mock worshiping of Mass in Latin for Paschal time (a season of joy, rebirth, and baptism).

43. The library episode "Scylla and Charybdis" comically presents dramatic discursive insets [9:893–34 and 9:1171–89], highlighting the Shakespearean topic under discussion by framing the interlocutors in the same dramatic discourse of much of Shakespeare's oeuvre. Sections of this episode are heavily laden with dialogue; the episode is dialogically set on providing Stephen's inner thoughts that accompany the library conversations. In "Circe" there are no private inner thoughts narrativized in the way we see in the first six episodes of *Ulysses*, "Scylla and Charybdis," and "Nausicaa" (i.e., episodes that highlight the play between the inner thoughts and outward experience of Stephen and Bloom respectively).

months of composing *Ulysses* to make alterations and additions across the breadth of the manuscript.[44]

Set in Dublin's zone of prostitution after midnight, "Circe" expresses sexuality in mimetic and realist modes as well as symbolic and poetic forms. Generally, the pornographic impulse applied to language is the urge to articulate what conventionally cannot or should not be said or expressed. "Circe," especially through its dramatic form, seeks to express that urge: the characters "speak" directly what should not normally be expressed: their transgressive sexual desires which involve experiences of censoring. In the process, we witness repeated reworkings of desire to name sex and call it into being. Sex can be made repulsive, enjoyable, ugly, painful, erotic, enchanting. Joyce deploys language to negate sex, to judge and condemn it, to elide it, to dress it up with words, or to make it banal.

"Circe" synthesizes the aims of artistic and explicit treatment of sexuality. The dramatic action depends on the creative-destructive cycle of bringing sexuality into words and censoring it. Moreover, the obscene components or aspects are compensated by several extenuating, far-reaching values and qualities. First, "Circe" is one part of an aesthetic whole, one portion of a work of art conceived in integrating terms of character, time, space, and themes. In terms of the novel, "Circe" gains a heightened status for its strong role in organizing the whole work by sweeping its two central but generally disparate and discrete characters together into a climactic vortex of nighttime adventure and self-revelation. Thus, "Circe" has a constitutive purpose for the novel as a whole, and provides significant understanding and amplification of Bloom and Stephen and their conflicting motives and desires.

In broad terms of the whole novel, "Circe" might be said to represent the literary Thing. It is outside the ken of the rest of the episodes and characters, but is known by Bloom and Stephen, the novel's two main characters. Moreover, the apparent marginal zone of "Circe" to which these two "escape" is paradoxically a deeply interior and integrated site—their home, memories, fears, and desires.

---

44. In her chapter "From Typology to Typography," Frances Restuccia provides an excellent discussion of how Joyce's accretive method helped to create numerous prolepses and analepses in *Ulysses* in order to create a discursive system of typology: "Modeled on the principles of typology, *Ulysses* not only aligns itself with Christian figural realism by virtue of its referential language that is simultaneously self-referential, thus producing an anagogic level hovering over a literal base; but it specifically, architectonically, imitates the Bible, Auerbach's paradigm of figural realism" (23).

My discussion of "Circe" and *Ulysses* complements Restuccia's argument in that her conception of the discursive system of *Ulysses* is a specialized variation of my more general application of Bahktin's conception of the novel as a dialogic discursive system that uses internal references or self-referentiality, intertextuality, and heteroglossia.

In terms of discursive strategies, "Circe" makes exterior psychic scenes, configuring these intimate personal states of mind into a pornographic scene of the prostitution district. This staging then transmits meaning on several levels. On one level of thematic plot (the quest), the theatrical production describes the subject's (Bloom's; Stephen's) epistemic search for the sexual Thing. On another level, the subject introduces himself into his own theater of judgment. The quest for escape and liberation from societal and personal constraints leads back to the questing subject: the quest for self-knowledge through one's desires and one's judgment of those desires. This theater produces his desires for him in a series of phantasmatic scenes of contradictions and reaffirmations of desired objects. Curiously, while the transposition of these literary figures into dramatic mode would seem to liberate them on the one hand, on the other, they seem to lack even more agency in this theater world in which one cannot retreat to inner, private thoughts because these are made exterior and dramatized for a judging spectatorship.

Furthermore, the repeated acts of being judged and the examination and avoidance of acknowledging motivation are central to our understanding of how "Circe" represents censoring through the character zones of Stephen and Bloom. In my view, the subject's frequent phantasmatic enactment of judgment represents censoring forces and indicates the subject's repetitive pleasure and need.

In Nighttown, man's quest to get beyond himself and beyond societal restraints, to liberate himself into fantasy and knowledge of the other's sexuality leads him to self-examination, possible self-discovery. This circular quest is akin to the quest to achieve an artistic goal. Both quests cause the subject to collide with and confront the Law and himself. The character-zoned censoring action in "Circe" can be seen as creatively productive, imitating the creation of dreams and of art. In general, Bloom and Stephen have multiple encounters with the Law. For Bloom, he at times transforms himself into the Thing or *res* of the Law, while Stephen attempts to master the very pen of the Law.

8. FANTASY AND THE LAW: FATHERS AND SONS

Ulysses is a response or supplement to the Law. In "Circe," we find censoring conflicts come to the fore, highlighted in the dramatic mise-en-scène of Nighttown, the prostitution district tolerated and regulated by representatives of the Law (Dublin's municipality, the corporation, the Church, the society as a whole). As Stephen and Bloom enter this demarcated zone, they do not become free agents, but rather become confronted with both the Law and the regulated lawlessness of the place. They consequently become aware of their own complicity and paradoxical motives for being there. Their fantasies about and conflicts with the Law and its symbolic forms provide much of the episode's content, action, and resolution—for example, the conflicts with the night watchmen and the soldiers, the confrontation with the brothel madam, Bella Cohen, and the grandiose fantasy instances of rising to power by both Stephen and Bloom and their respective symbolic falls.

Trials and judgment with liminal qualities pervade "Circe." Rituals of initiation, transformation, and death are part of the action leading the subject through passages of judgment or censoring. The erratic plot of two erring subjects is structured much like the fantasies of a subject who counteracts or "corrects" his desires with authoritative controls by the superego. These corrective maneuvers are accomplished through attempts to name, to give voice to, to transform, to elude, to allude to the Thing. Expressions of wish fulfillments and their negations or alternatives through modes of displacement and condensation—all serve to dramatize the subject's alternating desire to transgress and to be judged. Moreover, the staging of the subject's conflicts with the Law invites the reader's participation to judge. The theater of judgment that is "Circe" expresses the subject's desire to confront the Law and elicits the reader's response to judge. The reader's sense of ethics is activated because the text ensures some ambiguity about what is at stake at any given moment. The reader necessarily can appreciate how Bloom and Stephen experience difficulty in distinguishing between right and wrong, between right and good, between good and pleasurable. Moreover, Bloom and Stephen act in ways contingent upon the actions of others; whether in the brothel or on the street, they are not presented as able to determine situations, but neither are they passive characters.

Bloom's and Stephen's liminal experiences in Nighttown center on the doing and undoing of masculinity in its various forms—filial, paternal, homoerotic and homophobic, heterosexual and standardizing, homosexual and transgendering. These forms often intersect or combine in unexpected ways. For example, the combination of familial relationships with sexual ones creates taboo tension, often humorously. My discussion of "Circe" focuses on paternal-filial and masculinity conflations. Clearly homoeroticism and transgender eroticism are key elements of the Circean explorations of masculine selfhood.[45]

---

45. Meanwhile, in "Scylla and Charybdis" and especially *Finnegans Wake,* fraternal incest motifs can be discerned. See, for example, Susan Sutliff Brown's "The Joyce Brothers in Drag: Fraternal Incest in *Ulysses*"; a few points in her discussion remain moot, such as the connection between

The dilemma in ethics is found in the subject's conflict between desiring the *objet a* and wanting to do or possess the good. In the irrational terms of the ego's drives, what promises pleasure and what is good are equated. But these two aims are not necessarily related when considered from the point of view of ethics, when we include the superego and our awareness of the world and others' needs. The dilemma can never really be completely resolved; the decision between the libidinal good and the ethical good necessarily involves the subject's negotiation. Part of that conflict arises for the subject precisely because, even if he did not have to consider an ethical good, he would still be unable to apprehend fully the good in the Real. Thus in writing such as "Circe," what is dramatized, what is made exterior and viewable, is the subject's thwarting of his own attempts to apprehend his object(s) of desire. The closer he comes to seizing that object, the more ingenious become his stratagems to "save" himself (deny himself that first pleasure). Censoring of sexuality comes from within as well as from social forces.

The motivations for the two main characters' actions are complicated. Bloom goes in search of Stephen, ostensibly to keep a fatherly eye on the drunken and careless young man; yet Bloom has been avoiding his return home all day and evening, knowing that Molly has had a romantic rendezvous with Boylan at four o'clock. Stephen seems driven to lose himself in drink and revelry; to lose his money which he both badly needs and despises; to lose his dignity to the English; and to forget about his parents and his filial behavior, possibly in search of a kind of Dionysian release and artistic discovery. His inebriation attempts to censor unwanted memories and to tear away from cloying, confining local Irish rules and roots. While he seeks the proximity of prostitutes, his drunken state forecloses the possibility of performing sexual acts with them. He desires to lose himself in the illicit Nighttown and its associations as a setting for ritual masculine initiation. It is also a site in which the proto-Real social and economic circumstances of 1904 Dublin are made explicit. Stephen, as prodigal son returned from Paris, may seek a site of permissiveness, but Nighttown is conditioned by colonial Dublin morality.

Bloom's motives complement those of Stephen. He takes a paternal interest in the younger man. Bloom's pursuit and care for Stephen demonstrate a desire to behave ethically. Thus far in the novel, Bloom's sym-

---

Joyce's personal relationship with his three brothers and the possible referencing of them in his various works from *Stephen Hero* and *Exiles* to *Ulysses* and *Finnegans Wake*. For example, she identifies Bello as "recalling Isabel, Georgie Joyce's incarnation in *Stephen Hero*" (19); this somehow means that when Bloom has a form of anal intercourse with Bello that Bloom is enacting fraternal incest (presumably because Bloom should be equated with James Joyce)."

pathy and empathy for others, be they women, children, animals, or the disadvantaged, have been well established. Yet paired with that kindness is his desire to be wanted, needed, loved (to compensate for his knowledge of his wife's adultery). Moreover, Stephen possesses several qualities that Bloom intensely admires: Stephen speaks Italian and French fluently; he has been educated at some of the best Irish institutions and is well-read (the results of Simon's loving, lavish investment in his eldest son); he has traveled abroad; he possesses an exquisite voice apparently similar to Simon's squandered, but still lovely tenor. In the episodes following "Circe," Bloom's additional interests in Stephen become apparent, complicating his basic ethical impulse toward the young man.

In "Circe" itself, Bloom's motivation to help Stephen appears to be less (consciously) mediated by other concerns. Aside from wishing to befriend and protect the young man, Bloom hopes to postpone his own return home to Molly ("Hohohohohohoh! Hohohohome!" as Kelleher's carriage horse gently mocks Bloom's white lies about why he is in the prostitution district [15:4879]). Ever since the morning when Bloom learns that his wife will have a sexual rendezvous at home with Blazes Boylan around four o'clock in the afternoon, Bloom has wavered between entertaining and banning thoughts of that meeting. He repeatedly catches sight of Boylan around town; various interlocutors ask Bloom about his wife's upcoming singing engagement, prompting him to have to try to avoid mentioning Boylan while expressing excitement for his wife's performing career. The actual adulterous scene is one key episode in *Ulysses* that remains decidedly offstage but returns repeatedly to the text and Bloom's speculation. Part of his mutual delight and torture in thinking of the adultery derives from his doubts about it actually happening. His oscillation between knowing and not knowing is essential to his masochistic enjoyment in the fantasy and the reality. Aside from the adulterous affair Molly has with Boylan, any other interloping lovers belong more to the husband's imagination (or hallucination) in "Circe" than to actuality.

The adulterous scene between Molly and Boylan is an informative theme throughout *Ulysses*. Bloom predicates much of his movements, thoughts, and fantasy on the premise of this scene. Adultery rated as a sin and a crime in the Dublin of 1904. Some of Bloom's excitement about it derives precisely from the fact that it is a forbidden act; his wife is breaking the law. Other aspects of his excitement stem from the basic pleasure that he takes in having a fairly unconventional woman like Molly as his wife.[46]

46. By having a semiprofessional stage career, Molly approximates the status of an actress; in Great Britain at that time, society regarded an actress as having questionable personal morals and habits; in Ireland, with its censorious audiences, such regard might be harsher.

A proud husband, Bloom also takes pleasure in having other men admire his wife's beauty, voice, wit, and other charms. Although he himself looks for erotic pleasure both inside and outside of his marriage (in postcards, literature, masturbation, voyeurism, impersonation in correspondence), his sexual object remains Molly. She provides the source by which other lesser objects are measured. The recurrent Spanish motif—Molly as the Mediterranean temptress—particularly resonates with Bloom. The motif is developed discursively in several erotic ways: the *Sweets of Sin* heroine offering her "heaving embonpoint" and other bodily gifts to the Latin lover Raoul; the *señorita* and the *torero;* the nun and the priest; Zerlina, the peasant bride, and Don Giovanni ("*Là ci darem la mano*" [15:469]). Bloom does not exactly insert himself into the place of the man in these pairings; he is more excited by imagining the desired woman being enjoyed by a desirable man, possibly a rogue, a risk-taker or lawbreaker.[47] Bloom's fantasies clearly illustrate Lacan's observation that man's desire is the desire of the other: indeed, Bloom's desire predicates itself on two others, the desirable man and the desiring woman.

Meanwhile, Bloom imagines himself as lacking in sexual desirability in some respects. In his Circean fantasies, one desirable masculine quality is a certain measure of lawlessness. Such a modality of pleasure also might hark back to an Oedipal scene which shocks, offends, and excites the childish spectator. Such an oedipalization allows a subject like Bloom to imagine the father as the transgressor as well as the lawmaker. We could recall that

47. Andras Ungar shows how the novel *Ruby* is related to the lost son Rudy (phonemically similar; the novel, a gift to Molly) and to Bloom's attempt to compensate for the internalized guilt for Rudy's death and also for Boylan's possession of Molly (through the *Don Giovanni* topoi): "[Bloom's] bestowal of a ruby ring on the phantom of his old flame Josie [Powell] Breen is tantamount to a magical effort to deny the irreparability of the past, and to reestablish himself with a woman in a prelapsarian state. Along with the gift, he quotes a snatch from the song of seduction from *Don Giovanni,* 'Then we'll go hand in hand,' which was an item in the program Boylan was to deliver to Molly in the afternoon. By appropriating the song—Boylan's gift to Molly—and making it an accompaniment of his gift to Josie, he is, in effect, substituting for Boylan in his courtship of Molly, and, vicariously, displacing the rival. The ruby ring magically perfects the union as the birth of Rudy should have fulfilled his marriage" (494).

In a further development of the Rudy-guilt motif, Bloom becomes in fantasy the prostitute novice Ruby Cohen, and Bello "places a ruby ring on her finger," claiming "with this ring I thee own" (15:3067–68). Ungar suggests that in this instance, Bloom "has made good the demands of the ring symbolism and the lack in his marriage in the figure of his own body" (495).

In addition, I recognize the implied incest in the fantasy of Bello Cohen and Ruby Cohen, as well as the analogy of prostitution to marriage. In this fantasy, Bloom can "correct" or align his marriage with Molly.

Ungar points out a third fantasy involving the ruby ring: Bloom, becoming Leopold the First, "puts on a ruby ring" (15:1490). Ungar sees this moment as Bloom's ability to transcend the Molly-Rudy preoccupations of the other two fantasies. However, Ungar seems to overlook the sequence of the fantasies: Bloom with Josie Breen; Bloom as Leopold the First; Bloom as Ruby Cohen.

the primal scene corresponds symbolically to the adulterous scene.

Inferred by the dramatic structure of "Circe," Bloom produces as well as experiences a series of hallucinated figures, events, and scenes which express his conflicting thoughts and emotions, desires about himself and his relationships. The dramatic form of directions and direct speech make these fantasized figures exterior, giving them flesh and voice; in the mimesis and diegesis of the play, Bloom dramatizes his struggle between a wild striving after the objects of his drives and an achievement of control, serenity, or power by mastering those unruly, irrational drives. His desire for control bifurcates into a desire to be dominated, especially in masochistic sexual situations (e.g., with Bella/Bello), and a desire to dominate, as seen in his visions of becoming the ingenious Lord Mayor of Dublin, glorious Catholic king of Ireland, reformer-inventor-arbitrator-ladykiller, Christ-like martyr and Egyptian mummy, and psychoanalytic and medical case study of the new womanly man.

Bloom's fantasizing repeatedly relies on amazing transformations in dress, identity, manner of speech and language associated with his subjectivity (e.g., the collection of Irish emblems—the nymphs, the yews, the waterfall, and Poulaphouca, the site of the high school excursion). In his fantasies, he speaks and interacts with others, things, and even concepts related to his memories, relationships, knowledge, and wishes. For example, Bloom speaks of his "halcyon days" (when in his "teens, a growing boy," he needed little to get excited, "a jolting car, [. . .] and the dark sexsmelling theatre unbridles vice" [15:3319–24]), and shortly after, the "halcyon days" emerge as a discoursing composite character, cheering, "Mackerel! Live us again. Hurray!" (15:3331).

Central hallucinated figures such as Virag, which are extensions of Bloom, also tend to change in appearance and voice; these changes are forms of artistic censoring. The parenthetical dramaturgic directions strongly emphasize the constantly changing character of Bloom's representations. The need to change stems from two drives or needs: first, to censor or change what is being said or shown because it has become too unbearable for the conscious; second, to find pleasure in the multiplicity of creative representation. The two impulses develop themes of censoring and knowledge of the self gained through judgment and liminal experiences of initiation, transformation, and death.[48] The language works at naming, and then

48. Paul Schwaber suggests a circuit of maternal-sexual associations (Bello/Bella; his mother, Ellen Higgins; Molly; his mother's potato [Bloom's moly]) and its surrender to and recovery from Zoe Higgins, the prostitute with his mother's maiden name (150). In this analysis, "Bloom's brooding about demons, whores, menses, smells, and animals suggests condescension and animus, which qualify (and by reaction-formation, ironically, may enhance) his awed respect. The depressive link

renaming or transposing (techniques of metonymy and displacement); the dramatic language, the words refer to Bloom's life, experience, and desires. The discourse in this sense is realistic. But it is actively mimetic of the subject of Bloom, making him into a part of many elements of the "play." In this way, the transformations and judgmental actions are part of poetic discourse, not realist prosody.

The play of "Circe" tends toward a dramatization of "full" disclosure of desires and usually unspoken thoughts, truths, memories—generally pertaining to the men's sexuality and sexual life. Earlier I mentioned the importance of the father in the formation of fantasies. Bloom's fantasies often allow him to take the position of the desiring son. Additionally, a looming but largely unarticulated fantasy is that of being the loved father. We can discern this fantasy in the overall plot of "Circe," the interaction of Bloom and Stephen and the symbolic father-son relation that is tantalizingly approached but not developed. For Bloom, his vision of his dead son, Rudy, contains a promise of secret knowledge, which is not articulated; full disclosure cannot be given.[49] At the chapter's conclusion, in a moment of rest from frantic search and change, emerges the serene phantom vision of loved and loving lost son, Rudy, imagined at age eleven (if Rudy had survived),[50] immersed in the reading of a mysterious Hebraic book, kissing its

---

to women who betray, moreover, is worth flagging. The magical quality of his thoughts on the strand [in "Nausicaa"] will connect to his fantastic confrontation with Bella/Bello in Nighttown and to the image of his mother there that instantly gets superseded by Molly. Leopold's frantic internalized mother has almost no representability in his thoughts."

We could compare the concept of an "internalized mother" with Bloom's womanly masquerade and his masculine masochism.

49. The same holds true for Stephen, whose vision of his dead mother does not yield the desired, unknown (unknowable—unnamable) Word (the Thing). He asks, "Tell me the word, mother, if you know now. The word known to all men" (15:4192–93). But her disappointing response is to reintroduce the issue of prayer and repentance which he has already rejected (4194–98).

Patrick McGee notices the patriarchal features of May Goulding's ghost speech:

The silent word speaks as the discourse of the other, the capital Mother, the institution of woman's silence, of her confinement to the body in which she is dispossessed of her word by the law of the patriarch. Stephen's mother speaks and her word covers the silence that covers her death. She cites the law: "All must go through it, Stephen. More women than men in the world. You, too. Time will come"; but she also reminds her son of what subverts the law, of her word in his mouth: "You sang that song to me. *Love's bitter mystery.*" Stephen wants to appropriate her word, to translate it as the logos. (139)

50. Molly and Leopold both misremember Rudy's date of birth: actually, he would have been ten and a half years old on June 16, 1904. The mistake may be due to Rudy's death at eleven days, and the association of the number eleven with death. See Rickard's discussion of textual memory, including Hugh Kenner's interpretations of eleven (Rickard, *Joyce's Book of Memory,* 149).

pages. Rudy is not a discoursing subject in the play, but instead hovers as a poetic apparition of the lost love object of the loving father (and the fantasy image of a loving, mystical, faithful Jewish son who finds satisfaction in the secrets of the Judaic father that Bloom and his family have renounced). The Rudy apparition visually and metonymically mirrors Bloom's paternal and filial desires (idealizations of the son he lost and of the son he never was), without making these desires speak directly.

The strong aspect of (symbolic) fatherhood of Bloom's mental life is further exaggerated by his extensive Circean hallucination of his grandfather Virag Lipoti of Szombathely as a diabolical, cynically candid old man. This phantasm sketches out what Bloom imagines to be his ancestry, which he must carry like an embarrassing burden and a kind of badge of pride. Virag does not just represent paternal law, but also the wily, unwritten codes of necessity adopted by some Jewish foreigners to forsake some of that heritage in order to assimilate into society.[51] For example, Virag implies his conversion to and subsequent abandonment of Roman Catholicism, a series of actions demonstrating a kind of pervasive unbelief in religion and a pragmatic critical outlook ("Why I left the Church of Rome"). Virag's name itself strongly reminds Bloom of his partially lost (and therefore partially nostalgically longed for) ancestry, of the unsentimental practice of adjusting one's name to local standards, and the feminine side of his sexuality. His garrulous ancestor is also shown as a source of sexual knowledge, alternating between semipornographic and quasi-academic language. In one instance, Virag stands in place of a Sigmund Freud or Havelock Ellis as the author of a long book series entitled "Fundamentals of Sexology or the Love Passion" (U 15:2423); in another instance, Virag weaves into his discourse the Sanskrit words for human genitalia in a hilariously mock-serious, mock-pornographic description of sexual congress: "Woman, undoing with sweet pudor her belt of rushrope, offers her allmoist yoni to man's lingam. [. . .] Man loves her yoni fiercely with big lingam, the stiff one" (15:2549–50).

Bloom's mutable and mutated name and person throughout "Circe" (and elsewhere in *Ulysses*), such as through the figure of Virag, show that the power of naming relies on censoring in terms of the creative, expres-

---

51. Many of the Jewish signifiers in "Circe" represent Bloom's lost heritage and his association of it with familial love, affection, attachment, belonging, and knowledge; many also reflect contemporary attitudes and understanding of Jewishness. For an extensive review of Joyce's usage of Jewish references, see Ira B. Nadel's *Joyce and the Jews*. Nadel argues that Joyce, "in mythologising history, most notably in 'Cyclops,' 'Circe' and the *Wake*, [. . .] solves the dilemma of the emptiness of fact and the poverty of historical meaning. By turning to fantasy, fiction and repetition—in short, myth—into history, Joyce not only revitalizes history but gives new energy to myth" (43).

sive substitutions (names can function as metaphors or metonyms). The creative naming and impersonation—and in general the fantastic dramatic discursive signifying system of "Circe"—are evidence of Bourdieu's structural conception of censorship:that is, that censorship is "constituted by the very structure of the field in which the discourse is produced and circulates. [. . .] [I]t is the structure of the field itself which governs expression by governing both access to expression and the form of expression" (138–39).

Moreover, "Circe" personifies signifying systems of discourse, rendering the theme of censoring into a series of harsh or judgmental characters. Upon Virag's introduction (15:2304), he is called "basilicogrammate," meaning "king of letters" or even "a lord of language." Thus Virag connotes for his grandson Leopold Bloom a mastery of language, of living in the symbolic, of overcoming the hurdles of rules by ruling language. In a certain sense, Virag is an imagined master of the Law. In keeping with this role, he carries a roll of parchment (which later discloses cures for memory, warts, sexual drive), and two quills adorn his ears. His verbosity curtails Bloom's own usually wordy pronouncements, while Virag's modes of inquiry sympathetically coincide with those of his grandson. At one point, Bloom reflects, "It has been an unusually fatiguing day, a chapter of accidents" (15:2380). Virag then calls upon Bloom to use his memory ("Exercise your mnemotechnic" [2384–85]) in an effort to unearth and analyze his sexual desires, preoccupations, tastes.

While Virag seeks to be at once explicit, academic, and humorous about sexuality (and notably never fully succeeding in his disclosures by virtue of his digressions or substitutions), Bloom responds in choppy, short, and evasive phrases that combine diachronic action with existential contemplation [e.g., past + present; present + future; present + future + past]: "I wanted then to have now concluded. Nightdress was never. Hence this. But tomorrow is a new day will be. Past was is today. What now is will then tomorrow as now was be past yester" (15:2408–10). In these metasyntactic associations and other instances, Bloom struggles to master memory and how history is formulated from perceptions of the past, present, and future. By summoning the specters of his dead father (Rudolph [15:248–79]) and mother (Ellen [15:281–90]), grandfather (Lipoti), and son (Rudy), synchronizing discrete temporal instances of being, Bloom can fulfill the role of the son, grandson, and father in this series of fantasy.

Unlike the mystical silent discourse of Rudy and the garrulous language-master Leopold, Bloom's father, Rudolph, symbolizes the Law in terms of the fearsome father barking unbearable constraints associated with anti-assimilation; Rudolph's horrible image and harsh words reflect symbolically

Bloom's fear, love, and respect for him. Among Bloom's first encounters in Nighttown, Bloom meets his "stooped bearded" father, dressed as an "elder in Zion" and streaked with yellow poison (15:248–51). Rudolph scolds him for going with a "drunken goy" and Bloom reverts to a mealy "crestfallen" child, "*Ja, ich weiss, papachi.*" Perhaps more important, the father confronts him for entering Nighttown: "What you making down this place? Have you no soul? (*With feeble vulture talons he feels the silent face of Bloom.*) Are you not my son Leopold, the grandson of Leopold? Are you not my dear son Leopold who left the house of his father and left the god of his fathers Abraham and Jacob?" (15:259–62).

Rudolph's confrontation underscores the fact that, despite Leopold's awe, the beloved son chooses to defy the father. From various passages in *Ulysses*, we know that the anniversary of Rudolph's suicide is quickly approaching, one which will take Leopold away from Dublin for a ritual trip. Thus, the evocation of the father at the threshold of taboo territory (Nighttown) symbolizes not just the corrective voice of the Law (in terms of faithfulness to Jewish tradition and family), but also Bloom's preoccupation with the anniversary of the loss of his father, a thought not openly discussed, bearing the double pain of loss and shame of suicide (a sin in most religions, and particularly in Catholicism). Another coincidence will occur in the near future: Molly and Boylan's upcoming concert tour, in which they would be able to enjoy more illicit sex together, will overlap with Bloom's father's suicide anniversary.

9. BLOOM ON TRIAL

> (*An official translation is read by Jimmy Henry, assistant town clerk.*)
>
> JIMMY HENRY The Court of Conscience is now open. (*U* 15:1629)[52]

Readers of *Ulysses* tend to admire Bloom's conscience—his ethical sense of justice and judgment. His clear sense of balance, fairness, and kindness is not commonly found in his diegetic Dubliner counterparts. Thus he is set apart from the rest not only as a Jew, but also as an unusually levelheaded,

---

52. While Gifford notes the conventional connotation of this office, "the court of chancery [...]; also the court of requests, small local debt courts that fell into disuse toward the end of the nineteenth century" (478), there may be a theatrical meaning, too. In his history of Dublin theater, Fitzgerald reports, "In connection with the Dublin theatres were certain well-known supper-rooms. Sam's Coffee House was kept by Sam Lee, leader of the band at the Crow Street Theatre. Isaac Sparks, the actor, founded a jovial meeting in form of a Court of Justice, wherein he presided in robes as Lord Chief-Justice Joker." Sparks's mock court might provide a historical underpinning for the theatrical framing of "Circe."

fair-minded person. From the novel's early chapters involving Bloom's interior monologues, we learn that he often thinks in comparative terms, weighing and counterbalancing arguments and observations. He also accumulates facts and arguments, revealing a tendency to catalogue and classify. Throughout the day, Bloom must strategically defend himself in various ways, whether it is to win approval or to avoid ugly scenes at the funeral in "Hades" or to score some cheap points against the pub nationalists in "Cyclops."

In "Circe," his many fantasies about justice and judgment often stem from his need to justify himself for being Jewish in Ireland. While Bloom does not practice Judaism, he summons Jewish names, dress, identity, subjects, Hebrew and Yiddish phrases, and other trappings in order to glorify, distinguish, or defend himself. His diverse collection of things Jewish at times betrays his lack of consistency or knowledge, but it also shows the arbitrary and myriad ways in which Jewishness can be (mis)apprehended, even by someone who is Jewish.[53]

Bloom's concern with Jewishness also involves some of Judaism's recurrent motifs of judgment: persecution and guilt complexes; belonging to the chosen yet shunned people; and within this topoi, the concept of Moses as redeemer and savior (as Nadel states, "a natural Messiah for the Jews, embodying qualities of spiritual redemption and political salvation" [98]); being defined by blood; accepting or rejecting Mosaic Law. This harsh law of retribution is perceived as being cruel but fair, and becomes reconfigured in various fantasies about persecution and retribution.

In some instances in "Circe," the Mosaic Law functions as a kind of transformational and regulatory logic in fantasy akin to censorship. In the first fantasy trial, when Bloom is questioned by the night watchmen, Bloom's initial defense is to say, "I am doing good to others" (15:682). Later in the courtroom, Beaufoy attacks Bloom's "moral rottenness": "(*to the court*) Why, look at the man's private life! Leading a quadruple existence! Street angel and house devil! Not fit to be mentioned in mixed society! The archconspirator of the age!" (15:853–55). Ad hominem attacks and digressive arguments abound in this trial; even the codes of law are in battle, as J. J. O'Molloy, Bloom's defense attorney, remarks: "The Mosaic code has superseded the law of the jungle" (15:969–70).[54] Here, the Mosaic code triumphs over the law of the jungle paradoxically on the terms of the latter.In "Circe, "the motif of Jewishness artistically censors sexuality in at

---

53. See Ira Nadel's outstanding *Joyce and the Jews* for extensive discussion of Jewish topics in Joyce's work.

54. Note that Bloom encounters J. J. O'Molloy at the newspaper offices in the morning and reflects upon the barrister's decline from a once promising career.

least two ways, both of which stem from the episode's heteroglossia and the inner discursive system of meaning. First, in terms of male ancestry, Bloom hallucinates images and dialogues of his father, grandfather, and son, all of whom display Jewish features or signs (e.g., the Hebraic book, the Zionist garb, the Yiddish or German utterances). In addition to their status as lost loved objects, they can be regarded as cherished but censored other selves of Bloom. Jewishness itself can represent some lost, loving environment. Furthermore, Bloom's symbolic fatherhood and filial attachments are apprehended as judgmental, discursive, and scholarly. Assimilation achieved in part through sexuality is embedded in the censoring of his other selves: his marriage to a goy (Molly), his extramarital dalliances (with more goys), and his visit to Nighttown (part of 1904 Irish heteromasculine rituals). In this way, Bloom's sexuality rejects or makes impossible his Jewishness, and in turn his fantasized Jewish ancestors confront him with this rejection, condemning his sexual conduct and desires in particular.

Second, he indulges his sense of guilt (about his sexual desires) and of persecution (the unfair mistreatment of him by others because of his Jewish heritage) in fantasies involving judgment. Most notably, in one extended fantasy, Bloom, through his roguish solicitation of obscene correspondence with upper-class Dublin women, eventually achieves universal popularity; by direct consequence, he is acclaimed as the charismatic, reasonable, inventively practical ruler of Dublin. In the fantasy with Mrs. Yelverton Barry, Mrs. Bellingham, and the Honourable Mrs. Mervyn Talboys, Bloom's improper written advances (reflective of *Venus in Furs* discourse, as well as the Parnell-emulation fantasy) are replied to with shame punishments that emphasize the class inequality (e.g., "I'll scourge the pigeonlivered cur as long as I can stand over him. I'll flay him alive" [15:1082–83]; "Geld him. Vivisect him" [1105]; "I'll flog him black and blue in the public streets ..." [1115–17]).

This masochistic sexual imaging contrasts with Bloom's subsequent elevation as Dublin's Moses. He performs a series of miracles and enacts laws, much like a Messiah, lawgiver, and sage. In one of his many energetic acts of leadership, he opens a court of conscience which shares qualities of the biblical court of Solomon and Portia's court in *The Merchant of Venice,* two courts noted for their ingenious fairness. Bloom's eventual downfall occurs because, in their frenzied adulation, many distinguished women commit suicide for him (a fantasy metaphor for surrendering themselves sexually to him). This flurry of feminine death causes the mob to condemn Bloom. His Christ-like martyrdom includes a marked lack of just consideration and an extended masochistic death sequence by lynching, burning, and crucifixion. Nadel interprets this scene as one that connects Christian codes to Jewish ones:

> Following his exposure, the Moses/Messiah figure becomes the crucified Christ set ablaze to a chorus of six hundred voices until, carbonised, He disappears. Bloom becoming Moses becoming Christ is the enactment of the typology Joyce has borrowed from the Old and New Testaments expressed vividly in the surrealistic psychological world of "Circe." (100)

One strand of suppressed meaning in this hallucination is Bloom's triumphant, erotic enjoyment in his marriage with Molly. We can consider the Blooms' marriage a defiance of common contemporary bigotry (i.e., Dubliners' perception that she could have "done better for herself" than marry a Jew; his father's and grandfather's disapproval). Bloom's enjoyment is derived, in part, from Molly's mysterious hybrid origins (Moorish, Jewish, Spanish, and Irish), the "ubiquitous mystique of the Jewish woman, Oriental in character" (Nadel, 168), as seen, for example, in Bloom's Circean fantasy of Molly as a Turkish concubine.

Themes of censorship and sexuality complement each other in Bloom's masochistic tendencies. In "Circe," these tendencies are strongly conveyed, often in terms of persecution, punishment, pleasure, and pornographic and diegetic cliché, particularly in his extended hallucination of his erotic encounter with the brothel madam Bella Cohen. In this encounter, Bloom and Bella quickly trade genders (although Bloom seems to retain oneirically his male genitalia while gaining the female apparatus).

With Bella/Bello, Bloom indulges in several punishing fantasies. First, he occupies the position of a young, naïve, sexually exploited woman (a general character type whom he often lusts after in his everyday life, be she a housemaid or a girl on the beach). By fantasizing that he is a novice prostitute, he enjoys not only pain and degradation that might accompany the position, but also the pleasure of wearing pretty but constraining women's clothes. His fantasy also reveals how his lustful feelings toward the subaltern woman conflicts with his empathetic awareness of her hardships. Thus his sexual urges collide with his sense of just kindness. In the theatrical discourse and heteroglossia of "Circe," his ability to insert himself into the subaltern woman's role allows him to delight in erotic identification and desire to be subjugated and to bear punishments in the place of the usual victim.

Throughout *Ulysses*, and intricately diversified and elaborated in various dimensions in "Circe," adultery—Bloom's own and his wife's—is the focus of thematic developments of sexual and ethical crime. His trials under "Beauty's" (Bello's) domination also involve cataloguing the "many," "hundreds" of his sins of the past and staging some of these. Significantly these sins involve pursuing and writing obscene propositions to women: adultery enacted discursively. Bloom is also confronted in a fantasy with his daughter Milly, whom he mistakes for Molly, a possible indirect allusion to incestuous desire or involvement. Furthermore, in a Rip Van Winkle moment, Bloom helplessly surveys how Molly has become a prostitute in his exaggerated twenty-year absence (as opposed to his daylong one), and then he pleads to return to set things right. Bello responds:

> As a paying guest or a kept man? Too late. You have made your secondbest bed and others must lie in it. Your epitaph is written. You are down and out and don't you forget it, old bean.
> BLOOM: Justice! All Ireland versus one! Has nobody . . . ? (*he bites his thumb*)
> BELLO: Die and be damned to you if you have any sense of decency or grace about you. (15:3197–3205)

The masochistic fantasy of dying as a pleasurable punishment issues from the dialogue between Bello and Bloom. In Bello's harsh response is a promise of redemption in death ("if you have any decency or grace about you"). In the immediately subsequent punishment, Bloom will be buried along with some other supposed cuckolded husbands. Bloom berates himself, "My willpower! Memory! I have sinned! I have suff . . ." (15:3214–15). Then, in a Jewish ceremony by the Wailing Wall, a group of Jewish men ("the circumcised") "wail in pneuma over the recreant Bloom" (3224–25); the chant of the Circumcised—a common Jewish prayer to be repeated by every Jew before he dies—is sung at all Jewish services and prayers at home. While the ceremony in the fantasy links Bloom to Jewish masculinity and to his heritage in general, the motif suggests a kind of censoring of his other non-Jewish self. These men's names all derive from Jewish Dubliners of the 1904 period, citizens ranging from a librarian to a rabbi, and who were "neighbours" of the fictional Bloom when he "lived" in Lombard Street West (Gifford, 415; Nadel). This ceremony marks a sacrificial death of Bloom to atone for his sexual sins, the second fantasized death in this chapter. In this second instance, he sins for being a cuckolded husband, a statement of his failure as a man.

Thus, one censoring motif, the liminal transformations of Bloom (ritual punishments for his transgressions and shortcomings), becomes attached to another censoring motif, his rejection of Judaism. Both motifs are connected discursively to contextual cultural referents, a fusion of realism and fantasy (e.g., the transposition of Bloom's Dublin neighbors to an imagined scene in Jerusalem; the cuckoldry punished by the Judaic heritage that he both admires and rejects).

The textual plot and character development describe and dramatize poetically and mimetically the creative process of censoring. Bloom self-censors his wishes and fears about his love life with his wife. Sexuality is not repressed, but rather censored, in the sense of transformation (metaphor or metonym): even the burial involves throwing "dead sea fruit" upon Bloom.

This condensation serves as a stratified metaphor for unsatisfactory pleasures and an inversion of his sensual plenitude at the conclusion of "Lotus Eaters" (i.e., his luxurious bathing moment in which his sex floats flower-like); "dead sea fruit" refers in a dialogically stratified way to the qualities of the Dead Sea explored in Bloom's diverse morning thoughts. On the one hand, in "Calypso," he associates the Dead Sea with the Jews as wandering from one captivity to another and with barren feminine sexuality ("It lay there now. Now it could bear no more. Dead: an old woman's: the grey sunken cunt of the world" [4:226]). On the other hand, at the beginning of "Lotus Eaters," his associations turn to concepts of buoyancy, symbolic and real, reading, masculine ease, self-sufficiency, and introspection (his memory of a photograph of a man "in the dead sea, floating on his back, reading a book with a parasol open. Couldn't sink if you tried" [5:39]).

Thus, in "Circe," "dead sea fruit"—and by metonymic extension the burial of Bloom in this particular scene—supplies a dense condensation of masculinity and femininity (the "fruit" the antithesis of "dead," and metaphor for sex) and notions of sexuality as uplifting (another antithesis of death) and source of historical, geographic origins of humanity. The water associations are then countered by the burning of the body in funeral pyre. The passage relies on a dialogism conveyed not through dramatic dialogue, but through the narrative (diegetic) aspect of the dramaturgic directions. The scene connotes the antithetical idea of pleasurable suffering through punishment, resurrection, and self-preservation even in the dire crises of punishment, death, and condemnation. The individual subject, Bloom, is ritually disposed: a motif of censoring and liminality through punishment, death, crematory purification.

The narrative of Bloom's fantasy series in "Circe" mimics the artistic process of censoring in discourse. The fantasy episodes are joined by association, digression, substitution, all circling and closing in on the themes of sexuality (especially in terms of sexual difference, adultery, masochism) and censoring of the subject by judgment and punishment, and all circling around the subject of Bloom, self-knowledge, his sensuality, and conflicting ethical interests or aims.

An example of the linking of fantasy series can be noted in the nymph Calypso, the fresh sexual symbol that immediately emerges from the funereal blaze of Bloom's second death in "Circe" (the new symbol also harks back dialogically to the narratives of Bloom's morning action and thoughts). The Circean figure of Calypso is derived from the representation of the nymph that hangs over the Blooms' matrimonial bed. The nymph's entry onto the dramatic scene of "Circe" at this juncture in Bloom's series of fantasies signals a reaffirmation of sexual desire in marriage as well as various blush-inducing private acts performed under the nymph's gaze ("O I have been a perfect pig. Enemas too . . ." [15:3397]).[55] Thus one judgment and condemnation (the second death scene) give birth to new sexual inquiry and pursuit of the desired object. The references such as the Dead Sea and Calypso resurrect the happy matrimonial morning before Bloom's discovery of Boylan's letter in the mail, thus depicting wish-fulfillments to regain and transform a recent, but unrecoverable instance of marital infidelity.

When his burst trouser button temporarily breaks the spell he is under, Bloom regains his self-control to a large extent (and handily recovers his talismanic potato from Zoe), and the focus of phantasms shifts to Stephen, with Bloom standing by as a fatherly protector. Bloom's apparent recovery of self-control, however, does not prevent several more negotiations with his insistent desires and censoring response. In one hallucination, Molly (or Marion) appears with Boylan, who invites Bloom to witness the adulterous scene (15:3756–3816). Bloom behaves as a boyish servant to the arrogant imposter. Even in this instance, the artistic censoring—transformation or substitution of the truth—does not allow full disclosure. The sexual act is only alluded to: first by way of Mina Kennedy's and Lydia Douce's mediating reportage of the romantic action; then by Cohen's prostitutes' giggling; and then by the offstage voices of Boylan and Marion. Thus, Bloom's censoring practices manage to keep the adulterous scene offstage and distanced from him, so that he can safely enjoy or reckon with its masochistic meanings and effects ("[*his eyes widely dilated, clasps himself*] Show! Hide! Show! Plough her! More! Shoot!" [15:3815–16]).[56]

---

55. See Eric D. Smith's article for intertextual references to pigs in *Ulysses*, especially "Circe," and elsewhere. He argues that "the pig represents a threat to modernism that transcends notions of mere sanitation and sexuality or the pig's carnivalesque tradition" (138).

56. Suzette Henke sees Bloom as "author/actor/director of this play of infidelity. Through the dual role of playwright and spectator, he is able, like Sacher-Masoch's fictive Severin, to reduce his ignominious situation to an absurdly masochistic drama. In the course of 'Circe,' Bloom becomes author and reader of his own domestic narrative, gaining artistic control over emotional trauma by recreating the dread event in exaggerated detail on the stage of a highly charged erotic (and perverse) imagination" (119).

I differ from this reading. The masochist does craftily organize his scene of pain and degradation

10. THE CLOTHES OF THE SIGNIFIER

"Circe" is a circuit of desire. Fantasies are represented through their discursivity of censoring and the deployment of parody, negation, metaphor, personification, and allusions. Various brands of humor are called into action. Irony is especially prized as it provides the twist or contrast of opposing values or aims. Sometimes the humor is painful, humiliating—as seen in Bloom's various modes of fantasized dying, and especially in his grotesque bout as a female prostitute. But these tragicomedic forms are also cathartic in dramatic and psychoanalytic senses. Bloom's fantastic reconstitutive selves are resurrected time and again, assume new voices and tonalities, don different clothes, and interact with the novel's catalogue of personae—all demonstrating Bloom's inventive, censoring stratagems to explore pleasurably his particular preoccupations with sexuality and judgment. As with all discursive modes of the Imaginary and the Symbolic, Bloom's operation veils access to knowing the Real. "Circe" does provide instances of the Real that are both significant in their intervention in the plot and their impermeability: examples of diegetic pieces of Real are the popped button of Bloom's trousers, the smashed lamp, and the English soldier's blow that levels Stephen.

Bloom's changing clothes and roles veil his own subjecthood while also indicating or performing aspects of his sense of it. He is the central protean character of "Circe." In a complementary way, and in keeping with the discursive system of signification in this text, many other actants and props in the episode prominently feature a striking mutability. For example, the proverbial dog in the street (reminiscent of the Everydog depicted earlier in "Proteus") recurs and recurs again in all manner of pelts and barking. This mutable dog can also stand for the presence of God as everyday Real being, just as Adonai's offstage call "Dooooooooooog" and its inversion "Goooooooooood" imply (*U* 15:4710–16).

The issue of gender performance versus essentialism is synthesized in "Circe" through multiple instances of gender mutability and androgyny. In his scene with the doctors, Bloom is celebrated as the "new womanly man," a triumphant hybrid of masculinity that does not fear or degrade the feminine, and corrects the problematic masculinity with the pleasures of the feminine.[57] Bloom's "new womanly man" suggests an optimistic mod-

---

for his own enjoyment (cf. Deleuze; Silverman; Stewart). But, the narrativized dramatic structure of "Circe" does not endow Bloom with a director's kind of authority nor does the scene necessarily win him control.

57. Harly Ramsey examines Bloom's pain in sympathy for Mina Purefoy ("Kill me that would" [*U* 8:377]) and compares it and his mourning for Rudy with the "Circe" scene of Bloom's birthing

ern social trend (and possibly ethical condemnation of misogyny), while this version of the self also offers masochistic functions.[58] Previous to the Nighttown scene, we have learned of Bloom's particular love of fashionable, flattering clothing, especially women's undergarments and stockings. In Nighttown he gratifies this love in various fetishistic ways.[59]

The combined narrative and theatrical discursive modes of "Circe" allow for extensive use of costume and other trappings (an exaggeration of a real feature of theatrical productions) and identity change and revelation (a central theme in dramatic stories). The dress fetishism extends to Bloom's fantasy male octuplets: "handsome, with valuable metallic faces, wellmade, respectably dressed and well conducted [. . .]. Each has his name printed in legible letters on his shirtfront: Nasodoro, Goldfinger, Chrysostomos, Maindorée, Silversmile, Silberselber, Vifargent, Panargyros" (15:1823–28).

The changing of clothes can be seen as a special form of artistic censoring, a mode in which the subject is creatively veiled in the guises that reveal, conceal, or emphasize aspects of his masculine and feminine selves. In addition to the creative censoring involved in representing wishes and

---

of eight children (shortly after the doctors' examination of the womanly Bloom). In the birthing scene, according to Ramsey, Bloom experiences a kind of self-inflicted pain of hallucinatory childbirth. Bloom manages to imagine pain "when he fantasizes himself as the maternal body, the maternal object" (67).

While I agree that Bloom is certainly fantasizing the maternal body (and the doctors' examination of it), I find that Joyce downplays or even elides the experience of pain in the birthing scene, for Bloom merely embraces Mrs. Thornton tightly and miraculously pop out his eight "male yellow and white children" (*U* 15:1818–22) Joyce comically deflates the enormous feat of labor, distancing Bloom's fantasy experience from the excruciating one that Mina Purefoy has endured in "Oxen of the Sun."

58. See Restuccia's *Joyce and the Law of the Father* for an extended discussion of masochism vis-à-vis Bloom and Joyce himself (154). In this book, Restuccia discusses Deleuze's *Masochism* in comparison to Joyce, Joyce's work, and psychoanalytic conceptions of masochism (especially those developed in Deleuze). Deleuze, Joyce, and Freud develop in part their conceptions of masochism through *Venus in Furs* (Sacher-Masoch); diegetically in *Ulysses*, *Venus in Furs* is an artistic text that informs Bloom's and Molly's reading interests and part of the overall discursive economy of *Ulysses*.

59. Guided by Georg Simmel's studies of fashion and class-marked commodities, Mark Osteen discusses the "chapeaugraphy" of "Circe," reminding us of that episode's rapt attention to headgear, especially that of Bloom (to name a few, a boy's alpine mobcap, a red school cap, a purple Napoleon, a dinged silk hat, a red fez, a caubeen, a drooping sombrero, and so on). Osteen notes that in Bloom's female guises he wears no hat:

> Here Bloom's symbolic castration is dramatized by his hatless femininity [. . .]. Bloom's Circean chapeaugraphy dramatizes the roles he has already played (or hopes to play) in *Ulysses*: the outsider, the "Oriental," the cuckold, and the Jew; the patriot, the political reformer, the society maven, the lover. Whereas the former grouping indicates how others view him, the latter batch suggests how he views himself. (277)

wish fulfillments, the changing of clothes can demonstrate the constitutive aspects of psychic identity itself. Circean costume drama shows the subject's mode of separation, in the sense that the (barred) Subject, in his relation and drive toward the *objet a* ($ ◊ a :* Lacan's formulation of phantasy) moves toward the object (alienation) and twists back again toward himself (separation) (*Four Fundamental Concepts,* 210–15). Lacan explains how "separation" should be understood in a complex way, in terms of "to dress" and "to engender." He explains the etymology of "separation":

> *Separare, to separate*—I would point out at once the equivocation of the *se parare,* of the *se parer,* in all the fluctuating meanings it has in French. It means not only to dress oneself, but also to defend oneself, to provide oneself with what one needs to be on one's guard, and I will go further still, and Latinists will bear me out, to the *se parere,* the *s'engendrer,* the *to be engendered,* which is involved here. How, at this level, has the subject to procure himself? For that is the origin of the word that designates in Latin *to engender.* It is juridical, as indeed, curiously enough, are all the words in Indo-European that designate *to put into this world.* (214)

In this complex sense of separation, dressing or separation provides a self-signifying mode for the subject in terms of juridically bringing himself into the world. By assuming a certain dress, appearance, or voice, one assumes a significance both for oneself and for the other (*objet a*). Separation, conceived broadly as dressing and engendering, is the movement toward the self after circling around the other (in the circuitry of desire, the other cannot actually be achieved or obtained, only approximated, desired, and reflected or return back to the self, i.e., the barred Subject).

Subjecthood in "Circe" is dramatized in part according to Lacan's formulation of phantasy, in the initial movement of alienation and the subsequent one of separation. The emphasis on separation and dressing indicates, in an uncanny way,[60] several of the key aspects of "Circe" and the censoring,

---

60. The uncanny (Freud's *das Unheimliche*) is a familiar motif and point of discussion for many Joyce scholars (e.g., Brivic's *Veil;* Devlin's *Wandering;* Spoo). See Michael Bruce McDonald's article for an assessment of earlier approaches (e.g., Ellman; Ferrer), as well as his own suggestion of the exchangeability of things and people in "Circe." He maintains that Joyce's rendering of the *Unheimliche* tends to create comic effects (and thus, prompting smirks and complacency in the reader) rather than provoking "a shudder"; he suggests that, for example, "the ungainly spectral forms of Virag and Gerty provoke more mirth than alarm" (53).

However, I counter that it is possible to be both alarmed and amused by Virag and Gerty. The comic features in Joyce's work merit more examination, especially in terms of veiled aggressivity. Mark Shechner, along with other scholars, considers how Bloom establishes his "moral heroism" by way of comic, but at times disturbing self-denigration, and how Joyce uses "Circe" as a way to "violate the canons of social and personal taboo without being struck dead by censorship or

yet productive, gendered and engendering subject. In the chapter, the subject (Bloom; Stephen) goes through multiple alienations and separations of self through changes of dress, gender, and other role-playing. These diverse modes of separation—the subject draping himself with various signifying objects—aim at the impossible task of closing the gap of the perceived missing, never knowable part of the other. We know Lacan's basic premise that the subject desires the desire of the other. "Circe" repeatedly dramatizes how desire is necessarily predicated on the fact that the subject cannot know fully that desire, especially if the *objet a* is to remain desirable. In his quest to discover and recover the unknown, the lost object, the desire of the other, the subject must foreclose for himself through censoring strategies the procurement of that unknown factor, the Thing. The desire of the other and the Thing are perceived through their lacks and gaps, glimpsed at or felt in their signifying matter.

In "Circe," a central unifying discursive feature is a special hybridized novelistic style, a fantasy narrative-theatrical form, appropriate to "show" and "tell" psychic drama: the protagonists Bloom and Stephen externalize and stage their inner thoughts, preoccupations, memories, observations, and desires, using a narrative structure of fantasy (alienation and separation).

11. HALLUCINATED MEMORY: STAGING JUDGMENT

In the psychic system of checks and balances, there is a need or demand to create order, to make things right; this economy is regulated by an ethical drive. This drive obliges an awkward negotiation, as the subject cannot come to terms with crude reality as such. One of the subject's basic needs in living is to cope with his demand to make sense out of the nonsense or impression of arbitrariness of lived experience; he requires value and structure to provide a foundation for lived experience. But value and structure (i.e., language, the Law, the power of the signifier) are achieved at the cost of acceptance, recognition of a community, submitting oneself and others to judgment of common laws. In turn, admitting to values, structure, and community (even to reject, be indifferent to, or be intolerant

---

guilt" (101–4). In Zack Bowen's reading of *Ulysses* as comic novel, he notes that "[t]he methodology of Circe was almost inevitable if Joyce were to attempt to include Rabelaisean excesses in a modern novel. What better vehicle than to trace their logical origins in a Freudian unconscious?" (81). Bowen emphasizes how "Rabelaisean comic grotesquerie" is "played off the realistic scene in Bella's brothel. Joyce could blend modern realism with comic surrealism [. . .]." The contrast of the comic Bloom with the "would be tragic" Stephen lends to comic incongruity (88–89).

of these) establishes a basis and need for judgment (to censor, punish, assert, condone).

The Circean hallucinations, along with the paths of action taken by the characters, generally involve the subject's sense of displeasure with a state of affairs and crises with conflicting values and community codes. Both Bloom and Stephen grapple with issues that trouble them because they cannot easily apply a given value; the issues present conflicting and paradoxical facets which are only judged with harsh applications of the Law or by subversive elusion, delay, or disavowal of the Law. Moreover, we can see that the ethical drive that prompts or motivates the hallucination of these issues (in dramatic form for a jury of spectators) also involves a process of creative discharge.

BELLA (*almost speechless*) Who are. Incog! (*U* 15:4307–8)

The hallucinatory technique deployed in "Circe" can be compared to the compromises between our perceptions and our thoughts. In *The Ethics of Psychoanalysis,* Lacan makes several observations about the opposition between perception ("linked to the activity of hallucinating, to the pleasure principle") and thought ("psychic reality") (33). "Circe" expresses Bloom's and Stephen's experiences in Nighttown on a plane of realistic situations and a plane of hallucinated situations.

Bloom's role tends to dominate the chapter's structure and themes (e.g., the creative and productive functions of censoring and sexuality). Meanwhile, Stephen provides a strong additional perspective to personal hallucinatory processes. As a complement to Bloom's paternal identity, Stephen embodies symbolically a son. Bloom has an unspoken wish for an irretrievably lost son (Rudy). The two men are connected through mourning of a lost loved one (Bloom for Rudy and his father; Stephen for his mother) and by a kind of masochistic stance before an intolerant society. In Stephen's fascination with Shakespeare and other influential writers (e.g., Yeats), he prioritizes the dream of a transcendent masculine procreative ability, emblematic of a young artist's dream of self-sufficiency and his resistance to qualification of his sexual preferences. In conflict with his idealization of his mother, art, and elusive and illusory independence, arise censoring fantasies that incorporate his preoccupations with fatherhood, guilt, maternal love and punishment, religious duty and rituals, Catholic dogma, Irish and colonial history, and the threat of imitation in influential literature.

Stephen's censoring strategies differ in some respects from Bloom's maneuvers, and thus add to the chapter's discursive system examined so far. Stephen's strategies aim at partial condemnation of his parents and other influences of his youth (e.g., Catholicism). His most notable difference from Bloom is the relative lack of protean transformation: Stephen tends to remain relatively unchanged amid the metamorphosing world of "Circe" (with a few exceptions).[61]

Hallucinated apparitions that speak to him, or confront him in some dialogic way, represent that which Stephen wants to cast aside. These apparitions dramatize judgment in several ways, in hybridized speech and action reworking words and ideas used elsewhere in the novel, or from inferred moments in Stephen's past. Bloom's artistic censoring of the self results in his recreations, versions, and resurrections, whereas in Stephen's case the censoring motifs tend to result in a rejection of the stifling social, national, and religious influences in his past and an affirmation of an intellectual, sexually transcendent self (that is nonetheless dependent upon deep personal influences).

This is a self created in the sense that Stephen must fashion this self by peeling off the layers of the personal influences once dear to him. But it is not a self that promises new creation, in the way that Bloom's self tends toward playful, associative recreation and reformation of psychic drives. As Stephen's layers of experience are peeled off, so they are heaped back on in metamorphosis, with a punishing vengeance which negates or censors the self. For example, at the brothel, Stephen thinks of performing his father's act ("Play with your eyes shut. Imitate pa. Filling my belly with husks of swine [. . .] I will arise and go to my" [15:2495–96]. The last two phrases are from the parable of the Prodigal Son, Luke 15:16 and 15:18). Shortly after, the prostitute Florry remarks to Stephen, "I'm sure you're a spoiled priest. Or a monk" (15:2649). The conversation condenses the images of Stephen, his father Simon, hypocritical masculine authority, and blasphemous procreative masculinity based on sins and prodigality. The result of the conversation can be seen in the hybridized and dialogic apparition of the "Cardinal":

61. Stephen does demonstrate some protean transformation; for example, in the hallucinated encounter with his mother, his mother's cancer attacks and transforms him:

> THE MOTHER [. . .] Beware! (*she raises her blackened withered right arm slowly towards Stephen's breast with outstretched finger*) Beware God's hand!
> (*A green crab with malignant red eyes sticks deep its grinning claws in Stephen's heart.*)
> STEPHEN (*strangled with rage, his features drawn grey and old*) Shite! (*U* 15:4217–23)

Through this horrible encounter he momentarily becomes an old man, a condensed indication of symbolic effects of his mother's death and disease. The ironic metonym of "God's hand" and the metaphoric "green crab" (cancer) show Stephen's critical view of Irish Catholicism, God, and death of a loved one. In addition, the mother's warning to fear God is linked to death: if Stephen were to obey and fear God, he would die, too.

LYNCH He is. A cardinal's son.
STEPHEN Cardinal sin. Monks of the screw.[62]
(*His Eminence Simon Stephen cardinal Dedalus, primate of all Ireland, appears in the doorway, dressed in red soutane, sandals and socks. Seven dwarf simian acolytes, also in red, cardinal sins, uphold his train, peeping under it. He wears a battered silk hat sideways on his head.* [. . .])
THE CARDINAL [. . .] I'm suffering the agony of the damned. [. . .]
([. . .] *imparts the Easter kiss* [. . .]. *The dwarf acolytes, giggling, peeping, nudging, ogling, easterkissing, zizag behind him. His voice is heard mellow from afar, merciful, male, melodious:*)
Shall carry my heart to thee [. . .] (15:2650–88)

Cardinal Dedalus suggests a comically doomed version of the failed father, whose beautiful voice (much like Stephen's) has been heard earlier in "Sirens." The seven-dwarfs-as-acolytes motif mockingly represents a son's doomed imitation of the father (through sinning and hypocritically playing the mock-exemplary father). The acolytes also connect censoriously to Stephen's earlier argument in the library of the son's "apostolic succession" of the father[63] because the acolytes in this fantasy frame are clearly mocking, undesirable forms of paternal imitation. In this way, Stephen's hallucination seems to censor (judge harshly and mockingly) both the father and suggested outcome of his previously proud argument. We can note the worldly degradation of lofty "apostles" and the implied Christ of the "Scylla and Charybdis" speech to the vainer images of cardinal and acolytes in "Circe." The ensemble of cardinal and acolytes presents a dramatic scene for Stephen's viewing (rather than Stephen directly in a state of metamorphosis).

Stephen's fantasies involve guilt toward his parents and family (their monetary sacrifices for him; their promotion of him as the privileged eldest to the detriment of his poor, younger siblings; his refusal to fulfill the role of the dutiful, religious son for his mother; an irrational sense of responsibility for May's suffering and death), justification of his choice for independence and self-fulfillment; and artistic superiority based on a

---

62. Jeri Johnson notes that the "Monks of the screw" were an eighteenth-century "nonreligious Irish pleasure-seeking fraternal society, also known as the Order of St Patrick" (936).

63. "A father [. . .] is a necessary evil. [. . .] Fatherhood, in the sense of conscious begetting, is unknown to man. It is a mystical state, an apostolic succession, from only begetter to only begotten. [. . .] Upon incertitude, unlikelihood. *Amor matris*, subjective and objective genitive, may be the only true thing in life. Paternity may be a legal fiction. Who is the father of any son that any son should love him or he any son?" (*U* 9:828–45).

modern concept of freedom and "the intellectual imagination." The liminal experience of visiting the brothel does not bring about a moment of ritual masculine initiation, although arguably the visit alone is sufficient to qualify. The current prostitutes do not attract him nor arouse sexual desire;[64] if anything, his response is one of festive repression and studied self-absorption. Paul Schwaber emphasizes Stephen's self-negating operations, especially regarding sexuality and art: in *Portrait,* the "adolescent whoring, God-terrified guilt, and answering piety and asceticism," the "Villanelle of the Temptress" that stresses woman's negative "ardent ways"; in *Ulysses,* the account of Hathaway "as sexual villainess and Stephen's own antisexual consubstantial wishfulness"; and in "Circe," his unwillingness to "let his mother go" (154). Additionally, we should recognize the repeated preoccupations with homoerotic relations, particularly through the associations of Mulligan, Cranly, and Best.

The "Circe" plot of Stephen's entry into Nighttown issues from the urge for escape and quest, or perhaps most aptly for Stephen, a quest for escape from responsibilities of adulthood and memories of childhood, a most liminal situation. Through excessive drink and banter, Stephen seeks oblivion and the company of paid women whom he does not have to woo or impress. In these actions, he renounces responsibility to himself and his family and emphasizes his strivings toward an illusory freedom and individuality. This denial or renunciation of Catholicism's ethical good is

64. His former lustful interest in prostitutes has transformed to a mocking nostalgia and melancholy. He learns that his once favored prostitute Georgina Johnson, "*la belle dame sans merci,*" "*ad deam qui laetificat inventutem meam*" (to the goddess who has gladdened the days of my youth) (*U* 15:122–23; Jeri Johnson [923] for translation of the Latin), has married a Mr. Lambe and moved to London.

> STEPHEN [...] And so Georgina Johnson is dead and married. [...] Wonder. Parlour magic. Married. Hm. (*he strikes a match and proceeds to light the cigarette with enigmatic melancholy*) [...] Sixteen years ago. Distance. The eye sees all flat. (*He draws the match away. It goes out.*) Brain thinks. Near: far. Ineluctable modality of the visible. (*he frowns mysteriously*) Hm. Sphinx. The beast that has two backs at midnight. Married.
> ZOE It was a commercial traveller married her and took her away with him.
> FLORRY (*nods*) Mr Lambe from London.
> STEPHEN Lamb of London, who takest away the sins of our world. (15:3618–38)

In this exchange, Stephen combines his mocking interest of conjugal coupling and prostitution; his former femme fatale has "deceived" him, with Stephen taking the position of a cuckold. The exchange also joins the idea of marriage to English colonial economy: Georgina Johnson, once a prostitute bought by men, especially English men, has now been subsumed into the heart of the Empire. The imperial husband Lambe is a mock Christ who removes the prostitute from Ireland, or Stephen's goddess. Jeri Johnson notes that Stephen blasphemes in the earlier Latin reference to Georgina by changing the usual "Deum" (God) to "deam" (the goddess).

to be replaced by his allegiance to a new Law and its own ethical good: "The intellectual imagination! With me all or not at all. *Non serviam!*" (15:4227–28).[65]

Stephen and Bloom share a self-portrayal of themselves against the world (their Ireland; Dublin). Stephen's "With me all or not at all" echoes and refashions inversely Bloom's "Justice! All Ireland versus one!" The two utterances dialogize different aspects of alienation, the subject reaching out to the *objet a* (and the general existential sense of alienation, a consciousness of inability to secure that *objet a* or effectuate the desired relationship). In Stephen's case, he takes an aggressive, didactic position toward the community (it must join him, and not vice versa), whereas Bloom often positions himself as a legal thing, an embattled solitary subject judged by the community. Both speech acts do not directly solicit a verbal response, but rather imply a decision or action of an inferred collective.

Stephen's pursuit of a free, individual status does not correspond to the Lacanian drives of alienation and separation as identified for Bloom. Instead, Stephen's wavering between perception (hallucination) and thought expresses creative censoring activity. Two different examples of how Stephen censors himself will suffice. Both reveal the subject's conflict in reconciling actuality with hallucination.

First, at the climax of the ludicrous "My Girl's a Yorkshire Girl" whirligig scene with the prostitutes, Lynch, and Bloom, Stephen grabs his ashplant as a partner for his ironic, high-kicking "pas seul" ("step alone"; "dance alone"; "not alone") (15:4120–35). Amid this whirling frivolity (to a song which celebrates unfaithfulness), Stephen's extempory act of symbolic self-mastery and self-sufficiency provokes the horrible specter of his dead mother, the "once beautiful May Goulding" (along with the phantasms of a "choir of virgins and confessors" and Buck Mulligan as jester and parodic ideal son). "The Mother" judges Stephen harshly (censors him) in direct speech as well as through the poetic image and action. This phantasm lavishes on her son irrational feelings of responsibility for her death and nagging guilt about his stubborn resistance to play-act her brand of Catholicism to appease her. The implication is that, if he does not comply, he will be denied her love: the conditional tyrannical love of the mother condemns her son whether he obeys or disobeys.

The cancer-ridden corpse is an awesome, repulsive counterpart to wom-

---

65. Stephen's exclamation, echoing his stated position at the conclusion of *A Portrait of the Artist as a Young Man,* aligns him with artistic heresy and Lucifer's sin of pride, his refusal to serve God. In *Portrait,* he exclaims, "I will not serve," in explaining to his friend Cranly his refusal to oblige his mother's wish that he take Easter communion (260). By not receiving communion at least once a year and that once during Eastertide, Stephen breaks church law (325).

an's reproductive abilities and desirable charms. Somewhat like a female vampire, May Goulding stands as a doubly symbolic barrier to Stephen's access to a suitable, loving partner of his own, as well as more generally to a (pro)creative artistic ability. She is arguably indicative of the Thing, a body of dissolution, where sexual gender gives way to formlessness (cf. the prior discussion of the mother sea). Christine van Boheemen considers how *Ulysses* develops "[t]his (Lacanian) confrontation with the absolute nullity of the self through the maternal imago" (*Joyce, Derrida, Lacan*, 186), reminding us that as early as "Telemachus" May Dedalus is conceived by Stephen as an "orientalized vampiric spirit," such as when he addresses her with: "Ghoul! Chewer of corpses! No, mother! Let me be and let me live" (1:278). Also indicative of her role as barrier to Stephen's artistic development is the fact that she does not divulge "the word [. . .]. The word known to all men" (15:4192–93).[66] In addition to love, Stephen presumably refers to knowledge from the other world. Already earlier in the day, Stephen has resolved not to return to Martello Tower and even to leave Ireland. His midnight dallying among prostitutes cannot prevent him from recalling his decision for self-exile, and even serves as a dress rehearsal. In a fearful response of self-defense (or aggression) to the hallucinated censoring appearance of his mother, Stephen raises his ashplant and smashes the parlor light, thus destroying the specter and attempting to break with guilty memories that consume him.[67]

66. In her editorial notes, Jeri Johnson mentions that "[i]n the *Rosenbach Manuscript* (*RM*) holograph of *Scylla and Charybdis*, Stephen knew the answer: 'Love, yes. Word known to all men' [. . .] the 1984 *Ulysses* reinstates the phrase there" (791).
At the end of "Proteus," Stephen initiates the question while meditating on a woman's soft hand: "Touch me. Soft eyes. Soft soft soft hand. I am lonely here. O, touch me soon, now. What is that word known to all men? I am quiet here alone. Sad too. Touch, touch me." (3:434–36).

67. Restuccia elaborates on the sadistic and masochistic uses of sticks, canes, and whips and their overall connotation as phallic weapon in Stephen Dedalus's world ("From Whip to Reed"). Benjamin Harder views Stephen's stick as a prop of virile display (thus, stick as lack); Harder notes that the stick is left behind after the lamp-smashing incident, ostensibly because Stephen "has discovered the lack elided in its use and his participation in the violent phallic order that is betrayed when he strikes" (247). Harder sees THE MOTHER conflated with Christ. While this reading is problematic (consider how both Stephen and Bloom act out roles of Christ in "Circe"), I do agree with Harder that scholars' tendency to interpret Stephen's smashing of the chandelier as a sign of success should be questioned (251).
Christine van Boheemen notes that the maternal threat haunting Stephen throughout *Ulysses* includes the threat of "drag[ging] him with her into death" (186). Van Boheemen contemplates how the lamp smashing represents "a turning-point in the relationship between 'son' Stephen and 'father' Bloom, [and] suggests in its dramatization that the threat of the materiality of the mother is only to be laid to rest by the accepted risk of an Absolute Nothing beyond materiality, giving presence to death-in-life: in short, transcendental mourning" (187).
This canny interpretation perhaps overlooks the fact that Stephen's turning point may not turn him from his mother, especially if we consider his final moments in the episode, when, as he is

Furthermore, in this condensed episode, Stephen's German utterance "*Nothung!*"[68] ("Needful!") and his smashing action appropriate in mimetic and mock-epic fashion Siegfried and his magic sword *Nothung* (Wagner's opera *Der Ring des Nibelungen*). Siegfried destroys with his sword the dragon Fafner and gods; Stephen's speech and act express a similar impulse, to lay waste to the Law (The Mother, and by extension, God and Duty). The hybridized speech—"*Nothung!*" belongs simultaneously to Stephen and to naming Siegfried's sword—creates an unusual circuit of heteroglot meaning in the zone of Stephen's character.

A second example of self-censoring, also related to Stephen's negating renunciation of values of his origins and experience, arises shortly after this scene of the Mother. The example deploys various literary discourses, particularly Biblical discourse and those associated with Stephen's Jesuit education. He flees Bella Cohen's brothel and is confronted by two off-duty English soldiers, Privates Carr and Compton, and Cissy Caffrey (who have briefly crossed paths with Stephen at the beginning of the episode). In this example, Stephen directly confronts a representative of the irrational, nationalizing force of the British Empire. Carr cannot understand Stephen's slippery double-talk about the king of England and Cissy the

---

reviving from Carr's knockout blow, he murmurs the words of Yeats's song "Who Goes with Fergus?" Stephen has sung this song for his mother at her deathbed, a fact he recalls in "Telemachus" as Buck, unknowing, sings part of the song to coax Stephen from his moping ("His head vanished but the drone of his descending voice boomed out of the stairhead: /—*And no more turn aside and brood / Upon love's bitter mystery / For Fergus rules the brazen cars.* /[. . .] Fergus' song: I sang it alone in the house, holding down the long dark chords. Her door was open: she wanted to hear my music. Silent with awe and pity I went to her bedside. She was crying in her wretched bed. For those words, Stephen: love's bitter mystery" [*U* 1:239–53]). The song is from Yeats's play *The Countess Cathleen;* Oona, Cathleen's nursemaid or "foster-mother," sings the song to Cathleen to console her as Cathleen hears of the people's famine and trouble. The song unites the wood, sea, and stars. While Cathleen is inspired, hearing Fergus's horn in her heart and calling, Oona claims not to understand the words. In contrast to Stephen's conceptions of vampiric, bloody, or formless femininity leading to the Thing or nothingness, the song of "Fergus" celebrates "the white breast of the dim sea" (as reflected in Stephen's inner thoughts in "Telemachus" [1:244–45]). "Fergus" briefly returns (1:264) just before Stephen contemplates his mother's death and his attempt to dispel her as "ghoul."

68. The Irish dimension should not be forgotten in this scene of resistance to the mother's demand. Colin MacCabe maintains that Stephen resists an identification with the Croppy Boy in his "cry of 'Nothung!' (not hung like the Croppy)" (130) and again toward the end of "Circe" when the grotesque spectral image of the hanged betrayed patriotic boy from the song rises up during the Apocalyptic series of hallucinations to join Stephen in his flight down the street; MacCabe explains how the "Croppy Boy stands for all the disastrous demands made in Ireland and from which the only release is death. [. . .] The Croppy Boy achieves death and, in that moment, the signifier returns against the mother's demand: 'Horhot ho hray ho rhother's hest' (forgot to pray for his mother's rest)" (130). MacCabe explains how the "Croppy Boy moves through the pages of *Ulysses* as a warning to Stephen of the fate that awaits him if he assumes the identity that the mother urges on him" (129).

whore, but stubbornly insists on his own right to be right (even if that "right" negates itself: "I'll wring the neck of any fucking bastard says a word against my bleeding fucking king" [15:4644–45]). We can note in the street encounter satiric aspects of Commedia dell'Arte, particularly the style of playing the "grotesque mask." In the commedia, the "archetypal masks of the ancient and medieval carnival [are melded] with the stereotypical traits of types from the Italian society" (Wylie, 71). As Wylie explains, "[t]his union produced sociotypes which were employed to enact dramas centering on the social differentiation of personality structures and on the conflicts and tensions engendered by the socio-cultural system." It would seem that Joyce has such an objective in mind in his presentation of the redcoats, the prostitutes, and bystanders who dramatize the sociopolitical and cultural tensions of colonial Ireland. Carr's mask is particularly grotesque in its extreme exaggeration, violent gesturing and discourse, and pent-up libidinal attitudes.

Stephen's ecstatic, poetic address to Cissy as though she were a "mort,"[69] a Gypsy "free woman" ("White thy fambles, red thy gan / And thy quarrons dainty is" [(15:4654–56]), echoes his morning solitary meditation on the beach when he also considers final judgment, symbolically free women, and the army.[70] In "Circe," his recitation of the poem inserts a hybridized artistic text, using specialized poetic language (fambles = hands; gan = mouth; quarrons = body) to praise the woman's body, an elliptical expression of sexual desire, an eroticized address which seems superseded by his ecstatic attitude and the closed circuit of reference. It is unlikely that any of the

69. Jeri Johnson notes the origin of the poem or "canting," in the notes to "Proteus": "mort: 16th–17th-c. cant for 'woman'; first allusion to canting to 17th-c. canting song 'The Rogue's Delight in Praise of His Mort' (printed in Richard Head's The Canting Academy [1673] . . .)" (790). Jorn Barger provides most of the song with translation; here is the stanza initiated by Stephen:

White thy fambles, red thy gan,
And thy quarrons dainty is,
Couch a hogshead with me than,
In the Darkmans clip and kiss.
[Trans:]
Thy hand is white and red thy lip,
Thy dainty body I will clip.
Let's down to sleep our selves then lay,
Hug in the dark and kiss and play.

70. The prostitution of young Dublin women in this period was at a high level of activity, the combined result of the presence of the British military and Irish poverty (high prostitution levels generally being an indicator of poverty and a strongly marked social divide). Bloom and Stephen's presence in Nighttown is an ethical choice; by being there, they are no different from the English soldiers.

characters can understand the meaning of Stephen's coded recitation (the language of canting was once used by gypsies, thieves, etc.; ironically this language in theory could be understood by Carr and Cissy, but in practice has fallen out of common usage). Similarly the people in the street do not understand Stephen's other ruminations on the king and money; they take him for a professor. His speech is refracted in comments by Biddy the Clap and Cunty Kate, in ironic imitation of academic and ceremonial speech: respectively, "He expresses himself with much marked refinement of phraseology" and "Indeed, yes. And at the same time with such apposite trenchery" (15:4442–45). These two speeches must be hallucinated or imagined by Stephen (terms imported from "Aeolus"), for the prostitutes could not realistically imitate or produce this specialized language. The irony of these utterances is that the artist Stephen cannot make himself understood to the common people for all his fine words.

The encounter with the soldiers and the prostitute extends the anticipation of Carr's assault on Stephen. Within that stretched-out anticipatory moment, the dialogic exchanges take place. A hallucination of King Edward the Seventh develops in a dramatization that cannot be apprehended by anyone but Stephen. The stage directions narrate a series of apocalyptic actions. On the street in Nighttown, voices call for the police and distant voices announce that Dublin is burning: these voices, summoning the law and fire, also raise the enormous specter of Armageddon and related allusions to Judgment Day, the ruinous aftermath of the Crucifixion (the culmination of the mob's terrible judgment and renunciation of the good).

Irish and British nationalist imagery commingles with religious and feminine references, creating a chaotic obscene hodgepodge of the censoring action on the damned. At one point in a mock Mass, the figure of Mina Purefoy (the naked goddess of unreason), representing repulsive, burdensome Irish pregnancy, looms forward, accompanied by Buck (Malachi) Mulligan, a mock priest who reworks his blasphemous shaving mass scene from the novel's beginning. Mulligan's role as mock priest, aided by Haines, dramatically recapitulates some of the homoerotic elements of Mulligan's relationship with Stephen, as witnessed in previous scenes in "Telemachus," "Scylla and Charybdis," and "Oxen of the Sun." In a condensed way, Purefoy and Mulligan represent inversions of entities once loved by Stephen: his now dead, unreasonable mother (who like Purefoy had a surplus of children); his once dear, now rejected friend; his church and nation. Mother, friend, church, Ireland: these are all objects of renunciation for Stephen, and thus to be censored and condemned (while they in turn negate him). As Bloom, offering the ashplant, pleads with Stephen to renounce the standoff with Private Carr, Stephen resists, saying, "Stick, no. Reason. This feast of pure reason" (15:4735). The unreasonable, reactionary Carr finally delivers the long-awaited punch, knocking Stephen unconscious.

This combination of real event and fantasy-hallucination temporarily satisfies Stephen's quest for self through negation. But while the soldier's unfair assault might provide his victim with a sense of dimly fatalistic superiority, the more important censorious struggle with the inextricably intertwined issues of sexuality, family, country, and faith has been hallucinated before Stephen reaches the violent entry into unconsciousness. The Judgment Day motif is embellished and complicated with a rebellious vision of destruction and blasphemy—the law of God being flaunted as Dublin burns.

The narrative-dramatic qualities of this sequence reveal an imperative or urge to destroy the past and all the foundational values that have created the young artist Stephen. The dramatic action leads the character to a parodic state of a-heroism. The destructive erasure of the past is a creative fantasy, deploying an epic cast and scene, and implies a condemnation of most of what has made Stephen who he is. On the one hand, breaking with one's past might be liberating and even empowering. The powerful leveling of Stephen's Dublin aligns him authorially with God himself. In this sense, his hallucinated fantasy authorship signifies a censoring action: Judgment Day is Stephen's Judging Day. On the other hand, he is not just the censor but also the censored. The symbolism of the judgment sequence and conclusion reduces the character to a liminal, naked state, ready for some initiation moment.

His creative censoring of his past–together with its values and representatives in the fantasies of judgment day—relies on religious and national discourses. He deploys the languages of church and country in order to judge and condemn these spheres. But his censoring is entwined in sexuality. These spheres are connected to his erotic economy, if we take into account his history as outlined in *Ulysses* and more extensively in *Portrait of the Artist as a Young Man*. In *Portrait*, Stephen's coming of age is explicitly connected to his initial eroticized participation in church life (e.g., his period of devotion to Mary), his sensual abandonment to sinful sensuality and explorations of his sexuality with prostitutes and in fantasy, his agonized confession, and his subsequent renunciation of Catholicism. His sexual awakening is informed by Catholicism's rituals and mariolatry on the one hand, and on the other hand by his pleasure in transgressing the Law. He relates sexuality to a forbidden space of freedom in which art and desire can be practiced.

In this way, the emerging artist's censorious leveling of the influential elements of his past (church, country, family) in a zone of prostitution in

"Circe" signals a possible creation of a creative space for the work of art and self-(re)creation. His fantasies involve pleasure in punishment of the self and martyrdom, as in Bloom's creative psychic rhetoric of masochism. The chandelier-smashing and loss of consciousness through Stephen's confrontation with Carr are only temporarily cathartic at best. As he revives from the knockout blow, he first frowns "Who? Black panther. Vampire," and then murmurs words from Yeats's song "Who Goes with Fergus" (15:4930–33 and 15:4941–43). This song reinstates the mourning of his mother (the song he sang to her on her deathbed; see earlier discussion). Interestingly, the poem offers a path for the young man (or maid) to join the legendary fallen king Fergus MacRoy, Yeats's poet-legislator, in the transitional space between woods (realm of dreams and poetry) and the political world: "Who will go drive with Fergus now, / And pierce the deep wood's woven shade, / And dance upon the level shore? / Young man, lift up your russet brow, / And lift your tender eyelids, maid, / And brood on hopes and fear no more. / And no more turn aside and brood / Upon love's bitter mystery; / For Fergus rules the brazen cars, / And rules the shadows of the wood, / And the white breast of the dim sea / And all dishevelled wandering stars."

Even though this song offers an incantation for resurrection from mourning, it beckons the listener to an indeterminate natural space ruled by a fallen king—a space of (internal) exile, a fairy Irish space of waiting? Upon Stephen's waking, the signs of his preoccupations return: the vampire (dead mother, a hypermasculine fantasy, the Thing) and black panther (a reference to the nightmare of the Englishman Haines, who usurps Buck Mulligan from whom Stephen is supposedly making a break that night). Hugh Kenner considers Stephen's supine moment as a sharing of death with his mother.[71] The resurgence of the fairytale pantomime element to

---

71. Kenner reads Stephen's first waking words as related to Bloom's hovering figure in the dark: Stephen sees Bloom as the black panther of Haines's nightmare or vampire: "he has opened his eyes and seen bending over him [. . .]. It has come. And in what he must imagine to be his moment of death he consoles himself not with Christian prayer but by murmuring Yeats's evocation of a redeemed time" (128–29). However, we should recall that the stage directions do not indicate that Stephen's eyes are open. If we take Kenner's idea without the scopic aspect, there is an acoustic apprehension. Stephen apprehends a voice calling him, for Bloom calls to him first as "Mr Dedalus!" then hesitantly twice "Stephen," "bring[ing] his mouth near the face of the prostrate form" (*U* 15:4927) May Dedalus calls Stephen by his Christian name. In this way, Bloom unwittingly positions himself in the place of the mother-vampire-panther, somewhat like Stephen's dream of his mother, remembered in "Telemachus," in which her ghost comes to him silently. Kenner notes how this scene "accords with [Stephen's] interest in *Richard Feverel*, early in which Richard wakes up 'to see a lady bending over him' (called a ghost, but really his absent mother, returned)" (38). Richard is only seven when this dreamlike event occurs in George Meredith's novel *The Ordeal of Richard Feverel: A History of a Father and Son* (1859), one of the nineteenth-century novels to deconstruct masculine heroism. While successful, the book caused some scandal in that Mudie's Circulating Library, followed by other lending libraries, would not carry it (see Sue Zlosnik's notes).

the drama is effectuated in Bloom's ethical intervention with the prone Stephen, along with Stephen's broken repetition of Oona's song to Cathleen in Yeats's play.

12. FRAMES AND CONCLUSIONS: INTERILLUMINATION OF CHARACTER ZONES

Most of "Circe" emphasizes the paths taken, and the fantasies and actions, of the two protagonists, Stephen and Bloom within the hybridized chronotope of Nighttown, the brothel and the street, two spaces of dialogic encounter. The street, marking the space of the beginning and end of the chapter, is the site for the circulation of the Law. "Circe" is framed and resolved by two pairs of recurring meetings with representatives of the Law. First, at the chapter's outset, the arrival at Nighttown, Stephen and Lynch pass Cissy and Privates Carr and Compton in the street, and at the chapter's conclusion, Stephen encounters this party again, this time more interactively.

In the second pair of meetings with the Law, two night watchmen meet Bloom at the outset of the episode (inspiring Bloom's first extended hallucination of a trial and judgment), and two night watchmen meet him again at the end. The circulating night watchmen humorously personify the dream censorship that functions between sleep and consciousness, between memory and the unconscious.[72] In Nighttown, they regulate the borders and inroads of the economy of sexual commerce, and in the narrative frame, they demarcate the character zones of Bloom and Stephen. Joyce is careful to portray Nighttown as regulated intermittently by the after-hours law of the Crown (off-duty redcoats Carr and Compton) and the local Dublin constabulary (the watchmen), and not as a zone of freedom.

The father and son are abandoned by an adulterous wife for the husband's friend, a poet (a situation that reflected aspects of Meredith's marriage: his wife left him for their friend, a painter). In *Richard Feverel,* the father and son are de-heroicized and somewhat feminized because of this situation. Benjamin Fisher notes how Meredith's novel deploys some gothic or sensationalist qualities (ghosts, fires, threats of madness, etc), but resists fulfilling these elements in order to pursue the psychological study of father and son, apprenticeship, and the oppressiveness of Feverel père's moral system.

Haines's nightmare of shooting the black panther is related to Stephen in at least three ways. It is a veiled threat, for Stephen wears only black, and Haines has brought his gun (in which case, Stephen is a threat to Haines). It aligns Stephen with Haines: both young men suffer from nightmares of threatening creatures; at the end of "Circe," Stephen seems to expect to share in Haines's nightmare. Third, the violence of the Englishman shooting the panther parallels Englishman Carr's punching Stephen, positioning violent action with colonial rule.

72. In Freud's *The Interpretation of Dreams,* he suggests the metaphor of night watchman for this censorship function.

The conclusion of "Circe" brings together Bloom and Stephen through converging narrative action (apocalypse, collision with the Law) and the aftermath, an enactment of a paternal-filial relation, that interilluminates these two characters, giving rise to the phantom vision of an idealized son. In dramatic action, converging are the encores of the paired encounters with representatives of the Law: Stephen with Carr, Bloom with the watchmen. Toward the end of "Circe," Bloom has finally partially achieved his intended, conscious quest: he has located and taken temporary responsibility for Stephen and his money in the face of danger. Stephen has resisted Bloom's coaxing to disengage from the encounter with Carr and now lies unconscious in the street.[73] Amid an uncertain crowd and approaching police officers, Bloom must protect this helpless, temporarily adopted son, deterring any further censorious condemnation from the actual local law. Bloom's steadfast levelheadedness, along with the lucky entrance of Corny Kelleher and his horse-drawn car, defuses the intervention of the night watchmen and the contretemps of the soldiers.

Bloom's resolute protection of Stephen, of acting out an ethical drive to achieve a good, produces a final magical reward—the fairy apparition of Rudy, silently reading and kissing the pages of a sacred book. Bloom might be prompted to think of Rudy because of Kelleher's brief intervention; at Paddy Dignam's funeral that morning ("Hades"), Kelleher has carried a funeral wreath along with an unnamed boy carrying another wreath. Also, as Bloom arrives at the cemetery, he glimpses a child's funeral taking place. At that moment, Bloom sees and thinks of these two events in direct succession:

Corny Kelleher stood by the opened hearse and took out the two wreaths. He handed one to the boy.
Where is that child's funeral disappeared to? (6:505–6)

This daytime sequence of thoughts and observations helps to prepare for the nighttime metonymic extensions made by the unconscious and coincidence of events. Kelleher even comes close to giving Bloom and Stephen a ride, an event which would have had ironic funereal parallels and further sealed the association of symbolic son and dead lost son. Bloom's ethical

---

73. Cf. Gabriel Conroy's deathlike trance in "The Dead" analyzed in relation to medieval (Dantean, Celtic, and Irish) vision literature in Peter Fjågesund's "Joyce's 'The Dead': Carnival, Eucharist and Medieval Visions." He explains that "vision literature [. . .] describe[s] a visit of the living to the world of the dead. The purpose is, generally, an edifying one: these medieval visions dramatize the consequences in the beyond of your life here on earth, both positively and negatively" (146).

care of Stephen is associated with responses to death and love of the son. The apparition of Rudy interilluminates the two distinct, but occasionally overlapping worlds and character zones of Bloom and Stephen.

All in all, "Circe" has the potential to make evident, purge, and sublimate worldly and often grotesque aspects of sexual appetite, guilt, desires, alienation. Censoring takes place in a hybridized theatrical-narrative form, maximizing the potential of hallucinations to dramatize discursively dominant mental preoccupations. The chapter's theatrical function invites the reader (imagining a production through reading) to suspend disbelief and to apprehend the action and discourse as mimetic representation of both actuality and psychic life. As we have seen, the Circean theater foregrounds sexuality in collision with artistic censoring, soliciting our further judgment of the characters and action. Part of our judgment involves a comparison of the characters' situation with what we know of their past. Another part derives from the dialogical possibilities of themes involving sons (Stephen's and Bloom's developments of the Christ theme; Bloom as son, grandson, and father; Stephen as son and thematic extensions of heroism and divine power, such as the Siegfried and apocalyptic intertexts). By their position in the family, sons are in the position of desiring, but not obtaining, of defying or fulfilling the Law of the Father and the Law of the Mother.

In the dénouement of "Circe," overlapping Bloom's and Stephen's personal preoccupations is the poignant and never fully realized encounter of a father and a son, in which the son is depicted ideally as a nascent artist-scholar-mystic in harmony with the unknown book, a sign of the Symbolic—language and the Law—but also love. In this encounter, the Father-as-Law is both personified as an indulgent, loving, separate spectator (Bloom) and symbolized as the book. This dreamlike father-and-son tableau also suggests a value of caring that prioritizes elements associated with the book—learning, reading, dialogue in discourse, creative expression and discovery. The dream of an alternative masculinity and the fantasy of death (manipulated by the child for the love of his parents), of an imagined harmony between father and son, are suggested by Rudy's appearance.

This boy's loving immersion in a book represents symbolically a desirable childhood (at that exquisite prepubescent moment of knowing and not knowing), one that Bloom himself could imagine that he never had. Death—and with it loss of the loved object—is creatively overcome by the fantasy's restoration of the pleasing son. Rudy's manner of reading is unusual: he reads silently, but the reading is enacted through kissing. This sensual reading, an eroticized oral and tactile experience, simultaneously connotes reverence and mystic symbolic action. Rudy's silence and the general lack of revelation of the mysterious book's contents represent an open or blank gap in which affirmative creativity and imagination can be conceived, within the context of a negation. This blank gap is comparable to Lacan's explication of negation in the unconscious, that is, that space of "no-saying (*non dit*)," "interdiction (*interdit*)," and the "intersaid (*entre dit*)" (Lacan, *Ethics*, 64–65).

The coincidence of the final Circean scene of Bloom (who represents variously son, father, lover) between two nonpresent symbolic sons, the phantasmatic Rudy and the physically present, unconscious Stephen, marks a climactic and potentially cathartic moment for the theater of judgment, a moment in which several discourses involving the son are interilluminated. Throughout the chapter, various symbolic laws and their representatives have been tried, transgressed, tested, razed, and rewritten. In this final moment, the Law of the fathers (language, religion, military and political codes, social laws, written or tacit) is subdued and brought into a momentary harmony by a poetics of filial love and identity. The dreamlike filial love, with its striving toward independence and knowledge, suspends the activity of judgment, the application and interpretation of the Law. The ecstatic suspension does not happen by a shattering act of violent force, but rather through an apprehension of sensual reverence, mystic contemplation, discovery and discursive creativity and sensuality. The filial encounter is a condensed metaphor that provides pleasurable relief and transcendence to the preceding series of weighty judgments and resulting punishments and destructions. Bloom's character zone mediates this fantasy (he is the son/father who apprehends the vision of Rudy), incorporating Stephen's zone (Stephen's scholarly and artistic aims and his complex filial relations and identifications; i.e., he is a product of values that he now rejects).

Bloom's production and apprehension of Rudy's image result from a negotiation to censor or cover up a more painful thing, the experience of losing a son. The literary operation here is comparable to how, in dream life, the psychic apparatus and particularly the superego can use a heavily didactic logic in producing expressions of wish fulfillments. The painful loss of an actual son (Rudy), a memory reawakened by associations with the death of the son (Kelleher's appearance and Stephen's temporary fall), is filled in by two final additions to Bloom's character zone: his actions of care toward Stephen and his hallucination of filial plenitude (Rudy kissing the book), both of which indicate an ethical imperative and resolution of the preceding action in Nighttown that heavily emphasize the subject's encounters and negotiations with sexual desire and judgment.

The quest for self promises an arrival at self-discovery. Many scholars see Stephen in *Ulysses* set on the edge of a new beginning. Through the novel, he has given several indications that he might leave the Martello Tower, Buck, family, Dublin, and Ireland. However, Joyce offers us a portrait of Stephen looking toward the *past* instead of the future. First, he is mired in the mourning for his mother. Second, the little literary creation Stephen develops (e.g., "A Pisgah Sight of Palestine, or The Parable of the Plums" [7:922–1058] and in *Portrait,* "Villanelle of the Temptress"; the poetic fragments, modeled on works by other poets) pales in comparison with the works of Shakespeare, Yeats, Meredith (by 1904, from Stephen's perspective, Grand Old Man),[74] the Gaelic poet of "My Grief on the Sea," the anonymous poet of the canting poem, and the many other authors who accompany his thoughts. In these other authors' works, women are often unfaithful, missing, or sacrificed (lost and mourned); their works speak to Stephen.

His repeated return to "Who Goes with Fergus" can remind us that this song is from Yeats's first play *The Countess Cathleen* (Joyce attended the first performance in 1899), which received harsh local criticism (reiterated by the reactionary university men of the *Freeman's Journal* in *Portrait*).[75] The play originally incorporated many mythical Celtic and non-Catholic elements, including the song, which Yeats later excised to make the play more appealing to censorious Dublin and Irish audiences. Thus, Stephen's insistent return to the "Fergus" song of *The Countess Cathleen* (about a

---

74. Zlosnik explains Meredith's status by late in his career: "By 1895 Meredith had achieved the status of Grand Old Man and was one of the foremost literary figures of the age. In 1892 he had been elected president of The Society of Authors, a position previously held by Tennyson. Visitors flocked to Box Hill to see the celebrity and, as the mood took him, Meredith held court and indulged his taste for witty conversation. In 1905 the Order of Merit was conferred upon him by King Edward VII and in 1909 the writer died [. . .]."

75. In chapter 5 of *Portrait,* on May 10, Stephen meditates on the play *The Countess Cathleen* he has just seen (May 8, 1899); his thoughts contrast sharply with the intolerant cries of his classmates:

Symbol of departure or of loneliness? The verses crooned in the ear of his memory composed slowly before his remembering eyes the scene of the hall on the night of the opening of the national theatre. He was alone at the side of the balcony, looking out of jaded eyes at the culture of Dublin. In the stalls and at the tawdry scenecloths and human dolls framed by the garish lamps of the stage. A burly policeman sweated behind him and seemed at every moment about to act. The catcalls and hisses and mocking cries ran in rude gusts round the hall from his scattered fellowstudents.
—A libel on Ireland!
—Made in Germany.
—Blasphemy!
—We never sold our faith!
—No Irish woman ever did it!
—We want no amateur atheists.
—We want no budding buddhists. (189–90)

woman's motherly sacrifice for the starving Irish people, selling her soul for food) provides a dually artistic censoring ending for his activities in Nighttown. The fragments of "Fergus" that he mumbles as he awakes from the redcoat's blow indicate his resurging preoccupation with his mother, and thus confirm his ties to the past and Ireland (and not to the illusory artistic future of "Non serviam!").

Second, he upholds Yeats as the towering literary figure of his time (how would Stephen near Yeats's achievements?). The reiteration of the poem also recalls Mulligan singing it to Stephen when they discuss his mother in "Telemachus." Mulligan uses the song to rally Stephen (as well as to signal Yeats's creativity in the face of Irish opposition), a variation of how Stephen has tried presumably to comfort his mother with the song, to no avail, as she cries at the lines, "And no more turn aside and brood / Upon love's bitter mystery" ("Silent with awe and pity I went to her bedside. She was crying in her wretched bed. For those words, Stephen: love's bitter mystery" [1:251–53]). If May Dedalus cries over "love's bitter mystery," Stephen seems to expect that the ghost of his mother might reveal what that mystery is.

Further, it would appear that Stephen's singing the song to his mother has been a form of educating her ("she wanted to hear my music" [1:251], raising her level of awareness beyond that of the average Irish Catholic who would react negatively to Yeats (as he tried to educate her with Ibsen in *Portrait*). In the play *The Countess Cathleen,* Cathleen's old foster-mother, Oona, uses the song not to educate, but to comfort and hearten Cathleen, who is indeed inspired by Fergus's calling horn and cars, but subsequently admits, "Oh, I am sadder than an old air, Oona; / My heart is longing for a deeper peace / Than Fergus found amid his brazen cars : Would that [. . .] / I could go down and dwell among the shee [fairies] / In their old ever-busy honeyed land"; Oona warns her of the "ill-luck" to say such things (Yeats, 308–9).

In Yeats's version of the legend, Cathleen's later decision to sell her soul to the merchant-demons in order to buy food for the people (and buy back their already sold souls) sets her in a "trilemma—heaven, hell, or fairyland" (Peter Smith, 143). While Yeats heightens the importance of fairyland in this play as the "realm of the imagination," Smith argues that "[i]magination is here seen as neutralizing the common man's dilemma, the dilemma of good and evil" (143) and that, ultimately, "[h]er escape is from fairyland: an escape into responsibility" (146). The Countess is not a commoner; her option of fairyland is not open to all; further, her soul is worth far more than the commoners' previously sold souls in the play.

In Stephen's repeated use of the song, he might recast his mother as the Countess Cathleen, who makes an Irish sacrifice. The ennobled, lovely, generous mother-as-Countess Cathleen can artistically screen (or censor) the horrible specter of the dying mother, the reactionary Catholic-cancerous ghoul, or the womb/tomb. But all these images in fact lead to a kind of pre-Oedipal maternal space where paternal law is dispersed or not yet present. Here we can consider the offer in the "Fergus" song. It is a call to go away with Fergus to a dispossessed indeterminate space of stars, woods, the "white breast" of the sea, and brood no more on worldly concerns such as "love's bitter mystery," a sign of vanitas. Is this not a call to return to a pre-Oedipal state in which Fergus and Cathleen will wander, not unhappily?

The song offers a place that transcends censoring and the Law of the Father, but it is a place that remains patently Irish, deep in legendary times. In Yeats's play, this song is a transitional interlude, not the play's conclusion: Cathleen chooses a Christian sacrifice. By contrast, Stephen and Mulligan focus primarily on Fergus's song, and not on the whole play.[76] It would seem that this Irish fairy path *not* chosen by Cathleen is the alluring one, framed, too, in enchanting song.

Complementing Yeats's song is Joyce's excerpt from the pantomime *Turko the Terrible* (1873),[77] provided in "Telemachus" in Stephen's reflec-

76. In *Musical Allusions,* Zack Bowen notes how for Stephen in Telemachus, there are associations between "love's bitter mystery," the Irish Sea ("bowl of bitter waters"), his mother's bowl of green bile" (67). He suggests: "the green thoughts of jealousy as the agenbite of inwit [take] on Oedipal overtones. The bitterness of her love and life with Simon is part of the bile as well as Stephen's rejection of his father-rival."

77. By the Irish author-editor Edwin Hamilton (1849–1919), adapted from William Brough's (1826–1870) London pantomime *Turko the Terrible; or, The Fairy Roses* (1868). Hamilton's version was an instant success at the Gaiety Theatre in Dublin during Christmas week 1873. It was repeatedly updated and revived in the closing decades of the century. Its frame was essentially a world of fairy-tale metamorphoses and transformations—as King Turko (Royce) and his court enjoyed the magic potential of the Fairy Rose.

Bloom thinks of *Turko* in "Calypso" ("Walk along a strand, strange land, come to a city gate, sentry there, old ranker too, old Tweedy's big moustaches, leaning on a long kind of a spear. Wander through awned streets. Turbaned faces going by. Dark caves of carpet shops, big man, Turko the terrible, seated crosslegged, smoking a coiled pipe" [4.86–90]); *Turko* is taken up again in "Circe" ("Major Tweedy, moustached like Turko the terrible" [15:4612]).

In November 1871, the Gaiety Theatre opened. Samuel Fitzpatrick notes,

[It] has been built, decorated, and managed in accordance with the most modern ideas. The old tradition of the stock company was abandoned from the commencement, and the management learned to rely entirely on the visits of London companies. Even in the time of O'Keeffe "theatrical summer birds of passage from London found very good pickings in Dublin," and this was now to be the invariable rule. In December 1873 was produced the inimitable pantomime of *Turko the Terrible,* by Mr. Edwin Hamilton, most versatile of Dublin literary men.

tion of his mother wanting to hear his song on her deathbed. This excerpt corresponds to Stephen's drive toward the self at the end of "Circe." In "Telemachus," Stephen recalls how his mother

> heard old Royce sing in the pantomime of *Turko the Terrible* and laughed with others when he sang:
> *I am the boy*
> *That can enjoy*
> *Invisibility.*
> Phantasmal mirth, folded away: muskperfumed.
> *And no more turn aside and brood.* (1:257–63)

The pantomime song celebrates the king's fairy ability to become invisible, thanks to the Fairy Rose (Gifford, 18–19). A boyish fantasy to be invisible connotes freedom. But invisibility in the case of May Goulding Dedalus has come to mean her death (invisible and absent). For Bowen, Stephen's memory combines his mother's "faded sensuality" with "his own childish fantasies" (67). Bowen goes on to assert that "once [Stephen] could identify with the boy who enjoyed invisibility, but now the modality of the visible as well as his guilt is inescapable, as Stephen's thoughts turn to his present dreams in which her coming to him, still with sensual overtones, is filled with horror and death."

Dovetailed with Stephen's Circean conclusion is Bloom's intervention with the young man and the simultaneous fairy vision of Rudy. Stephen's mourning of his mother is countered by Bloom's for Rudy. While Rudy has been contemplated several times through the novel, in this special instance in "Circe," Rudy is projected as a ghostlike image from the present, a dream fragment of how he would be in 1904, symbolically, if he had lived. This generative image situates Rudy in a hybridized realm of the paternal (Oxford; Hebraic learning; scholarly and devout ways), and interilluminates the tragic-pathetic filial position of Stephen (replacing Stephen's conflict of rebellion and desire for return to a thetic zone of creativity).

Stephen's mourning of his mother and Bloom's of his father and son are transcended temporarily through the dialogic sign that is Rudy. Men's mourning, along with masochistic fantasy, can be seen here as a variant of the quest for the self. In Henry Staten's study of a literary tradition of "thanatoerotophobic metaphysics [. . .] defined [largely] by male authors," he maintains that "Lacan, too [along with Nietzsche], presents the libidinal object as a disruption of the self's most authentic self-propiation, its drive to be only and absolutely itself" (16).

After the series of harsh and punishing maternal and paternal judgments meted out in "Circe," this final filial sign functions as a point of transcendent judgment in imaginary time, a sign that filters the masculine subject's desire to be his own true subject. The sign of Rudy transcends everyday dialogue, resorting instead to the pantomimetic field artistically embedded within the narrative. Along with Fergus's song, the sign of Rudy is the last segment of the hermeneutic code woven into the quest narrative of "Circe": identity is bound to mourning, judgment, and return to an impossible time and space of creative potential in sexual innocence or liminal edge of initiation.

3

Lolita

AMERICAN MIMETIC FANTASY, ETHICAL READING, AND CENSORING NARRATIVE

The confessions of Humbert Humbert, a "white widowed male," demonstrate the discursive lengths to which a subject could go to maintain his fantasy: the girl Dolores Haze and Humbert's fantasized nymphet "Lolita" inhabit the same body, but represent two distinct "others." Dolores performs a complex mimetic function, providing the sense of an artistic copy and a natural copy. The girl resembles earlier girl-child lovers, child-brides, femmes fatales, and fairies. In a sense, she looks like one of a series of feminine figures who enable a man's romantic and erotic discovery of his sexual life, and by inference, of his creative powers. The girl's similarity or commensurability to other children establishes that she is a tragic figure, subjected to a man's cruelty and indifference. The character-narrator's account of his relationship with this young person reveals his prolonged abuse of her as a sex slave. The narration presents this evidence along with his explications of his fantasies and desires. This aestheticization of his actions and thoughts provides a kind of screen censoring that involves the reader.

How to write of unspeakable desire? Humbert superimposes his nymphet "Lolita" over a still-discernable girl Dolores Haze. By maintaining the fantasy of the nymphet and his passionate relation with that fantasy, and by appealing to some readers' potential aesthetic and erotic sensibility,

Humbert largely screens or censors the reality of his actions and his situation. The irony of this extensive screening performance suggests that his actions are foul and that the reader must judge Humbert by transcending the confines of the box of solipsistic mirrors that constitute much of the narrative *Lolita*.[1]

In addition to the complex play of mimetic images and references, Humbert inscribes, from the beginning, a readership of judgment. In this way, the novel creates a disparate clash between ethical engagement with human subjects on the one hand and an aesthetic defense on the other. The conflation of two distinct arguments creates one of the most intriguing and ongoing problems in the criticism of this novel. Readers are placed in a highly precarious situation, bullied into taking sides, open to flattering appeals to their intellect or sophistication, curiously seeking erudite cultural and historical references.[2] While readers struggle with the task of interpretation, the dominating voice of Humbert organizes virtually the

---

1. Peter Levine's discussion also proposes this critical approach, for we are stuck with Humbert unless we "transcend his perspective" (39). Bordo advocates reading beyond Humbert's tricks. Rothstein reads allegory in reverse: "[*Lolita*] urges moral understanding upon us. In saying this later, I'm tying moral truth to truth in reading, both within Nabokov's radical nominalism. Only readers who perceive objects in their otherness may seize what Nabokov calls 'the secret points, the subliminal co-ordinates by means of which the book is plotted.' When they do so, a cognitive virtue leads to an aesthetic one. That is, normative truth in reading affords 'aesthetic bliss,' Nabokov says, 'where art (curiosity, tenderness, kindness, ecstasy) is the norm.' By this thesis, Nabokov naturalizes the normative with regard to art if he succeeds in naturalizing the normative with regard to truth in reading. Given his definition of 'art,' the cognitive and aesthetic virtues involve the moral" (43).

Herbold and Moore notice some of the censorship impulses in the novel. Moore is particularly adroit at showing how the novel, ironically through pompous Humbert, shows up masculinist strategies. For example, Moore points out that Humbert "exaggerate[s] the likely size of his penis by close to 100 percent: 'I was to her not a boyfriend, not a glamour man, not a pal, not even a person at all, but just two eyes and a foot of engorged brawn—.' The average length in its erect state of the white European male member is six and a half inches. This verbal enlargement of his small piece of flesh reduces to absurdity the legend of the phallus, depending as it does on a willing suspension of disbelief, a collusion to deny the reality that no penis can live up to its fabulous mythical importance. So Nabokov diminishes the singularity and power for which the phallus is generally a metaphor in male-centered literature in the same graceful and complex irony that cuts Humbert down to size" ("Seeing through Humbert," 103).

Scholars such as Fiedler, Trilling, and Greene may have been seduced by Humbert's masculinist strategies. In identifying Humbert's traps for readers, Ohi analyzes Humbert's sentimentalism, narcissism, and false transcendence (*Innocence*, 155–90 and 203–6).

2. Many scholars, particularly in the past fifteen years, have examined the problems of readers' reception of this work, although some fall into a trap of reading Humbert as Nabokov (e.g., Kauffman; Patnoe). Troubling, too, is some scholars' uncritical use of the name "Lolita" to refer generally to the girl Dolores Haze, indicating that they do not resist Humbert's characterizations of her as nymphet. Some of the best observations regarding readers' reception can be found in Bordo; Herbold ("'[I Have Camouflaged Everything, My Love]': *Lolita* and the Woman Reader"; "Reflections on Modernism"); Phelan ("Double Focalization . . ."); Pifer ("Nabokov's Novel Offspring").

whole narration, and in his confessions, reveals himself as a monster (or vampire, ape, spider; e.g., beneath his "boyish smile" lurks "a cesspool of rotting monsters" [44]; "my ape paw" [258]).

As a character-narrator, his character zone encompasses much of the novel (with the exception of John Ray, Jr.'s foreword). Humbert's character zone splits into discursive strands connected to his victims (Dolores Haze, Charlotte Haze, Clare Quilty); to diverse interlocutors (from educators like Miss Pratt to fellow pedophiles like Gaston Godin); to the heteroglossia of cultural, political, and social America and Europe; and to literary genres such as the fairy tale, the detective novel, and erotic fiction or pornography. The zone is dialogic, in that Humbert imbricates competing discourses with his own, many of which "show up" his own solipsism. In keeping with Bakhtin's theory of the novel, the confession of the "hero" opens up the possibility of "testing" his discourse (350 and 387–99). Moreover, the narrator creates a kind of personal dialogism. While Humbert confesses his aberrant state so plainly and repeatedly that some readers might disavow such a confession as ridiculous exaggeration, he is in fact revealing a central truth (and denouncing himself). Further, the gothic implications of his monster persona lead an interpretation of the work toward a self partially censored—Humbert as a postmodern Dr. Jekyll and Mr. Hyde—and censored or forbidden other—Dolores as a postmodern Peter Pan, the nymphet who should never grow up.[3]

In my discussion, the mimesis at stake is an order of difference, not similarity. In this usage, I concur with Arne Melberg, who explains that, for mimesis, "this ontological turn [in modernism] in favour of difference could be summarized in J. Hillis Miller's excellent formula as 'two forms of repetition.' One would be heading for similarity, the other for difference" (5–6). While Nabokov's novel sets before us a series of critical mimetic plays of difference, we can note how Humbert, the homodiegetic narrator, does not always value difference and is at times dazzled by apparent similarity. Melberg takes as examples Walter Benjamin's and Gérard Genette's discussions of the mimetic function of difference in Proust's work. Proust's analogies, affinities, comparisons, and contiguities make a break with "all traditional mimesis" and promote "his revolutionary use of temporality" (7). By contrast, we might see Humbert's narration of mimesis as a kind of crisis and abuse; his tyrannical approach to temporality—his exaltation of the erotic

---

3. Nabokov's lectures at Cornell University include his exploration of Robert Louis Stevenson's classic *Dr. Jekyll and Mr. Hyde* (1886) (*Lectures on Literature*); this lecture is excerpted to serve as the introduction of a Signet edition of the Stevenson novel ("The Strange Case . . ."). Later in this chapter, I will discuss how themes of childhood and censored adult subjectivity of the Stevenson novel and J. M. Barrie's *Peter Pan* coincide with similar threads in *Lolita*.

child and desire to lock her into that age forever—results in destruction of the other (Dolores). Nabokov, with *Lolita*, presents us with this highly flawed character-narrator in order to submit him to judgment, a judgment that has been prepared in the narrative ethically and aesthetically.

1. CRITICAL SYNOPSIS

Humbert Humbert writes a confession-memoir in prison over the course of some fifty-six days, ultimately dying before going to trial for murdering a playwright, Clare Quilty. His confession of the murder is only part of his story: its core is his relationship with a preteen girl Dolores Haze. Humbert has grown up in the south of France with a well-off family. His childhood has been blighted by the death of his mother, and later shaken, in 1923, by a romantic and sexual summer relationship with fellow child Annabel, who some months later dies. As he becomes an adult, he recognizes that he has a predilection for prepubescent girls. At first interested in psychiatry, he becomes an English literature professor and tries to find outlets for his desire by having, for example, sex with a teenage prostitute Monique. He then marries Valeria, but this relation lasts only until his wife has an affair with a White Russian and leaves him. Around 1939 or 1940, Humbert emigrates to America where he alternately works in his uncle's perfume company and undergoes psychiatric treatment and retreats, while also maintaining his scholarship.

When he decides, in May 1947, to rent a room in Ramsdale, New England, from a widow, Charlotte Haze, he becomes decisively obsessed with her twelve-year-old daughter Dolores (or "Lolita" as he prefers). Charlotte takes her daughter to summer camp, and confesses in a letter her love for her lodger. He decides to propose marriage in order to remain close to Dolores, whom he claims to be a "nymphet." While married, still that same summer, he contemplates murdering Charlotte, but cannot bring himself to commit the act. Not long after, she discovers by reading her husband's diary that he has been lusting for the child and has partly seduced her. As Charlotte tries to disengage herself from Humbert, she is accidentally hit by a car and killed. Humbert manages to retrieve Dolores from camp as her stepfather, and thence commences an unequal relationship and cohabitation of stepfather and stepdaughter, in which the girl is coerced into daily, frequent sex with her keeper. During this time, they take two wide-ranging road trips, staying in motels. In between the two trips, they stay in a college town, Beardsley, where Humbert can teach and Dolores can resume studies. At school, she rehearses a play written by Quilty, whom she has secretly been interested in for some time. She then convinces Humbert to take the second road trip. Quilty trails the couple, and eventually takes Dolores away from Humbert in 1949. This relationship does not last long, Dolores rejecting the life of debauchery on Quilty's ranch and, after working diners, finding a young war veteran to marry. Meanwhile, Humbert is crushed by being duped and attempts to search in vain for "his love" and rests in a Québec sanatorium. He settles for a temporary two-year relationship with a hapless Rita, until, late in September 1952, he receives a letter from Dolores ("Dolly," "Mrs. Richard Schiller"), requesting money. He meets with her, finding the couple living in relative poverty. He begs her to join him again, but she refuses. He then gives her money and leaves to confront and kill Quilty, having learned from Dolores how she escaped. When Humbert meets Quilty, the playwright refuses to admit any wrongdoing, pointing out that he was saving the girl from a monster. The two fight, with Humbert finally shooting him dead. The police capture Humbert, and he ends his confession by revealing some apparent feelings of remorse, eerily qualified by his insistent possessiveness of her, "my Lolita."

The novel features a fictional foreword (dated August 5, 1955) by one John Ray, Jr., Ph.D., who explains Humbert's raving quality; his dying wish is that his confession be made known only once Mrs. Richard Schiller has died. Ray suggests that the work "Lolita" can serve as a case study, and that, save for a little editing, he is presenting "this remarkable memoir" "intact" (3). Humbert has, in his will, allowed his lawyer, Clarence Choate Clark, Esq., to "use his discretion" in publishing "Lolita"; the lawyer has suggested during the composition certain additions, such as a clear account of the itinerary of the first trip. The lawyer has possibly been interested in recent psychiatric work published on "morbid states and perversions." Clark's and Ray's interest in the manuscript complicates its reception. Further, we learn from this editor that Dolores has died in childbirth (December 25, 1952) and Humbert has succumbed to heart failure while awaiting trial (November 16, 1952). Humbert's narrative takes up several narrative genres, from the confession, diary, and erotic story to the case study, legal document, and detective novel, and multiple layers and strands of parody and forms of irony, from hyperbole to extreme litotes. While he mainly writes a sequential narrative, it includes several overt and covert prolepses that signal a doomed ending. Despite the overall dark subject matter—the extended subjection of a girl to the sexual appetite of an egocentric man—the novel is shot through with humorous, satirical perceptions of human life, especially human carelessness, vanity, prejudices, and consumerism, and, as will be argued, a structure designed to be explored ethically by judgment.

2. JUDGMENT, NARRATORS, AND FOCALIZATION

Humbert presents a highly aesthetic picture of his passion which derives much of its edge from the inherent irony he knows makes that passion possible: society's collective prohibition of adults having sexual relations with children, and further, more specifically, the taboo of incest or sexual abuse involving parents and (underage) children. Humbert's alternating awareness and disavowal of his transgression are reflected in his testimony for a judge and jury. For example, he points to legal definitions of children, historical precedents of marriage of young people, including some lofty inferences (the Dante–Beatrice couple perhaps compares most parodically with the Humbert–Dolores pair). His narrative account is clearly submitted for judgment, but his defensive measures and humorous ploys complicate our interpretation of his actions and intentions. Herbold points out the various narratees and addressees the reader is supposed to model: gentlemen, "Gentlewomen of the jury," "Jurors!" "Human beings," a balding middle-aged man, "*Bruder!*" "Lolita," "my love," and so on.[4] The histrionic naming of multiple types of narratees (who would have conflicting interests in reading the story) prompts each actual reader to consider who he or she is (and the diversity of other readers, past and present), and whether the reader approximates any of the plural or singular narratees invoked by Humbert. Coyly, judgment reflects back on ourselves: who are we as readers, chuckling or fuming at Humbert?

James Phelan has noticed that a narrative challenge of *Lolita* is the reader's mastery of the dual narrator—Humbert as character and as teller of his tale, open to reflection and editorializing in the course of composition. Phelan explains:

> The more clear-sighted Humbert the narrator becomes about his past self, the more clearly does his violence against Dolores come through: he was "a pentapod monster," who offered a twelve-year-old girl who suddenly lost her mother only "a parody of incest" as he repeatedly coerced her into "hard and nauseous" acts of sexual intercourse. By the end of Humbert's narrative, he and Nabokov both want us to see that Dolores's life with him was a horror and that

---

4. In "'(I Have Camouflaged Everything My Love),'" Herbold sustains a compelling argument that the gender of readers has a critical and reflective, ethical value: "Paradoxically, *Lolita*'s manipulativeness, sexiness, and difficulty are as complimentary to women as they are insulting. [. . .] Nabokov challenges women not to remain victims and acknowledges his dependence on their considerable power, which is (like his own) greater for being concealed. Ironically, moreover, it is this double relation toward women that makes *Lolita* a complex and paradoxical 'masterpiece' of modernism—the same modernism that seems to establish its preeminence by exploiting and excluding women" (75).

Humbert was the agent of that horror. At the same time, the story of Humbert's gradual move toward greater clear-sightedness is a move to greater reliability along the axis of evaluation, and it indicates a greater respect for his audience. ("Double Focalization," 129)

This lucid separation of character and narrator and the idea of ethical progress or change in the narrator make a good case, and might align with an ethical reader's desire for the reformation of the criminal as well as with a suggested arc in Humbert's character development. However, in my view, Humbert's transformation remains moot, and the task of condemnation is left squarely to the reader. Nabokov's novel revisits a familiar motif of the criminal or sinner who, close to death or judgment, enacts his own confession and self-discovery: the motif is only suggested but not reperformed. Humbert does confess, but his confession and regret are overly belated and conditional on his maintaining ownership of his fantasy Lolita as his "love" and his "work of art" that is the homodiegetic narrative. In this way, progress or positive change does not gain purchase. This lack of a clear sense of redemption actually strengthens the ethical reading because the reader's task of evaluation is more complex and less obvious.

In addition to the dual focalization of Humbert the character and Humbert the narrator, readers need to transcend the narrator's levels of awareness altogether, and join the author in surveying the whole work from above, as well as join the character Dolores in terms of imagining the place of the other. Despite the deceptive invitation of immediacy and access to "truth" of the first-person narrator (Humbert), especially one who proves from the first pages to be wildly unreliable in his self-inflation and subversive motives, *Lolita* creates a strongly ironic experience of interpretation, forcing one to examine mirrored resemblances, to tear down deception, and particularly to study the access to pleasure through violence and aesthetics.

The constructions of fantasy intermingled with more straightforward narrative reportage refer to the Thing which is striven toward but cannot be known.[5]

3. HUMBERT'S CENSORED DOLORES

Humbert's narrative about how he comes to be, by force and cunning, the sexual partner of a twelve-year-old girl for some two years is built upon

---

5. For more discussion of Nabokov's relationship of the "Thing," see Alexandrov's exploration of his transcendent concerns in *Nabokov's Otherworld*.

conflicting desires: (1) to confess his actions and be judged by others, and (2) to recreate his fantasy love object, "Lolita," in order to savor his fantasy through the possibilities of language and establish his narrative as a work of art to live for eternity. The two conflicting impulses are imperfectly censored by him in various ways. He withholds certain facts, evidence, observations, and thoughts. This strategy causes the reader to delay in making judgments and to develop a degree of sympathy or tolerance for the narrator. At other times, Humbert presents conflicting evidence or observations which raise problems about judgment.

The girl herself provides the most favored area on which Humbert can map out his complicated fantasy: she is a screen on which "Lolita" appears. Apart from this splitting and eclipsing of the other, Humbert perceives and describes a conflicting range of qualities apparently possessed by his love object. Her qualities are generally beauty (involving womanliness, literariness, love, sophistication, power, memory, timelessness) and childishness (involving innocence, fantasy, animality, vulgarity, fragility or helplessness, androgyny, memory, time). This range of qualities is important as it reflects Humbert's conflicting wishes and intentions. The oscillating conflict signals self-censoring, attempts to justify, parry, bluff, on the one hand, and to reveal, confess, relish, on the other.

An important premise for his infatuation with "Lolita" is that she constitute a repetition/replica of his dead childhood love Annabel. In both the novel's introductory page (9) and in Humbert's first encounter with the girl Dolores (39), he emphasizes the fact that he perceives her as mimetic of Annabel, his "initial girl-child," "my Riviera love": "It was the same child—the same frail, honey-hued shoulders, the same silky supple bare back, the same chestnut head of hair" (39). Here and elsewhere, Humbert subverts the love of a child as love of a woman by deploying a *blason du corps feminin*—a poetic praise of the loved lady's physical qualities. The mimetic Dolores/Lolita appears to be a copy from nature. However, given Humbert's unreliable powers of apprehension, the mimesis is indebted to his desire for there to be a similarity.

The dolorean mimesis is one of difference, not of similarity. Similar appearances deceive rather than confirm prior knowledge and presuppositions. The narrator eventually discovers her difference and prioritizes it ("my Lolita"), but with a dual claim of marking the girl's originality and his love's authenticity, a conflation of interests. Appel notes how H.H. "sees himself in a line descending from the great Roman love poets [Propertius; Tibullus; Horace], and he frequently imitates their locutions" (e.g., "*this* Lolita, *my* Lolita") (Appel, *The Annotated Lolita*, 358, n 45/1). "Lolita" is further marked as original and a "true love" on many pages throughout the narrative,[6] with variations including "My unique Lolita" (183), "my American sweet immortal dead love" (280), "my lone light Lolita" (285), and "my conventional Lolita" (287).

This issue of a mimetic girl is central to Humbert's delusion and criminality. The nymphet mimics the natural, innocent child in appearance and actions; only a specialist like Humbert can discern the demon child among the normal ones. The argument, however, is not valid, in that a shrewd observer should be able to discern difference between two types of children, innocent ones and demon seducers. Further, if the difference is between innocence and knowledge, children are clearly more innocent than knowing, although the terms can become confused if we generally accept that children live in a state of becoming, rather than being tiny adults or naïve infants. Humbert's and other pedophiles' excuse is that the demon nymphets are different from other children; nymphets have the power to seduce, yet such a "little deadly demon [. . .] stands unrecognized by them [the wholesome children] and unconscious herself of her fantastic power" (17).

The deconstruction of this claim reveals that the situation is the reverse: the adult observer is the potential demon, the potential seducer. The ploy of offering nymphets as mimetic of other children appeals to a reader who desires to know or understand. Aristotle links mimesis to a basic desire to know, and sees both human learning and pleasure as connected to mimesis. Mimesis, however, can also provide the opportunity for finer discerning of difference. The witchcraft of the mimetic Dolores finds its source in the adult observer, as Humbert acknowledges his authorship of "Lolita," "[. . .] that little girl with her seaside limbs and ardent tongue haunted me ever since—until at last, twenty-four years later, I broke her spell by incarnating her in another" (15) (Humbert performs the action). In this passage, and others, Annabel is strongly represented as a modernist sexual being;[7] her haunting of Humbert involves the intense memory of an interrupted tryst in which the two children kiss and masturbate each other (14–15).

Later in the story, the comparative force of the overlaid images weakens

---

6. See examples of "my Lolita" on 32, 44, 53, 66, 79, 80, 92, 111, 115, 128, 134, 154, 166, 167, 176, 190, 198, 199, 207, 231, 241, 247, 267, 277, 278, 284, 293, 309, 311. "My Lolita" is often used as a form of direct address, in contrast to some variations, such as "my dear love's name" (32). The insistent possessiveness or ownership of "Lolita" disavows H.H.'s supposed "love" and repentance. Her singularity or difference (from Annabel, from any other person) is predicated on H.H.'s domination. We do not come across "my Dolores."

7. Annabel seems to derive intertextually as much from James Joyce as from Edgar Allan Poe. The emphasis on "limbs," "tongue," "seaside," and "ardent" recalls Stephen Dedalus's preoccupation with the "ardent ways" of the seductive woman in his villanelle composition in *A Portrait of the Artist as a Young Man* and *Ulysses*'s motif of the enchanting "seaside girls."

as Humbert is obliged to acknowledge differences between Dolores and Annabel.[8] But the narrative's early and repeated emphasis on the commensurability of the two images signals Humbert's irrational fantasy: he himself is no longer the child that he was with Annabel; twenty-four years separate him from that childhood relationship. He partially censors his transgressive desire for "Lolita" by exalting in the apparent sameness of the girls and in the effective force of fantasy that returns him to the boy or "faunlet" he once was, though disguised as an adult (and even as a signifying object that might appeal to Dolores: "a great big handsome hunk of movieland manhood" [39]).

But along with his own censoring defenses, which allow him to revel in his fantasy, he acknowledges that he is an adult with obscene aims. We can note, for example, the explicit but sly contrast of his two competing perceptions in the following passage: "A polka-dotted black kerchief tied around her chest hid *from my aging ape eyes, but not from the gaze of young memory,* the juvenile breasts I had fondled one immortal day" (39; my emphasis). The false synthesis, "one immortal day," would imply an ageless synchrony between girls Annabel and Dolores and a dominance of selfish blissful memory over the specific and important differences of two separate events in distinct contexts. Proustian memory in Humbert's narrative becomes an exercise in self-serving solipsism as opposed to a potential function for self-discovery and discovery of the deceptive appearances of others in childhood.[9]

Early warnings to the reader can be glimpsed in Humbert's various indications that he is aware of his transgressive and bad intentions: "my aging

---

8. For example, in Part One during the extended Enchanted Hunters episode, Humbert editorializes his confession, marking his awareness of difference: "But somewhere behind the raging bliss, bewildered shadows conferred—and not to have heeded them, this is what I regret! Human beings, attend! I should have understood that Lolita had already proved to be something quite different from innocent Annabel, and that the nymphean evil breathing through every pore of the fey child that I had prepared for my delectation, would make the delectation lethal. I should have known (by the signs made to me by something in Lolita—the real child Lolita or some haggard angel behind her back) that nothing but pain and horror would result from the expected rapture. Oh, winged gentlemen of the jury!" (124–25).

9. In contrast to Proust's narrator's voluntary and involuntary memory, Humbert the narrator identifies "two kinds of visual memory: one when you skillfully recreate an image in the laboratory of your mind, with your eyes open (and then I see Annabel in such general terms as: 'honey-colored skin,' 'thin arms,' 'brown bobbed hair,' 'long lashes,' 'big bright mouth'); and the other when you instantly evoke, with shut eyes, on the dark innerside of your eyelids, the objective, absolutely optical replica of a beloved face, a little ghost in natural colors (and this is how I see Lolita)" (11). This separation of the two girls is disingenuous, in that "Lolita" is often described in reference to her long lashes, honey-hued skin, and thin arms (i.e., the *blason*), as well as to her erotic allure. Further, how can her face be beloved to Humbert if he has abused her and remained indifferent to her suffering?

ape eyes"; "my gaze slithered over the kneeling child"; "the vacuum of my soul" (39); "like some predator that prefers a moving prey to a motionless one" (42); "my hot hairy fist" (123). By the end of Part I, culminating in the episode of the Enchanted Hunters and its immediate aftermath, the narrator has repeatedly and ostentatiously pointed out what should be condemned in him. It is not entirely clear how retroactive this self-awareness is (i.e., Humbert's view of himself from the cell; cf. Phelan). Humbert already seems to know how corrupt he is from the outset and to take pleasure in naming his grotesque qualities and acts. He particularly favors his comparison with an ape, which as a homonym supplies the additional signification of his tendency to pretend, copy, and perceive doubles.

Aside from rejoicing in the enchanting effect of reencountering a lost love object, Humbert delights in describing "Lolita" as an exquisite and vulgar creature. This seemingly incongruous combination is significant in two respects. First, masochistic pleasure around the cherished but tarnished fetish is a prominent feature in Humbert's perversion. Second, the paradoxical view of the girl simultaneously disavows and confirms Humbert's erotic drive and thus maintains his desire.

This antithetical characterization of the beloved object becomes sharpened in Humbert's accounts of, or allusions to, the contradictions in their sexual relation. According to him, she is a whore and yet a child; she does want sex (but not always with him, but rather with some jealously perceived other, such as Charlie Holmes) and she despises it (Humbert hears her cry every night of her confined life with him).[10] Humbert eventually pays her for sexual favors and then must constantly fear her saving up the money to escape from him. What lover would run away from paradise? Humbert creates an unwilling prostitute and then must work overtime to disavow that role. His defenses and denegation are elaborately recorded in his mode and aim of writing.

There is a metonymic relation to be found between Humbert's vulgar-exquisite object that is the nymphet "Lolita" and his literary efforts, *Lolita*.

---

10. Scholars as different as Pifer and Fiedler read Dolores as a willing, and at times even empowered (!), agent in the sexual exchanges between Humbert and her. Such readings do not recognize the completely unequal power in the relationship. A preadolescent girl (or boy), despite her awareness of her sexuality, can exercise little judgment, resistance, or power; in fact, her attempts to appear more adult through her sexuality can play directly into an abusive adult's manipulative plans. Humbert uses the child's susceptibility by luring her to consume tranquilizers through feigning that they are for him; he manipulates her into copying him or showing him the right way to kiss. While the screen image of the fantasy nymphet "Lolita" may give the impression of a seductress's agency, this illusion derives its power from Humbert's allusions to Eve, sirens, femme fatales from Carmen to la Belle Dame sans Merci—all who would be the downfall of a pitiful, naïve man or poet.

He has told us that he loathes vulgarity, but he relishes opportunities to make witty, trenchant remarks about the vulgar aspects of American culture. In his exposé of Americana he never really reproduces any actual coarse language, but he adores Lolita's "vulgar vocabulary—'revolting,' 'super,' 'luscious,' 'goon,' 'drip'" (65). By contrast, anything that could be seen as explicitly repugnant to a prudish reader's morals is effectively kept "off the scene."[11]

Conventional pornographic language finds no place in *Lolita*. That said, occasional narrative sequencing and lyricism (or purple prose) toy with the pornographic potential (e.g., Hubert's seduction of Dolores on the davenport has passages that read erotically, building to a crescendo). Frequently, references to body parts are curiously separated, detached from anticipated referents, described in poetic or metaphorically clinical terms, made strange, alienated, or fantastic. Body parts or inanimate objects often act as a grammatical subject ("The blond leg was pulled in . . ." [66]; "A polka-dotted black kerchief [. . .] hid from my view [. . .]" [39]). This mode of indirection conceals Humbert as the active voyeur. Nabokov contrasts *Lolita* to the subgenre of pornography:

> [. . .] in pornographic novels, action has to be limited to the copulation of clichés. Style, structure, imagery should never distract the reader from his tepid lust. The novel must consist of an alternation of sexual scenes. The passages in between must be reduced to sutures of sense, logical bridges of the simplest design, brief expositions and explanations, which the reader will probably skip but must know they exist in order not to feel cheated (a mentality stemming from the routine of "true" fairy tales in childhood). Moreover the sexual scenes in the book must follow a crescendo line, with new variations, new combinations, new sexes, and a steady increase in the number of participants (in a Sade play they call the gardener in) [. . .]. ("On a Book . . . ," 313)

Nabokov's afterword aims to orient the reader in a somewhat convoluted way toward an aesthetic appreciation of the novel and away from censure (i.e., an overly moralistic or prudish response). Yet, on top of the implication of publishers' censorship of the shocking Part One of the novel, Nabokov implies that the first four American publishers "W, X, Y, Z" also rejected it because the latter half of the novel lacked the erotic "techniques" of the first (a circular argument that cancels itself out). At first blush, the long passage cited above would explain why *Lolita* is not pornography (that is, because it does not dedicate itself to the mechanical code he describes).

---

11. For example, acts of oral sex are suggested via indirection or metaphor: the "nauseous" acts at the Enchanted Hunters or "[h]er brown rose tasted of blood" (240).

Prior to this passage, Nabokov mentions that, by contrast, in ancient literature as well as European literature, especially in French eighteenth-century works, "lewdness was not inconsistent with flashes of comedy, or vigorous satire." How should we understand, then, the mention of de Sade, apparently heaped in with pornographic novels? While Nabokov has not written a "Sade play,"[12] he has incorporated a degree of Sadean sensibility in his character Humbert, whose libertinism extends to repeated cruel abuse, debauchery, and abduction of a defenseless girl. The fourteen-year-old girl who runs away from Humbert to Quilty partially suggests the transformation of Eugénie of *La philosophie dans le boudoir* (but certainly not a complete transformation, for Dolores rejects Quilty's request that she "[blow]" ["*souffler*"] his boys[13]).

The pornographic genre thus operates in *Lolita* on dialogic and intertextual levels, in terms of narrative techniques and ironic intertextual character comparisons, but with subversive consequences. Through Nabokov's ironic treatment, Dolores is not a desiring pornographic fantasy lover, and her Sadean schooling with Humbert and Quilty does not empower her. Humbert and Quilty impose pornographic codes on her ("Lolita"), while largely screening or censoring out of the frame the girl Dolores.

In his afterword, Nabokov touches on generic conventions of three literary forms he borrows from to construct *Lolita:* the detective novel, the pornographic novel, and the fairy tale. These particular genres share motifs of sexual curiosity and discovery, fear, horror, transgression, and transformation. The erotic elements of the detective novel of the 1930s and 1940s (Hammett, Chandler, film noir) include the centrality of the male detective, duped by the femme fatale and potentially redeemed if he overcomes the archenemy or villain. The detective establishes or allows himself to enter into a kind of masochistic relation with the woman and criminals and makes dangerously tenuous his attachment to the Law. In

---

12. Sade's works are hybrids; for example, *La philosophie dans le boudoir* is presented as a play, but generally read as a novel, not performed on the stage. Dolores's recounting of the scene at Quilty's ranch reminds Humbert that "Sade's Justine was twelve at the start" (276). In *Justine,* the moral heroine, targeted for her virtue, is abducted and subjected to a lengthy series of abuses. Ironically, her suffering is comparable to Dolores's woes.

13. Contrary to Nabokov's claim, Part Two of *Lolita* continues to employ some of the "pornographic" techniques Nabokov identifies in his afterword (if we take away the term *pornography*, Nabokov might be cataloguing standard features of narration). For example, "new variations" and "new sexes" can be seen in the incorporation of Beardsley School; the drama *The Enchanted Hunters* and its supporting events; Gaston Godin and his taste for boys; the second road trip; the post-Lolita relation with Rita; the meeting with Dolores as Mrs. Richard Schiller; the revelation of Quilty's involvement; and the Pavor Manor scene, in which Humbert and his Doppelgänger roll in an embrace and Quilty lists his accomplishments in the realm of pornography, erotica, and his merging of his life with his "art."

Lolita, Humbert's detective persona becomes emphasized in Part Two, during the road trip and the post–"Lolita" period. The façade of nymphet crumbles, for his "bride" dupes him for another man. As H.H. is the criminal, his relocation as "wronged party" is ironic; he can hardly turn to the Law for support.

The fairy tale explores children's (and adults') fears and desires connected with sexual awakening, family rivalries and struggles, and identity, with children often pitted against some evil, predatory adult (e.g., Hansel and Gretel, Cinderella, Snow White, Little Red Riding Hood). The child must overcome the sadistic attentions of such an adult. The fairy-tale motif is integrated into *Lolita* in a number of ways, most notably in the application of "nymphet," "fairy child beauty," and variations of "fairy" and "daemon."

By Humbert's framing the child as fairy creature, childhood and the genre of the fairytale are pinned to each other in an unfamiliar way. Children read fairy tales and strange adventures that occur to *children.* For Dolores, the mask of the fairy or "nymphet" is imposed on her so as to celebrate the fantastic "Lolita"'s power to provoke desire (and to make it a disingenuous excuse as seduction). The nymphet living on "that intangible island of entranced time" (17) is comparable to J. M. Barrie's Peter Pan, who must live on an island forever (in Neverland) and who can only visit with other children.[14] While his children friends grow up, Peter remains always a child. In his state of imprisonment, his "freedom" is idealized, but it is also terrorized by Captain Hook, the phallic aggressor. We could also compare Dolores-Lolita to Alice of *Alice in Wonderland.*[15] But while that narrative's focalization is squarely on Alice, in *Lolita,* the girl is obscured (although perceptible with careful reading). This is a "fairy tale" told by a sadistic adult figure, the figure who craves the child (the wolf in Little Red Riding Hood; Hook in the various versions of *Peter Pan,* the play;

---

14. See Jacqueline Rose's extensive discussion of the tangled history of *Peter Pan.* While *Peter Pan* passes for children's literature, Rose explains that this work "first appeared inside a novel for adults, J. M. Barrie's *The Little White Bird* [...], as a story told by the narrator to a little boy whom the narrator was trying to steal. In order for it to become a work for children, it was extracted from its source, transformed into a play, and sent out on its own. *Peter Pan* emerges, therefore, out of an unmistakable act of censorship" (*The Case of Peter Pan,* 5). In a somewhat parallel situation, but on a homodiegetic level, we might consider how Humbert steals Dolores, the tale of which becomes a play for children by Quilty, *The Enchanted Hunters.*

15. Humbert's fantasies of nymphets in his "pre-dolorian past" included an image of a "half-naked nymphet stilled in the act of combing her Alice-in-Wonderland hair" (264). He describes Dolores as entering "my world, umber and black Humberland" (166), a grotesque variation of "wonderland." Nabokov was familiar with Carroll's *Alice in Wonderland* as he translated it into Russian (*Ania v strane chudes*) in the summer of 1922 (Boyd, *Vladimir Nabokov: The Russian Years,* 197).

the ambiguous adult narrator of the novel *The Little White Bird* [1902], the first version of the Peter Pan story).

In *Lolita,* the theme of eternal childhood assumes a sinister proprietary tone of the adult who enjoys children in "fancied adventures" (20). As Humbert recounts his years in Paris, he has frequented parks to be near the "nymphets play[ing] freely" (20). Echoing Peter Pan's fate of an eternal childhood, he rhetorically begs, "Ah, leave me alone in my pubescent park, in my mossy garden. Let them play around me forever. Never grow up" (21).

Kincaid and Rose discuss how *Peter Pan* posits the child as an erotic object for a desiring adult audience. In Kincaid's comparison of Peter Pan and the Alice books he suggests several "counters": "the child and the adult, the world of play and the world of power. Peter, the child, is lodged in the world of play and the adult is stuck in the world of power; Alice, the apparent child (actually the adult) is firmly in the world of power and the apparent adult (actually the child) is in the world of play" (276). Nabokov subverts the erotic child genre by using a monstrous character-narrator Humbert to have us question our possible enchantment with children. *Lolita* is obviously a book for adults, not a fairy tale for children.

Lolita engages these two worlds: Humbert's world of power encroaches playfully and cruelly on Dolores's world of play. Unlike Peter, Dolores is not a fantasy child and cannot escape the adult. Humbert often presents her as if she were such a fantasy child, a demoniac nymphet. He describes the type generally in fantastic terms: these "maidens" "reveal their true nature which is not human, but nymphic" to "certain bewitched travelers" (16); he substitutes "time terms for spatial ones. [. . .] I would have the reader see 'nine' and 'fourteen' as the boundaries—the mirrory beaches and rosy rocks—of an enchanted island haunted by those nymphets of mine and surrounded by a vast, misty sea." This "enchanted island" (later "coves of evoked islands" [257]) is commensurable with Peter Pan's Neverland island to the extent that it is the fantastic dwelling place for children suspended in youth, although not safe from predators. Captain James Hook, the pirate against whom Peter is pitted, is comparable to Humbert. Barrie's narrator describes Hook: "In manner, something of the grand seigneur still clung to him, so that he even ripped you up with an air, and I have been told that he was a RACONTEUR [storyteller] of repute. He was never more sinister than when he was most polite [. . .]" (chapter 5 of Barrie, *The Adventures of Peter Pan*). Humbert, too, has sinister, suave manners ("Old World politeness" [38]), considerable talents as raconteur, and a seigneurial manner (Dick and Bill might mistake him for a "viscount" [Part Two; Chapter 29]).

Nabokov uses techniques and allusions from these fairy-tale, detective, and pornographic genres to create a complex, ironic novel whose heteroglossia extends beyond a mediated range of social and cultural voices to a modernist hybrid. The friction or incongruity of genres emphasizes the ironic delivery. *Lolita* relies on some of the conventions of pornographic literature (as well as the detective and fairy-tale genres) in order to mock Humbert's and the potential reader's desire to make the story an untroubled, gratifying piece of pornography. The whole movement of Part One can be seen as a parodic development through short episodes toward a climax of consummation. Similarly, the narrative mimics the expressive first-person experience of anticipation of the detective-story genre. Humbert humorously builds up a crescendo in his recounting of Lolita's departure for camp in a breathless style of an erotic romance novel:

> A moment later I heard my sweetheart running up the stairs. My heart expanded with such force that it almost blotted me out. I hitched up the pants of my pajamas, flung the door open: and simultaneously Lolita arrived, in her Sunday frock, stamping, panting, and then she was in my arms, her innocent mouth melting under the ferocious pressure of dark male jaws, my palpitating darling! The next instant I heard her—alive, unraped—clatter downstairs. The motion of fate was resumed. (66)

Lolita's ironic use of pornographic motifs forces readers to decide whether or not they are offended by the complicated presentation and ironic poeticization of the plot, characters, and themes. The reader's ability to read and judge Humbert's attempts at disavowing or defending his actions (while recognizing his own pastiched but evil intentions: "ferocious pressure of dark male jaws," "alive, unraped") shows that Humbert has an ethical urge to supplement an aesthetic one of "ecstasy." His potential position as exalted male lover is deflated to the unglamorous quotidian layabout: "I hitched up the pants of my pajamas." These and other ironic contrasts also show the conflict and generation of meaning based on the reader's diverse expectations of literary narratives: the high and low; the ironic high road versus the worn discursive paths of pornographic, detective, and sentimental fiction, as well as the fairy tale; the literary, linguistic, or elite references amid common or popular modes of cultural expression; the awkward balance between lyrical passages, purple prose ("My heart expanded [. . .]"); sharp satirical turns, learned cultural references and allusions, and histrionic pomposity. The confession of a pedophile (who has once aspired to become a psychotherapist but who has then become a literary academic) is appropriately embroidered by these conflicting ethical and aesthetic discourses, each of which can be manipulated to present Humbert as the embattled, rather than guilty, party.

Legal and critical arguments over the definition of the obscene try to weigh the values of the aesthetic and the ethical. *Lolita* is based upon the conflicting assessment of these two sets of values, art and crime. The novel can be seen, for example, as a critical, cynical, and aesthetic rendering of a sexual transgression and criminally aggressive act. The choice of transgression, pedophilia, targets and questions a relatively recently enshrined value in our age: that is, the sanctity of childhood.

Humbert derives artistic pleasure in describing his destruction of the cherished middle-class American child. His dual pleasures in his transgressive behavior and aestheticized recounting of it distress many readers because of the potential confusion of the acts of transgression with the act of confession. The reader's judgment of Humbert is further troubled because he finds fault in the supposedly enlightened, liberal values of the contemporary middle class. Charlotte Haze and her peers are depicted as relatively permissive with children. Humbert judges the Beardsley teachers to be dangerously liberal, promoting "the four D's: Dramatics, Dance, Debating and Dating" (177) and a mainstreamed American interpretation of psychoanalytic concepts (194). Hypocritically, Humbert deplores the parents and teachers who are willing to accept their children as sexual beings. Meanwhile he himself obviously and consciously regards and uses Dolores Haze as a source of sexual gratification, but he wants her to remain a child with others. His attempts to keep "Lolita" for himself and to present to the world a sanitized or censored version of their actual relationship stem from his prudish nature and jealousy, as well as from the need to protect himself from the judgment of others.

However, his censure of the Beardsley educators is not without some warrant. First, Dolores is the victim of prolonged sexual abuse by her "step-father." Yet, despite the staff's openness and knowledge, no one is able to detect the cause of her suffering. In fact, they misdiagnose the girl as frigid ("morbidly uninterested in sexual matters" [195]), a rather premature evaluation, given Dolores's and her classmates' age. Second, the Beardsley teachers also devote far too much of their students' time to the four D's; the girls are hardly being prepared to become competent, intelligent, knowledgeable citizens, workers, partners, and mothers, but instead are encouraged to become alluring, energetic, eligible girls for decoration, fun, and breeding. Dolores is doomed both at home and at school, ill-prepared to do anything except acting and performing as a sex worker.[16]

---

16. Some scholars, such as Goldman, see Dolores in her final year as a young woman who has entered the ranks of middle-class suburban America through marriage and pregnancy.

Nabokov clearly indicates, however, that this is not the case. The destitution of the Schiller couple is signaled in their debts, humble lodgings and clothes, and their physical decay despite

The reader's perceived need to judge the novel's ethical and aesthetic aspects is reflected in the focus of much of the critical commentary on Nabokov's work. Some admirers of the book risk appearing as supporters of pedophilia.[17] The staging of judgment is complicated: in a sense, Humbert Humbert has already condemned himself and his actions, but he still delights in telling his story. He is witty, ironic, deeply critical, highly intertextual, enjoys using puns and foreign words and phrases: all of these qualities can delight and engage the skilled reader. He also spares the reader the most gruesome elements of his life, while frequently describing himself as a monster. The reader must try to take Humbert at his word when he identifies himself as the sexual predator, deviant, pervert. His self-deprecations ("pentapod," "Humbert the Hound," and "the doe in

---

their youth (he is a wounded war veteran and Dolores is "used" and "worn" and has "rope-veined [. . .] hands" [277]). They lack opportunities owing to little education and no family support, and as a result, they plan to relocate to Alaska. Formerly a resident of a depressed tenement house in Coalmont, this impoverished pregnant seventeen-year-old hardly approximates what Goldman calls a "typical housewife" and "quintessential American housewife," nor leads "a normal life as a housewife in American suburbia" (Goldman, 101). Nabokov is emphasizing the disastrous conclusion of Dolores's life (she will die shortly after her last meeting with Humbert). By contrast, Goldman suggests that Nabokov "presents readers with a portrait of normalcy that is undercut by the reader's knowledge of Lolita's supposedly deviant history."

Fortunately, Goldman identifies compellingly and critically some broader implications of Nabokov's narrative strategies in the discourses that cover up the girl: "By satirizing both Humbert's romantic, mythical construction of Lolita and the scientific view of Lolita as statistic who exhibits normal characteristics of 'mammalian' sexual development in the human female, Nabokov suggests the inadequacies of conflicting ways of knowing *Lolita*. [. . .] Nabokov reveals the damage that a misogynist myth can inflict on a young woman. [. . .] Clearly, though, Nabokov points up the way a scientific approach dehumanizes as well as 'normalizes' young women like Lolita" (102).

17. See, for example, discussions in Alexandrov, "*Lolita*"; Andrews; McNeely; Berman; Bloom; Clifton; Dennison; Frosch; Girodias; Geoffrey Green; Hiatt; G. M. Hyde; Johnson, *Worlds in Regression;* Rigby; Schneiderman; Stegner; Wood. The critical field is filled with debate about authorial intention, the tendency of some readers to overvalue the aesthetic or erotic aspects of the novel or to miss important but difficult points of ironic contrast (as Graham Greene and some others have done by delighting, for example, in a supposedly simple situation that the girl seduces Humbert).

By contrast, my discussion shows how Nabokov integrates discursively devices of artistic censoring (e.g., irony, the unreliable character-narrator Humbert, and the veiled but perceptible Dolores) to move us toward ethical understanding.

Some readers imagine the girl to be in her late teens in order to visualize her as a knowing seductress. In late 1950s France, Brigitte Bardot was associated with the fictional Lolita. This trend inspired Simone de Beauvoir's *Brigitte Bardot and the Lolita Syndrome;* after that, *Playboy* wanted to commission Nabokov to write an essay on Bardot (Nabokov declined) (see Boyd, *Vladimir Nabokov: The American Years,* 464). Beauvoir scarcely mentions *Lolita;* in her analysis of Bardot, she writes, "Her eroticism is not magical, but aggressive. In the game of love, she is as much a hunter as she is a prey. The male is an object to her, just as she is to him. And that is precisely what wounds masculine pride" (20–21). Bardot's sexuality is not commensurable with Dolores's; Dolores is always the prey, and the game is not love.

Tamir-Ghez explains rhetorical features of *Lolita* which persuade readers to support Humbert.

me, trembling in the forest of my own iniquity" [129]) can be so amusing that the reader must maintain an awareness that the laughter accompanies a serious significance.

The narrator's splitting of aims can be seen as a treacherous trap for the reader. Hiatt views the narrator as the author when he comments on Nabokov's attempts to manipulate our reception of Humbert: "It is a strange game for an author to play. If he wins, the reader loses the point of the book" (370). McNeely ventures further in his persuasive condemnation of the novel's structure:

> The aesthetic argument comes unfailingly to the floundering critic's rescue when his defence of the book on character grounds begins to collapse. The aesthetic argument holds that plot and character are irrelevant, in fact phony; the whole thing is a literary game—and that argument is absolutely correct. The plot has one justification and basis only—to trap the reader. (144)

These critics falter in their otherwise careful interpretation because they tend to see the author and the narrator as the same person. If we put aside this flawed approach, however, we are still posed with the challenge of depending mostly on H.H.'s narration for our interpretations (several other discursive perspectives include the fictional preface, reported direct dialogue, and the insertion of diegetic texts such as Charlotte Haze's letter). While Humbert certainly presents his own point of view, he records sufficient material for the reader to make further assumptions or observations beyond that point of view. Humbert is not the first criminal character, either fictional or real, who is capable of charming some readers or eliciting their sympathy.[18] Certain offenders can disarm us with a production of their own vulnerability and original sense of taste. At times they prove to us that they do have character (*ethos*), despite their awful crime.

Conscientious active readers should be deterred from accepting wholesale Humbert, his actions, and his version of events because the narrative ensures that his integrity and charisma are marred or made ridiculous by his seemingly boundless vanity and arrogance, as well as by his contradictions, evasions, exaggerations, attacks, and revisions. The narrative is presented as Humbert's confessional written in prison while he is awaiting his trial, and the confession directly addresses the "ladies and gentlemen" of the jury. These imaginary diegetic jurors or narratees help to define our own role as readers coming to the text.

---

18. In his *The Company We Keep: An Ethics of Fiction*, Wayne C. Booth reflects at great length on how readers have to appraise a variety of characters in fiction, many of whom can hardly be called virtuous.

Humbert's defense and explanation of his actions and motivations do not only refer to the diegetic world of *Lolita;* they also anticipate the work's diegetic reception by the Law and a reading public, as framed, for example, by John Ray, Jr. in the foreword and by Ray's cousin and Humbert's lawyer Clarence Choate Clark, Esq. For that purpose, Humbert marshals in defense an elastic mass of allusions to people, events, and literary texts. The reversible pliability of *Lolita*'s textuality activates our sense of censoring because we must evaluate the possibility of the references.

Perhaps most notably, we encounter and must assess seemingly innumerable instances of doubling and mirroring depicted in the novel, from the coincidence of the number of the hotel room and the street number of the Haze home to the false-true association of "Lolita" and Carmen (and variations Carmencita, *gitanilla* [little gypsy]),[19] to the commensurability of two literati perverts (Humbert and Quilty) who "entext" and "entre dit" themselves. These homodiegetic authors "entext" themselves by becoming embedded in their novelistic and dramatic discourses (the plots of the entrapments of Dolores), respectively. They "entre dit" ("say between," a play on the French "interdit" or "interdire," to forbid) by placing themselves in between the spoken and the permissible. Their obscene intentions are not directly articulated in their self-presentation to the world (e.g., Humbert's bogus roles as protective stepfather and artist manqué; Quilty's play *The Enchanted Hunters*).

Humbert's erudite allusions and comparisons largely serve to defend his actions and desires. But the attentive reader should be able to weigh these with care and come away with a sense of the incongruity of issues or objects which initially appear textually coherent. For example, Humbert alludes to celebrated literary love relationships involving girls, such as that of Dante and Beatrice, in order to justify and elevate his relationship with "Lolita." But Humbert's elaborate and excessive comparisons demonstrate

---

19. Freeman identifies Nabokov's early inspiration for the character "Lolita" in the novels by nineteenth-century American author Captain Mayne Reid. Part of her discussion elaborates a fresh Carmen connection: Merimée's Carmen as the American child-bride. In a comparison of *Lolita* and Reid's *The Scalp-Hunters* [1851], Freeman writes: "Hispanicizing Zöe allows him to imagine her as the agent of precocious desire rather than the victim of violence, a technique Nabokov uses with Lolita: Lolita, whose name is short for 'Dolores,' was conceived in Monte Cristo, lives in a house filled with 'Mexican trash,' and gets molested to the tune of a song about 'Carmen.' Humbert even calls her 'my little Creole' (*L,* 171)—as though her Americanness, reconfigured as a racialized creole identity, explains why she seduces him rather than vice versa" (870–71).

Freeman elaborates several important considerations for influence, including the fact that Nabokov, as a boy, read Reid's novels ravenously; at age eleven, translated Reid's 1865 novel *The Headless Horseman* into French alexandrine verse; and cited Reid's work as operative in his desire to travel to America (867). This information is confirmed in Boyd (*Vladimir Nabokov: The Russian Years,* 81) and Nabokov (*Speak, Memory,* 202).

his strong disavowal of his actual relationship with Dolores Haze, his desire to transcend the ruinous situation he has created, and his lack of ability to analyze himself.[20]

Humbert repeatedly sees mirrors, mirroring, analogies, and homologies where there is in fact no sustainable evidence for such comparisons. Many of his pairings and intertextual references often fail to produce a signifying relationship. For example, his "nymphets" reside on "mirrory beaches and rosy rocks" in a dystopic stretch of time, between the ages nine and fourteen (16). Some readers may become frustrated with the many cul-de-sacs in Nabokov's work, but his is an important depiction of the illusory qualities of human perception and desire. The novel highlights our need to determine value and meaning from these, however tenuous or arbitrary. In Humbert's case, his tendency to perceive repetition or doubling, shown even in his self-imposed pen name, eventually traps him within the bars of his own imprisoning passion and need to justify himself.

In *Lolita,* the tragic and the obscene depend on one another for context. The tragedy of a girl's ruined life is caused by the obscene desire and actions of Humbert. In various censoring stratagems, the narrator strives to exclude obscene description from his account. But it is the unarticulated, obscene context of *Lolita*—an intelligent, educated adult's coerced and repeated sexual use of a child for an extended period of time under the guise of parenthood—that informs the expressive content and framework of the narration.

The girl's character zone is heavily layered with Humbert's discourse[21]

20. McNeely correctly identifies Humbert's false comparisons, but he mistakenly confuses Nabokov with Humbert the narrator when he states the following: "In Humbert's famous opening rhapsody in praise of nymphet love, one of the ways Nabokov pretends to justify him is by associating his case with that of two of the western worlds most celebrated literary lovers, Dante and Petrarch, both of whose eternal loves first flowered when the objects of their passion were of nymphet age. The blatant falsehood in the comparison, known perfectly well to Nabokov [. . .], is first that Dante and Petrarch did not fall in love with Beatrice and Laura *because* they were children as Humbert does, but *when* they were children—the difference is crucial; as crucial as the second part of the analogy, the fact that *chastity* is a fundamental condition of the relationship in both the classical instances" (147).

I suggest that, since Nabokov would know the "blatant falsehood of the comparison," we can infer that he as author is knowingly creating a deceitful character-narrator in Humbert, perhaps the epitome of the unreliable narrator. Surely Humbert parodies the classical lover, child or adult. As children, Humbert and Annabel do not share a particularly chaste relationship; their two private rendezvous focus on having sexual congress.

21. Moore notes Humbert's discursive dominance as child abuser-narrator: "He either cannot or will not grant preadolescents and readers, events and language, and predominant values in and for themselves; they are manipulated only to keep them oppressed within his subjectivity. The pervert has to use perverted narration to realize his perverted world" (97). While I agree that the narrator is oppressive and solipsistic, he does not succeed entirely in blotting out Dolores Haze's voice, as I will discuss later in this chapter.

with his alternating references to tragic consequence and reconsideration and reflection ("Lolita" as "my love") and to obscene sexual action, references that emphasize the disparity of power in their relation (e.g., "*Seva ascendes, pulsata, brulans* [. . .]" [120]; "she was not quite prepared for certain discrepancies between a kid's life and mine. [. . .] I [. . .] had her have her way—at least while I could still bear it. [. . .] Anyone can imagine those elements of animality" [134]); his arranging the hotel room bed "in such a way as to suggest the abandoned nest of a restless father and his tomboy daughter, instead of an ex-convict's saturnalia with a couple of fat old whores" [138]; "This was a lone child, an absolute waif, with whom a heavy-limbed, foul-smelling adult had had strenuous intercourse three times that very morning" [140]; "a prison cell of paradise" [145]; "a particularly violent morning in bed" [160]; "I would lead my reluctant pet to our small home for a quick connection before dinner" [164]; "her morning duty" [165]; "her basic obligations" [183]; "our grotesque journey" [229]; "the dark life she led at home" [231]; "two years of monstrous indulgence" [257]; "my poor, bruised child" [284]; "after having had my fill of her" [285]).

The ethics of *Lolita* involves an inversion of an Oedipal story (the adult desiring the child), and uses the aesthetic presentation of the tragic and the obscene to complement and inform each other. Humbert generally avoids accounting for his lack of pity and compassion for his love object during their long cohabitation and his abuse. By contrast, as a narrator surveying himself and his deeds in retrospect, he recognizes and condemns his callousness to a degree. A strong element of his desire for the girl comes from his paradoxical conception and use of her.

"Lolita," like other kinds of degraded love objects and fetishes, acquires her particular appeal through both tragic and obscene treatment. Her names—Dolores ("sorrows, pain") and its diminutives (Dolly, Lo, Lola, and Lolita: fragments of "sorrows")—allude to the abject quality of the object of passion (from the Latin *passio* [suffering]). The association of passionate feminine sexuality with the Spanish "Lolita" masks the reality of a girl Dolores or Dolly, manipulated into a coercive sexual and emotional relationship. Whereas Dolores the girl icily rejects an amorous relationship with Humbert, the fantasized "Lolita" is cast as a cruel but consensual lover (such as Carmen) or exotic New World child-bride. Humbert's fantasy nymphet supposedly has power over her "lover," is a potential dominatrix, given her daemon-child talents. Meanwhile, the girl Dolores has no such agency, and her only self-defense is to affect a tough-girl attitude. Her tragic situation, the sorrows she experiences daily for some two years, is the obscene stuff of Humbert's fantasies, discourse, and enjoyment of his victim.

The usual family romance between child and parent becomes perverted in the Haze household because Humbert does not abide by his role as a father figure who can be safely desired in the child's fantasy. Humbert breaks the usual trust inherent in a family, the tacit agreement to maintain the incest prohibition, a point which is perhaps at the crux of our understanding of Dolores's destruction and despair.

He offers her a "parody of incest" (287), underlining his double abuse of the family triangle (he is not the father); he ironically argues with her: "But now, I am just your *old man,* a dream dad protecting his dream daughter" (149). For example, he recalls episodes during the "Beardsley era" which show his awareness of his destruction of familial trust and love: he and Dolores witness her school friend Avis and her father cuddle affectionately (286), whereas the life he offers Dolores is worse than "the most miserable of family lives" (287). Second, Dolores asks where her "murdered mummy" is buried, revealing her sense of loss and blame (286). The narrator recognizes these moments as evidence of his culpability in the tragedy of this child:

> Now, squirming and pleading with my own memory, I recall that on this and similar occasions, it was always my habit and method to ignore Lolita's states of mind while comforting my own base self. [. . .] But I admit that a man of my power of imagination cannot plead personal ignorance of universal emotions. [. . .] But the awful point of the whole argument is this. It had become gradually clear to my conventional Lolita during our singular and bestial cohabitation that even the most miserable of family lives was better than the parody of incest, which, in the long run, was the best I could offer the waif. (287)

Humbert's transgressions and his need to recount them activate his motivation to measure and censor these; strangely, in the mirror of language he reencounters himself and the Law. Noam Chomsky and Jacques Lacan have asserted that, in fact, "at the heart of language, and perhaps embedded in the unconscious [. . .], is not the impulse to transgression but the will to law"[22] (Joss Marsh, 245–46).

It is not without significance that Humbert himself is acutely sensitive to the strictures of moral conventions (as witnessed in his disgust with what

---

22. Such concerns are at the heart of two philosophers' work which examines the relationship between the law and writing, that of Derrida and Legendre. See Goodrich, also, for an exploration of these issues, especially regarding Legendre's work. While the law and psychoanalysis have been recognized foci in Derrida's work, Levinas's (ethical) influence on him should not be forgotten either.

he perceives as overly permissive attitudes in pedagogy and parenting in postwar America). His remarks reveal an awareness of his artistic censoring (screening) of the need and desire of the other (Dolores) at the time of his crime: "it was always my habit and method to ignore Lolita's states of mind." Habit and method represent conscious repetitive practice. Through Humbert's contortions we can perceive that what he is trying to say is that he knew at the time just how base his actions were ("I have still other smothered memories, now unfolding themselves into limbless monsters of pain" [284]; his pseudonym "Humbert Humbert" is chosen to "[express] the nastiness best" [308]). This circumlocuted admission of the degree of his guilt is a form of belated self-censure.

Humbert's oscillating disavowal and confession represent the artistic censoring of the (ethical) thing in art (Dolores). His written review of his affair with this girl is a defense and an aborted attempt at redemption because he professes a transcendent love for his object of desire (e.g., "my Lolita"; "she looked—had always looked—like Botticelli's russet Venus—the same soft nose, the same blurred beauty" [270]; "my American sweet immortal dead love" [280]; "*mais je t'aimais, je t'aimais!*" [284]).

Despite these professions of transcendent, aestheticized love, one has to question whether he has known what such a transcendent love would truly require. For his approach to the girl has been to blot out her emotional responses in order to allow his "own base self" to enjoy her. He has had to censor his powerful imagination so as to avoid generally recognizing what the other might actually desire and need. His censoring of the human response in the desired other, his refusal to hear what the other wants, is what produces the text of *Lolita*. Particularly toward the end of his testimony, it seems as though the exercise in writing and recalling causes Humbert to begin to touch upon "still other smothered memories, now unfolding themselves into limbless monsters of pain." His accounts of his initial actions and their consequences condemn him further, as he reports how he consciously decided not to allow his sense of ethics to interfere with his pleasure. He censors the other (Dolores) and her gaze so that he can enjoy his version of it; he finds his desire mirrored off the child. For example, he begins to recognize what he has recognized previously and yet has repressed: his knowledge of the child's utter despair with the helplessness and injustice of her situation with this man and her view of him as an inhuman thing that rapes. She cannot perceive him empathetically as an ethical, human other:

> There was the day, during our first trip—our first circle of paradise—when in order to enjoy my phantasms in peace I firmly decided to ignore what I could

not help perceiving, the fact that I was to her not a boy friend, not a glamour man, not a pal, not even a person at all, but just two eyes and a foot of engorged brawn—to mention only mentionable matters. (283)

Lolita does parody incest. The family romance between parent and child, which usually does not involve actual incestuous practices because of the incest taboo, becomes ruinously play-acted by Humbert and Dolores. Humbert's claim of transcendent love is subject to the parody. If H.H. and "Lolita" "may share" "the only immortality," "the refuge of art," then these characters are aesthetic figures within an artistic sphere, hybrids of the generic villain and tragic heroine. Humbert is deluded if he believes the "refuge of art" transcends in some way ethical interpretation. His discourse reveals his myopia, the limitations of his focalization, and provides signals for the reader to transcend the character zone of the narrator.

The tendency to perceive treacherous doubles is at the heart of the parody. When he meets her as Mrs. Richard F. Schiller[23] or Dolly Schiller, Dolores has moved further away from the palimpsestic guise of the nymphet "Lolita." At age seventeen, she has taken on the rudiments of 1952 American womanhood, marriage and pregnancy. Falling prey to seeing doubles, Humbert imagines that he can still win "Lolita" back. His delusion shows how he does not fully recognize the harm he has done to her. For Dolores, it is not possible to imagine living again with a man who showed her no true love or compassion. She does not see him mimetically doubled as lover, only the parody of a lover. While it might seem possible to feel that Humbert has in some way elevated his love and fused it with moral and communal categories, upon close inspection his supposed redemptive rebirth is a stillborn one. Nabokov ensures that Humbert receives a death bereft of heroic value.

The act of writing his confession and defense allows Humbert to reexpe-

---

23. Dolores seems to take refuge under the name of Schiller, an allusion to Friedrich von Schiller, German dramatist of the *Sturm und Drang* era. His plays involve themes of the psychology of people in crisis. His treatises on aesthetics include the *On the Aesthetic Education of Man,* which also serves as a moral treatise. In other words, for Schiller, aesthetics are not separate from moral issues.

In Schiller's essay "On the Sublime," we can observe a possible similarity between Humbert's "Lolita" and Schiller's explanation of the sublime:

> But in the sublime, however, reason and sensuousness do *not* accord, and precisely in this contradiction between the two lies the magic with which it captures our minds. The physical and the moral individual are here most sharply differentiated from one another; for it is precisely in the presence of objects that make the former aware only of his limitations that the latter is aware of his *power* and is infinitely exalted by the very same object that crushes the physical man to the ground. (199–200; emphasis in original)

rience at a distance his life in both its pleasure and suffering. The many ways in which he artistically censors his narrative and himself produce the text and activate judgment and assessment of value and blame, therefore giving it both aesthetic and ethical signification. His desire to relive his "love life" is countered by his ethical urge to defend himself and find higher, transcendent meaning and value in his actions. Upon reviewing the humorous, erotic, and ironic aspects of the events, the reader can recognize that the "artist" must account to a jury of moralists, headed by himself. Humbert's retelling of his criminal and troubled life enacts judgment. Dolores Haze figures as the legal, tragic, and ethical subject in much of this discourse (the abused child, the orphan girl),[24] while "Lolita," the fantasized nymphet superimposed over the girl, figures discursively as the erotic, pathetic, and doubled image of forbidden sexual desire and romantic love.

Part of Humbert's narrative method is based on his contradictory attitudes toward psychoanalysis, which represents another institution of the Law and judgment. He both relies on and rejects psychoanalysis in order to write his confession. On the one hand, his confession is written somewhat like material for a psychoanalytic case study.[25] The patient demonstrates

---

24. During their first cross-country trip, Humbert thinks, in "one pole of insanity," "that around 1950 I would have to get rid somehow of a difficult adolescent whose magic nymphage had evaporated" (174). As a legal person, Dolores does not fall into a clear category ("I somehow never managed to find out quite exactly what the legal situation was. I do not know it yet" [171]). Humbert "terroriz[es]" the girl with the prospect of the law: he would "go to jail" while she would face the "laws relating to dependent, neglected, incorrigible and delinquent children," becoming the ward of "a choice of various dwelling places [. . .], the correctional school, the reformatory, the juvenile detention home, or one of those admirable girls' protectories" (151).

During his lengthy harangue (149–51), he repeatedly emphasizes the girl's legal name (e.g., "Let us, however, forget, Dolores Haze, so-called legal terminology, terminology that accepts as rational the term 'lewd and lascivious cohabitation.' I am not a criminal sexual psychopath taking indecent liberties with a child. The rapist was Charlie Holmes; I am the therapist [. . .]" [150]). And, later in considering legal action to become her legal guardian, Humbert returns repetitively to the girl's full name, emphasizing a legal status: "fishy me and dangerous Dolores Haze"; "the case of Dolores Haze"; "her mother's small property was waiting untouched for Dolores Haze to grow up" (172). The instances in the novel of "Lolita" and "Lo" far outnumber those of "Dolores" or "Dolores Haze."

25. Linetski offers a comparative reading of *Lolita* as case study and Freud's Dora ("Fragment of an Analysis of a Case of Hysteria"), reminding us of Dora's symptoms related to the unwanted sexual advances of an older man. The shadow of Freud alternately looms up and fades away in *Lolita*. Many scholars (e.g., Berman; Geoffrey Green; Hiatt; Welsen; Schneiderman) have noted the aggressive abuse that Nabokov's protagonists such as H.H. heap onto psychoanalysis.

Berman, Green, and other critics have aptly noted how "He who hated Freud" is actually compelled to write about psychoanalytic themes: childhood sexuality, psychoses, perversions. Humbert's narration has been seen as "the supreme parody of the psychiatric case study" (Berman, 105). Yet "parody" does not encompass all the special uses of psychoanalysis of *Lolita*. The narration consists of a written confession of someone who has serious psychiatric problems and who has spent considerable time at clinics or asylums, as his pre- and post-dolorean periods attest.

a great deal of resistance to the exercise, yet is drawn to the practice of recovering and recalling his memories and assessing his actions. This psychoanalytic aspect of Humbert's narrative is emphasized by several factors: he has spent several years on and off in psychiatric clinics and retreats, trying to fool therapists; as a university student, he has once aspired to be a psychotherapist; he is mockingly conversant in and resistant to some psychoanalytic terms and concepts.

On the other hand, he is dependent on the premises of psychoanalysis to make his parodies, denials, disavowals, and investigation of his life. In his coercion of Dolores, the "therapist" Humbert instructs her: "the normal girl—normal, mark you—the normal girl is usually extremely anxious to please her father. She feels in him the forerunner of the desired elusive male [. . .]. The wise mother [. . .] will encourage a companionship between father and daughter, realizing [. . .] that the girl forms her ideals of romance and of men from her association with her father" (150).

Furthermore, his investigation leads him to uncovering the censored thing in his own "art," that is, the gothic grotesque truth about himself ("other smothered memories, [. . .] limbless monsters of pain") and the tragic victim of cruelty. All of these factors would indicate his unspoken acknowledgment of the possible validity or signifying value psychoanalysis might hold for him, thus explaining his conflicting motivations for writing *Lolita*. Humbert's will is a will to meaning, despite concerted discursive efforts to disavow, deny, or otherwise censor, a drive to make sense out of his acts and fantasy.

Lolita toys parodically with the drama of the psychoanalytic case study. Humbert explains how he once aspired to become a psychiatrist: "I planned to take a degree in psychiatry as many *manqué* talents do; but I was even more *manqué* than that; a peculiar exhaustion, I am so oppressed, doctor, set in; and I switched to English literature, where so many frustrated poets end as pipe-smoking teachers in tweeds" (15). Humbert's half-mocking attempts at self-analysis counteract his rejection of psychiatric aid and show that, despite his disavowals, he believes that there might be value in such analysis. Relying on the comical, distancing effect of a foreign language, Humbert's self-portrayal as "*manqué*" implies his serious lack in many areas, a kind of double lack, his constitutive defective or maimed quality. The confessional mode of the narrative is a form of legal defense for his crimes, but also a form of defense and resistance to psychoanalytic discourse and ideas, and to his own repressed desires. He "psychoanalyz[es]" his crazed poem, "Wanted, wanted: Dolores Haze," "notic[ing] it is really a maniac's masterpiece" (255–57).

Toward the novel's end, he even mentions the value he gained from a prolonged series of confessions made to a Catholic priest in Québec.

Michel Foucault, among other scholars, has emphasized the interrogatory strength of the Catholic confession, especially since the Council of Trent (*The History of Sexuality: An Introduction*). Catholic confession relies on a considerable surrender of the sinner and the probing detailed questions of the confessor. That Humbert has confessed, presumably in French, to an unnamed priest in culturally and politically remote Québec suggests that the man made a more explicit confession which will never become known, owing to priests' confidentiality. This French confession would probably have disposed of at least some of Humbert's overwrought style, allowing him to speak in his native tongue.[26]

Thus, Humbert's heteroglossia and strategies—including self-incriminating parody and shifting interpretation of himself as fiend and lover and his actions—rely upon the discourses of the law, psychoanalysis and popular psychotherapy, literature (e.g., the *blason;* the detective; the romance; the erotic and pornographic novel; drama; the fairy tale, myth, and children's literature), education, and religion for structure and meaning. Yet he also seeks in his writing to disavow or slip past the reach of those discourses: "Oh, my Lolita, I have only words to play with!" (32).

4. THE NARRATOR-ROGUE, DIALOGISM, AND CONFESSION

Lolita's confessional discourse is informed by the character-narrator's ironic role as a *pícaro* or rogue, as alienated underground man, as author of a psychoanalytic case study, and as pornographic confessee. The character-narrator's hybrid position at the intersection of these personae problematizes the veracity, honesty, and aims of the confessional text. In my view, these maneuvers by the character-narrator indicate his attempt to censor or block out our ethical apprehension of the abused child Dolores and tempt us to read her as an exotic, desiring, and desired other.

The picaresque genre in *Lolita* has been analyzed by other scholars, notably Freeman. In her exploration of "pedophiliac picaresques" in Poe, Hawthorne, Reid, and Nabokov (the first three influential in Nabokov's work), she identifies numerous comparative instances of the child-bride in the context of the American picaresque or road trip. The imperial and

---

26. The references to Canada sharpen the American context; on Dolores's fifteenth birthday, Humbert mails her abandoned things "as an anonymous gift to a home for orphaned girls on a windy lake, on the Canadian border" (255). At the outset of the narrative, early on in H.H.'s immigrant period, in order to recover from a breakdown, he spends some twenty months in arctic Canada with scientists on an expedition (32–34).

American masculine adventure, with its discovery and mastery of virgin lands, is sexualized and humanized by the male protagonist's relation with a young female object of desire. Authors like Hawthorne and Nabokov present the motif of the child-bride or child-lover in critical, ironic terms. Freeman explains how Hawthorne's "Little Annie's Ramble" (1834) "resolutely skews the nineteenth century's naturalized and sentimentalized image of the father-daughter relationship. Significantly, the tale refuses to reproduce the father-daughter dyad or to contain the child in domestic space" (880). In addition to the road trips in *Lolita*, Freeman reminds us of a scene of Dolores (884), who looks at naked mannequins and a worker ("a bald and armless child, an amputee bride, and a man vacuuming") in a bridal shop window and has a huge quarrel with Humbert. This scene reenacts the dislocation of the father-daughter dyad, placed picaresquely and incongruously in a market space for weddings. Freeman explains the comparative effect of the tableau: "While in Hawthorne the wedding to a child provides a momentarily safe image of communion with consumer culture, and in Poe and Reid it is the reward for conquest and adventure, in Nabokov the conjoined images of *intacta* bride and mutilated child cause a horrific 'blast'" (884).

Similarly, in *Lolita*, we can note rogue Humbert's various failed attempts to frame Dolores as his fantasy nymphet bride "Lolita," particularly in the two highly ironic road trips, Humbert's "honeymoons" and Dolores's rides through circles of hell. The narrator acknowledges from time to time how his attempt at a honeymoon (implied romance, legitimate and consensual consummation) is a sham, from his careful strategies to avoid detection by fellow travelers and motel attendants to his attempt to restage with Dolores in California his Riviera beach scene with Annabel (166–67), to the implied horror we "gentle drivers" would witness if "Komfy Kabins were suddenly drained of their pigments and became as transparent as boxes of glass" (117). The American landscape rejects his attempts at "rural amours" with Dolores, the Californian attempt even involving the censorious gaze of two beautiful children and their mother, an intrusion of idealized family life (169).

Humbert's picaresque narrative strategies unveil him as the rogue to be condemned, not the rogue who garners some sympathy (such as Lazarillo of *Lazarillo de Tormes* [1554]). Conventionally, the rogue's or *pícaro's* confession often reveals the faults of others as he moves through diverse social strata on his road trip. By contrast, although the ironic rogue Humbert's confession shifts blame and criticism to others (e.g., parents, teachers, psychiatrists) and does reveal social flaws (e.g., racism, anti-Semitism, commercialism), he himself is clearly the most at fault. Further, the true *pícaro* of *Lolita* could have been in fact the young Dolores, the orphaned waif, who must serve a cruel master, not unlike Lazarillo's painful apprenticeship under cruel paternalistic masters. But Dolores does not recount her story like other *pícaros* do (and Dolores's narrative would not be entitled *Lolita* but rather some variation of *Dolly of Pisky* [her fictional town of birth in the western United States]).

Lolita's homodiegetic narrator's solipsism bears some resemblance to the solipsism of Dostoevsky's misanthropic, neurotic Underground Man (*Notes from Underground* [1864]). The two narrators write "from underground" and obsessively review their lives and the flaws of others. They both seek to persuade, while the overall narrative arrangement and the characters' self-presentation inspire caution in careful readers. Dostoevsky's novel opens with the memorable confessional lines, "I am a sick man . . . I am a spiteful man. I am an unpleasant man" (3). Nabokov acknowledges an influence when he has Humbert mention how he feels "a Dostoevskian grin dawning" (70).

For Bakhtin, the internally persuasive discourse (such as a first-person narrative) poses a challenge for readers, for they must try to resist its dominating, authoritarian effect. The unreliable narrator (Humbert) who manically attempts to persuade narratees and readers evokes literary comparisons. His attempts to live "according to literature" ironically resemble those of famous literary characters such as don Quijote or Madame Bovary (*Dialogic*, 413). Yet, Humbert falls short of acting as a don Quijote, for his actions are not intended for a greater good, but instead for selfish pleasure.

Humbert as narrator sets himself at a crossroads between the narrative of trial and temptation, and confession and the memoirs of the *pícaro*. Bakhtin writes of the picaresque hero: "[he] is faithful to nothing, he betrays everything—but he is nevertheless true to himself, to his own interpretation, which scorns pathos and is full of scepticism" (408). It would seem that Nabokov seeks to revive some of the qualities of the picaresque narrator in Humbert. Bakhtin outlines some of these qualities: "[t]he hero of such novels, the agent of gay deception, is located on the far side of any pathos—heroic or Sentimental—and located there deliberately and emphatically; his contra-pathetic nature is everywhere in evidence, beginning in his comic self-introduction and self-recommendation to the public (providing the tone of the entire subsequent story) and ending with the finale" (406).

Nabokov revitalizes and further ironizes this picaresque tradition by reinstating a pathetic and realist factor—the abused child Dolores Haze—who is censored (screened over) partially by the rambling artistic discourses of her abuser. The literary motifs—those of the lover, the femme fatale, the fairy or witch—are superimposed over, or censor, the girl in crisis beneath. The dialogism of the narration helps us to perceive this person, not unlike the dialogism of *Notes from Underground* that allows us to apprehend the abject situation of the prostitute Liza and the narrator's cruel intensification of her abjection.

Bakhtin's explanation of the dialogic voices of Dostoevsky's characters can be generally related to Nabokov's character-narrator Humbert. Bakhtin explains the struggle with another's discourse in Dostoevsky:

> The acute and intense interaction of another's word is present in his novels in two ways. In the first place in his characters' language there is a profound and unresolved conflict with another's word on the level of lived experience ("another's word about me"), on the level of ethical life (another's judgment, recognition, or nonrecognition by another) and finally on the level of ideology (the world views of characters understood as unresolved and unresolvable dialogue). What Dostoevsky's characters say constitutes an arena of never-ending struggle with others' words, in all realms of life and creative ideological activity. (349)

Humbert as character and narrator, too, along with the characters' speech he reports, makes possible such "acute and intense interaction." Humbert's language comes into intense, sustained conflict with others' language ("and I *am* speaking English" [150]), including the reader's language. Ultimately, the conflicts are activated through our critical readership.

Lolita's character-narrator shares some similarities with other nineteenth-century characters that express profound dialogism in terms of conflict or clash of values, such as Dr. Jekyll and Mr. Hyde. Nabokov lectured on Stevenson's novel frequently at Cornell, and his lecture notes emphasize themes that are commensurable with Humbert. Humbert, without a magic potion, perhaps embodies a modern Dr. Jekyll and Mr. Hyde, outwardly an educated, mild-mannered bachelor while inwardly a twisted madman with shady desires (Nabokov describes Hyde's desires: "sadistic—he enjoys the infliction of pain" [196], dark deeds, and an "ape-like fury").

In Stevenson's novel, the female child is the first witnessed object of Hyde's cruel abuse. Mr. Enfield reports how he sees in an empty street the accidental pedestrian collision of the man (Hyde) and a girl of "eight or ten," resulting in "the horrible part of the thing; for the man trampled calmly over the child's body and left her screaming on the ground. It sounds like nothing to hear, but it was hellish to see" (Stevenson, 40). Nabokov notes how Enfield's anecdote has artistic resonance, inspiring the "hidden artist" in both himself and his interlocutor Utterson (193). Nabokov also points out that the novel relies on Jekyll's confession, preparing for a possible trial of Hyde for his various fiendish deeds.

Jekyll's confession ("Henry Jekyll's Full Statement of the Case") illuminates the twisting, turning mystery narrative initially explored through the focalization of Enfield and Utterson. His confession before death can be compared with Humbert's. I suggest that, despite the possible awakening of the "artist" in men like Enfield and Utterson (they can witness and imagine), it takes the actual criminal Jekyll/Hyde to compose the narrative that will reveal the mysteries of evil, which point to some kind of essential flaw in man, magnified by Jekyll's potion, as well as the "profound duplicity of life (103), an allusion to the "irregularities" he has been guilty of even before devising the potion. Of this pre-Hyde period, Jekyll states, "from the high views that I had set before me, I regarded and hid them [the irregularities] with an almost morbid sense of shame" (103). In contrast to Jekyll's confession, Humbert's occupies almost the whole novel; his narrative encourages the reader to awaken the witness or inner "artist." The shadowy "irregularities" of Jekyll[27] become explicit in Humbert's nympholepsy and abuse of Dolores. In this way, the potential ethical reader—the one who can imagine another's suffering, the girl's suffering—is implied in *Lolita,* activated through the dialogic confession.

Especially since the late nineteenth century, but dramatically demonstrated earlier in the example of the revised practice of confession, as Foucault has noted, the project of writing about sexuality, of articulating a project of sex, virtually necessitates both a disavowal (of a pornographic project) and an assertion of one's purpose (an epistemic goal). While pornography is not as transparently straightforward in its aims and fantasies as it appears to be, involving as it does its own ideology,[28] creators of works of art or science about sexuality strive to disassociate themselves and their work from the obscene or lascivious.

Within the homodiegetic text of *Lolita,* Humbert's narrative, Humbert as narrator and literary academic encourages readers to associate his writing and life with those of other actual historical writers. He tries to use intertextual aesthetic references to elevate readers' interpretation of his narrative.

---

27. In Stevenson's novel, the "irregularities" remain conveniently vague to allow the reader to imagine any monstrous qualities and activities, although I tend to agree with Nabokov that sadism is Jekyll's likely vice.

28. The apparent transparency of pornography deceives not only its consumer but also its opponents. Some of MacKinnon's cause-and-effect arguments illustrate the protesters' misunderstandings about pornography. For two important examinations of the psychic operations involved in the production and consumption of pornography, see Randall and Kaite. Aside from the personal sphere (of fantasy), Randall also examines pornography in the public sphere of communications, community, and law; his bibliography is excellent.

Yet some of the intertextual references, such as the subtitle "Memoirs of a White Widowed Male," teasingly imply a comparison of his confession or memoirs with literary works with a strong pornographic flavor such as John Cleland's *Memoirs of a Woman of Pleasure* (or *Fanny Hill*). This cunning and treacherous use of what are often false leads shows the lengths H.H. is willing to go to try to impress and captivate his readers, as well as his investment in the power of words and references ("I have only words to play with"). For example, although *Lolita* is no *Fanny Hill,* the intertextual irony produces other correspondences of signification: Cleland's novel is a fantasy, for real prostitutes provide pleasure for others, not usually for themselves; Humbert's memoirs are those of a Man of Unpleasure, a man who coerces a child into a sexual relationship for his pleasure and her pain; Dolores Haze serves as a novice "woman of pleasure" or prostitute for him, but she does so through suffering and coercion, not through the lighthearted enjoyment shown by Fanny. Unlike Cleland's novel that highlights Fanny's narrative voice, Dolores's voice is only mediated through H.H.'s narrative, and does not provide a confession or memoir of her own. Whereas the pornographic enjoyment of Cleland's work is evident in the prostitute's cheerful recounting of her work and adventures (the male fantasy: she is a desiring subject who could desire him; she really wants sex and takes pleasure in it), the desiring woman's voice is tellingly censored in *Lolita*.[29]

As a writer, Humbert attempts to create an artistic haven for the discourse of sexuality and a discursive morality. He uses absences and gaps, as well as twisted, ironic comparisons, in order to regulate his discourse and demonstrate a sense of judgment (i.e., a recognition and application of ethical values). Our active reading of the complex narrative, combined with our sensitivity to the indications or inferences of obscene or transgressive acts that hurt the child, should show us how the obscene thing shifts through the motley gradations of relatively better or worse alternatives. That is, obscenity necessarily belongs to the realm of ethics, although it is not anchored to a particular normative value. *Lolita*'s production of ethical meaning and value is enacted through the twisting modes of confession, cynical subterfuges, contrasting discourse, and censoring of Dolores as a human subject. While H.H. would seem to begin his narrative with an ecstatic (i.e., displaced), erotic frame of reference, he pays for the pleasure he gains from writing about his life and transgressions by submitting his confession to a complicated, discursive evaluation, beginning with the very

---

29. Annabel's voice is largely unreported; Dolores's voice is presented in terms of pleasing or conflicting with Humbert's desires; Charlotte's desiring voice is largely ridiculed or avoided by Humbert. It is to Humbert's advantage to downplay the desiring woman's voice as he attends to his own desires; he does not truly attend to the desire of the other.

first words and ending with concluding ominous statements such as "my story [. . .] has bits of marrow sticking to it, and blood, and beautiful bright-green flies" (308). We could consider H.H.'s confession as a process of arriving at an awareness of his authentic self if we compare *Lolita* to the confessional mode as assessed by the philosopher Peter Sloterdijk: "In motley reality, all talking about oneself necessarily ends up in the vicinity of a blackguard's confession or a criminal's testament, a sick report or a story of suffering, a witness's statement or a confession. That is the condition of authenticity in a situation of the unavoidable ethical overtaxing of oneself" (303).

Self-censorship, in keeping with the etymology of the economic aspect of "censor," can in effect be conceived as an "unavoidable ethical overtaxing of oneself." Writing, and especially the confessional mode, brings to the fore these concerns. Through writing, one might arrive at a possible authentic self: the self who has meaning and value, who is not incidental or superfluous, an original self.[30] The confession can be authentic because it is accomplished by the subject. In the case of the character-narrator Humbert, his act of writing accomplishes an artistic censoring of the self that makes possible ethical judgment. We might agree that the effort of writing the homodiegetic text *Lolita* taxes her torturer enough to prompt an early death through heart failure.

5. DOLORES'S TEXTUALITY AND CENSORING PATTERNS

The character Dolores Haze is difficult to perceive amid the crisscrossing discursive screens Humbert lays over her. These screens—"Lolita" as nymphet, lover, the beloved, work of art, goddess of love, daemon, fairy, witch, dominatrix—almost censor out the girl. There are some competing discourses that issue from this character, including cinema, comic books and magazines, children's literature, and drama or theater. By contrast, the fairy-tale allusions belong more to Humbert than to Dolores, and provide an intersecting discourse that tells the tale of his abuse and delectation and her suffering.

Dolores's discourses emphasize image and illusion, and involve imitation or mimesis and, at times, education. These discourses are not unique or special to this one girl, but relate to common interests of American middle-

---

30. "Authentic" derives from the Greek *authentikós,* original, primary, at firsthand, equivalent to *authéntes,* one who does things himself, a doer.

class preadolescents and teenagers of the 1940s. The cinematic discourse of Hollywood presents stars as idols to admire and possibly emulate. In Dolores's bedroom, she has a poster of a male movie star who, H.H. claims, resembles him. While Humbert's report may be unreliable, perhaps more narcissistic wishful thinking than reality, he does insinuate himself, however clumsily, into the discourses with which Dolores is familiar. In his early seduction of the girl, when she leans over his writing, he guesses that he could "kiss her throat or the wick of her mouth with perfect impunity. I knew she would let me do so, and even close her eyes as Hollywood teaches" (48). Ironically, he does not take this supposed opportunity. Later, as the pair near the Enchanted Hunters hotel, they pass a cinema and Dolores begs to see "that picture" "right after dinner" (116); Humbert intersects her desire for film with his own secret gothic vampiric plans: "knowing perfectly well, the shy tumescent devil, that by nine, when *his* show began, she would be dead in his arms" (116). In Ramsdale, on the road, and at Beardsley, Dolores maintains a strong interest in cinema and drama (e.g., she studies the book *Dramatic Technique* by Baker [198]).[31]

For Dolores, film and drama provide sources of education and possible life narratives. During the first road trip, she has favorite films, "musicals, underworlders, westerners," as explained by Humbert (170). None of her favorite genres are featured in Humbert's competing array of dominant artistic discourses. The films favored by Dolores offer stories of transformation and triumphant resolutions. In the musicals, "real singers and dancers had unreal stage careers in an essentially grief-proof sphere of existence wherefrom death and truth were banned" and where the finally triumphant showgirl is applauded by her "initially reluctant father." The underworld genre also offers a "world apart": here, crime and justice are exaggerated, with villains chased by "pathologically fearless cops." The westerns involve heroic manhood in action, surviving effortlessly various crushing physical challenges, and two versions of femininity, the "prim pretty schoolteacher" and the "gorgeous frontier bride" (171).

Apart from the escapism of all three genres, attractive to many young viewers, but even more meaningful for an abused, trapped child, each genre seems to play out possible desires of Dolores. In the case of the musical, the girl who performs and pleases others, including her father, triumphs. The musical's story line deflects the "nauseating" and "unspeakable" daily performances with her "dream dad." In the underworld, villains like her stepfather will be discovered and punished. In the westerns, two conventional and

---

31. First published in 1919 by George Pierce Baker, a Harvard professor and playwright, *Dramatic Technique* remains a classic.

attractive feminine roles—the educator and the wife—are glamorized in a safe way ("prim pretty"; "gorgeous [. . .] bride"), in stark contrast to the role of the child sex-slave that Dolores performs daily for two odd years.

Meanwhile, horror films featuring vampires or other monstrous male figures are absent from her favorites. Cinema appeals to Dolores, offering imaginary paths that lead away from her daily hell with Humbert. When she finally flees from him, Humbert believes that her interest in film and acting will take her to Hollywood in search of a screen career. Quilty wants Dolores to act in his Sadean "film." Charlotte argues that her daughter "sees herself as a starlet" (65). The Beardsley teachers delight in her talent ("She was such a perfect little nymph in the try-out" [196]). Yet, despite this dramatic talent, Dolores does not seek to be an actor, but rather is interested in realizing some of the dreams or possible identities that filmic discourse offers (e.g., to be approved by her idealized father; to have the villain stepfather punished and to escape from the underworld of his abuse; to marry someone and move to a frontier of new possibilities—her marriage to Dick Schiller and their plans to move to Alaska, an ironic 1950s frontier).

Dolores's reading materials—comic books, magazines, children's books like *Treasure Island*—also offer some insight into her character and desires, outside Humbert's censoring discourses. The comic books are the everyday stuff of childhood, showing stories through pictures and text, emphasizing humor. The comics her mother buys for camp are consumed before Dolores leaves. The language of comics, popular magazines, and movies can be heard echoing in some of Dolores's utterances: "kiddo," "it's a sketch," "dull bulb," "stinker."

The magazines, particularly one, offer a study in contrast. Dolores's usual magazines are about movie stars. In the davenport scene, a different magazine emerges, found in the hands of Humbert. Dolores takes the magazine from him and shows the image "she wished Humbert to see. Found it at last. [. . .] Dimly came into view: a surrealist painter relaxing, supine, on a beach, and near him, likewise supine, a plaster replica of the Venus di Milo, half-buried in the sand. Picture of the Week, said the legend. I whisked the whole obscene thing away" (58). Couturier suggests that the photograph is of the painter René Magritte: "Magritte made a series of paintings on this theme [of the Venus di Milo with the artist on the beach]." It is also possible that the tableau in the magazine evokes an amalgam of Salvador Dalí's painting (Venus di Milo, a perennial subject of his), Luis Buñuel's early surrealist films including *Un chien andalou* (1928), and tongue-in-cheek photographs that surrealists made of themselves. In *Lolita,* the artist posing ironically with his subject, the half-buried Venus, deflates the ethereal qualities of the muse of love, and grounds her, literally, as the artist's modern, but inanimate partner in the production of art and tourism. Dolores offers the image as something to decipher, whereas Humbert censors the "whole obscene thing." The surrealist artist's self-ironic, deconstructed attitude toward sex, love, and art challenges the seduction Humbert the "artist" is poised to enact.

As Dolores has been interested in this magazine photograph prior to the davenport scene, it stands to reason that she has been interested in its deconstruction of the happy erotic couple. For a preadolescent interested in the mysteries of sex, the photograph offers possible lessons that could allow her not to be blinded by romantic veils of seduction. If an artist poses on the beach with a plaster image of a woman, what value does an actual woman have in art and in life? As an inexperienced reader of such photographs, Dolores might miss such lessons and irony and instead consider imitating the Venus's disempowered role as object. In comic-book discourse and slippery visual stories in magazines, the child is invited to consider modes of imitation.

We can capture an impression of Dolores's interests in the discourse of children's literature, especially Stevenson's *Treasure Island* (184) and the unknown book ("some trash for young people" [286]) about a motherless girl Marion. As in much of children's literature, the children characters in these two books operate in an environment largely separate from the adult world. In the case of Stevenson's adventure tale for boys, Dolores might find empowering alternatives to the crushing limitations of an orphan coerced into daily sex with her stepfather. She keeps her prostitution earnings in this book. The female child's attempt to store her escape money in a book that glorifies male children's sunny civilized autonomy from adults shows poignantly her interpretation and investment in the book and its idealistic promises.

In the case of the book about Marion, who has lost her mother, Dolores plainly tries to interpret or make sense of her own life through Marion's story. The book suggests to Dolores an alternative reading of her mother Charlotte with whom she has had frequent rows. With her mother dead and Dolores subjected to Humbert's will, the book invites a positive reevaluation of her mother.

Both books offer stories told by the children in retrospect, suggesting to a young reader like Dolores that there might be a different future life, beyond the current life of abuse she endures with Humbert. These kinds of children's discourses are largely censored out, of course, by Humbert, for he is not using Dolores's preferred discourses to tell the story, but rather his own.

Finally, we should consider the discourse of drama or theater at the point where Dolores's horizon or character zone crosses with those of Humbert and Quilty. Her talent for acting is recognized early on, and is particularly capitalized during her lengthy cohabitation with her stepfather. She pretends to lead a "normal" family life, while she is actually suffering in an abusive relationship. Her year at Beardsley School initiates her into more formalized dramatic training, "dramatics" being one of the cornerstones of the school's education. Pratt has little serious theory to defend the school's approach: "it [participating in dramatics] is all part of the fun of being young and alive and beautiful" (196). Dolores studies a chapter on "Dialogue" in Baker's *Dramatic Technique* (198); her investment in dialogue contrasts with the lack of authentic dialogue in her life with Humbert. Further, by perfecting her dialogue skills she can learn how to deceive him.

Acting can offer an education on how to be someone else, to assume others' roles. Dolores's participation in the school play *The Enchanted Hunters* by Clare Quilty, as well as her later deception designed for her escape from Humbert, shows her active involvement in discourses that counteract the beautiful-sublime lover/beloved motifs of Humbert's story lines, while allowing him to maintain her as deceptive image. Of course, the play dupes Humbert. He is more concerned that "male parts" be "taken by female parts" (196) to avoid Dolores mixing with boys.

"The Enchanted Hunters" play is almost a *mise-en-abyme* text. Its title derives from the hotel's name; Quilty has stayed at this hotel at the time of Humbert's full induction of Dolores into his dark world. The play's story does not retell the gothic action of the hotel, but rather reverses the culpability. From the point of view of the "hunters" Humbert and Quilty, they are enchanted by the witch or nymphet "Lolita." The play reproduces the theme of acting and allusion: "a farmer's daughter who imagines herself to be a woodland witch, or Diana," using "a book on hypnotism," puts several hunters into a trance and then falls herself "under the spell of a vagabond poet" (200). The action involves the hunters as transformed, remembering "their real lives only as dreams or nightmares from which little Diana had aroused them" (201). The postmodern, self-reflective part of the play includes the seventh hunter, the Young Poet, who argues that he has invented Diana and the rest of the scene. She leads the poet out of the Perilous Forest and to the paternal farm and ends the play with a kiss "to enforce the play's profound message, namely, that mirage and reality merge in love" (201). This play poses a trap to Dolores as Diana: it seems to promise a discourse of agency and a fusion of invention and reality. The role of Diana offers Dolores the illusion of autonomy, power over the other hunters. However, if the poet (Quilty) claims authorship over her and the whole scene, then none of it can reflect

Dolores's desires. Instead, she is seduced into a role that leads her into the kiss with the poet, back at the paternal door.

Humbert's impressionistic appreciation of the play (200–1) identifies literary precedents from fairy tales such as *Hansel and Gretel* (by the Brothers Grimm), *The Sleeping Beauty* (by Hans Christian Anderson), *The Emperor's New Clothes* (Grimm), and to "echoes" of "Lenormand and Maeterlinck and various quiet British dreamers"[32] (201). The first two fairy tales portray children victimized by nightmarish women. In *Hansel and Gretel,* a wicked old witch in a sugar house is preparing to consume them. In the second fairy tale, a vengeful thirteenth wise woman locks Beauty in a trance of youth. The child in the third fairy tale points out what others cannot see, a sly allusion to the construction of a blind Humbert, the Emperor.

The influence of the British dreamers on the play *The Enchanted Hunters* has more to do with Humbert's reception (and Quilty's authorship). Humbert compares the play to artistic works that portray the child as an aestheticized erotic object of the desiring adult gaze. The difference is that *The Enchanted Hunters* does not so much concern children (neither the farmer's daughter and Diana nor the hunters are children). The desiring gaze of the adult takes place in the *narrative setting:* Dolores and Mona Dahl are child actors playing adult roles scripted and directed by adults, including Quilty.

The erotics of children playing roles for the adults' world of power—children playing at being enchanted adults—is at stake. Ironically, although Dolores's participation in the play allows her to get close to Quilty and plot an escape from her stepfather, the escape is illusory in the sense that her collaboration scripts her into the powerful realm of another desiring and abusive adult and then alone to forge her way in the world ("I have gone through much sadness and hardship" [266]; Dick Schiller thinks she "had run away from an upper-class home just to wash dishes in a diner" [271]; when Quilty kicks Dolores out of the ranch, "[t]hat winter 1949, Fay and she had found jobs. For almost two years she had—oh, just drifted, oh, doing some restaurant work in small places" [277]). The games of mimicry do not extend much of their power to Dolores in real life.

The fantasy narrative of transformation and enchantment that structures Barrie's and Carroll's works can be seen in *Lolita,* but in an ironically dialogic way. For example, in *A Kiss for Cinderella,* Jane, an impoverished London domestic, lives in squalor with four orphans during World War I; her hardship is alleviated by her rich imagination. By comparison, Dolores lives in great hardship under her monstrous stepfather, later on her own, and

---

32. I.e., J. M. Barrie and his *Peter Pan* (1904) and *A Kiss for Cinderella* (1916) and Lewis Carroll and his *Alice in Wonderland* (1865).

finally with Richard Schiller. Plays that portray escape from the real world into the enchanting fantasy of the imagination, together with a dove-tailed ending of romance with a prince charming, are appealing to readers like the young Dolores. However, the intertextual trap of *The Enchanted Hunters* is that it offers no true escape, but rather drives her deeper into the clutches of Humbert's Doppelgänger Quilty, the "American Maeterlinck" (301). Quilty's play offers Dolores the means to act as a witch, Diana (with its empowering associations with the Roman goddess Diana, patron of hunting and virginity), but she is really acting the role of the farmer's daughter acting Diana. Just as the name "Lolita" largely blots out the real name of the child Dolores, so the name Diana basically covers the name of the farmer's daughter. The real subject in both cases is lessened or reduced in value compared to the creatively empowered but fantasized "Lolita" or "Diana."

In *S/Z*, Roland Barthes has noted that "the character and the discourse are each other's accomplices: the discourse creates in the character its own accomplice" (178); discourse plays with characters, "to obtain from them a complicity which assures the uninterrupted exchange of the codes" (179). Barthes's observations complement Bakhtin's concept of dialogism. In *Lolita*, Humbert and Dolores produce competing heteroglossia. Humbert's play of discourses is more dominant and almost overwhelms those of the child.

As we have seen, Dolores's discourses of film, theater, magazines, comics, and children's literature are marshaled to answer, or counteract, those of Humbert. Her discourses offer alternative happy narratives for the child subject, casual comic-book language that excludes the adult from the child's realm, and lessons in conflict with evil, confrontation with male desire in the guise of the artist or the "enchanted hunter," imitation, performance, dialogue, and mimesis. However, his discursive strategies largely censor the child, as he himself recognizes occasionally (for example, "It was something quite special, that feeling: an oppressive, hideous constraint as if I were sitting with the small ghost of somebody I had just killed" [140]; "living as we did, she and I, in a world of total evil" [284]).

Owing to Humbert's lack of curiosity about the girl, he can only report fragments of her speech, with an emphasis on the moments of seduction, rows, sarcasm, and the final reunion. He does "not know a thing" about her mind, when he hears her discussing the solitude of death with her friend Eva Rosen, and he thinks "that quite possibly, behind the awful juvenile clichés, there was in her a garden and a twilight, and a palace gate—dim and adorable regions which happened to be lucidly and absolutely forbidden to me" (284). These new landscape tropes are still suggestive of the fairy-tale world, or even an eden and heaven. They allude to the humanity and otherness of Dolores, not to be apprehended through the predatory filter of Humbert. In this way, his victim, an absolute other, is inaccessible to him, no matter what cruelty he subjects her to.

As we have seen through the discourses of the two main characters, Humbert and Dolores, in *Lolita,* patterns of censoring can be apprehended in the textual composition and strategies. The tension between control and freedom of expression that varies from chapter to chapter, paragraph to paragraph, envelops the reader in Humbert's own battle with revelation, artistic creation, resistance, and repression. Although Humbert has chosen to write his confession and defense and supposed homage to his love object, often under supervision, the process of writing reveals that he assesses his behavior and life in complex, conflicting ways.

Writing out his story is, in a sense, a process of both self-discovery and attempted manipulation of the reader's sympathies. We tend to judge him in two ways: first, by assessing his "progress" in his narrative (as reflecting, creative narrator) and the linear order of events (as character); second, by recognizing his stubborn points of resistance and blind spots. Some readers view the example of Humbert's account of his epiphany at the abyss over the prototypical good town (307–8) as a redemptive moment; Dolores's voice is missing from the concord of children's voices. That supposed moral awakening occurs shortly after her escape from Humbert's custody. It does not explain why he then continues to search for her and desires to kill Quilty, nor why he continues to desire "nymphets."[33] Despite the event at the abyss not constituting a lasting epiphany at the time, it has a generative or extendable effect because Humbert chooses to displace that episode, inserting it into the end of his narrative. Encountered at this late juncture, the epiphany allows the reader to imagine that perhaps Humbert has gone through some incomplete awakening during the process of writing his confession in prison.

6. CONCLUSION: ETHICAL OTHERS

The act of reading this novel makes one particularly conscious of how one is forced to make judgments as one reads—judgments about oneself, Humbert, and the narrator. The fictional situation and language might tempt some

---

33. He admits that his loss of "Lolita" does not "cure" him of his "pederosis" (257). In his New York flat shared with Rita, he has a "view of gleaming children taking shower baths far below in a fountainous arbor of Central Park" (260). When he is in search of Dolores and her husband, Richard Schiller, in Coalmont, he looks for nymphets ("The ancient beast in me was casting about for some lightly clad child I might hold against me for a minute, after the killing was over and nothing mattered any more, and everything was allowed" [268]).

readers to revel in the aesthetic allusions so much that their enjoyment may distract them from ethical concerns of the human subject. Readers' reliance on an unreliable, darkly comic narrator can lure some into becoming too invested in and sympathetic with the rogue Humbert. As I have demonstrated, Humbert's intertextual ploys develop motifs of "Lolita," beneath which lies partially censored the figure of the abused child Dolores.

One of the central organizing features of *Lolita* is the open appeal to judgment; that appeal involves a challenge. Through artistic patterns, H.H. refuses to provide easy confirmation of a reader's assumptions or evaluations. His narrative comprises an active but imperfect process of self-examination, veering from astonishing egotism to grave abjection. Given his suspicious inconsistency and the gravity of his crimes, we should distrust and read against such a narrator who heavily manipulates our reception of him.

Some philosophers of ethics, such as David Parker, have recognized that a novelist must be able to set aside his or her "fixed moral identity" "in the process of imagining" (46). Parker goes on to explain that, "in so far as the novelist clings to a univocal morality, the work will tend to repress and distort all that threatens to resist it. Keats's phrases 'Negative Capability' and 'chameleon' identity indicate the fuller kind of self-recognition achieved by the greatest writers" (204). Nabokov's *Lolita* does not cling to a univocal morality, has "no moral in tow," but rather sets into play, through the imaginary character Humbert, a series of questions about the responsibility of the reader and the homodiegetic narrator.[34]

If we conceive of H.H. as a kind of novelist of his life, he presents a challenge to Parker's view of the ethical role of the artist. However, Nabokov frames Humbert ironically so that we can apprehend him as a failed artist, or not even as an artist at all, just a character mimetic of an artist. As a writer of his life, Humbert seems to be able to set aside a "fixed moral identity" and adapt a chameleon one. *Lolita* shows how the narrator is a chameleon not only in his writing, but in his actions and intent as he manages to infiltrate the suburban American home and ends up gaining a child to abuse.

H.H.'s identity is predicated upon his ability to maintain and change masks, on his ability to censor his moral self. His crisis with his Doppelgänger Clare Quilty radicalizes the lack of responsibility in the figure of the artist. Humbert and Quilty present themselves as artists. This chapter has explored Humbert's role as artistic censor of sexuality, the private artist

34. My interpretation loosely aligns with Andrews's in *Aestheticism, Nabokov, and Lolita*. Andrews notes how "Nabokov's *Lolita* fulfills [John] Dewey's conception of art" (129), the most pressing concern of which is art's impact, "an ethical impact deriving from the perceiver's energetic participation in the aesthetic experience."

preparing his work for the world's judgment. Meanwhile, Quilty serves as his foil, the public celebrated playwright. Humbert's aim to destroy Quilty is ironically self-reflective; in his desire to avenge Dolores's "abduction," his nemesis reminds him that the girl has not been cared for by a responsible protector. Quilty reminds Humbert of the lack of responsibility: "I saved her from a beastly pervert. [. . .] I'm not responsible for the rapes of others" (298); and "you were not an ideal stepfather, and I did not force your little protegée to join me. It was she made me remove her to a happier home" (301). Both men, posing as artists in different ways, cover up their abuse of Dolores. Art here seems to be an excuse for cruelty, even pleasure in cruelty.

We have noted that Humbert uses his parodically artistic text to censor and censure himself. Nabokov frames Humbert in a metanarrative of condemnation. For Humbert, confession constitutes pleasure and suffering, and writing intertextually allows a more developed experience of his life.[35] Through writing, Humbert articulates, revises, refines both his acts and judgments. In the reprehensible segments of this refined confession, he does not divulge all of his secrets—the worst details—but instead edits them out of the text, or indulges in highly aestheticized renderings of the obscene act which leave a lingering idea of harsh judgment. His editorial censoring (or omissions) helps to indicate how the sexually obscene transgression is just there, in the margins of his writing, and within the ability of the reader's apprehension and imagination of human experience. His avoidance of, yet allusion to, the naturalistic depiction of sexual processes (i.e., his avoidance of sexual actuality) alerts wary readers to the unpleasant reality being veiled in his language. Our awareness can lead us to censure Humbert and his actions.

The omission of specific details pertains to sexual taboo and obscenity. By omitting these crucial pieces of information, the subversive narrator attempts to make his narrative more aesthetically pleasurable and less censurable. Paradoxically, the provocative *Lolita* is practically defined by its lack of articulation of naturalistic portrayals of sex: "Anybody can imagine those aspects of animality," Humbert shrugs (134). This narrator, generally so verbose and precise, is carefully vague with all such troubled and reprehensible episodes (e.g., the davenport scene; the Enchanted Hunters seduction episode and its aftermath; the daily sexual use of Dolores for some two years; the payment to Dolores for sexual favors). Meanwhile, the persistently ethical reader will discover sufficient details to judge Humbert

---

35. For an expansion of this interpretation, see Michael Wood's *The Magician's Doubts: Nabokov and the Risks of Fiction*.

and his acts as being loathsome. Part of this discovery also involves noting Humbert's prudery about privacy and sexual matters: "Despite my manly looks, I am horribly timid. My romantic soul gets all clammy and shivery at the thought of running into some awful indecent unpleasantness" (53).

Humbert's artistic leanings are detailed in the text-within-a-text, his diary. This literary genre promises confession and revelation. The reproduction of his diary kept during his days in Charlotte Haze's house is an extraordinary act of memory (chapter 11, 40–55). Although the practice of diary writing is parodied, it also relays important information about his early efforts to inscribe Dolores as "Lolita." His dual pleasure of writing and self-censoring is evident in the following explanation:

> I remember the thing so exactly because I wrote it really twice. First I jotted down each entry in pencil (with many erasures and corrections) on the leaves of what is commercially known as a "typewriter tablet"; then, I copied it out with obvious abbreviations in my smallest, most satanic, hand in the little black book just mentioned. (40)

He thus describes the interdependent act of censoring in the creative process of his forbidden pleasure. He is compelled to write down repeatedly what he feels and experiences in the Haze household because he must find some way of deriving pleasure from the girl's proximity. The transcribing of his drafts into his little black book with his tiny, "most satanic" longhand[36] repeats the pleasure of the experience of writing his forbidden fantasy. The laborious, punctilious, encoded (thus decodable) methods he uses to write his diary prolong the enjoyment and enact censoring strategies ("many erasures and corrections," "abbreviations," "my smallest [. . .] hand"). Humbert's drafts indicate his desire to achieve a perfected text and to censor words or phrases which do not agree with his view of his fantasy and reality. His "obvious abbreviations" also denote his desire to conceal and reveal meaning. These weak efforts of self-effacement during the inscription of his desire do not prevent Charlotte Haze, upon discovering the diary, from apprehending the enormous danger that her husband poses to her child.

As he presents with a parodic flourish "Exhibit number two," Humbert emphasizes that we, the readers, must decide whose side we belong to. This diary is produced by him in prison for what would be the third time (another repetition of pleasure). Are we complicit with his interests and investigations or are we situated beyond the enemy line when he announces

---

36. Humbert's description of his handwriting of a censurable text remarkably complements the way in which Sade wrote *120 Days of Sodom* in prison: "in an almost microscopic hand, on a single roll of paper forty feet long" (Randall, 75).

that, like a spy, he will now regurgitate his consumed fantasy?

The *mise-en-abyme* of the diary as a 1947 exhibit within the confession emphasizes the question of implied reader by bringing the act of reading to the arena of judgment and possible seduction. I have already suggested that Humbert writes for his own pleasure, perhaps for himself as the ideal reader. The diary is not rewritten from the point of view of Humbert of 1952 a man in prison, looking back with regret and pleasure. But his diary-keeping of 1947 also seems already to imply an ideal projected reader as ambiguously complicit judge or fellow traveler who might enjoy it.

The homodiegetic judge, Charlotte Haze, is the first reader and censor of the diary. Our condemnation of her as unwary mother cannot be total (as a single mother in late 1940s America, Charlotte's tenuous hold on a "respectable" middle-class life makes her vulnerable to schemers), but her vanity and lack of care signal despair for the child. Retrospectively, Humbert seems to intend that the messages in the diary reach the narratee-judge. Humbert makes several blunders which awaken Charlotte's curiosity to discover the "old love letters" hidden in the locked drawer. For a character noted for his meticulous scheming, such gaffes can be read as an early sign of his conflicting desire to be discovered and judged harshly (as opposed to enjoying his transgressive sexual desire without detection) and to have the law applied to him, especially before it is too late, and to have that law applied by Charlotte herself.

His own writing in the form of the diary initially condemns Humbert in the eyes of a single critical reader, Charlotte. His mocking treatment of her letter of response belies the serious reception he makes of her written judgment. His later book-length expansion of that diary which largely is the text of *Lolita* addresses a wider array of potential judges and jurors. Charlotte is a flawed reader and judge, for, although she condemns her husband harshly, she suggests the possibility of reconciliation. Her outrage seems to stem more from jealousy and bruised vanity than from protectiveness for Dolores. Does Charlotte want a man so much that she would sacrifice the well-being of her daughter?[37] Or does she not read Dolores as a child anymore, but as a woman? Her references to Dolores as "my little girl" (68) and "that miserable brat" (96) indicate that Charlotte sees her daughter as a child. Charlotte's condemnation of Humbert is not firm and clear ("after a year of separation we may [. . .]"), signaling ironically further misfortune for Dolores.

Humbert's career choice of literature and literary history over psychiatry

---

37. Nabokov's portrait of Charlotte shows both sympathy for and criticism of the modern mother, and a particular awareness of the social and economic strains on a single mother. In terms of the story, Humbert stumbles upon an ideal target, the single mother.

does not preclude analysis (and judgment) from his preoccupations. His efforts in self-analysis (to read the narrative of his life) lead him to, in his words, "surrender to a sort of retrospective imagination which feeds the analytic faculty with boundless alternatives and which causes each visualized route to fork and refork without end in the maddeningly complex prospect of my past" (13). Humbert's self-criticism shows preoccupation with the law and a desire to live by it. His inner conflicts are repeatedly emphasized from early on in the confession (e.g., "law-abiding poltroon" [18]; "[t]aboos strangulated me"; "[h]e had the utmost respect for ordinary children" [19]; "my criminal craving" [23]; married life might allow him "to purge myself of my degrading and dangerous desires" [24]; "as naïve as only a pervert can be" [25]).

Some kinds of writing claim or appear to unify meaning, provide wholeness and closure, and do away with gaps. Conversely, Humbert's text, just like his exploration into the many-forked routes of his elusive past and psyche, offers a wealth of discursive fragmentation, drawing on several conflicting genres. This nonunifying structural aspect of *Lolita* conveys both richness of signification and Humbert's own meandering revelations and severe (self-)censoring. The narrator repeatedly avoids or defers assuming responsibility for (and recognition of) his deeds, despite his occasional acknowledgment and acceptance of his crimes. His quest "to fix once for all the perilous magic of nymphets" (134), stated at the crucial and sensitive point in his narrative of his and Dolores's first act of sexual intercourse, is quixotic, not even realized in writing. He does not find a way to describe her "magic." At the same juncture, he claims not to be concerned with so-called 'sex' at all: "[a]nybody can imagine those elements of animality" (134). The narrator cannot narrate that "magic" because the effect would be grotesque. The various fragments of information or observation show how H.H. must vigilantly and artistically censor in order to derive signifying pleasure and a lasting work of art from his obscene fantasy and transgression: "The beastly and beautiful merged at one point, and it is that borderline I would like to fix, and I feel I fail to do so utterly. Why?" (135).

In a striking screen of censoring of sexual conquest, Humbert, in place of recounting directly a rape scene, explains his abuse of Dolores by exotic analogies of incongruous pairs. He catalogues fragments of fantasized imagery of a mural that he might have painted for the hotel's dining room (134–35). For example, a sultan, "his face expressing great agony," "help[s]" the "callypygean slave child to climb a column of onyx." Such an image remains ambiguous in ethical terms: while the sultan and slave child pair clearly indicates inequality, the sultan's "agony" and his "help" superficially seem to reduce the sultan's supremacy. Yet, as code words for his orgasm (agony) and abuse of a child (help to scale something far beyond the means of the child), Humbert's fantasy mural would not seem to entail any moral transformation or awakening but rather a desire to reinscribe his act in exotically erotic terms. However, his imaginary mural also includes damning points of contrast, and thus indications of some condemnation of his acts: the mural would have included fragments of Dolores's childhood world, within and beyond the influence of Humbert ("juke boxes"; "camp activities [. . .] in the lakeside sun"; "poplars, apples, a suburban Sunday" (an oblique reference to his earlier "seduction" of Dolores one Sunday morning on the davenport).

Later, H.H. relinquishes this aim of "fixing" the nymphet's magic, for his recounting of the story seems to furnish him with more aspects of the reality of his life with Dolores Haze than with his fantasy of them. The painful shifts in memory and perspective allow us to glimpse through his censoring the actuality of a grotesque, incongruous pair and the pain caused through his cruelty. Richard Rorty's analysis of the cruel narrator uncovers Humbert's exaggerated indifference to others. Through this indifference to much of the pain felt by others, especially Dolores, Humbert's narrative excludes authentic notes of love and compassion. It is not necessary to portray pain directly; in an ethical act, we can also imagine it. Nabokov encourages us to engage in this ethical activity of imagining the pain of the other, but from the difficult vantage point of the one who inflicts the pain.

Aligned awkwardly with John Ray, Jr., Ph.D. and his cousin, the lawyer Clark, we as readers are left the task of judgment. The most central of the potential homodiegetic readers of *Lolita* are not available (i.e., the main characters have all died). *Lolita* consumes the characters it engenders. When we are first-time readers, our judgment becomes reinforced by our gradual and retrospective awareness that the main characters (Dolores, Charlotte, Quilty, Humbert) have died in some tragic or premature way by or around the time of Humbert's completion of the manuscript. The confession is intended possibly to serve as his defense at a trial; neither he nor Dolores Schiller would live long enough for such a trial.

Death is emplotted in the narrative of *Lolita* to signify censoring of the failed or false artist. Literary death often provokes judgment of the dead one or of the one who contributed to that death. A series of women (Humbert's mother, Annabel, Valeria, Charlotte) dies in accidental ways which nevertheless symbolically connect to Humbert. Humbert comes closest to enacting that symbolic role of murdering a woman in his dealings with Charlotte, prompting readers to condemn his evil intentions. H.H. recoils from an opportune moment to drown Charlotte. Yet the residue from Humbert's murderous plans lasts in the effect that a proto-incestuous crime has been committed. Dolores asks about her "murdered mommy," blaming him for the accident.

That accident has after all brought about a strange inversion of an Oedipal wish fulfillment. The parody of incest runs as follows: instead of the male infant's desire to kill the father and have the mother, in *Lolita* it is the (step)father who "kills" the mother in order to have the female child. Dolores's orphaned state is emphasized. In their cross-country trips, Humbert superstitiously avoids her place of birth, the place where the original Haze family was once intact. Dolores's own death is doubled, in that she and her newborn die: the destruction of this child is complete through her premature ruin and fatal attempt to bring new life, another girl, into the world. The enchantment, bride-lover, and fairy-tale motifs, with their narratives ending in safety from impending disaster, contrast ironically with the deglamorized death of Mrs. Richard F. Schiller in Gray Star, an outpost in the "remotest Northwest" (4), a conclusion noted at the novel's outset.

If the death of women and female children signal a negation of beauty, life, and goodness, then Humbert's role in these deaths might be that of a censor. The culminating though anticlimactic murder of Quilty fixes H.H. as a murderer. He interrogates, wrestles, and kills his despised, grotesque double. Before writing his confessional narrative as an act of judgment, self-discovery, and artistic censoring of sexuality, Humbert uses murder as an act of censoring judgment on a fellow pervert. Furthermore, death functions as a censoring motif because Humbert, in setting the conditions for the publication of his confession on the premise of his and Dolly Schiller's death, predicates the entire exercise of our reception of his confession on their absence by death from the worldly scene of transgression.

H.H.'s realm of language comes to imprison and condemn him. Language as the *habitus* of the self turns out not to be a trustworthy refuge of uncritical pleasure and nostalgic memory. Humbert insists in his text on pleasure and fantasy to have meaning. Ironically, his pleasure and fantasy resonate most strongly in reference to his crimes. His fantasy of the nymphet forecloses the recognition of ordinary little girls. The nymphet is supposedly a primarily sexual being. Her physical beauty, precocious flirtations with older men, and her vulgar taste combine to feed into the pedophile's fantasy of a knowing, demon prostitute disguised as innocent child. The nymphet image is at heart the fantasy of the unattainable, pure woman who secretly really wants sex. She is unattainable because she is a child and should not be sexually available for an adult.

Projecting that fantasy is the desiring male subject, posing disingenuously as the artist. He creatively imagines and perceives a secretly desiring and knowing other. In order to produce such a fantasy as "Lolita" Humbert must persistently confront himself as the grotesque thing that this child must desire. His many deprecating references to himself (e.g., "Humbert the Wounded Spider") reveal a heightened, yet ironic awareness of his degraded or base self-image and motivations. Yet, as the recounting of his story lengthens and gains in detail, analysis, and retrospection, the reader can become increasingly aware of the attempts of foreclosing obscene acts and moments. H.H.'s artistic deployment of censoring of the sexual subject and an ecstatic experience of confession, might appear designed to deflect harsh judgment. But, ultimately, the text *Lolita*'s signification derives from its originator's will to be judged. His many discursive subterfuges and acts of censoring of the child Dolores Haze with the fantasized "Lolita" (disavowal, resistance, ironic devices such as parody and doubling, digressions, etc.) *add* to the meaning of his character-narrator and lend gravity to the baseness of his acts. In these ways, Nabokov's novel appeals to readers to activate our powers of judgment, to transcend the focalization of the rogue character-narrator Humbert, and to gain a critical view of the censoring patterns enacted in his narrative that seek to cover up the girl's character zone and, with it, the other as the abused child Dolores.

4

The Masochistic Pleasure of Censoring Modes of Fantasy

ALIENATION, CANCER, AND JUDGMENT IN *TIEMPO DE SILENCIO*

In Luis Martín-Santos's *Tiempo de silencio* (*Time of Silence*) [1961], the protagonist Pedro fantasizes about negated modes of sexuality by using censoring strategies of production (such as displacement, disavowal, condensation).[1] His crisis and alienated perspective of himself and others dramatize sexuality as a potentially positive, reproductive, or sensually pleasing element that becomes negatively mired by imagery and instances of disease, pain, cutting, death, and exile. Moreover, these censoring motifs are often associated with the deficiencies of contemporary Spanish life. While this novel's plot, characterization, and ironic and modernist narrative modes and styles depart from the postwar trend of the *novela social*, Martín-Santos retains a social consciousness or Sartrean *engagement* (*compromiso*) by integrating Pedro's personal crises into the specific historical context of 1949 Madrid. Pedro finds erotic satisfaction or masochistic pleasure in producing censoring images which emphasize disease, pain, suffering, castration, and ecstasy. As a failed critic of others and society, he, along with the omniscient narrator, incorporates dominant Spanish fictions and ideological codes in his interior monologues and other sections of the

---

1. All translations of quotations from this novel and other sources in Spanish are mine unless otherwise indicated. I have consulted the English *Time of Silence* translated by George Leeson, but it contains too many errors and inaccuracies for quotation purposes.

narrative. But he does not master these fictions and codes outwardly in his everyday life, nor achieve his worldly goals of making a career. Pedro and the sexuality portrayed both receive censoring, negating stylistic and plot treatment. Surrendering to a kind of Spanish-inflected fatalism, this protagonist denies himself agency, opting ultimately for a defeatist enjoyment of a passive, masochistic state of being.[2] The narrative discourse reflects the complication of agency. Pedro's voice is one part of the novel's discourse, and he is not the first-person narrator of his own story. His character zone reaches the other segments and characters of the novel. This multilayered presentation of the failed hero and negated sexuality suggests a profound social and political criticism of Franco's Spain. The novel's juxtaposition of sexual fantasy, medical research, disease, moral and criminal transgressions (e.g., abortion, prostitution, incest, premarital sexual relations, murder) prompts the reader to consider ethical judgments or evaluations.

The publication of this novel signaled an initial "liberalizing" shift in Spain's censorship policy in the early 1960s. The censored editions between 1961 and 1966 did not prevent readers from appreciating the novel's pervasive and varied aspects of sexuality and its sophisticated, critical treatment of social, artistic, philosophical, and psychological questions. The editorial restorations of 1966 (most notably the two brothel scenes) and those of subsequent years allow a heightened awareness of the novel's potential significance. In this chapter, I discuss how *Tiempo de silencio* elaborates artistically motifs of censoring sexuality.[3]

---

2. Fatalism is a common feature in Spanish literature since the Middle Ages: one is unable to control one's own destiny. This motif takes on various political, religious, and moral nuances, but by the modern era there is an additional idea that simply "being Spanish" predetermines one's outcome in life. The motif is further Hispanicized by the representation of engrained national and regional customs, traditions, and sets of beliefs. For example, in *Tiempo de silencio,* when Pedro and Dorita dance at the feria, they seem to be caught in a pattern of acts that they cannot avoid performing, which lead to her stabbing.

3. In my discussion, if not otherwise indicated, I use the "edición definitiva"'definitive edition' of 1980 (reprinted in 1993). The 1966 and 1971 editions are basically identical. In 1966, most of the censored passages were restored.

Where necessary in this chapter, I indicate some differences in editions. The manuscript was first reviewed by the censor several times in 1961, resulting in a very late approval for publication (November 1961). I consulted the manuscript in the archive, the censor's reports, and requirements for changes, and I compared this early censorship with the resulting editions. I was not able to locate a copy of a 1961 edition; the 1962 edition bears the same censorship as recommended in the archive file, so it can be assumed that the first edition of November or December 1961 is the same as the edition of 1962. From 1961 to 1965, the editions show the more rigorous early censorship. In 1966, after the editor's appeals made in 1965 to the censor, a new, much less censored edition was published. This edition continued to be used through 1971 and until 1980.

The "definitive edition" of 1980 (and subsequent reprints) is longer in pagination, but does not seem to restore any previously censored passages according to my comparison of segments. The difference in length can be accounted for in the change of formatting to improve readability

Sexuality informs a multitude of problems and desires of the non-hero Pedro and those around him. Sexual reference is made in scientific, intertextual, metaphorical, and ironic language and imagery. Martín-Santos presents sexuality as a source of knowledge and research, even while some of that knowledge is ultimately either unknowable or forbidden. This orientation toward sexuality is expressed by the narrators, especially by Pedro and the third-person narrator, the two most prominent voices, but also by key character-narrators such as the pension owner ("*la vieja*" [the old woman]) and Cartucho, for whom sexual forces and strategies motivate their actions and preoccupy their inner thoughts. Feminine sexuality and man's desire for woman are largely de-etherealized. In strong contrast to the dominant ideological idealization of the wholesome Spanish Catholic woman in Franco's Spain, the novel's female characters' sexuality is characterized by prostitution, economic and class factors, and medical, biological, philosophical, literary, religious, and anthropological discourses. The prostitution motif is not limited to doña Luisa's brothel, but also extends to the realms of the pension owner and the shanty town. This pessimistic approach to feminine sexuality emphasizes the extent to which human relations in Spain are debased for interests of money, status, and survival.

Given that the novel focuses on the elaborately reported, conflicting inner thoughts and wishes of Pedro and his dubious moral conduct, readers are engaged to judge the contents of the novel critically, to activate their sense of ethics, and to find sources of meaning or knowledge in the book. In this way, *Tiempo de silencio* invites readers to question social and individual dilemmas and desires which are defined by alienation. The

---

(fewer words on a page). The first page of the definitive edition has twenty-four lines whereas the 1971 edition (and others between 1966 and 1979) has thirty-one. The first section of the 1980 edition runs from page 7 to 15; in the 1971, it runs from page 7 to 13. This formatting accounts for the growth in pagination (1971 edition runs from page 7 to 240; 1981 edition from page 7 to 295). According to my comparisons of the texts, the "definitive edition" does not include additions from a manuscript or notes that were never submitted to the censor.

Chapter 4 is informed by my comparisons of the 1962, 1966, 1971, 1980 [1993] editions as well as the manuscript and censor's instructions from the file on Martín-Santos at the Archivo General. Because this is an interpretative study of the whole novel (with an awareness of the passages that did offend the Francoist censor) and not a historical analysis of the manuscript and its editions, I am not dividing this chapter into separate discussions of the censored, less censored, and uncensored editions.

For a compact study of the comparison of the manuscript and editions, see Ronald Rapin's article. His findings generally coincide with mine. He notes translator Leeson's omission of certain passages, especially sexually explicit lines, indicating a possible additional censorship outside Spain. I disagree with some of Rapin's interpretations of the Spanish editions. In this chapter, I maintain that, although the early 1961 censorship damaged some signification of the editions from 1962 to 1965, the damage was not so grave as to cause the novel to "fail to capture much of the ambience and [. . .] much of Martín-Santos' criticism of the socio-economic situation" (Rapin, 242).

novel does not use overly didactic or erotic modes of expression, both of which would have invited a heavier treatment by the censor (if not outright banning), and would have shifted the values from the ethical to the propagandistic or sensual.

1. CRITICAL SYNOPSIS

In Madrid in the autumn of 1949, Pedro, a graduate student of oncology, has just discovered that his supply of experimental mice, specially imported from the United States with a strain of cancer, has expired. In a quest for replacement black-market mice raised by the laboratory's former employee Muecas, Pedro and his lab assistant Amador meet Muecas at his home in the slums on the city's outskirts. There Muecas breeds the mice with the help of his two teenage daughters (one named Florita) and wife, Encarna (or Ricarda). Nothing is clearly resolved at this meeting.

Pedro, a middle-class young man from out of town with pretensions and ambitions, lives in a shabby pension run by a conniving old woman (*la vieja*) along with her daughter Dora and granddaughter Dorita. The old woman is intriguing to entrap the naïve student into marrying Dorita and thereby guarantee all three women some kind of decent life through his future status as a doctor and perhaps researcher. Pedro is well aware that the beautiful but vapid Dorita is enticing. He goes out one Saturday night on a drinking spree with his distinctly upper-class friend, Matías. The young men's night out sets the stage for their reflections on art and life, such as their exchange with a German-Jewish neo-expressionist painter, and ends with an unconsummated visit to doña Luisa's brothel.[4] Pedro staggers home and succumbs to his temptation to have sexual relations with Dorita, whose bedroom strategically neighbors his. *La vieja,* who has made certain to stay awake, greets Pedro in the hall when he returns to his own bedroom, thus ensuring an engagement of obligation.

That same night or early morning (now Sunday), while Pedro meditates drunkenly in his own room, he is summoned by Muecas to come to the aid of his fatally hemorrhaging daughter, Florita, made pregnant by him. Muecas and a kind of medicine man, *el mago* (the magician), have botched an abortion. Ostensibly owing to the late hour and his drunken state, Pedro, assisted by Amador, agrees to try to remedy the disaster by performing an abortion on the virtually dead girl, but the "scraping" is done in vain. Flo-

---

4. Palley finds several comparisons to make between *Tiempo de silencio* and *Ulysses*, including noting a resemblance between the two novels' brothel scenes.

rita is dead, and Pedro leaves the scene without issuing a death certificate or summoning any authorities.

On the Sunday night, Pedro visits Matías at his luxurious home, meets and is attracted to the beautiful Matilde, Matías's mother, and admires Matías's reproduction of painter Francisco Goya's *El Aquelarre o El Gran Buco* (*Witches' Sabbath or The Great He-Goat*) (1797–1798).[5] On the Monday night, Pedro and Matías attend a lecture given by a famous philosopher, "el Maestro" (the Master, modeled parodically on Ortega y Gasset and Goya's "gran buco"), and the subsequent soirée hosted by Matilde.

Pedro is then pursued by the police, who are investigating the cause of Florita's death, and by Cartucho, her jealous lover (who believes that Pedro has been both Florita's lover and murderer). Pedro takes refuge at doña Luisa's brothel, but the police soon find him there by following Matías. The police interrogate Pedro and keep him in prison on suspicion of murder until Encarna tells the police categorically that he did not kill her daughter. He is released from prison, but the institute's director dismisses him for the disgraceful involvement in the assisted abortion. Cornered into an engagement with Dorita, Pedro takes his fiancée out with her mother to an open-air fair where Cartucho manages to stab Dorita fatally, in mistaken revenge for Florita's death. After taking his civil servant exams, Pedro travels out of Madrid and toward an undemanding, mediocre life as a village doctor.

2. ALIENATION AND SEXUALITY UNDER THE SCALPEL

In *Tiempo de silencio,* Pedro's alienation dramatizes censoring. His inner monologues and his actions are framed within an ironic narrative of an omniscient third-person narrator. Pedro's character exudes social estrangement and self-estrangement. As the solitary subject of the middle class, he has no social peers in the novel's setting and action, and his encounters with

---

5. In a disorienting linguistic turn, the novel cites the painting's title in French; it also provides in French ("Musée Lázaro") the original painting's location in Madrid. This museum (Museo Lázaro Galdiano) still houses this Goya painting, among many others. The *Aquelarre* of 1797–1798 is a brighter version of the same theme carried out more than twenty years later in Goya's "black paintings" at the Museo del Prado (*Aquelarre o El gran buco,* 1821–1823).

For Pedro and Matías in 1949 Madrid, the Museo Lázaro Galdiano would have been a precious novelty in a relative cultural desert, for the collector José Lázaro Galdiano died only two years earlier in 1947, and legated his rich collection to the state as a foundation (see the foundation's Website for the history and views of the collection: www.flg.es). By buying the painting's reproduction and admiring it in his room, Matías shows some depth of culture and education.

those from other classes and callings emphasize uncomfortable, and even alarming, differences in values, conduct, and states of being. Estrangement and "making strange" are also stylistic elements of the narrative, especially its use of irony. For example, Pedro's inner thoughts are organized along a rhetorical path of a university student's logic: "Deseando: Haber vivido algo, haber encontrado una mujer, haber sido capaz de abandonarse como otros se abondonan. Deseando: No estar solo, estar en color humano, ceñido de una carne aterciopelada, deseado por un espíritu próximo. [. . .] Temiendo: Nunca llegaré a saber vivir, siempre me quedaré al margen" (112) (Desiring: To have lived something, to have found a woman, to have been capable of abandoning oneself as others abandon themselves. Desiring: Not to be alone, to be in human warmth, pressed against a velvety skin, desired by a kindred spirit. [. . .] Fearing: I will never get to know how to live, I'll always remain on the margin).

In this scene, each assertion or meditation is introduced by a depersonalized gerund structuring the thoughts into semimock inductive and deductive reasoning: for example, "Afirmando," "Interrogando," "Reflexivo-recordante," "Incisivo-perdonador," "Acusador-disoluto," "Conclusivo" (112) (Affirming, Interrogating, Reflexive-remembering, Incisive-forgiving, Accusative-dissolute, Conclusive). The omniscient narrator might ridicule the student's desires and his education, as well as mock reason's inability to treat such psychic states as desire and alienation. Pedro tries to overcome his alienation ("siempre me quedaré al margen") by combining fantasies about his research and women's sexuality. But the unpleasant, violent, or blood-related aspects of cancer research and women's sexuality create a censoring fantasy of pain, distancing, and disavowal. He fantasizes about censoring his desires.

His character (his thoughts and his actions in the plot), the narrative oscillations among the omniscient narrator and character-narrators and place of action (the chronological sequencing of the novel remains fairly coherent), and irony all heighten his lack of engagement or agency (while not taking that lack as a given). The narrative modes and ironic devices provide fundamental foci for the reader to make critical judgments about the action, characters, and ideas presented in the novel, just as the seemingly paradoxical title prompts an assessment of its appropriateness.[6]

6. For example, how can one write about a time of silence, a time in which there is no sound, no speech, and thus no words to record? Or, how can one express silence, when silence can imply an absence of expression, a lack, a void? Does "silence" mean censorship, death, repression? In psychoanalysis, an analysand's silence usually signifies the moment when he has reached an area of resistance and cannot (or does not want to) find words to articulate the repressed thing. Is that time of silence not the moment when the subject confronts his own sense of censorship on the

The novel establishes an inner discursive logic of several zones of silence: Pedro's cancer research, the cancer that silently waits to be discovered; the shanty town and its mysterious ways of life (Muecas's ability to raise the laboratory mice; the unexplained pregnancy and incest; the heavy segregation and disparity of power in gender relations; the people's pathetic ingenuity in the face of crushing poverty); the pension and the triad of la dueña, her daughter Dora, and her granddaughter Dorita as they attempt to entrap Pedro ("un silencio prolongado envolvía a los cuatro actores del drama" [49] [a prolonged silence enclosed the four actors of the drama]; "[d]esde este silencio los sobreentendidos de las tres mujeres se volvían más claramente perceptibles para Pedro, como si las tres parcas hablaran musitando lo que el hilo de su vida significaba" [from this silence the implicit exchanges of the three women became more clearly perceptible to Pedro, as though the three Parcae were talking, musing over what the thread of his life signified]); the brothel and the unspoken and silent rituals of election ("El silencio que envolvía la escena, las reducía a pesar de su objetividad palpable y olible a un amenazante aspecto de fantasmas prestos a desvanescerse" [102–3] [The silence enclosing the scene reduced them, despite their palpable and smellable objectivity, to an threatening appearance of phantasms about to disappear]) and the silent understanding between the police and brothel owners; the silence that characterizes Encarna's lack of narrative voice, despite her importance in the plot, and her new painful silence after the autopsy of her daughter (239); and so on.

Alienation connotes the separation from oneself or from others, one's heightened sense of otherness or of being different or disassociated from the rest. In Marxist terms, alienation implies the worker's lack of involvement in the means and results of his labor or production. In loosely existentialist terms, alienation can be taken as the separation of the individual from his society, his sense of *mauvaise foi* or even nausea toward himself and the people around him.[7] In the scenes involving the German artist and the Ortega y Gasset character[8] (among others), *Tiempo de silencio* pursues the problems of the subject's (Pedro's) conflicting sense of logical or rational perception.[9] Knowledge or assessment of an object depends on one's posi-

---

frontier of the unconscious?

While there are many possible significations of silence in the novel, the word appears to have few positive connotations such as tranquility, serenity, purity, a higher state of consciousness gained through meditation.

7. See Schacht and "Alienation."

8. See Pérez-Magallón for a detailed discussion of the Ortega character and his symbolic function as an emissary of the failure of the Spanish intellectual world.

9. With this character, Martín-Santos alludes to the evolution in German philosophy of the concept of alienation, starting with Hegel and on to Feuerbach, Marx, and Heidegger. Lacan and

tion. In Lacanian terms, one's position can be sensed as unclear because of one's awareness of the Cartesian limitations beyond which lie the Real and the barred subject (or subject as lack). Although alienation is popularly perceived to be a negative state of being, in Lacan and elsewhere it is seen as a necessary state for the subject's entry into the Symbolic and thus into language and being in the world.

The alienation developed in *Tiempo de silencio* is an interplay of powerlessness, meaninglessness, social isolation, normlessness, and self-estrangement. Pedro seems to be trapped in his alienation, propelled by events and his repressed impulses instead of taking clear decisions and actions. He generously applies negating condemnation of certain social conditions and practices while failing to be adequately critical of his own shortcomings. He also fails to achieve a sustained dialogue or relationship with the various people whom he encounters. To compensate for his lack, the novel incorporates these other characters in dialogue, monologue, or focalizations. His language is usually arrested in an interiorized space, framed by the ironic omniscient narrator. Indeed, his only long verbal communication occurs when a police detective is manipulating him for a confession of guilt. In a gush of words not unlike a Catholic confession, Pedro takes his chance to explain to a willing listener the details of his research project and how his plans got entangled in Muecas's world.

Pedro's alienation and lack of ability to overcome it provide a basic motivating force of events and character in the novel. This trend is modified by the novel's repeated references to fate or destiny, a traditional topos of Spanish literature. The idea of inevitability and lack of agency informs negatively Pedro's goal to excel at medical research. Chance and destiny oppose conventional scientific deductive practices. The mystic or reactionary Spanish tendency to attribute occurrences and states of being to fate, destiny, and chance counterweighs a more modern outlook of possibility and responsibility. Pedro's alienation stems from a deep conflict between his sexual desire and sense of self. His cancer research is presented as a personal epistemic project, an impulse to know and discover, and cloaks a more primal drive to acquire sexual knowledge. His thoughts often shift their emphasis from the scientific to the sexual, and often merge the two streams into an ironic, hyperscientific, literary, or hyperbolic way.

Martín-Santos share a strong interest in this stream of philosophy. Martín-Santos's philosophical interests include Dilthey, Jaspers, Sartre, Marx. See, for example, his *Libertad, temporalidad y transferencia en el psicoanálisis existencial: Para una fenomenología de la cura psicoanalítica* (1964 and 1975) and *Teoría marxista de la revolución* (1977). For a comparison of Martín-Santos's psychiatric and philosophical works and his fiction, see especially Labanyi's *Ironía e historia en* Tiempo de silencio (83–116).

The Masochistic Pleasure of Censoring Modes of Fantasy ▪ 169

For example, in the novel's opening interior monologue, he laments the expiration of his precious supply of imported mice and considers their special origin:

> Hábilmente seleccionada a través de las familias de ratones autopsiados, hasta descubrir el pequeño tumor inguinal y en él implantada la misteriosa muerte espontánea destructora no sólo de ratones. Las rubias mideluésticas mozas con proteína abundante durante el período de gestación de sus madres de origen sueco o sajón y en la posterior lactancia y escolaridad. [...] Traídos del Illinois nativo los ratones—machos y hembras—separados los sexos para evitar coitos supernumerarios no controlados. Con provocación de embarazo bien reglada. (9–10)

> Skillfully selected across the families of autopsied mice, until the little inguinal tumor is discovered and in it implanted the mysterious, spontaneous death, destructive not only to mice. The blond Midwestern girls with abundant protein during the gestation period of their mothers of Swedish or Saxon origin and in the lactation and school years [...]. Brought from their native Illinois the mice—males and females—the sexes separated in order to avoid uncontrolled supernumerary coitus. With provocation of well-regulated pregnancy.

This passage is disorienting because Pedro unexpectedly couples scientific and extrascientific interests (tumors, cancer, mice, reproduction versus blond Midwestern girls and their mothers and reproduction). We can note, too, the grammatical dependence on past participles, passive and disjointed subjects, and incomplete sentences and fragments. This style conveys a choppy stream of consciousness of the character's associative thoughts. Pedro's mind expresses itself in this associative, fragmented form, reflecting the incompleteness, hesitance, passivity, resistance of his later thoughts, problematic reasoning, and actions. While the setting is a laboratory for cancerous mitosis, the narrative focus is on an inner laboratory of dramatic, sexually charged reflections of the American Midwestern mice with tumors, cancer, women, fertility and reproduction, and death.

Pedro's recurring preoccupation with sexual reproduction, ruled and unruly,[10] is cloaked in sarcasm and feigned indifference as he manages to associate his cancer research with his sexual digressions. After this opening scene, Pedro often continues to view women derisively, defensively, and

---

10. Scientific or clinical terms of control and regulation like "provocación" (from the preceding quotation) contain an erotic double meaning. Provocación in a sexual context indicates seduction or aggression (i.e., unruly sexuality).

with a conflicted aggression and lust on the one hand and on the other a desire for a sensually spiritual communion ("deseado por un espíritu próximo") or soul mate at the end of his chosen path ("otra clase de mujer, de la que lo importante no será ya la exuberancia elemental y cíclica, sino la lucidez libre y decidida" [116] [a woman of another order, for whom what is important is not some cyclical, elemental exuberance, but rather a free and decided lucidity]). In the opening laboratory scene and elsewhere, he sometimes tries to express dispassionate thoughts that he thinks a worldly man of learning should think.

Just as he meditates on blond virgins of the Midwest (as well as their older counterparts whose "fresh flesh" is also destroyed by the cancerous mitosis he is trying to study[11]), so does he remain fascinated by the virginal Dorita (whose blondness and "juiciness" ["lánguida y jugosa"] attach to his fantasy about faded foreign virgins who are "never sexually satisfied"). Dorita is compared to a flower more than once (e.g., "cuerpo joven siempre floreciente" [ever-flowering young body]), and Pedro the invading fly ("No debe caer en esta flor entreabierta como una mosca y pringarse las patitas" [116] [He should not fall on this half-opened flower like a fly and dip his little feet]).

Such passages emphasize Pedro's negating fascination with reproduction, fertility, and planned prevention of coitus. The cancer of the groin which he studies seems to attack women alone, allowing him to dwell on their sexual attributes and possibilities. The mention of exquisitely autopsied mice foreshadows Pedro's dual fantasy of castration and of finding the inguinal cancer transmitted to Florita by way of autopsy, an operation he actually approximates when he later performs the abortion on her. Such a miraculous discovery of cancerous contamination would lead to Pedro excelling in his research, perhaps leading one day to the Nobel Prize.[12] He models himself after histologist Santiago Ramón y Cajal, the then sole Spanish Nobel recipient for scientific achievement. The study of organic

---

11. "[E]sa mitosis torpe que crece y destruye, igual aquí que en el Illinois nativo, las carnes frescas de las todavía menopáusicas damas, cuya sangre periódicamente emitida no es vida sino engaño, engaño" (8) ([T]hat sluggish mitosis that grows and destroys, the same as here as in its native Illinois, the fresh flesh of the already menopausal ladies, whose periodically emitted blood is not life but rather deception, deception).

12. After the writing of this novel, the 1960s saw a succession of progress in cancer research, including the discovery of the viral transmission of some cancers. Fifteen percent or less of all cancer is hereditary; most forms of cancer have environmental causes. For these overviews of cancer, see "Cancer" in *Britannica Online*.

Still, there is a curious node of relations in the origin of cancer that is reflected in Pedro's merging of thoughts about environmental and hereditary factors. The emphasis on hereditary factors stems from an ingrained Spanish attitude toward fate or inevitability and cultural determinism via hereditary transmission.

tissue is closely related to oncology. Pedro follows the Francoist regime's promotion of Ramón y Cajal almost to the letter.[13]

Aside from the autopsy-abortion association, the description of the family of mice provides other imaginary and literal links to Muecas and his family. Pedro's pursuit of the mice into the shantytown leads him to a family who do not sleep separately like the Illinois mice. The result for the Muecas family is incest, Florita's unwanted pregnancy by her father. The solitary observer, Pedro is fascinated with the strength of hereditary factors, blood lines, ethnic differences. Impoverished families like Muecas's seem to keep some secret of fertility. Muecas manages to raise the lab mice possibly by using the female body heat of the women in the family. While Pedro's preoccupation should be cancer, he is as fascinated by sexual reproduction.

Recurrent references to blood seep into several discrete areas of the narrative, which have in common the female body—virginity, menstruation and menopause, abortion, autopsy, and death. While these situations or states of being refer to different women, for Pedro, the images and associations often become mixed or cross-referenced; one experience or fantasy is fused onto another. A prominent example of this process of fusion or bleeding is found in the almost contiguous and closely chronological episodes of Pedro's sexual congress with Dorita and his operation on Florita early Sunday morning. While there is no direct consequential relationship between these two events except chronology and the coincidence of the young women's similar names and ages, for Pedro's guilty mind there is much more at stake. His ostensible rape of a virgin ("mujer [. . .] siempre vigilante, aun en la hora de la violación en la alta madrugada a manos de un borracho irresoluto" [117] [woman, ever vigilant, even at the hour of rape in the wee hours by an irresolute drunk]) mirrors ironically his performance of a belated abortion on another young woman. He sees both women as objects of study—sexual exploration and cancer research. Also, an imaginary sense of causation and remedy is at play: phantasmatically he seeks to undo with Florita (repair the damage of an abortion) what he has done with Dorita (possibly impregnated her). The fact disclosed later that Dorita will die a bloody death by the less surgical knife of Cartucho eerily completes a series of images associated with Pedro's guilty feelings about blood, female sexuality, and ambition.

Pedro's anxious obsession with virginal-siren types is not the only preoccupation with women. Mature women—from the "first and second gen-

---

13. In a way different than mine, Pratt's fine book explores both the writing of Ramón y Cajal and his significance in *Tiempo de silencio*.

erations" of the pension and doña Luisa to Matilde (Matías's mother), and to a lesser extent Ricarda—also compete for his attention, and the novel's microcosmic space offers this variety of feminine subjects, ranging in class and age. Altogether, most of the women who touch on Pedro's life suggest mystery and secret knowledge, power, fertility, seduction and betrayal, and possible pleasure at the cost of pain, contamination, and degradation.

3. CENSORING STRATEGIES IN SPANISH MASOCHISM

The male masochist in twentieth-century European literature as an ironic hero rejects the dominant ideology in favor of pursuing his own punitive course. Suzanne Stewart and Kaja Silverman, among other scholars, observe the portrayal of the masochistic male subject in twentieth-century literature and film. Freud suggested the masochistic tendencies may be more prominent in men than women ("Economic Problem of Masochism"). For Freud and later Deleuze, the male masochist does not necessarily surrender all power as he submits to pain. They argue that the masochist operates the scene of his painful submission, somewhat like playing both the director and lead actor in a play.

Masochism can be seen conceptually elaborated in art. Over the centuries, Spanish art and literature often celebrate suffering and martyrdom, aligning with an austerely grandiose strain of Spanish Catholicism, as evidenced in the style and taste of Philip II and depictions of the Inquisition, stages of martyrdom, and the crucifixion. In these portrayals, the (male) body suffers painful punishment from worldly social forces. Martín-Santos makes use of these Spanish aesthetic traditions and emphasizes the masochistic psychic and symbolic forces at play in the novel's characters, particularly Pedro. Pedro positions himself increasingly as a mock Spanish martyr or masochist, who orchestrates in part his own downfall and thus aligns himself with a dominant discourse of Spanish fatalism, failure, and austerity.

Pedro is not a masochist strictly along the lines of Severin in Leopold von Sacher-Masoch's *Venus in Furs,* who worships Wanda and begs her to act as his dominatrix in an extended play of his fantasy. The fantasy of Pedro's punishments extends into his professional goals and values. He submits himself to female power. He is manipulated by "las diosas" (the goddesses) of the pension; he entrusts himself briefly to doña Luisa, the brothel madam; and he is dominated by erotic yearnings for sirens. His thoughts and actions cohere to some degree with those of a moral masochist.

In the novel's final episode, Pedro's interior monologue as he leaves Madrid on the train for the provinces, two examples of censored passages demonstrate Pedro's preoccupation with female sexuality and state as the defeated-triumphant male subject. His only reference to either of his parents comes at the end of the novel, "la puta que me parió" (240) (the whore who gave birth to me),[14] and indicates his self-conception as base being.

As moral masochist, Pedro imagines the exalted scenes of his defeat in the village where he will practice medicine. The scenes position him both as a sufferer (no longer a medical researcher; exiled to the province) and as erotically enjoying his new position as doctor. For example, he imagines a patient in his future practice in the village: she will be female, pretty, will politely thank him, and will spread the good word about the new doctor, and he will diagnose her with having "prurito de ano" (pruritus of the anus). This example demonstrates his habitual association of (attractive) women with medical conditions involving an erogenous zone. His moral masochism allows him small triumphs of conquest.

Pedro frequently uses medical terminology and practice to censor or sanitize his thoughts, allowing him to fantasize without articulating directly his desires.[15] The subterfuge is so pervasive that it becomes an activity of erotic pleasure. In fact, Pedro seems aware of his tendency to screen (censor) his lascivious yearnings behind medical terminology when he first fantasizes about his village practice:

¿Es que voy a reírme de mí mismo? Yo el destruído, yo el hombre al que no se le dejó que hiciera lo que tenía que hacer, yo a quien en nombre del destino se me dijo: "Basta" y se me mandó para el Príncipe Pío con unas recomendaciones, un estetoscopio y un manual diagnóstico del prurito de ano de las aldeanas vírgenes. Escatológico, pornográfico, siempre pensando cochinadas. Estúpido, estúpido, las nalgas del mozo [. . .]. (236)

Is it that I should laugh at me myself? I, the destroyed, I, the man whom they would not let do what he had to do, I who was told in the name of destiny: "Enough" and was sent via Príncipe Pío with some recommendations, a

---

14. Until 1966, the censored version is "the mother who gave birth to me."
15. Unlike the English medical usage of "pruritus," the Spanish word has established figurative and idiomatic meanings: an itch, an urge (to perfectionism); *tener el prurito de* + inf. means "to have the urge to" + inf.; *por un prurito de exactitud* means "out of an excessive desire for accuracy." The introduction of the medical term in the text is complicated by the verb *tener*, thus blurring the lines between having an urge of the anus (the sexual longing) and having an itch (as in the medical condition).

stethoscope, and a diagnostic manual for pruritus of the anus of the village virgins. Scatological, pornographic, always thinking filthy things. Stupid, stupid, the buttocks of the cabin boy[...]

Pedro pursues his fantasy of his future practice with the doubly satisfying image of his power, ease, and skill (image of his successful masculine performance) and his future female patient's reciprocal admiration and praise: "Tú la diagnosticarás sin esfuerzo, le recetarás lo que necesita. Ella dirá, es simpático el nuevo" (239) (You will diagnose her without effort, you'll prescribe her what is needed. She will say, he's nice, the new doctor). This cynical, proud statement reflects Pedro's reductive conception of women as sexual beings, whose sexuality is unclean, dangerous, contagious, or cancerous, or whose disease or ailment is linked to sexuality, i.e., sexual organs and urges (the prim sounding condition "pruritus of the anus" in lay terms might read as "itchy ass"; itchiness can be readily associated with sexual arousal as well as disease).

The novel's final episode, with its flowing associative language of Pedro's inner monologue, continues and elaborates the main features of his negative character ("yo el destruido") as evidenced throughout the novel as various sorts of alienation—his lack of power or agency before the Law and institutions; his inability to assert his goals of self-realization as a researcher nor to gain understanding of others (e.g., his relationship with Dorita is highly superficial); his social isolation (ranging from the upper class of Matías's world to the lowest rung of the ladder, Cartucho and Muecas, the world of the *chabolas*). Pedro's self-estrangement in the final episode is expressed in his oscillating focus of attention. In one moment he is complacently enjoying his fantasy life as a successful village doctor which includes excellent partridge hunting and inspecting virginal girls' bottoms. In another moment he is luxuriantly torturing himself in masochistic fantasies, three of which are particularly striking—his being a salted piece of meat left to cure in the sun or salted tuna ("mojama," "se amojama"); his being toasted alive like the martyr Saint Lawrence; and his letting himself be castrated.

Pedro's narrative revisits recent thoughts in spiroid fashion, building an effect of contiguity, repetition, and elision. At times he bitterly criticizes the backward Spanish pueblo and arid plains (236) (Spain is infertile and lacks a concept of the future: a criticism developed since the publication of *Don Quijote* three and a half centuries ago). Alternately, he reflects on Florita and Dorita (their fertility and life have been cut short). Perhaps most indicative of his self-estrangement is his recurrent questioning of why, when matters seem to have gone so wrong, he is not despairing. I suggest that he lacks authentic despair, for he actually enjoys his end and is looking forward morbidly and ironically to his future. The straightforward life of a village doctor appeals to his abilities and supplies his desire for respect and some sexual rewards (partridges and submissive village girls [237]) combined with his masochistic pleasure of martyrdom (presumably he can imagine his martyred identity as stemming from his mission to cure cancer and win the Nobel Prize, but rationally he cannot be considered a martyr).

Pedro's final vision of this village life marks a transition from his far-fetched aspirations at the novel's beginning for the Nobel Prize, to follow Ramón y Cajal's example and surpass the usual fatalistic barriers imposed on Spaniards. In this way, *Tiempo de silencio* strongly reflects the pessimistic messages of Pío Baroja's story of a young man, Andrés Hurtado, who struggles to become a doctor and is dismayed when he goes on to practice medicine by the backwardness, corruption, and apathy in Spanish society (*El árbol de la ciencia* [1911]; *The Tree of Science*).[16] While Baroja's protagonist ends his life despairingly in suicide, his ironic counterpart Pedro in *Tiempo de silencio* will not experience that kind of moral agony, perhaps immune to it. In this way, Martín-Santos builds on Baroja's well-informed, panoramic pessimism and contributes to the long literary tradition of criticism of Spanish backwardness (e.g., Cadalso; Larra; Pérez Galdós; Pardo Bazán; Unamuno; García Lorca; Baroja).

Pedro's self-estrangement is expressed in several maneuvers that connote negation of a hopeful, modern life in Spain. He begins and ends his narrative by picturing himself as a protagonist in a series of story lines. On the one hand, he will become a village doctor and enjoy an indulgent, complacent life as a big fish in a little pond; he will be a potent hunter of birds and girls (the repeated references to hunting fat partridges curiously echo the Caudillo's own obsessive love of hunting, particularly partridges, which was amply reported in the press). This almost parodied macho Castilian self-image is Pedro's self-interpellation into the dominant fiction of Spain at the time: he will become the epitome of the rural Spanish doctor, complacent and apathetic about social changes and politics. On the other hand, he will be an ironic martyr—an exalted role in Spanish

---

16. Other critics compare in greater detail these two novels. See, for example, Jerez-Farrán, who also notes other ironic intertextual uses of literary precursors, such as don Quijote/Alonso Quijano and don Juan (*El burlador de Sevilla*). This scholar argues that "Martín-Santos quiere desmentir la idea erróneamente sostenida de que el hombre es dueño de su destino" (Martín-Santos wants to refute the erroneous idea that man is master of his destiny) (121).

In my view, while Martín-Santos's narrators emphasize the concepts of fate and destiny, this emphasis is ironic, at least in part, in order to question the logic and sustainability of a Spanish tradition of giving into "fate" and "destiny" as excuses for lack of change and modernization. The omniscient narrator frames Pedro in these Spanish intertexts, showing how he does not cohere; he is far removed from the romantic ideals of don Quijote and the seductive powers of don Juan.

history, hailed by the Spanish-Francoist narrative of splendid isolation and Catholic martyrdom, as seen for example in San Lorenzo de Escorial, Philip II's monastery-palace for his monkish retreats.[17]

The conclusion's preoccupation with castration functions in several censoring ways on a symbolic plane. First, castration reinforces the concept of martyrdom while also suggesting a more general male self-denial in keeping with a priest's or monk's life. Second, the loss or absence of testicles connotes an important aspect of Pedro's alienation, his feeling of lacking power and meaning (and of course directly related to the Spanish expression of possessing potency and courage, *tener cojones* [or *huevos*], "to have balls"). Third, his recurrent fantasy of castration, along with his conflicting desire and disgust with women, speaks of a fantasy to rid himself of his maleness and become asexual or even female (his repeated focus on both his future diagnoses of pruritus of the anus and on various "phallic men" and their buttocks). Fourth, Pedro's allusion to eunuchs, who were castrated by the Turks to serve in harems and whose cries could be heard by navigators and taken for the voices of sirens, suggests a self-perception which opposes the scenario of the smugly successful village doctor. For a doctor-eunuch would watch over the virginity of the harem of village girls, not exploit it. If as a eunuch he is taken for a siren, he reinvents his recurrent fantasy about sirens (a phallic/virginal/sexless woman—the paradoxical pre-Oedipal object of desire) by inserting himself in the place of that phantasmatic object.

In other words, some of Pedro's fantasies about male prowess (hunting, exercising diagnostic and general medical knowledge, conquering virgins) are offset or negated by the sporadic but insistent resurgence of fantasies about lack, loss of agency, enjoyment or self-realization in pain and suffering. Yet both oscillating sides of his discursive fantasies satisfy a particular requirement: to be the hero in his story, however desperate, squalid, banal, or arid or dismally Spanish and self-defeating that fiction might be. The castration imagery, combined with frequent mentions of "silence" in this final episode, provides strong metaphors for textual censoring—from the point of view of lack of agency or authorship, as well as the cutting out of the "best bit."[18]

The words or phrases deleted or altered by the Francoist censor in this last episode relate to some of the sexually allusive or explicit areas and themes just discussed. Yet even the censored version of the text retains most

---

17. Since Pedro leaves from Príncipe Pío train station, he is leaving Madrid westwards, into Castilla and its meseta, and past the Escorial, a prominent monument from the train.

18. See Michael Levine for an extended discussion of Heine's and Freud's use of this castration metaphor in allusions to censorship.

of its allusive and referential force. Officially censored words in the pre-1966 editions of this episode include: "prurito de ano" (page 221 [1962]);[19] "la puta que me parió" which was made "la madre que me parió" on page 222 [1962]); "a ese sanlorenzaccio que sabes, a éste que soy yo" (which was altered to read simply as "a ése que soy yo" on page 222 [1962]).[20]

Two longer passages in this final monologue were censored until the 1966 edition when they were fully reincorporated. They reflect or repeat ideas and images used elsewhere in this last episode, so their inclusion makes the text more forceful, nuanced, complex, and condensed rather than adding completely new meaning or thoughts. The condensation is notable because Pedro does not always keep the two main streams of fantasy discrete. Also the excision of these two passages was not as apparent to pre-1966 readers as were those passages involving the first brothel scene. In the final monologue, the censored passages do not create a confusing gap. These two longer passages were suppressed because the censor considered them as too emphatic or as becoming too explicit in describing potentially lascivious thoughts. Let us now examine these passages in greater detail to discover how they dramatize dynamics of censorship for Pedro.

The first passage deals with Pedro's self-projection into his future village life with the village girls:

> Miraré las mozas castellanas, gruesas en las piernas como perdices cebadas y que, como ellas, pueden ser saboreadas con los dientes y con la boca o bien ser derribadas al suelo de un bastonazo donde se quedan quietas y no se retuercen como gusanos obscenos, sino que permanecen catatónicas, stelltotenreflex, reflejo de inmovilización, todo a lo largo de la escala animal, el insecto, el sapo, la gacela, la entamoeba haemolithica, todas quietas, vírgenes purulentas, esperando. (290)

> I will look at the Castilian girls, with plump legs like fattened partridges and who, like these, can be savored with the teeth and with the mouth or even be knocked down onto the floor with the blow of a stick where they stay still and do not squirm like obscene worms, but rather remain catatonic, stelltotenreflex, reflex of immobilization, all throughout the animal scale, the insect, the toad, the gazelle, the hemolytic entameba, all motionless, purulent virgins, waiting.

---

19. But the first mention of "prurito" a couple of pages earlier remained uncensored in all editions.
20. "That saint-lawrence-type, that one who I am" was altered to read simply "that one who I am."

Pedro self-censors his sexual desire and object through the recourse to violent, degrading action (in the passive voice) and then medical, psychiatric, or scientific language as his fantasy approaches dangerous limits suggestive of rape, death, blood, the squirming worm (a vision of repellent female desire or sexual pleasure and therefore "obscene"[21]). The artistic censoring occurs also in his imagined transformation of his sexual object into food, animal life, disease-carrying cells, or disgusting, unclean females ("vírgenes purulentas" [pus-filled virgins]).

These allusive screens are all censoring strategies. What starts as a seemingly safe, distancing practice of voyeurism ("Miraré . . .") leads successively to sadomasochistic transformations of his distinctly passive object of desire, one image madly replacing the next, building an extensive network of excessive negation. The twinned objects of desire, shapely legs of the girls and the birds, are important factors here, especially noted for their fullness and fatness, a point to which I shall return shortly. Also outstanding is the fact that precisely after this passage, Pedro shifts his focus to ask himself why he is not more despairing, why he is letting himself be "castrated" ("¿Por qué me estoy dejando capar?" [291]). Now he posits *himself* as the imaginary passive object of mutilation and transformation, replacing the Castilian girls.

Thus, by having the full text restored, readers can appreciate how Pedro's fantasy of his savoring of partridges and village girls becomes metaphorically self-censored by his immediate reactions of revulsion and diversion toward images about beating, medicine, biology, castration, and death. Pedro's fantasies and narrative turn from the object of sadistic desire toward the self as masochistic object in terms of sexual and physical negation. Unlike Severin, Pedro is not punished by a dominatrix. The punisher or castrator remains unseen, thus providing a complicated sense of moral male masochism. Pedro describes his pleasure in defeat and silence, a result of censoring: "¿Y por qué no estoy desesperado? Es cómodo ser eunuco, es tranquilo, estar deprovisto de testículos, es agradable a pesar de estar castrado tomar el aire y el sol mientras uno se amojama en silencio" (293) (And why am I not in despair? It's comfortable to be a eunuch, it's peaceful, to be deprived of testicles, in spite of being castrated it's pleasant to take in the air and sun as one hangs out to dry in silence).

---

21. Note that the worm imagery first emerges during Pedro's gyroscopic meditation in the brothel's visiting room (105). At that juncture, the "gusano-cuerpo" (worm-body) seems to refer to Pedro's own bodily experience of drunken disorientation, nausea, and contact with imprisoning masses. The hermaphrodite imagery of a worm is flexible enough to imply a grotesque vision of the penis. This, too, is an implication of Humbert's reference to his "hairy hermaphrodite."

4. A SUBJECT'S AGENCY AND ETHICS TRANSGRESSED

Pedro's readiness to cross the threshold of ethical practice reveals his moral and scientific laxity and his unconscious aims: to gain forbidden knowledge, to derive pleasure from inflicting pain and imagining receiving that pain, to flaunt regulations and procedures and perhaps be caught. Thus he enjoys a masochistic experience of being reprimanded by the Law. His decisions show his strong tendency to associate scientific pursuits to sexual contact with human subjects. The epistemic drive (his desire to know, think, express, create freely) connects these two discrete areas, diminishing his research skills in science while suppressing (censoring) his sexual desires.

Tiempo de silencio presents a phantasmatic circuit between the animal and human world, involving warmth and bodily contact. The circuit comprehends reproduction, both mouse and human, and the viral transmission of cancer, a disease then generally thought to be inherited (another effect of reproduction). Pedro senses and reworks this chain of signifiers many times metonymically and irrationally throughout the novel. In both his mental life and his life of actions and decisions, he often operates by assuming cause by virtue of contiguity and chronology. My point in recognizing this series of associations and operations is to emphasize the complex and creative censoring dynamics at work in the very discursive production of this text. Through such a text, readers are engaged in a discovery of unethical practices based on an aestheticized censorship of desire and sexuality.

While science and medicine are important to Pedro as sources of epistemic activity and sublimation of sexual desire, much of his emotional investment in his studies stems from his desire to ascend to the small, highly respected, highly educated class of people and to receive honors and signs of respect. As "don Pedro," he is someone in Madrid. When the research institute's director dismisses Pedro from his research, Pedro temporarily loses some status, but upon becoming a regular doctor he maintains at least an ordinary respectability.

During the action leading to his fall, Pedro is a magnet for those who might gain in some way by contact with a doctor: Muecas, Amador, Florita, the old woman of the pension, Dorita, doña Luisa, even Matías and his mother, Matilde. Steven Marcus points out that part of American society's conception of a doctor involves "primitive fantasies of magical powers, priestly privileges, and esoteric knowledge" (256). A modified version of this conception can be seen in Spain, where the doctor stands in distinction to the pueblo's rituals and superstitions which persisted strongly into the Franco period (Muecas's initial recourse to *el mago* shows this divided loyalty).

Thus, Pedro's own desires to be valued are fulfilled to some extent in the attention he receives from various people he meets. But they do not necessarily value him in the way he desires. For some (Amador, Muecas, doña Luisa, Matilde), Pedro is esteemed for the medical function he can practice, and for others (Dorita, Dora, and grandmother), he is coveted as a long-term investment and a ticket to bourgeois respectability.[22] Pedro is not valued for "who he is"; in terms of love, no one longs for him.

This protagonist's alienated stance toward himself and others casts him into an apparently passive state; he *appears* to lack agency.[23] Part of his inability to love and be loved stems from his emotional barrenness (lack of affection, appeal, warmth), cynical detachment, and questioning of artistic, social, and philosophical questions.[24] In many ways, Pedro functions as a kind of panoptic element which gets acted upon by others and mitigating circumstances. Things seem to happen to him, with others giving or taking things away from him.

Our impression of Pedro's passivity is cunningly crafted through both narrative techniques and Pedro's own self-perception as a thinking, but not acting subject. Pérez Firmat notes how Pedro is deaf to calls at crucial moments, and that this repeated inability to hear and respond creates a kind of narrative symmetry. Pérez Firmat explains, "If one passes from the beginning of this episode [the abortion] to its conclusion one discovers that it ends in a symmetrical manner. As Pedro is leaving the hovels after Florita's death, Amador tries to detain him by shouting, '¡Don Pedro! ¡Don Pedro! ¡El certificado!' The episode is framed by two calls directed at Pedro; an initial acoustic stimulus is succeeded by an auditory lapse. The narration

---

22. Rodríguez García explores how these three women's use of Pedro constitutes the "lucha por la vida" (the fight for their lives) (272).

23. Labanyi offers an in-depth study of the multivoicedness of the text in relation to character.

24. Fernández notes the scientific coldness of Pedro compared to the more ethical, empathetic fictional precursors in novels such as Pérez Galdós's *Misericordia*. In one example, Fernández comments, "Galdós y sus personajes burgueses no descienden a los barrios bajos sólo por curiosidad científica, sino también por la posibilidad de redimir a los que allí habitan" (56) (Galdós and his bourgeois characters do not descend to the lowly neighborhoods merely out of scientific curiosity, but also for the possibility of redeeming those who live there). Fernández maintains that Pedro sees Muecas's daughters as human incubators. I differ from this assessment in that such scenes are presented by the third-person narrator. Pedro's attitude toward others is not always clearly conveyed, as Pedro's focalization is often overlaid by the language of the ironic omniscient narrator; Pedro is also critical of Muecas, who is after all the mastermind of this reproduction plan. In the case of Muecas and his daughters in the highly awkward meeting in the humble shack, bourgeois don Pedro hardly knows where to look without seeming impolite. Florita's act of baring her chest to show the bites from the mice is not a conventional mode of behavior during a visit. It is also a true that Pedro, despite his embarrassment and stiff manners, is fascinated with the possible scientific implications of the human incubation.

of Dorita's murder falls into the same pattern" (209 n. 17). Pedro does not hear Dorita's scream ("nadie se enteró") just as he does not understand the telephone caller ("No me he enterado bien") at the novel's outset. I have noted some other occasions of this deafness as a sign of resistance and self-censoring. When a pale, nervous Matías comes to Pedro to warn him at Matilde's party, Pedro's deafness creates a silence: "Las capas de silencio son tan gruesas que la voz de Matías apenas llega. Adivina lo que ocurre por sus gestos" (173) (The layers of silence are so thick that Matías's voice scarcely reaches him. He surmises what is happening by his gestures). This deafness and silence coincide with Pedro's contemplation of a phantasmatic image of the cadaver of Florita.

Pedro's apparent passivity, however, should not prevent us from apprehending his active role in the narrative. He is the researcher and decision maker, while others offer tempting and unethical opportunities for him to choose from. It is Pedro who decides to try to purchase the black-market mice (instead of reporting the theft and racketeering to the institute's director). This one remarkable decision shows how promptly Pedro is willing to abandon the tenets of both ethical and scientific practice and enter the ranks of dilettantes. After all, the mice raised outside known, controlled conditions of the experiment cannot be used as research subjects unless the premises of the experiment are changed radically; the human incubation process in Muecas's *chabola* also problematizes use of the mice for further experiment.

By transgressing scientific and ethical practices, Pedro shows that he is prepared to buy his status for a price set by Muecas, a man uneducated, unprincipled in wartime combat and in postwar survival,[25] a member of the most marginalized part of society. Moreover, Pedro links himself damningly to the world of the *chabolas* by agreeing to operate on their terms and thus putting himself on par with Muecas himself. Therefore, from the novel's outset, the reader observes that Pedro fails to meet standards that he probably would have criticized in others.

---

25. Amador explains to Pedro, on their way to the first meeting in the shantytown, that even he would not sublet his home to Muecas and his family, stating, "Porque aunque le aprecio comprendo que es muy burro. Es exactamente un animal. Y siempre con la navaja encima a todas partes" (38–39) (For although I appreciate him I know that he's a donkey. He's simply an animal. And he's always got the knife out everywhere). Amador lists extensively Muecas's lack of character, abilities, and trustworthiness. If all these are not sufficient signs that Pedro should not do business with such a desperate, shady character, Amador mentions that he himself charges Muecas a "tarifa" for each job he gets, as a kind of commission (40). If Amador stands to gain monetarily from the possible transaction of the mice, then the integrity of the mice is further in question. Surely, with all this information acquired *prior* to the meeting, a less naïve or more scrupulous person than Pedro would not continue considering conducting business with Muecas and Amador.

Of course, all of these assessments are never articulated by Pedro who does not generally conceive of himself as an active, decision-making subject. In a defensive, self-censoring operation he manages to supplant his sense of wrongdoing by asserting to himself that there is a valuable, new research factor to be explored (a new research proposition, in fact), one which he considers in detail in the opening episode (i.e., before meeting Muecas's family at their *chabola*): the possible transmission of the cancerous strain to Muecas's daughters because of their close contact with the (supposedly) cancerous mice and curious ability to sustain the growth of the mice. "¿Qué poder tienen las mal alimentadas muchachas toledanas," speculates Pedro, "para que los ratones pervivan y críen?[26] ¿Qué es lo que les hace morir aquí, en el laboratorio?" (13) (What power could the malnourished Toledan girls have so that the mice would survive and breed? What is it that makes them die here, in the laboratory?). As if in answer to this question, in the first meeting at the *chabola*, Florita shows everyone how the female mice in heat have bitten her chest (62).

The illegal negotiation with Muecas presents a considerable and untenable shift in Pedro's research aims: although cancer research's ultimate goal is to cure and prevent cancer in humans, Pedro's own research is reasonably limited to a project on a few controlled animal subjects. By embarking on the prospect of human experimentation outside of controlled, authorized limits, he takes on a responsibility he cannot properly account for. Moreover, he, by inference, assumes that certain human subjects such as those from the subhuman world of the *chabolas* (Florita, whose incest is one of the expressions of her family's phantasmatic, animal, nonhuman status) are more expendable than others. Pedro's subterfuge or self-censoring is to use the excuse of the pursuit of freedom of inquiry in the name of science, social justice, and the difficulties of overcoming inherent Spanish inferiority. The laboratory-mice deficit (blamed on Spain's poverty) is countered with the following grandiose but weak argument:

26. Significantly, one meaning of the verb *criar* is "to suckle, feed," while the basic implied meaning in this passage is "to breed" or "to grow." The word's suggestiveness is further developed by both the reference to the girls' own malnourished state and by Florita's revealing the mouse bites on her breasts gained from bearing the female mice in a sack around her neck. The implication feeds into a metonymically irrational thought that the mice actually suckle from the girls, thus completing a phantasmatic circuit between the animal and human world. This circuit involves warmth and bodily contact, and it (allegedly) produces reproduction, both mouse and human, and the viral transmission of cancer, a disease then generally thought to be inherited (another effect of reproduction); Pedro senses and reworks this chain of signifiers many times metonymically and irrationally throughout the novel. In both his mental life and his life of actions and decisions, he often operates by assuming cause by virtue of contiguity and chronology.

Hay posibilidad de construir unas presas que detengan la carrera de las aguas. ¿Pero, y el espíritu libre? El venero de la inventiva. El terebrante husmeador de la realidad viva con ceñido escalpelo que penetra en lo que se agita y descubre una lidia.

It is possible to construct some dams that would hold back the flow of water. But, what about the free mind? The source of inventiveness. The piercing smell of living reality with a restrained scalpel which penetrates that which moves and discovers a bullfight. (8)

These inventive statements do not get corroborated later by Pedro's serious involvement in work. They do reflect, however, his uncomfortable awareness of the disquieting aspects of using live animals for experiments, alluding indirectly to the basic practice in histology of taking tissue samples from live subjects. His early, somewhat dismissive assessment of the arid "vientre toledano" (11) (Toledan womb) is later contradicted by his contact with the strangely prolific population of the *chabolas*, which, despite hunger, disease, unsanitary conditions, inadequate shelter, and transgression of incest taboos, manage to sustain growth (unlike his experimental mice in the laboratory). Florita's Toledan womb is not arid; moreover, she possibly provides incubational warmth for Muecas's breeding mice which hang in a plastic pouch between her breasts.

An additional artistic censoring can be noted in Pedro's fetishistic thoughts on the bullfight. The metaphor of the corrida is deployed several times in the novel, notably in Pedro's meditation on how he succumbed to his desire for Dorita (see discussions in sections 5 and 7). Labanyi points out that in Martín-Santos's analysis of the psychic symbolism of the bullfight the people unconsciously wish for the bull to win; the bull becomes a subtle object of identification. Using this analysis, I would suggest that Pedro's vision of a "lidia" (bullfight) beneath the microscope sets up a distancing situation of self-observation, a kind of erotic voyeurism of the self in conflict.[27] The bullfight is developed in greater detail in a segment narrated by the omniscient narrator during Pedro's stay in prison (223–25).

---

27. Labanyi notes that in the novel the bullfight can represent the people's desire for destruction; alternatively, if the public desires the death of the torero, it sublimates its antiauthoritarian tendencies (105–6). The institutionalization of the bullfight (in the eighteenth century) and the bullfight itself confirm the power of authority, "al representar la incapacidad de llevar a cabo el parricidio. De ahí que la policía, la prensa, las fuerzas armadas, la Iglesia y el Gobierno Civil colaboren en el rito" (106) (by representing the inability of accomplishing parricide. From there the police, the press, the armed forces, the Church and the Civil Government may collaborate in the ritual).

5. IN THE ARTIST'S STUDIO: NUDES, FLOWERS, THE HOLOCAUST

Pedro's character zone incorporates the world of painting and with it, a set of contrasting aesthetic theories. For some, art can tap into Dionysian power and inspiration; for others, it can present difficult ethical meditation. Art can be nationalized or nationalist, or cosmopolitan. In the mid-twentieth century, avant-garde painting in Spain tended strongly toward the semi- or nonrealist and abstract (e.g., the Barcelona group Dau al Set [1948], from which Antoni Tàpies emerged), in part in keeping with international trends and in part to remove itself from issues of Spanish censorship.[28] In *Tiempo de silencio,* Spanish painting (unabashed nudes smiling "stereotypically") and German-Jewish neo-Expressionist painting (a bombarded city overshadowing masses of tiny human subjects) are presented together in a private studio in central Madrid. The Spanish nudes would not have been able to sell on the public market in 1949, not just because they deploy stereotypes and "vulgares recetas del arte combinatorio" (87) (vulgar formulae of the combinatory art), but because they depict two women in combination instead of one, increasing the fleshiness and potential pornographic interpretation. The German-Jew's painting is described as "realmente muy malo" (really very bad), with dark browns and reds showing a "desesperación colectiva" (collective desperation) and with a "carácter fecaloideo" (fecaloid character) and whose protagonists have a wormlike quality ("vermiculosidad") (88–89). Neither art is excellent; rather, each shows an artistic aim, either

---

28. Gubern explains the postwar art movements in relation to the late 1940s and early 1950s when many Spaniards were trying to effect changes: the plastic arts were "less explicit in political content" and

> expresaron su ruptura con el desesperante academicismo, la atonía y la rutina dominantes, con un intento de enlazar con las corrientes de anteguerra, como ocurrió con la inspiración surrealista animadora del grupo barcelonés Dau al Set (1948), [. . .] o adhiriéndose a las corrientes informalistas en boga en Europa—grupos El Paso (1957) y Equipo 57, de Madrid—mientras otros pintores cultivaban la temática social con espíritu «comprometido» (José Ortega, Ricardo Zamorano) (119).

> expressed their break with the dominant, despair-inducing academicism, atony [lack of tone], and routine, with the intent to connect with the prewar trends, as occurred with the animated surrealist inspiration of the Barcelona group Dau al Set (1948), [. . .] or by adhering to the informalist trends in vogue in Europe—groups El Paso (1957) and Equipo 57, of Madrid—while other painters cultivated a social theme in the "engagé" spirit (José Ortega, Ricardo Zamorano).

By contrast, the paintings explored in the studio in *Tiempo de silencio* do not pursue these trends, indicating these artists' distance from the avant-garde. Matías's aesthetic criteria of "magma" opposes the dominant trends of "academicism, atony [lack of tone], and routine."

to please or to provoke protest.

In this regard, the reactions of the diegetic viewers Pedro and Matías are central to understanding the function of the paintings in the novel, for neither type of art would have been shown in contemporary Spanish galleries for reasons of censorship. The nudes would offend Catholic morality; the bombed city and antlike people ("seres aparentemente humanos, pero más bien formiciformes" [apparently human beings, but rather ant-formed]) might be construed as counterpolitical. Martín-Santos creates an ironically dialogic conversation in artistic themes and techniques: the nudes exaggerate the limbs and fleshiness of the female bodies while the collective-despair painting reduces the human subjects to masses in a not-to-scale miniature stature. In the first case, human subjectivity is erased as the eye is drawn too close to the flesh, while in the second human subjectivity is minimized, too, but now its features are indistinguishable. Both genres of painting see the human subject as animalistic.

The scene opens a discussion of what art should achieve. Ironically, the young men are viewing and commenting on forbidden art, albeit poorly executed art and not master works. In response to the lavish nudes, Pedro and Matías have various defensive censoring strategies. These strategies are not simply negating, but transformative, producing signifying interpretative fantasies that dramatize issues of sexually charged desire, judgment, and punishment. The subject of human experimentation resurfaces as Pedro and Matías utter showy compliments in Latin. Then the conversation takes an unusual turn:

> —El número de desnudos que pinta indica el nivel alcanzado por la represión de un pueblo—opinó confusamente Pedro pensando en sus propias represiones. Resultaba grato permanecer en el vasto invernadero de opulentas peonias, en lugar de caminar hacia un presunto Dachau masturbatorio.[29]
> Como un telepático pendant, exclamó Matías:
> —Nada me ha recordado más las cámeras de gas.
> [. . .]—Imagen espantosa de la muerte, no turbes mi reposo—recitó Pedro—. Yo no estoy muerto ahí entonces. Yo estoy vivo aquí ahora. (87–88)

> —The number of nudes that he paints indicates the level reached by the repression of a people—Pedro opined confusedly, thinking of his own repressions. It proved to be pleasant to remain in the vast greenhouse of opulent peonies, instead of walking toward a presumed masturbatory Dachau.

---

29. Note that the adjective "masturbatorio" until 1966 was censored to read "inevitable" (cf. 70 [1962]; 72 [1966]).

> Like a telepathic pedant, Matías exclaimed:
> —Nothing has reminded me more of the gas chambers.
> [. . .]—Awful image of death, do not disturb my repose—Pedro recited—. I am not dead there and then. I am alive here and now.

Here the thoughts of the two young men bifurcate. Pedro identifies himself with the Spanish painter of nudes; he thinks often and chromatically about women as fleshy beings. For him, the death camp Dachau represents metaphorically his own awful sexual solitude; masturbation is apparently a punishment comparable to the suffering of camp victims. We can note the implied passivity and hyperbolic victimhood in the Dachau-masturbation imagery. The masturbator's necessary fantasy might be a Nazi imposing torture or death on a Jew. Pedro's other analogies express elsewhere similar masochistic tendencies (the torero and the bull; the scalpel and the live specimen; the hunted and cooked prey). Masturbation is also a punishment for not having a woman. He contrasts the Dachau image with the image of heavy-petaled flowers (peonies). He recurrently uses floral metaphors for naked women. In the subsequent scenes later that night, first Dorita and then Florita are described as flowers, their legs being petals. The initial meeting with Florita at the *chabola* had perhaps set off the recurrent sequence of floral metaphors.[30]

In this studio scene, Matías, meanwhile, develops different sexual fantasies about Nazi death camps: the numerous paintings of various groupings of naked women give the impression of there being one large mass of naked bodies, which he associates in turn with images of a mass of naked Jewish women before being exterminated in the gas chambers. Matías seems to attempt to censor or displace his own lascivious feelings by expressing some contempt for the Nazi atrocities through indirect criticism of the paintings that he thinks are done by a German artist. As the Nuremberg trials were coming to a close in 1949, the fairly recently disclosed, grim details of the Holocaust would have been a newsworthy subject. In a grotesque turn, Matías possibly is stating that any woman's body is erotic for him. Despite Matías's initial negative criticism of the nudes, he subsequently praises them for having the sublimated artistic power of "magma" (90–91). This second assessment may be a nationalist one, resulting from confirmation that the nudes were painted by a Spaniard.

Pedro's and Matías's changing comments and reactions to the nude paintings (praise of erotic beauty expressed in Latin, an erudite way to cloak,

---

30. See Pérez Firmat for further discussion on floral metaphors and sequencing in *Tiempo de silencio*.

elevate, and laugh at one's prurient response; politicized, moral revulsion; Golden Age intertextual references ["Imagen espantosa de la muerte, no turbes mi reposo [. . .] Yo no estoy muerto ahí entonces. Yo estoy vivo aquí ahora"[31]]; explication of aesthetic primal energy) all show a continuous effort to reinterpret and distance themselves from the overwhelming effect of the paintings. The various strands of their discourse intertwine, suggesting a pleasurable recourse to the safety of erotically and intellectually charged talk amongst men. Indeed, their whole bacchanal is a refuge of masculinity, sporadically punctuated by the specter or presence of women as sexually desirable and threatening figures. Feminine sexuality is safely considered in the artist's studio.

The Spanish artist's painting of nudes offers a Dionysian orgiastic promise and the quality of "magma," Matías's scientific-metaphysical term for the painting's "pregnante realidad" (pregnant reality), "protoforma de la vitalidad que nace" (the protoform of nascent vitality), and "fuliginosa pegajosidad del esperma" (the darkened stickiness of sperm) (90). Pedro may find an opposing quality in the paintings: his statement "Imagen espantosa de la muerte" identifies the lavish female nude as a death sign,

31. In the quoted passage, Pedro recites a fragment from "Al sueño," a sonnet by Golden Age poet Lupercio Leonardo de Argensola. The sonnet begins thus: "Imagen espantosa de la muerte, / sueño cruel, no turbes más mi pecho [. . .]" (Frightful image of death, / cruel dream, my breast no longer set in turmoil [. . .]). Pedro's own words spoken just after his recital, telling of his desire to live in the here and now, resonate with his recitation. The sonnet deals with the entangled themes of death, dream, sleep, and contrasts the vanity of the tyrant or rich miser with the glories of love.

This citation further develops the earlier notion of Pedro's desire to postpone indefinitely a return to his masturbatory hell, solitary bed, and struggles with sleep or dreams. His words foreshadow the idea that he is someone to be judged harshly, especially by his conscience, but we know not yet of any crime, except for the tentative transgression of his scientific project (which has a deeply symbolic function as well as a resounding narrative set of consequences—his "seduction" of Dorita, abortion of Florita, potential complicity as accessory (251), evasion of the police, incarceration, condemnation by himself and by the Director, and demotion to some rural outpost).

In his dealings with women and his encounters with the Law, Pedro parodically contrasts with don Juan, another transgressor in Spanish literature.

Among the novel's references to Tirso de Molina's *El burlador de Sevilla,* perhaps the most notable intertextual reference is "no hay plazo que no se cumpla ni deuda que no se pague" (285) (there is no term that does not finish nor debt that does not get paid); the intertext virtually repeats its source, for in Tirso's play the voices from the beyond and the ghost of don Gonzalo warn don Juan and those who fear God's punishment "que no hay plazo que no llegue / ni deuda que no se pague." See Act III or Jornada III, 2729–32, 2749–58, and 2773–74 for variations. Jerez-Farrán (122) discusses the Tirso intertextuality in terms of Northrop Frye's conception of the "anxiety of influence."

The moral implications are communicated in the economy of time and debts: don Juan and Pedro are similar in their transgressions of ethical standards combined with their lack of regard for others' feelings and their desire to remain in a pleasurable, idle present; their crimes are not all necessarily punishable by a worldly code of law.

intimating the idea of death as corporeal, based in the body, and the body as site of desire and love. While the young men are drawn to these nudes for sexualized truth and vitality, these qualities remain framed as private fantasy as opposed to possible reality.

The studio scene is not the only place for the contemplation of art. Elsewhere, Pedro's thoughts on paintings turn to the medieval period and its fantastic and moral currents, such as the allegorical elements of these paintings (e.g., yellow for envy, 170) and Bosch's paintings of the garden of delights (178). In these paintings, at least two levels of signification are maintained, the worldly and vain on the one hand and, on the other, the apocalyptic, fantastic, and eternal. Pedro is not able to grasp the lessons of such paintings, although his thoughts of them signal an attempt to interpret. The Goya painting of "el gran Buco" similarly enchants him without enlightenment. The Spanish intellectual's lack of understanding of the wealth of his cultural heritage in the arts is ironically noted by the omniscient narrator: "a visitar el museo de pinturas con una chica inglesa y comprobar que no sabemos dónde está ninguno de los cuadros que ella conoce excepto las Meninas" (17) (to visit a museum of paintings with an English girl and realize that we don't know where any of the paintings are located that she knows except for las Meninas). Here the collective "we" of educated Spain scarcely knows the famous collection of the Museo del Prado where Velázquez's *Las Meninas* and other masterpieces from Bosch to Goya are housed. The lack of familiarity signals a forgetfulness of Spanish heritage and apathy. The art of Bosch, Velázquez, and Goya exemplify critical perspectives of society and the individual, but Pedro cannot fully interpret these signs.

6. THE SPECTER OF THE VIVISECTION: A MASOCHISTIC FANTASY

Pedro's self-censoring produces fantasies involving pleasure in pain or subjugation. In these fantasies, the administration of pain or judgment masks his pleasurable enjoyment of it and expresses a censored sexuality. One of his deepest obsessions is the specter of the vivisection, an image from his laboratory practice which functions as a metaphor for his fear of or repulsion from sexual intercourse and contact. The vivisection also serves as a metonym for his fear and pleasure in the practice of medicine, which involves touching and cutting living human beings. When Pedro thinks about or is confronted with aspects of sexuality, he often mentally transforms or renames them as scientific images, study, procedures, language (animal and plant life serving as objects of scientific study).

These fantasy-transformations involving science express a sense of censoring because Pedro's conception of science is largely based on fear, coldness, objectivity, lack of caring, cutting away, operating, conducting autopsies. This conception about the harsh, cutting side of scientific practice is masochistically pleasurable. As a physician or scientist Pedro seems actually afraid to practice (but apparently performs very well). He gains pleasure by imagining the (live) object of the experiment. This pleasure is heightened by his imagining himself in the place of the object of desire (*objet petit a*); his dependence on masochism is maintained by avoiding love relationships which would involve a rather different investment of affect.

Paradoxically what Pedro seems to want at bottom—human warmth and contact ("deseado por un espíritu próximo")—is what he is bound to avoid. He avoids warmth and contact because these might close a gap or fill a lack which he finds pleasurable in delaying satisfaction. Pedro *enjoys* being separated from the rest; he derives a sense of satisfaction from his self-imposed alienation and denial. Moreover, warmth and contact are closely linked with contamination.

Throughout the novel, the specter of the vivisection remains perhaps the most pervasive and profound expression of Pedro's fixation on the entangled concerns of symmetry, wholeness, lack, cutting, sexuality, and life's struggle against death, disease, and other threats. References to the vivisection recur frequently, along with its closely allusive counterparts of the autopsy, castration, abortion, stabbing, and genital intercourse. The vivisection alludes metonymically to histology, the study of tissues; histologists must take tissue samples from live animal subjects. It is pertinent to note that Ramón y Cajal was a histologist, the Spanish scientist Pedro would like to emulate. Pedro's cancer research is closely related to histological practices. The vivisection thus also connotes the possibility of scientific discovery and access to achieving worldly ambition.

The vivisection evokes both the infliction of pain on a suffering, live animal and the sharp, exacting investigation of the mysteries of the flesh (and of disease). The "animal desnudo" (naked animal) under the scalpel, and by extension its blood, organs, tissue, and connective tissue, haunts Pedro's associative flow of thoughts as he leaves Madrid at the end of the novel:

> el animal desnudo con su aspecto de persona muerta antes de que se le mate, sólo las lentejas circulando por la red venosa del mesenterio, la vivisección. Esto es, la vivisección, las sufragistas inglesas protestando, igual exactamente, igual

que si fuera eso, la vivisección. Ellas adivinan que son igual que las ranas si se las desnuda, en cambio Florita, la desnuda florita en la chabola, florecita pequeña, pequeñita, florecilla le dijo la vieja, florecita la segunda que ... ajjj ... (288)

the naked animal with his look of a dead person before one kills him, only the platelets circulating through the venous network of the mesentery, the vivisection. That's it, the vivisection, the English suffragettes protesting, exactly the same, the same as though it were that, the vivisection. They intuit that they are the same as the frogs if one strips them, while Florita, the stripped little flower in the shack, the little wee flower, tiny, little flower said the old woman to her, little flower the second one that ... ayyy ...

Evidently the memory of his participation in Florita's abortion has come to represent vivisection for Pedro. The connection is important because he feels guilty about wanting to use Florita as an actual scientific subject in his cancer research; the abortion through the careful scraping of the uterus walls with the scalpel phantasmatically mirrors the vivisection, the action of cutting into or dissecting a living body in order to advance pathological knowledge. The fact that Florita dies shortly after Pedro begins the operation increases his sense of guilt. While he is not responsible for her death, he feels the weight of the automatic sense of cause and effect of contiguous and sequential action.

The protagonist's ruminations over these images and events present a neurotic, even hysterical, impression. He seems to know logically that he is not to blame, but nevertheless he sustains a secret, irrational sense of guilt. Moreover, he has early thoughts about vivisection which are presented in the first passage of the novel, long before he ever sees Florita in the *chabola* or assists in her abortion. Although he renounces research to take up medical practice, he does not abandon the prospect of cutting up live subjects. Indeed, as a doctor, he will be dealing almost uniquely with live human subjects, conducting surgery and other practices on their bodies. While dismissing Pedro from the research institute, the director tries to console him by pointing out the young man's leading asset—good hands: "Puede usted hacer un discreto cirujano" (259) (You could make a shrewd surgeon).

It would appear that Pedro's talent lies precisely in the area he might prefer to keep at a distance or disavow. This talent is also an outward expression of his personal desires: to be in direct contact with people, especially women, in some powerful function; to delve into the human body; to achieve a position of respect and importance in the society.

7. NARRATIVE TECHNIQUES: SPLITTING POINTS OF VIEW

Tiempo de silencio's narrative techniques help to enact censoring strategies and produce negating fantasies. These techniques also encourage the reader to judge Pedro and Spain critically for their reliance on dominant fictions, negating fantasies, and overlooking their unethical behavior or attitudes.

Most of the novel is composed of passages narrated by Pedro or by a diegetic third-person narrator. In addition, there are occasional fragments of interior monologues by *la vieja*, Cartucho, the police detective don Similiano, and Matías which lend a mimetic, heteroglot depth to the multiperspective text. Critics have paid much attention to the uncertain split in narrative between Pedro and the third-person narrator.[32] In my argument, this technical achievement expresses the ambiguous borders of a subject's consciousness, his sense of separation from himself, and his sense of being narrated.

A few important sections are unambiguously presented as Pedro's interior monologues (e.g., the novel's opening and closing narratives, Pedro's reflections just after having sexual relations with Dorita and those during his solitary confinement in the Madrid prison). These monologues strategically approach but avoid touching upon forbidden meaning; or they tend to transform the sensitive thought or image into something more acceptable.

Pedro's first-person narrative segments at times refer to him as an other, as a character in a story, as the subject of a history. This inner-diegetic effect shows both his ability and desire to gain distance from himself at times, in order to disassociate himself from unpleasant thoughts and actions. For example, during his postcoital interior monologue, Pedro reflectively counters his knowing, moral self with the libidinal, lawless self: "Yo aquí con mi ser conciencia, claridad, luz, conocimiento. Yo aquí con mi kikirikí borracho. Como el asesino con su cuchillo del que caen gotas de sangre. Como el matador [. . .]" (119) (Here I am with my conscience-being,

---

32. See, for example, Caviglia; Feal Deibe; Jerez-Farrán; Margaret Jones; Knickerbocker; Labanyi; Spires; Rey; Roberts; Ugarte. Jones remarks on Martín-Santos's technique of "monólogo dialéctico" (dialectic monologue), which "allows a double plane of reality to be present simultaneously: the sequential narrative of an episode along with an interior monologue providing the character's commentary, reaction, and feelings on an internal level. From this point of departure, it is not difficult to construct a theory of dialectical realism pitting one element against another, offering a dynamic conflict and movement toward change or resolution, while portraying a synchronic conception of reality" (87).

clarity, light, knowledge. Here I am with my cock-a-doodle-doo drunk. Like the assassin with his knife from which fall drops of blood. Like the matador [. . .]).

From this point the monologue produces a long chain of images about a bullfight, developing his initial thoughts without further mention of Pedro as "I." This chain involves the phantasm of a stabbed bull who refuses to die and instead grows and grows, enfolding him in its black matter like "un pulpo amoroso" (an amorous pulp) (a recreation of his recent penetration of Dorita). In the subsequent paragraph, the third-person narrative seems to take the place of Pedro's first-person expressions to describe how he washes his face at the basin in his room and observes himself in the "pequeño espejo rajado" (little cracked mirror) above it (120). Curiously, the omniscient narrator (or Pedro?) reports the persistent vision of Dorita. As is often the case in his "real-life" actions which are presented as passive or observational moments, Pedro is not described as thinking thoughts, but rather positioned as the recipient of thoughts:

> La imagen de la belleza de Dorita seguía flotando en la confusión de su mente. No como la de un ser amado ni perdido, sino como la de un ser decapitado. Ella había quedado allí, [. . .] unida a él por una historia tonta que no podía ser tomada en cuenta, pero que le perseguiría inevitablemente. La cabeza flotaba—como cortada—en el embozo de la cama. ¡Era tan bella! Ella dormía. Todo era natural en ella.[33] (120)

> The image of Dorita's beauty continued to float in the confusion of his mind. Not like that of a being loved nor lost, but rather like that of a being decapitated. She had stayed there, [. . .] united with him through a silly story which could not be taken into account, but which would inevitably pursue him. The head was floating—as though cut—at the top of the covers. She was so beautiful! She was sleeping. Everything was natural in her.

Pedro's various modes of self-censoring create a fantasy vision that reinterprets what has just transpired between Dorita and him. In his elaborate, recreative, censoring fantasy, he compares himself to various dramatic transgressive counterparts: the boastful, crowing rooster, a bloodthirsty

---

33. We can compare this passage with the later intrusion of the specter of Florita's bloody, naked body in the middle of Matilde's soirée (173). Both moments represent the reemergence of Pedro's repressed thoughts from his unconscious. In an uncanny coincidence in terms of plot, Florita's body is exhumed in the episode immediately following the soirée one. The narrative contiguity of events provides a sense of causation and psychic coincidence.

assassin, the bullfighter (note the recurrent image of blood, the knife or scalpel, and death, live victim or experimental animal, and genital intercourse).

The spectral image of Dorita's beautiful head functions as a double reproach. He feels guilty of decapitating her, that is, of separating her from her innocence and virginity. The decapitation motif also implies how he admires her beauty, but not her as a person ("¡Era tan bella!"). The motif serves as a kind of self-identified metaphor of castration and a double denial: the separation of head from body is a way to desexualize his carnal knowledge of her and to reassert her innocent, sleeping beauty. He translates their sexual encounter into a kind of fictionalized narrative event: their being "united" (which carries sexual and marital nuances) somehow has come about through "una historia tonta" (a silly story). The narrative itself meanders from first person to third person, expressing Pedro's self-alienation and rejection of his responsibility or sense of agency, but also his flickering attempts at self-analysis.

The narrative presents two focalizations of the same character. The shifting in narrative voices in this example and elsewhere is important because it shows more than one perspective or point of view, offering contrasts for comparison and judgment. Because Pedro sees himself at times as an other, the reader is prompted to evaluate Pedro's assessments. Indeed, the narrative offers a sense of the psychoanalytic relation in which the analyst must listen to the analysand's story. The third-person narration, with its spectacularly ironic and intertextual effects, further distances the subject Pedro while deepening the novel's contemporary themes, characters, and setting.[34]

The reader's role as judge is encouraged by the pervasive use of an omniscient, somewhat unreliable, critical, and at times extravagantly ironic third-person narrator. While this narrator describes Pedro and his thoughts and actions in detail, the reader is not seductively persuaded to identify or commiserate with the protagonist nor with the other characters, but rather to compare and judge him and them. This distancing effect is achieved in part through the generous and varied use of irony, such as metaphorical and literary-inspired hyperbole and the adoption of various seriocomic elements (e.g., the ridiculous notion that Muecas is a gentleman farmer looking after his livestock and family in some agrarian utopia [67]; the cunning analogy of the Pedro-Amador relationship with that of don Quijote and Sancho Panza).

---

34. For discussions on intertextuality in Martín-Santos, see, for example, Franz, Palley, Caviglia, Luna, Jerez-Farrán, and Labanyi.

The third-person narrator plays with official discourse, dominant fictions, and the like in a mocking or deadpan tone. This use makes us aware of dominant Spanish themes and myths (and their fragile foundations), many of which fueled the country's self-conception in the mid-twentieth century, some belonging to a long continuum of national myth, ideology, and tradition. At various narrative moments, mention is made of Spain's heroic-pathetic isolationist stance (personified in the lone *caballero* [knight]) and the country's strong sense of difference from other nations and peoples. Just as Pedro views himself at times from an outsider's standpoint so is his pueblo held up to a critical gaze. The third-person narrator and Pedro repeatedly mention Spain's identity traits of race, blood, hereditary features, geography, and ingrained customs: Iberia's non-European status and position; its primitive or uncivilized practices comparable with African tribes, Australian or South Pacific aborigines; its racial inferiority to the Nordic peoples in terms of diet, intelligence, work patterns, sexuality, and art.

What is at stake in these discursive reworkings of national myths, self-perceptions, and neuroses is a recourse to blame one's shortcomings or failures (Pedro's or Spain's) on supposedly hereditary or permanent factors. By pointing to apparent fatalism, one could be divested of responsibility (and self-determination or free will). The dubious heroics of preordained self-defeatism is a strategy to derive some dignity and pleasure from lack of agency. *Tiempo de silencio*'s reworking of Spain's dominant fictions through the medium of Pedro and the omniscient ironic narrator shows how these fatalist fictions are both negating fantasies and part of social reality, serving as a self-fulfilling prophecy and as a fixture in personal and social self-perceptions. These fictions also play a censoring role in that they protect or screen the subjects from actual self-perception or analysis, thus divesting them of a sense of agency and ability to initiate transformation.

Dominant fictions help to occlude, erase, or write over (to censor), as in a palimpsest, the actuality (and the Real). The Francoist regime's ideology promoted to a strong degree certain idealizations about Spain and a selective, glowing history; that promotion was the prescriptive aspect of the Spanish censorship, especially from 1939 to the early 1950s.[35] *Tiempo de silencio,* through its ironic and extensive use of these fictions and accompanying discursive language, helps to expose the censoring function of these. This function is at once useful and debilitating for the subject. Perhaps the most telling aspect of the complex censoring mode is the deployment of Francoist-inspired discourse about national myths and fictions based on

---

35. See Herzberger and Carr for sustained discussions of the regime's rewriting of history and use of propaganda. Gubern explains how, in each period of the dictatorship, the censorship helped to support these dominant ideologies.

negated identity. For example, in the novel's final pages, Pedro links together in a metonymic chain associations of sexual ecstasy (displacement), racial differences, and Spanish alterity. Beginning with remarks about the hypnotic effect of the train's rhythm, comparable to that of the drums of "tribus primitivas" (primitive tribes), who, during their nights of dancing festivals, achieve the "famoso éxtasis" (292) (famous extasis), Pedro thinks that:

> Si llegara al éxtasis [. . .] podría convertirme, atravesar el lavado necesario del cerebro prevaricador y quedar convertido en un cazador de perdices gordas y aldeanas sumisas. Pero no somos negros, no somos negros, los negros saltan, ríen, gritan y votan para elegir a sus representantes en la ONU. Nosotros no somos negros, ni indios, ni países subdesarrollados. Somos mojamas tendidas al aire purísimo de la meseta que están colgadas de un alambre oxidado, hasta que hagan su pequeño éxtasis silencioso.

> If I would arrive at that ecstasy [. . .] I could convert myself, pass through the washing of the prevaricating brain and remain converted into a hunter of plump partridges and submissive village girls. But we are not black, we are not black, the blacks jump, laugh, shout, and vote to elect their representatives to the UN. We are not black, nor Indian, nor underdeveloped countries. We are stretched, dried tunas in the ultra-pure air of the meseta which are hanging from an oxidized wire, until they make their little, silent ecstasy.

Note the grammatical (and imaginational) shifts (displacement) in this passage, ironically and phantasmatically highlighting themes of alienation (sense of difference, separation from one's self, loss of power and meaning): Pedro shifts from being an active subject to a semi-disembodied passive recipient (his lying brain needs washing—a double allusion to censoring practices—to lie, to wash). Also the subject grammatically changes number in a contiguous, associative chain—I, he, they, we, they. This passage ironically employs tell-tale references to Franco and certain dominant fictions: the avid partridge hunter (el Jefe); Spain's identification with and distancing from Africa and evaluations of superiority; the "healthy" need for brainwashing in an authoritarian country; Spain's masochistic celebration of its isolation and martyrdom. All of these references are predicated on the ideas of erotic masculine self-negation, displacement, and resolute passivity which produce an impoverished little pleasure. In turn, these ideas and the (psychic) dynamics that bring them to light are related directly to artistic censoring.

The novel's narrative style complements Pedro's alienation, providing the connective tissue for sexually related metaphors and metonyms that notably evoke censoring dynamics. Indeed, the narrative often functions as an extended metonymic expression and elaborate irony (a rhetoric of economy and excess). Many passages in *Tiempo de silencio* are remarkable for their long, intertwining, baroque syntactic structure. Pedro's meandering, associative thought processes are reflected in the third-person narrative. For example, we can note a rich array of such rhetorical figures in the episode involving Pedro's dismissal from his research by the institute's director. Instances of elaborate anaphors accumulate in the opening sentences:

> Que la ciencia más que ninguna de las otras actividades de la humanidad ha modificado la vida del hombre sobre la tierra es tenido por verdad indubitable. Que la ciencia es una palanca liberadora de las infinitas alienaciones que le impiden adecuar su existencia concreta a su esencia libre, tampoco es dudado por nadie. Que los [. . .] (253)

> That science, more than any other of humanity's activities, has modified the life of man on earth is taken for an indubitable truth. That science is a liberating lever for the infinite alienations that keep him from adapting his concrete existence to his free essence is also doubted by no one. That the [. . .]

This passage also identifies grandiose conceptions of science and its mission, and it expresses thoughts in the hyperbolic way in which Pedro would expect science to speak. Here, as often elsewhere, the narrator's ironically elevated and overly assured tone and choice of words cause the reader to maintain a wary surveillance. The passage goes on to stipulate that the protagonists of the study of science must be worthy and consummate. We know that Pedro is far from meeting those standards; thus the voice of judgment increasingly makes itself felt. The institute's director later supports this conception of scientists, reminding Pedro that their profession is a "sacerdocio" (258) (priesthood). The opening passage of the meeting with the director also articulates notions held tacitly by Pedro—that science would indeed be for him the liberating device (in lieu of a sexual one) that would help him overcome his sense of alienation.

8. CANCER AND CONTIGUITY IN NARRATIVE

The novel's narrative style involves excessive elaboration, extended and recurrent metaphors and images, and other modes of displacement and condensation. This excess of language is expressed, in part, in one of the novel's organizing themes: cancer and its associated motifs of disease, contamination, tumorous growth, reproduction of cells (mitosis), and the psychic association of cancer with sexual contact, reproduction, and pregnancy (tumors, division of cells upon conception). The theme of cancer that metaphorically impregnates writing, scientific research, reproduction, and sexuality is negatively productive: cancer grows, but it is bad. In *Tiempo de silencio,* cancer is associated with potentially good things (writing, reproduction, sexual functions, attributes, and desire) and it contaminates them, rendering them bad. This negating effect of the cancer motif is another form of artistic censoring thought in the production of fantasy and writing.

Before entering the literary café on his Saturday night out, Pedro thinks that he would prefer to continue "evocando fantasmas de hombres que derramaron sus propios cánceres sobre papeles blancos" (78) (evoking phantasms of men who spilled their own cancers onto white papers). Writing, creativity, fantasizing, masculinity, masturbation, and cancer are thus condensed into a strong metaphor. During this solitary walk, Pedro's mental attempts to unravel the moral logic and irony of don Quijote also spill forth like cancerous growth, the signifiers piling up in an often seemingly random sequence or "espiral" (spiral) but containing a convoluted logic.

The metonymic linking of signifiers, even if not logically or rationally related or consequential, shows how Pedro often thinks and how meaning is produced in the narrative in general. The power of contiguity to generate associative meaning can be seen at the syntactic and paragraph level, as well as by theme and episode. Pedro's guilt is expanded, like a cancerous growth in itself, by the contiguous episodes of his Saturday night. That night, time becomes a malleable, contagious property,[36] reflected in the narrative play of a generally irrational logic. Meanwhile, Pedro is fueled that night by the narcotic, distorting effect of alcohol and is susceptible to committing logical fallacies. Like the cancerous metastasis he studies, his thought processes (and the narrative) spread into and link usually discrete areas.

Motivated by illusions of self-aggrandizement, and blind to the lack of ethical balance in his approach to research, he depends on contiguous reasoning which leads him astray. Already at the outset of the novel, he shows his readiness to alter his research on the basis of unrelated factors. Too much trust in contiguity often works on the premise that "one thing leads to another." Pedro's contact with the world of the *chabolas*—initially simply through his powerful imagination fueled by some details from Amador—inspires him to envisage a sexualized set of causation that would provide remarkable, new research results. Pedro conveniently overlooks the scientific strictures of hypothesis. Properly methodological research cannot

---

36. "Era un sábado elástico que se prolongaba en la madrugada del domingo contagiándolo de sustancia sabática" (122) (It was an elastic Saturday which was prolonged into the early morning of the Sunday, contaminating it with sabbatical substance).

be attained through prejudiced anticipation of certain results alone. The fantastic nature of Pedro's leap into speculation is expressed in the following culminating sentence in a series of anaphors:

> ¡Oh qué posibilidad apenas sospechada, apenas intuible, reverencialmente atendida de que una—con una bastaba—de las mocitas púberes toledanas hubiera contraído, en la cohabitación de la chabola, un cáncer inguinoaxilar totalmente impropio de su edad y nunca visto en la especie humana que demostrara la posibilidad—¡al fin!—de una transmisión virásica que tomó apariencia hereditaria sólo porque las células gaméticas (inoculadas ab ovo antes de la vida, previamente a la reproducción, previamente a la misma aparición de las tumescencias alarmantes en los padres) dotadas de ilimitada inmortalidad latente, saltan al vacío entre las generaciones e incluyen su plasma íntegro—con sus inclusiones morbígenas—en el límite-origen, en el huevo del nuevo ser! (34)

> Oh! what a scarcely suspected possibility, scarcely intuitable, reverentially heeded, that one—one would suffice—of the adolescent Toledan girls would have contracted, in the cohabitation of the *chabola,* an inguinoaxilar cancer totally inappropriate for her age and never seen in the human species which would demonstrate the possibility—finally!—of a viral transmission that assumed the hereditary appearance only because the gamete cells (inoculated *ab ovo* before life, previously to reproduction, previously to the same appearance of the alarming tumescences of the parents), gifted with unlimited, latent immortality, leap into the void between the generations and include their whole plasma—with their diseased inclusions—in the limit-origin, in the egg of the new being!

Pedro's willingness (even desire) to discover a connection between hereditary and viral factors in cancer shows his susceptibility to the suggestion of false causation and false symmetries. Part of this seductive mode of reasoning derives from his guardedly eroticized ways of referring to the pubescent girls. The ecstatic, breathless, accretive effect of the passage also conveys a pornographic excitement. Pedro's thoughts are not entirely irrational; disease and sexuality are comparable on a metaphorical or conceptual level, and are at times directly related on an actual level.[37] These associations fuel our personal fears about contamination and coincide with irrational thought processes or inner logic related to our mental life established in infancy, when the perception of causation is based on a limited point of view and the observance of contiguous events or actions.

---

37. Many diseases can be transmitted through sexual contact; some diseases are hereditary and thus handed down to offspring through (sexual or artificial) reproduction.

Cancer is a particularly intriguing disease to compare pathologically with sexuality: pregnancy (cáncer inguinoaxilar), division of cells (células gaméticas), penile erection (e.g., tumescencias alarmantes en los padres), even the plump legs of Castilian girls can be (irrationally) misapprehended as tumorous growth. The cancerous strain from Illinois is vaguely described as cancer of the groin (cáncer inguinal) supposedly found in virgins and premenopausal ladies, a repeated reference which never becomes more explicit, a fact suggestive in itself of Pedro's dual interest and revulsion with his research. The novel makes no direct mention of ovarian, uterine, or cervical cancer. The strain of cancer is connected to certain female types at certain stages or types of sexuality (virginal, prostitute, maternal, pre- or postmenopausal). It seems that Pedro is driven to categorize women, limiting them to their sexual function, a maneuver that at once keeps them at bay and increases the tension of the controlled attention he fixes on them.

Pedro's reliance on explaining speculated causation by contiguity is curiously reinforced in a different way by the character Muecas. When Pedro visits the *chabola*, Muecas demonstrates that he, too, has intriguing beliefs based on contiguity. The secret of his success with breeding the mice is apparently based on the premise that the female mice should only breed when in heat. These mice can be brought to heat by being warmed by the "female heat" emanating from the breasts of his daughters. Muecas's female-heat theory in turn provides an alternative solution for the mystery of Pedro's lab mice's extinction—they have lacked heat, not vitamins.[38]

Pedro is, of course, not abandoning rational thought entirely when he posits hypotheses about cause and effect. Many diseases are contagious, and contagion can transpire in obvious and obscure ways. But he spoils the potential of his research before he can get it seriously underway because he is apt to act or make assumptions hastily, on impulse, or think too broadly or narrowly. These responses foreclose his ability to develop as a researcher. Through his self-sabotage, he gives up that scientific work based on careful use of time, testing, repetition, measured practice in order to live in the here and now and a defeatist Spanish fatality.

Closely related to Pedro's, and often the omniscient narrator's, tendency to conceive of contiguity in terms of cause and effect is their perception

---

38. My own suggestion is that Pedro's mice have had cancer, while Muecas's mice (reputedly stolen from Pedro's batch) are an unknown type (they may have been bred from a stolen pair of healthy control mice). Pedro's mice have died because they had cancer; Muecas's mice survive and breed because they do not have it. We never discover the condition of Muecas's mice, for Pedro never buys them to test them under the microscope. If Muecas's mice are descendants of the mice with the cancerous strain, then the irony lies in their ability to survive in the Spanish destitution of the shantytown along with people reduced to subhuman living standards.

of symmetry. Various concepts, people, or actions lead to the production or perception of various false symmetries. Examples include Dorita and Florita; Príncipe Pío train station as the "principio" (beginning) and end; San Lorenzo asking to be toasted evenly on both sides and Pedro's identification with that saint. The creation of a symmetrical form, pair, or group can be thought of as yet another censoring defense against an unwanted truth or desire. Symmetry, much like a cause-and-effect chain of signification, presents the appearance of wholeness or completeness. The fulfillment or creation of a link, part, or counterpart to fill in a perceived lack or incongruity is a satisfying strategy to disavow that lack or flaw.

Cancer, along with the related use of contiguity and symmetry, helps to organize sexual reference or allusion in many ways in *Tiempo de silencio*. Like the creative psychic censorship in the productions of dreams and fantasies, sexual reference is artistically concealed by the repulsive, forbidding, enigmatic nature of the disease itself and its ostensive purpose in the novel of providing a serious aim for the protagonist to pursue. What could be further removed from sex? Yet, as we have seen, for Pedro, sexuality is profoundly related to science and medicine; these are disciplines of control, regulation, penetration, and discovery. In fluctuating obsessive neurotic patterns, he is attracted to and repulsed by sexuality just as he is with his scientific research and his future medical practice. He seeks knowledge in sex, but in trying to grasp "it" he only seems to prolong his alienation, which is produced from his obsessive neurotic oscillations between conflicting impulses. This sort of oscillation acts as a censoring function in that it forecloses attainment of his goals or self-discovery. Instead, at the end of the novel Pedro narcissistically glorifies in his self-identification with San Lorenzo or a castrato, among other masochistic-heroic images. While there is surely some bitter irony in these thoughts, there is also a marked repeated emphasis on his pleasure in this nondefeat.

In fact, Pedro is more closely aligned with the dominant ideology than he might care to recognize. His language often borrows from Francoist discourse in glorification in one's martyrdom, heroic isolationism, and self-denial. Pedro demonstrates a censor's reaction to the sexual object—a combined sense of attraction and repulsion.

9. PROSTITUTION: THE BROTHEL AND A DESIRING SELF

Prostitution in literature signals a crisis of sexuality in the twentieth century. Man's desire is problematized by the humanization and empathy for the prostitute, the marketing and commodification of sex and the female body, and the uncertain integrity of the male subject. While writing about prostitution is not new in literature, I suggest that the nineteenth- and especially the twentieth-century literary explorations of prostitution make men's pleasure increasingly complicated and at times negated, and emphasize the socioeconomic conditions that determine prostitution on the one hand and, on the other hand, stress the male subject's psychic life, history, and conflicting desires, his inner self in a kind of erotic contemplation and interrogation.

Similar to the "Circe" episode in *Ulysses,* the brothel scenes of *Tiempo de silencio* dramatize the censoring production of fantasy about desiring and negating that desire for sexual satisfaction, fullness, discovery.[39] Martín-Santos integrates the concept of a personal odyssey in Pedro's trajectory including the episodes of the Saturday and Sunday. The brothel scene loosely parallels Joyce's "Circe" brothel scene, including hallucinatory street scenes that frame the visit to the brothel.[40] The brothel scenes stage a confrontation of Pedro with himself and his fantasies about facing sexuality and the Law.

These scenes (which were originally censored in 1961 and then largely restored in 1966) do not contain descriptions of actual sexual intercourse, and the women are not represented in a notably prurient way. Pedro, Matías, and the other customers certainly go to the brothel to satisfy sexual urges (physical and emotional). But the narrator does not present an idealized or pornographic fantasy of the Spanish brothel, and such rhetorical mentions of "celebración de los nocturnales ritos órficos" (99) (celebration of nocturnal Orphic rites) are counterbalanced by such ironic reductions as "el estéril intento de aplacar la bestia lucharniega" (the sterile attempt to

---

39. Several critics (e.g., Palley) explore the Joycean influences in *Tiempo de silencio.* Among the most recent efforts, see Rodríguez García, who discusses the impact of Joyce and Conrad on Martín-Santos's work. Martín-Santos incorporates British modernist trends in his novel, making it in 1961 a late example of modernist literature.

40. In a more distant analogy, the abortion episode is called Pedro's "Nausicaa" ("a reemprender los periplos nocturnos hacia la aún no explorada Nausicaa" [125] [to resume the nocturnal wanderings toward the yet unexplored Nausicaa]). In *Ulysses,* the episode Nausicaa portrays the dual subjectivities of a young woman at the seaside, Gerty MacDowell, and Leopold Bloom. During her flirtation with him from a distance, he surreptitiously masturbates and she, too, achieves some kind of pleasure. Her youth positions her symbolically as a daughter. In Homer, Nausicaa is the lovely unwed daughter of King Alcinous; she helps Odysseus by providing him with clothes, oil, food, and counsel, which leads him to Alcinous's welcome. In the abortion scene of *Tiempo de silencio,* the Nausicaa figure of Florita is made pathetic and drained of agency. The unwed Florita, while perhaps once lovely, is dying of a failed abortion. Her tragic body, especially her uterus, offers Pedro a difficult segment of his odyssey that will result in more troubles. This Nausicaa's father, Muecas, is a degraded parody of Alcinous.

placate the battling-negating beast). In general, the brothel represents a paradoxically forbidden, yet well regulated, zone in society. In 1949 Madrid prostitution was commonplace, there being an excess of women without employment or marriage possibilities. Brothels provided a regular recourse for working-class men in particular, and Martín-Santos's descriptions of the clientele and the brothel's situation in the city are in keeping with this social history.

The text involving the brothel shows strategies of artistic censoring to regulate sexuality, to keep it from overflowing well-maintained practices. The novel itself partitions the two brothel scenes neatly into their own sections, and the residents of the brothel do not appear in other settings or episodes. Within this domain of the brothel, doña Luisa carefully maintains order. In a psychoanalytic sense, her function is that of a censor or "mujer-esclusa" (101) (woman-floodgate), and on the Saturday night Pedro is an item requiring censoring. Doña Luisa removes, transforms, or displaces unseemly elements from the scene. Her editorial, calculating, and managerial function is stressed in the text. On Pedro's first visit, because of his and Matías's social standing as gentlemen, they are displaced to the visiting room, out of the way of the normal transactions of the night. On his second visit, Pedro is again allowed to remain as long as he hides himself away in one of the rooms (a kind of plotlike condensation and transformation). Doña Luisa hopes in the short term to disguise the fugitive as a client and in the long term to gain him as a doctor who will perform occasional abortions for her employees. The irony of Pedro's involvement with the brothel is that it represents for him a refuge from the law and the "real world," while for doña Luisa and the police it is a domain doubly bound by internal and external laws. The brothel is not a romantic or idealized maternal haven, nor a rebellious or bacchic escape into freedom and lawlessness, as Pedro's illusions and actions would suggest at times.

If anything, the brothel is subsumed in the law, something which is emphasized clearly by Luisa's repeated references to the police, the authorities, the municipality's control of water and electricity in relation to her business hours. The nature of her business's relationship with the authorities is corroborated by don Similiano's visit and arrest of Pedro, events which show the police's matter-of-fact acknowledgment of Luisa, her trade, and their collaboration and mutual support. In the brothel, sexual transactions are strictly regimented by in-house procedure, economic interests, and municipal and police forces. The women who work as prostitutes do so out of economic need and lack of ability to work elsewhere, owing to their low or fallen social status, lack of education, and the state's fairly openly discriminatory policy regarding women's employment and education. The austere effects of the Civil War and World War II and the mismanagement of Spain's economy in the 1940s resulted in the surplus of unemployed, unmarried women, as well as unemployed, unskilled laborers in general. Both groups gravitated toward the cities, contributing to the cancerous growth of the impoverished masses.

Tiempo de silencio's detailed portrayal of prostitution and the people of the shantytown can be read as a social history, although a pointedly non-social-realist approach is used.[41] It is notable that the brothel elicited more shame for the 1961 censor of the manuscript than did the far more damning and strongly developed episodes concerning the shantytown and the conditions mediating the illegal lab mice, the Muecas family, and the abortion.[42]

The brothel is regimented by inner laws and practices that are alternately focalized by the omniscient narrator and Pedro. In the "salón," the "ceremonias de la elección" (ceremonies of the choice) take place (102–3). The prostitutes' highly ritualized choosing of their clients from the hushed

---

41. Fernández compares the social and geographical strata of Madrid, "la fractura del espacio urbano" (the fracture of urban space), and the socioeconomic investigations in the literature of Galdós and Martín-Santos. He argues for the increased separation of the public and private spaces in the 1949 setting of Madrid; he does not mention the brothel scenes. If he had, he might agree with my assertion that these brothel spaces suggest a point of continuity in Spanish life, sharing some of the earlier Galdosian period's intermingling of the classes and of the public and private. On the other hand, Fernández's idea of the fracture of urban space is also operative for the 1949 brothel situation of Madrid, given the specific social, political, and economic circumstances of that era that caused a huge rise in prostitution.

42. See Carr and Preston for accounts of postwar Spain's rise of prostitution and shantytowns coupled with the phenomenon of urban growth. Carr explains how Spain's poor and subaltern were negatively affected by the grossly inadequate public medical services, labor laws and practices, and autarky. *Tiempo de silencio* is conveniently set in 1949, one of the "years of hunger," and thus does not seem to criticize the Spain of the early 1960s (the time of the novel's reception). Franco's broadcast to the nation at the end of 1948 was a speech of self-congratulation. As Preston aptly points out, at this 1948 juncture, Franco

> was oblivious to the fact that, in working class districts of major towns, people in rags could be seen hunting for scraps. Outside Barcelona and Málaga, many lived in caves. Most major cities had shantytowns on their outskirts made of cardboard and corrugated iron huts where people lived in appallingly primitive conditions. The streets thronged with beggars. State medical and welfare services were virtually non-existent other than the soup kitchens provided by the Falange. Hardship, malnutrition, epidemics, the growth of prostitution, the black market, corruption were consequences of his regime's policies. [. . .] (585)

And yet the shantytowns were still the shame of Spain in the early 1960s; Franco's negligence was made evident by his shocked reaction to that reality when Sevilla's governor took the Caudillo on a visit to that city's borderline slums during his tour of Andalusia in 1961; he was equally surprised to learn then that Madrid and Barcelona had similar shantytowns (Preston, 689–90). Therefore, Martín-Santos's apparent distanced exposition of 1949 prostitution and poverty were commensurable with the conditions of the early 1960s when he was writing and publishing *Tiempo de silencio*.

group of shyly waiting men is described in part as a religious ceremony, a casting of a spell, and a leading into a trance. The scene's silence ("un discreto silencio avergonzado" [an embarrassed, discreet silence]) bears a "litúrgico" (liturgical) air (104); the "deseo mudo" (mute desire) of the men is expressed in their partly concealed faces (102). The silence also seems to reduce the women to threatening phantasms on the verge of disappearing, "a pesar de su objetividad palpable y olible" (in spite of their palpable and smellable objectivity). Like unwanted or unseemly elements in a dream, Pedro and Matías, the "pareja sacrílega" (104) (sacrilegious couple), first drunkenly disrupt this ceremony of choosing clients and the "sagrado del lugar" (sacred nature of the place) and then are transferred from the scene by doña Luisa's lackeys to the visiting room.

The passage emphasizes the mysterious methods of elections and the spectral fantasy of the women, making desire a coded, liminal event for the initiated, with women who reduce their gestures to essentials such as a shockingly "mirada franca" (frank look) and a "un entreabrir la boca [. . .] perverso" (mouth perversely half-opened) and men who are muted and dissimulating (102); the young men Matías and Pedro do not cohere to this ritual.

The narrative strategy in the brothel episodes involves a predominant third-person voice that occasionally gives way to the inner workings of Pedro's mind or voice. The third-person narrator relates the drunken, disoriented mode of perception experienced by Pedro. This separation helps to distance the reader from the scene, showing in part Pedro's unsuccessful use of alcohol to get beyond himself. By way of the third-person narrative, the reader follows Pedro closely through his introduction to the brothel to his relegation with Matías to the visiting room. In the visiting-room scene, the narrative abandons regular syntax and breaks into a chain of associative or disruptive thoughts and images (104–6). This flow of thought presumably issues from Pedro, although the third-person narrator remains in place.

Thus, the brothel is refracted through several points of view, mostly thanks to the ingenious narrative manipulation. On the one hand, the reader follows Pedro's experience and non-Orphic descent into silent contemplation of himself and life, including the mysteries of the female body bared to its biological core. On the other hand, the narrative also alternately embeds the perspectives of Matías, doña Luisa and her employees, and workings of the brothel, thus resisting a completely subjectivized presentation of the brothel. The two brothel episodes depict it largely as a place of work (regulated by the state and in-house religiously kept rituals) and a place of residence. The relations between clients and prostitutes are strictly regulated and marked by a lack of detectable pleasure and excessive desire. Pedro's identity upon entering the brothel becomes that of the censored object (he becomes hidden or camouflaged), and his own reverie narrates the edges of the unconscious and his repressed thoughts.

The Francoist 1961 censorship of the first brothel scene and a large portion of the second scene shows the censor-reader's intolerance of the prostitution theme. The censor's ideologically correct upholding of the special taboo status of prostitution seems remarkable in retrospect because he was, by contrast, willing to tolerate a good number of other taboo or unsavory subjects treated in this novel (incest, abortion, poverty, and so on), which were certainly not tolerated widely by Francoist censorship for general reading in the early 1960s.[43]

After the restoration of the brothel-related passages in the 1966 and subsequent editions of the novel, a reader could begin to judge the brothel passages' relevance to the novel as a whole. While the main story in the censored version (1961–1965) was reasonably comprehensible, the complete versions (editions from 1966 on) supplied a richness of association because of Pedro's initial visit to the brothel and his subsequent flight to it from the law. In episodic terms, the first brothel scene is important because, if it is read in sequential order, it seems to be the ironic culmination of Pedro and Matías's drunken night on the town. Surely nothing more exotic or out of the ordinary could occur after the brothel visit? But the brothel only marks at best the half-way point in Pedro's trajectory and serves as a kind of psychical launching pad for further actions. Having come away dissatisfied from the brothel, he returns home and succumbs to carnal instincts and poor judgment to have sexual relations with Dorita, who has been positioned as "bait" by her mother and grandmother. Moving from the zone of regulated prostitution, Pedro in the pension enters a zone of amateur prostitution, the stakes of which are as important for the survival of "las tres generaciones" or "tres diosas" (three goddesses) as for the women working for doña Luisa.

Moreover, the symmetry between doña Luisa and her brothel and *la vieja* and her pension is established in the editions of 1966 on. This sense of association organizes Pedro's orientation to some degree and presents to the reader an important zone of the subaltern, the counterpart to the shantytown (and female characters' subaltern position in that world). Also, the pension owner, a celestina figure,[44] mirrors doña Luisa's own

43. I will explore the Spanish censorship's changing criteria in the 1960s in a forthcoming book on Spanish writers and censorship under Franco.

44. The medieval-Renaissance Spanish character la Celestina is a procuress, a wild, conniving, witchy older woman, immortalized in a twenty-one act, narrativized play *Comedia de Calisto y Melibea* or popularly *La Celestina* (1499) (or *Tragicomedia* in a new version by 1502) by Fernando de Rojas, and reincarnated variously over the centuries in Spanish literature.

pretensions about running a respectable establishment. Doña Luisa and *la vieja* are comparable in a number of ways: unmarried, vain, of dubious morals and unrealistic aspirations in the face of grim basic reality, impoverished, catering to single men.

The brothel functions in part as a sign of Pedro's feelings of guilt and desire to be found guilty. Thither he flees from the authorities, and it is his refuge there that further incriminates him in the point of view of the police and various high-ranking officials appealed to by Matías. The narrative clearly presents the brothel as a site of taboo. But, in addition, the narrator insists on including other perspectives which depict the brothel as doña Luisa's business, home (the second brothel scene has a distinctly domestic air), and a place carefully regimented by her according to the hour and purpose. In this way, the economy of the brothel is multiproductive. While its articulated purpose as the site of the traffic in women is considered obscene to the dominant ideology of Francoist Spain, the brothel setting is in fact an integrated part of the social scene. Upon entering or escaping to this domain, Pedro becomes a dubious entity which must be controlled by his own conscience and by others; he becomes a potential thing requiring censoring. Doña Luisa treats him as a desired-undesired entity and disguises or displaces him accordingly, and when an agent of the law (don Similiano) finally intrudes, she instantly cooperates with the Law and relinquishes Pedro.

Pedro's censoring of sexual desire is dramatized through the specter of prostitution: his oscillating attraction and aversion to virginal, nubile, young women and older, mature maternal figures. His censoring interest involves women's reproductive ability. That mysterious life-giving source fascinates him, as though secret knowledge (about sex, life, his authentic self) can be attained through the female body. His occasional yearning for maternal warmth and contact (and in some cases even a desire to return to an infantile or *in utero* dependency) is counteracted by his revulsion in sensing the underlying sexual tension or danger in that contact and by his censoring (screening) of his sexual desires and thoughts with scientific language and ideas. His censoring struggle with his desires can be noted in the stream of associations he makes while drunkenly meditating in the brothel's visiting room:

> calabozo inmóvil donde la soledad del hombre se demuestra, cesto de inmundicia, poso en que reducido a excremento espera el ocupante la llegada del agua negra que le llevará hasta el mar a través de ratas grises y cloacas, calabozo otra vez donde con un clavo lentamente se dibuja con trabajo arrancando trocitos de cal la figura de una sirena con su cola asombrosa de pez hembra, vigilada por una figura gruesa de mujer que la briza, acariciada por una figura blanda

de mujer que amamanta, cuna, placenta, meconio, deciduas, matriz, oviducto, ovario puro vacío, aniquilación inversa en que el huevo en un universo antiprotónico se escinde en sus dos entidades previas (105)

motionless prison where man's solitude is demonstrated, barrel of filth, dregs in which, reduced to excrement, the occupant awaits the arrival of black water which will carry him to the sea, past grey rats and sewers, again a prison where with a nail slowly, picking laboriously away bits of lime, the figure of a siren with her astonishing tail of a female fish is drawn, guarded by the stout figure of a woman who strokes her, caressed by a gentle figure of a woman who is suckling, cradle, placenta, meconium, deciduas, oviduct, womb, pure empty ovary, inverse annihilation in which the egg in an antiprotonic universe splits into its two former entities.

This passage introduces the conflict between man and woman, man's arrest in scopophilic trance vis-à-vis the impossible phallic woman, the siren, the mythical creature of male invention that overcomes the oedipal crisis of discovering the mother's lack (of a penis). The thought, tellingly situated as man's solitary imprisonment in creative disavowal, oddly anticipates Pedro's forthcoming incarceration and subsequent scratching of the siren's image on the prison wall. Some of his guilty feelings (e.g., the repeated mention of "calabozo" [prison] anticipates confrontation with the Law) *thus precede any actual action* taken on his part with Dorita or Florita (or any attempt to flee from questioning). In a later episode, when Pedro is actually in prison, the association between the siren and Dorita becomes far more evident. In the brothel, Pedro's thought of the siren is accompanied by the initially forbidding character of the "mujer gruesa" (big woman) who caresses the siren and transforms into a "figura blanda" (gentle woman) who suckles. This phantasmatic relationship between the older, maternal woman and the siren-virgin with the astonishing tail structures part of Pedro's desire, his drive to insert himself into that position of being cared for by that mother and thus in some way to become that siren, that phallic woman (a woman who is really a man).

In the brothel narrative, as Pedro's thoughts break into a progressive inventory of features of reproduction, they veer to a split or cleavage predicated on the notion of a negation or separation of reproductive forces. There is a striking homology between the first mention of the solitary man's excremental state of being washed away by black water and the subsequent mention of the female reproductive features. The fetus-newborn is also a solitary being, and the placenta, meconium, and deciduas are all matter that become excrement at birth.

Thus, even the phantasmatic "matriz" (womb) offers no satisfying haven or source of plenitude. The further censoring reversal of the train of thought undoes through signifying links the concept of conception itself: "pure empty ovary," "inverse annihilation," "antiprotonic universe," the separation of sperm and egg. Reproduction produces excrement (the abject subject), a form of negation which expels man into an excremental world. Women are responsible for this depressing state of affairs: the deceptive siren; the mother figure to whom one cannot return; even the lowly aging prostitute Charo whom no one else has wanted and who keeps the two drunk young men company.

The womb-siren passage also emphasizes Pedro's lack of presence or subjectivity. His fantasy thoughts seem to erase his presence. The third-person narrator seems to relate Pedro's thoughts (or Pedro narrates himself in the third person). This ambiguous, distancing narrative effect thus provides us with a sense of observing Pedro's psyche. In addition, this effect is achieved through the occasional use of the Spanish reflexive mode ("se dibuja") which translates into English as the passive voice ("it is drawn") and which dispenses with the need to cite the acting subject. These censoring yet desiring views of the feminine body, and Pedro's confrontational relationship to it, recur in his responses to various women throughout the novel. Women's reproductivity is important to him in negative and narcissistic ways. His perceptions of his room at the pension—his "masturbatory Dachau" or "su alcoba ascética de sabio" (116) (his ascetic bedroom of a scholar)—reflect frustration and feelings of superiority. Although he is not notably religious, Pedro has absorbed Spain's Catholic views of female sexuality as dirty, dangerous, sinful. He supplements that basic standpoint with his creative use of language and his scientific studies.

The female body threatens to become a prison of excrement, a site of silence, disorder, unwholesome growth (pregnancy through incest and inguinal cancer). The female body also serves as a combined worker and product in the sale of sex and artistic work. It therefore presents the site for imposition of a network of disciplines: the law and science in particular, but also economics, art, literature. These disciplines help to suppress and regulate female sexuality, allowing the male subject to have a sense of empowerment over it, being able to censor or denigrate it when it seems too dangerous. At the same time, these disciplines and the censoring functions they provide also help to create the circumstances for the subject to experience erotic desire. Censoring in this sense produces and shapes aesthetically our perceptions and experience of sex.

10. FLORITA'S INCESTUOUS PREGNANCY

If sexual relations are strongly overlaid by screens of prohibition and danger, then pregnancy, the fruition of those relations, is a site of problematic meaning in *Tiempo de silencio*. In Spanish literature, pregnancy, legitimate or illegitimate, often indicates the future or destiny of the parents or a generation. Pregnancy out of wedlock concretizes a conflict with societal norms, such as Fortunata's and Adela's self-destruction through pregnancy (the respective fallen women characters of Pérez Galdós's *Fortunata y Jacinta* and García Lorca's *La casa de Bernarda Alba*). Florita's death also dramatizes a social conflict. Her incestuous pregnancy is caused by the backward patriarchalism and dire poverty of her father and general grotesque milieu of the *chabolas*, and serves as a critique of Franco's mismanagement of Spain. Her pregnancy offers further specialized motifs in terms of aesthetic censoring of sexuality.

Pedro's fascination and disgust with women and their bodies are demonstrated in various overdetermined ways in his mental life, and he deploys strategies of metonymy and metaphor to censor thoughts that are not acceptable to his harsh superego. The ascetic side to his medical practice is a forced façade, disguising lascivious desires as well as providing him with an auxiliary source of self-satisfaction with a social status he has had to work to attain (unlike the privileged Matías). Florita's incestuous pregnancy offers a dramatic instance in which Pedro makes a regulating, surgical intervention which has serious ethical repercussions.

Pedro's negating association of women's bodies with filth finds a fertile source for elaboration in the shantytown, an obscene counterpart to the brothel. In a self-reflexive moment as he surveys the world of the *chabolas*, he recognizes his murky, erotic, nonscientific fascination with this domain outside the Law:

> Allí, en algún oculto orificio, inferiores al hombre y por él dominados, los ratones de la cepa cancerígena seguían consumiendo la dieta por el Muecas inventada y reproduciéndose a despecho de toda avitaminosis y de toda neurosis carcelaria. Este pequeño grumo de vida investigable hundido en aquel revuelto mar de sufrimiento pudoroso le conmovía de un modo nuevo. Le parecía que quizá su vocación no hubiera sido clara, que quizá no era sólo el cáncer lo que podía hacer que los rostros se deformaran y llegaran a tomar el aspecto bestial e hinchado de los fantasmas que aparecen en nuestros sueños y de los que ingenuamente suponemos que no existen. (53)

There, in some occult orifice, inferior to man and dominated by him, the mice of the cancerous strain were continuing to consume the diet invented by Muecas and reproducing in spite of all avitaminosis and all incarcerative neurosis. This researchable little cluster of life sunk in that rough sea of modest suffering moved him in a new way. It seemed to him that perhaps his vocation had not been clear, that perhaps it was not only cancer which could make the faces deform and assume the bestial and swollen look of the phantasms that appear in our dreams and of those who we ingenuously suppose do not exist.

It is difficult to determine from the passage whether it is sympathy or a kind of creative relish that Pedro feels. What could Pedro's clear vocation be? Priest, anthropologist, psychiatrist, social or political reformer? The shantytown people and homes, "oníricas construcciones" (oneiric constructions) cobbled together out of odd materials, appear fantastic to the outsider.[45] The people have become "immunized," as Amador explains, by living in so much "filth" (41). Described in ironically anthropological terms, these inhabitants' sexuality is apparently unruly, incest is prevalent, and any morality in marriage is disregarded (51). Yet these and many other statements by the third-person narrator must be treated with caution. The irony functions both to criticize the shameful social state of affairs (Franco's negligence) and to play into the educated reader's readiness to assume that these impoverished people have lost all sense of humanity, and are leading instead a solely primitive or animal existence.

The point is supposed to be taken both ways critically. Despite the fact that there *is* a case of incest (Florita and Muecas), it eventually turns out that that case is not taken lightly or obliviously (as animals might). The father finds it imperative to try to induce an abortion; his surviving daughter hates her father for his actions; his wife denounces him to the police. During and after the abortion and Florita's death, the *chabolista* neighbors flock around the Muecas home, out of voyeurism and empathetic interest (particularly on the part of the women). Mistakenly connected to Florita's pregnancy, Cartucho goes to great lengths to gain revenge on Pedro, thus showing that his feelings for Florita went beyond a purely physical sexual instinct. These *chabolistas* are not mere animals, although some of their actions and responses are clearly flawed.

The incestuous pregnancy also significantly coincides with Pedro's intervention. He suspects that he could find a cancerous tumor in Florita's groin,

---

45. The passage recalls Luis Buñuel's documentary film *Las Hurdes*: the extradiegetic narrator observes the physical deformation and suffering experienced by the film's subjects in Extramadura, owing to extreme malnutrition, lack of hygiene, poverty, inbreeding, and severe degrees of ignorance.

contracted through a viral contact with the mice. It is not clear whether Pedro knows that what is growing in Florita is the result of contact with her father. The implied parallel between the unclean pregnancy and the mice's cancerous multiplication (and possibly contamination) is extended by the fact that both take place in Madrid's cancerous growth of the shantytown. When Pedro performs the "scraping" of Florita's uterus, he helps to complete the negation of the pregnancy and approaches the womb as a void (135).

The death of Florita in post-abortion serves as a sign of censored or negated knowledge and sexuality. During the police interrogation, Pedro articulates his interest in the girl as a possible scientific subject because of her contact with the mice. After her death, her image haunts Pedro, such as the scene at Matilde's soirée in which Pedro has a phantasmatic vision of the bloody naked body of the Toledan girl (173). Her cadaver, along with its damning blood, appears like a censored thing:

> Obstinadamente desnuda deja que su sangre corretee caprichosamente entre los muebles y entre las piernas de los desmesurados contertulios. Sin duda es uno de los objetos que éstos no deben ver, pues aunque pasen a su lado o bien lo pisen distraídamente, no lo advierten. Entre las leyes de este mundo de dioses y de pájaros hay alguna referente a los cadáveres.

> Obstinately naked it lets its blood run out capriciously amid the furniture and the feet of the unrestrained guests. It is doubtlessly one of the objects that these people should not see, for although they walk by it or even distractedly step on it, they don't notice it. Among the laws of this world of gods and birds there is one that refers to cadavers.

In this passage, the upper-class world is consumed with fashion and philosophy. Florita's death reminds Pedro of his complicity in the occlusion of the girl's death.

Her body as censored thing is further dramatized by its burial, subsequent exhumation according to a mysterious court order, and autopsy. Finally, her body is doubled in the murder and subsequent autopsy of Dorita.

11. CONCLUSION: THE PARADOXICALLY PRODUCTIVE ORGAN OF CENSORING: TISSUE, FOLDS, AGENCY

The fabric of the text emphasizes contiguity of elements which are not necessarily related on a logical or realistic plane, but which imply powerfully significant symbolic and psychic meaning. The folds in the narrative bring together and exclude certain features in a way comparable to censoring processes. The term "pliegues" (folds) is referred to several times in *Tiempo de silencio,* as well as "capitoné" (quilted). By using narrative organization, especially metonymic, sequential, and contiguous linking, the quilted, folded aspects of language and narrative are emphasized so that apparent incongruities or oppositions reinforce each other or offer screening (censoring) effects.

By recognizing the text's capacity to fold in on itself, to be inwardly self-referential and outwardly intertextual, we can note that this tissue-text functions as a paradoxical site of reproduction, a place which generates censoring meaning. And this emphasis is reinforced by the novel's preoccupation with the themes of sexuality and cancer, two dangerous elements capable of unruly reproduction if not regulated in some way through censoring strategies.

Together with the omniscient third-person narrator, Pedro acts as the agent of exploration across this folded, quilted fabric. Pedro's complex character and modes of thinking organize the erotic economy in the novel. His personal erotics are not limited to a private and inner sphere, although it is from that inner space of consciousness that much of the narrative focalization issues. Pedro's erotics are related to social and political conditions of 1949 Spain, the tension among competing Spanish discourses in literature, philosophy, and national mythology, and the ironized ambiguous motives of science and medicine, two domains that would supposedly offer knowledge, enlightenment, and therapy.[46]

Part of Pedro's importance is that he be apprehended by readers as a flawed agent (and not some middle-class intellectual or moral hero or healer).[47] While he is a privileged agent who can move around many *madrileño*

---

46. Margaret Jones suggests how medical research attaches to concerns of national determinism: "[T]he narrow field of Pedro's research embraces a national allegory with the implication of determinism (essential historical character) versus self-determination (possibility of change). Cancer becomes a metaphor: if it is viral, there is hope for change, since a remedy may be possible with a vaccine; transmitted genetically, there is no hope for cure" (92).

I suggest that such a national allegory is part of Pedro's point of view, and not one necessarily shared by the author or reader. The narrative sets these issues up critically to allow us to question Spaniards' overinvestment in essentialism.

47. Barry Jordan views Pedro as a "totally ridiculous, superfluous character, as much an embarrassment in the salons of the bourgeoisie as in the *chabolas* of the sub-proletariat, by whom he is mercilessly used and exploited" (180).

I would try to modify this view by pointing to the *mutual* exploitation at play in the relations between Pedro and others. Pedro shows little if any evidence of being "[g]enerous, kind-hearted, full of good intentions" (Jordan 180); as an ambitious but naïve young man, he seeks to use medical research to advance his status and even achieve greatness. Medical research has further erotic and

worlds, that unstable, gyroscopic mobility signals his lack of belonging. We know through his experiences and perceptions that he often disavows his ability to wield some agency. His weak-willed character does not mean that he has no will at all. He has a will to achieve certain limited goals of masochistic enjoyment. We can count a number of examples of his exercise of will: he censors unwanted elements and thoughts using unpleasurable imagery and scenarios in his fantasies (which he then perversely enjoys); he agrees to marry Dorita, even though it is not his desired match with a kindred spirit, but a fall into the suffocating, cloying sphere of the "tres diosas" and their taste for popular Spanish entertainment, pretentious classism, and general vulgarity (a marriage which he would enjoy despite these tortures because Dorita is so beautiful and Pedro, in spite of himself, as a Spaniard, shares in some of their vulgar taste); in his "fall" from the institute, Pedro does not let himself fall into destitution and despair, but rather writes his exams and assumes a conventional career as a provincial doctor.

Meanwhile, the narrative's grammar and syntax tend to present Pedro as being out of control or abdicating his position of relative or potential power. Decisions are made for this seemingly passive, receptive subject out of hand, whether they be by the director of his institute, the women in his pension, the people of the *chabolas*, the police, Matías's lofty world (including his mother and the philosopher), or doña Luisa's world of the prostitutes. Unlike Pedro, these other people reside in comparably stable places which provide some coherent social meaning and structure.

Pedro's internalized struggle with Spanish societal and ideological codes is narrated in the novel's framing device of the interior monologue at the beginning and conclusion: the grandiose fantasy of an embattled Spaniard who will win the Nobel Prize and prove his sense of value. The plot and setting support the portrayal of Pedro's conflicting desire for sexual contact, warmth, and sensual satisfaction in beauty. This desire is artistically screened or censored by masochistic interests in cancerous contagion, impregnation, being cut, or inflicting that pain. The balance between his two urges is an unsteady one, producing alternately creative disavowal, displacement, recourse to transformational images of negation, cutting, castration, barrenness, anesthesia, burning, being dried out, and powerful zones of silence. His censoring fantasies transform, for example, his desire for female warmth into a masochistic-heroic fantasy of a solitary and distancing achievement of painful pleasure through other heat sources: being toasted (San Lorenzo) and being dried out in the sun (*mojama*), two intertwined national images at the novel's end.

---

censoring personal connotations for him vis-à-vis the other, as established in this chapter.

Labanyi suggests how Martín-Santos performs a psychoanalysis of the Francoist society in a kind of complex dialectic:

> Martín-Santos sugiere que el español, por sentirse impotente, se deja castrar por la autoridad, y así confirma su impotencia. El miedo al fracaso lleva al fracaso. El complejo de la inferioridad crea la inferioridad. Martín-Santos enriquece el análisis sartriano de la dialéctica social, al añadir la nueva dimensión de lo inconsciente, que impulsa al hombre a buscar lo que más teme. (115)

> Martín-Santos suggests that the Spaniard, by feeling impotent, lets himself be castrated by authority, and thus confirms his impotence. The fear of failure leads to failure. The inferiority complex creates inferiority. Martín-Santos enriches the Sartrean analysis of the social dialectic by adding the new dimension of the unconscious, that compels man to seek what he most fears.

My discussion expands Labanyi's interpretation. I explain how the failure and inferiority experienced by Pedro and in the various plot outcomes, especially the deaths of Florita and Dorita, result in a kind of masochistic pleasure and embittered enjoyment of coherence with Spanish mythologization of failure, punishment, fate or destiny, isolation, and determinism. My discussion differs from Labanyi's on the issue of the unconscious. Martín-Santos makes conscious or legible desires, perceptions, and censoring operations in his narrative. In his *Libertad, temporalidad y transferencia en el psicoanálisis existencial,* he makes a chart of correspondences between "orthodox" Freudian concepts and their existential counterparts. For the Freudian "Inconsciente" (Unconscious) he posits the existential "Conciencia no tética" (non-thetic consciousness) (54).

On a conscious, linguistic, and narrative level, which often grazes the conscious borders of fantasy, the omniscient narrator and Pedro elaborate a complex censoring of sexuality. As we have seen in this chapter, sexuality's positive connotations of life, fertility, pleasure, and love are screened or censored aesthetically with discursive references to negative qualities. Martín-Santos's dialectical narrative presents a series of wrongful and flawed actions and situations, all tied to sexuality, which require critical judgment of Spanish life under Franco.

5

Apocalyptic Beauty, Russian Sublimity

VIKTOR EROFEEV'S *RUSSKAIA KRASAVITSA*

*In*stead of a synthesis of East and West, Russian literature often offers contrasts and paradoxes of the contiguity of the two influences, suggesting a crisis of coherence, a schizophrenic split of values, and judgmental and negating attitudes. Some of the prominent features of this literature are the fascination with dangerous and powerful beauty, a tendency toward fatalism and apocalyptic reasoning, the characterization of weak, ineffectual, superfluous, or marginalized (underground) male protagonists, and variations of the strong woman, ethereal woman, and the fallen woman.[1] Some literary Russian fallen women of the nineteenth century (for example, Tolstoi's Anna Karenina and Dostoevsky's Nastasya Filippovna) are tragically idealized, foregrounding a social crisis of conflicting or outdated values. For all their beauty and allure, such women are directed toward a doomed ending. Their suffering and death can be interpreted variously: a punishment for sin; a sign of Christ-like greatness, lending to a general trend of martyrdom narratives in Russian literature; an

---

1. Russian fatalism is comparable to Spanish fatalism in their stress on national or regional attributes and customs; Dostoevsky is interested in innate characteristics and how these can inexorably lead to certain outcomes that seem predestined (e.g., Smerdiakov's parricide or Filippovna's Russian beauty that leads to her downfall). Erofeev, as we shall see, taps into beliefs of Russian fatalism.

indication of repressive and hypocritical society; a crisis of incompatibility of love and sexuality.

The confessional mode of Viktor Erofeev's novel *Russkaia krasavitsa* (1990 and 1994) (*Russian Beauty*)[2] emphasizes the creative and repressive functions of writing about the sexual subject under censorship. Irina Tarakanova, the protagonist and first-person narrator, provides in her confession a portrait of an apocalyptic, censored self. Her character and life are defined by the censorious Soviet world around her and her desire to connect with it. Mediated through Irina's point of view and her body, the novel offers a candid, multifaceted portrait of the late Soviet period. The novel's narrative meaning also depends upon the pornographic fantasy of encountering the desiring woman's voice in the confessional writing of a woman defined by her sexual beauty and relations. The narrative anticipates and ironically uses the presuppositions and dynamics of that fantasy to represent an alternative portrait of a feminine subjectivity as sublime artistic creativity. *Russkaia krasavitsa* parodically derives meaning from such pornographic pre-texts as the merry or wise, reformed prostitute's confession (e.g., Cleland's *Memoirs of a Woman of Pleasure* or Defoe's *Moll Flanders*). Furthermore, artistic, literary, and historical intertextuality reinforces the idea that Irina is a censored subject, a Russian beauty, with a paradoxically national heroic and tragic aesthetic status.

Erofeev's oeuvre forms part of what has been termed Russia's alternative prose (*alternativnaia proza;* or new prose, *novaia proza*). This literature, emerging in the late 1980s during glasnost' and the early 1990s, before and after the coup that ended the Soviet era (1991), is distinguished for its ostensible break from Soviet literary traditions on the one hand and, on the other, for its continued interest in pre-Soviet Russian literature and less sanctioned or censored Soviet-era literature as sources of exploration of collective identity, ethics, and aesthetics. Alternative literature emphasizes brutal and obscene effects, creating a kind of shock value and clear break from Soviet-era puri-

---

2. In this discussion I refer to the uncensored, post–Soviet *Russkaia krasavitsa: Roman, rasskazy* (Moscow: Molodaia gvardiia, 1994) and the English translation, *Russian Beauty*, by Andrew Reynolds, and cite passages from each by their respective page number. The first edition of *Russkaia krasavitsa* (Moscow: Moskovskii rabochi, 1990) was lightly censored; several sexual or other offensive words (such as "blow job" or "whore") were replaced by dashes or ellipses. See Ermolaev (252–57) for his careful, concise assessment of the censorship of the first edition of *Russkaia krasavitsa*. A comparison of the censored and uncensored editions of *Russkaia krasavitsa* shows that, by 1990, Soviet censorship was virtually over. If we take into account the far stricter Soviet censorship and publishing scene at any time before 1988, it is little wonder that Erofeev could not find a publisher for his first novel until the late 1980s. *Russkaia krasavitsa* was the sort of novel that either had to be refused publication permission altogether or published virtually in its entirety; the integration of sexuality throughout the text makes it almost impossible to delete or remove sections without seriously interfering with the meaning.

tanism that had become embedded in cultural production and reception. *Alternativnaia* or *novaia proza* offers an exorcism of Stalinism.[3]

Erofeev's early career and *Russkaia krasavitsa*, his first novel, were shaped by censorship and the emerging literature of the *alternativnaia proza*. Together with a group of writers unable to publish their avant-garde work owing to the censor's refusal to shift criteria of acceptability, Erofeev helped to compile with Vasilii Askenov an uncensored literary almanac at the end of the 1970s, *MetrOpol'*, which was denounced in the Soviet Union while published abroad. For this transgression Erofeev lost his membership to the Writers' Union, thus falling outside the pale of sanctioned writers. He completed *Russkaia krasavitsa* during this internal period as a persona non grata in the publishing world. He did not succeed in publishing the manuscript until extremely late in the glasnost' era.

The novel can be read as a wild confrontation with censored subjects in Soviet Russia, with a brilliant integration of intertextual references to Russian and non-Russian art and literature, as well as politics and society. *Russkaia krasavitsa* represents Bakhtin's modern dialogic novel in its incorporation of heteroglossia and narrative structures, and parodies and analogies of earlier Russian trends in art and literature that present a critical view of the state of collective life in Russia. As a postmodernist novel, it makes strong and highly elaborate uses of parody and analogy for characters and plots. It sews together long-term Russian preoccupations with the apocalypse and forms of endings (as opposed to beginnings), with the schism between love and sexuality, and with the role of art and beauty in social, political, and spiritual life. In a series of inversions, negations, and displacements, the heroine embodies an amalgam of nineteenth- and twentieth-century Russian poetic ideals involving beauty, love, art, and sexuality, while, in terms of plot, she plays out actions that have usually pertained to masculine roles of the superfluous or marginal man, the martyr, and the writer.

The complex combinations of parody and ironic analogy in characterization and plot indicate an ongoing concern with censorship of free expression and with Russian freedom and identity in general. As such the Russian beauty Irina Tarakanova is more than a heroine; her character provides a markedly self-reflective, subversive, and disruptive investigation of Russianness which is premised on forms of censoring, harsh judgment, including apocalypse, and negative sexuality.

---

3. For discussions of this exorcism, see Porter; Gillespie; Deming Brown; and Shneidman's excellent series of overviews of the late Soviet and post-Soviet periods of Russian literature (*Soviet Literature in the 1970s: Artistic Diversity and Ideological Conformity; Soviet Literature in the 1980s: Decade of Transition; Russian Literature, 1988–1994: The End of an Era; Russian Literature, 1995–2002: On the Threshold of the New Millennium*).

1. CRITICAL SYNOPSIS

Russkaia krasavitsa's first-person narrator, Irina Tarakanova, writes a swirling, nonsequential confessional tract. She reviews her life, jumping from one event to another, interjecting frequent critical, ironic asides, and paying special attention to the events of the last two or so years. Irina as writer is the antithesis of the Soviet norm, a unionized male writer. She comes from the countryside, has only a patchy high-school education, and leads a dubious life in Soviet Moscow. She acquires further learning and culture by living in Moscow and by deftly using her magpie skills of copying, observing, and taking on mentors. She has a nondescript job in a collective; her "real" life takes place mostly outside of work. A party girl, and possibly an occasional prostitute, the beautiful Irina tries to live a glamorous, alternative life. Her beauty, which has a strong sexual quality, attracts men and women. After a string of lovers, she finds her match in Vladimir Sergeyevich (his last name is withheld), who is an older married man and a prominent Soviet writer and cultural figure. She affectionately nicknames him "Leonardik," comparing him to Leonardo da Vinci, because she respects his image as a Soviet Renaissance man.

Irina and Vladimir Sergeyevich embark on an adulterous affair which lasts some two years. Her status as lover, courtesan, or sexual partner remains ambiguous for much of the novel partly because Vladimir Sergeyevich cannot decide what he wants from her. Like many "other women," she aspires to having more than brief, secretive sexual encounters. She would like love, marriage, stability, a certain respectability, and perhaps children.

When Vladimir Sergeyevich suddenly dies during sexual intercourse with Irina, her role as his lover becomes exposed to the public in the Soviet Union and abroad. Her fame expands because of her extraordinary sexual beauty and the unauthorized printed dissemination of its image beyond the Soviet borders. Vladimir Sergeyevich's widow attempts to exclude Irina from the funeral proceedings and even banish her from Moscow. In reaction, Irina agrees to be interviewed by foreign journalists and pose for some photographs, thus disseminating her image and her sexual relationship to this famous, late great Soviet figure. She attempts to assert and define her identity in others ways. With the aid of a group of Muscovite intellectuals, she tries to become a national heroine through a fantastic, porno-graphized, postmodern Soviet-Russian mimesis of Joan of Arc.

These flamboyant efforts exhaust her, and she falls sick with a fever, alone in her apartment. In her hallucinatory state, the ghost of Vladimir Sergeyevich visits her. He has changed, and now wants to make love to her and even marry her. In a comic, semipornographic scene of intercourse, he inseminates her. From this juncture, Irina's tendency toward a psychotic vision of the world and herself becomes emphasized. Once she realizes that she is pregnant, she is conflicted in her desire to have the baby or to abort. The pregnancy produces a growing smell of rot, obliterating her once famed uterine fragrance of a bergamot forest. Even her attempts to be cleansed by a Russian Orthodox baptism and a Russian witch do not improve matters. Finally, in triumphant despair, she agrees to become Vladimir Sergeyevich's bride in death, invites all of her friends and acquaintances to her wedding, and hangs herself in her bathroom at the age of twenty-three.

2. RUSSIAN BEAUTY: THE RUSSIAN HEROINE

Russkaia krasavitsa's emphasis on subjectivity and parodic and ironic intertextuality aligns it with postmodern world literature. Linda Hutcheon explains how postmodernist textual reflexivity involves awareness of nature and historicity. "This complex awareness" has been produced in part by poststructuralist theory. She adds, "[F]eminist theory and practice have problematized poststructuralism's (unconsciously, perhaps, phallocentric) tendency to see the subject in apocalyptic terms of loss or dispersal, for they refuse to foreclose the question of identity [. . .]" (37). In keeping with this postmodern sensibility, Erofeev's feminist and poststructural use of Irina as reflexive female voice positions the apocalyptic theme critically and openly in the text.

Erofeev's novel embraces the postmodernist desire to reexamine and include former Russian master narratives, especially poetic and pre-Soviet ones. But this embrace involves both suspicion and subversion. Notably, by situating Irina as the narrating subject, Erofeev distances her from the beautiful and apocalyptic Russian women of the past (in lyric poems by Pushkin, Tiutchev, Blok; in philosophy, like Rozanov and Soloviev; in novels by Chernyshevskii, Dostoevsky, Tolstoy, and Pasternak). Irina incorporates within her self and her narration pre- and post-revolutionary literary characters, implying repetitions and unreliable copies. By making Irina the messy but central and centralizing force in terms of character and action, Erofeev draws into center stage the woman who is usually marginalized and censored, the one who usually disrupts the plot and does not end up married. From the first chapter, Irina presents herself in apocalyptic terms, and by chapter 2, most of the story is known, at least in embryo. Each subsequent chapter provides a circling narrative that tells some more details of her story, while there is no methodical structure of a chronological memoir (e.g., beginning at the beginning, or starting a retrospective by going back to the beginning). The resistance to a historically organized development redistributes priorities in the narrative. Irina as subject, although the centralizing narrator, creates a body of words that whirl and disperse, including various intertextual references and anecdotal digressions. The effect is one of centralized displacement. As we consider the heroine's primary features, her "genius" of beauty and love, we might recall their embedded problematization.

Irina defines beauty on various cultural levels. She is the "Russian Beauty" sung of in the old popular folk song.[4] Within the nineteenth- century perspective of poets Alexander Pushkin and Fyodor Tiutchev's, poets evoked repeatedly in *Russkaia krasavitsa,* Irina's beauty is comparable to the entrancing women of the poem "K A.P. Kern" (1825) (To A. P. Kern) and "O, kak ubiistvenno my liubim" (c.1851) (How murderously we love).[5] Irina reads Tiutchev, and Vladimir Sergeyevich compares himself with him; V. S.'s affair with the young Irina is not unlike that of Tiutchev's with Elena Aleksandrovna Deniseva. With this much younger mistress, in his autumn years and after two previous marriages, Tiutchev wrote some of his finest poems but lost favor in court circles; his mistress had his children out of wedlock and suffered from a lack of social respect. Tiutchev's poem, "O, kak ubiistvenno my liubim," speaks of the passion of such difficult love affairs, referring to the *coup de foudre* first meeting and the social censure and doom awaiting the lover:

O, kak ubiistvenno my liubim,
Kak v buinoi slepote strastei
My to vsego vernee gubim,
Chto serdtsu nashemu milei!
[...]
Ty pomnish' li, pri vashei vstreche,
Pri pervoi vstreche rokovoi,
Ee volshebnyi vzor, i rechi,
I smekh mladencheski-zhivoi?
[...]
Sud'by uzhasnym prigovorom

---

4. Porter comments: "we have parody: the title [of the novel] would seem to derive from the words of a folk song: 'After all, not for nothing is renowned / The Russian beauty' (*Ved' nedarom slavitsya / Russkaya krasavitsa*); yet one might detect a pun similar to the one in Pasternak's unfinished play *The Blind Beauty*—both authors, in very different ways, are writing about their Russia as a whole, charting her attributes as well as her considerable deficiencies" (150).

5. See Porter, Dark, and Rylkova for discussions of Tiutchev and other intertextuality in *Russkaia krasavitsa*. See Gregg and Zeldin for commentary on Tiutchev's work and life.

Tvoia liubov' dlia nei byla,
I nezasluzhennym pozorom
Na zhizn' ee ona legla!
Zhizn' otrechen'ia, zhizn' stradan'ia!
[...]
I na zemle ei diko stalo,
Ocharovanie ushlo ...
Tolpa, nakhlynuv, v griaz' vtoptala
To, chto v dushe ee tsvelo. (1–4, 13–16, 21–25, 29–32)

O how murderously we love,
How in the stormy blindness of passions
We most surely ruin that which is
Dearest of all to our heart!
[...]
Do you remember at your first meeting,
At your first fateful meeting,
Her magic gaze and words
And lively-maidenly laughter?
[...]
Your love for her was a terrible sentence of fate,
And like unmerited shame
It has lain upon her life.
A life of abnegation, a life of suffering!
[...]
And she has become like a wild thing on the earth;
The charm has passed ...
The crowd, having burst in,
Has trampled in the mud
That which blossomed in her soul. [6]

6. Translation by Gregg (Tiutchev, 163).
Tiutchev's preoccupation with a personalized apocalyptic beauty is explored in other poems. For example, we can see the poet's recognition of the destructive quality of his desire for his blossoming lover in the short poem "Sizhu zadumchiv i odin" (1836) (I Sit Pensive and Alone). The poem ends with these lines: "No ty, moi bednyi, blednyi tsvet, / Tebe uzh vozrozhden'ia net, / Ne rastsvetesh'! / Ty sorvan byla moei rukoi, / S kakim blazhenstvom i toskoi, / To znaet bog! ... / Ostan'sia zh na grudi moei, / Poka liubvi ne zamer v nei / Poslednii vzdokh" (22–30) (But you, my poor, my pallid bloom, / There will be no renewal for you, / No blossoming. / You were plucked by my own hand, / And with a joyful pleasure and anguish / God only knows! / Stay then close beside my heart, / So long as love's last sigh still lingers / On within it). If Irina or Leonardik would read this poem, each might identify with the man's ruining of the young woman, "my poor, pale flower" (moi bednyi, blednyi tsvet), through his desire; the poem's ending is reflected in the love-in-death embrace that ends the novel.

Similarly, Irina and V. S.'s first meeting is auspicious; ironically, they each die in their lovers' embrace, at different moments, not exactly murderously, but with a kind of violence and inevitability. Ostensibly, Leonardik's love for Irina is a "sentence dire." This poem was one of Aleksander Blok's favorites, another poet read by Irina during the course of the narration. In Tiutchev's final cycle of poems, he frequently laments how his love crushes his lover, or how their love involves a duel or other forms of aggression. One can also see how Irina's character is not limited to a comparison with the young mistress; Irina is also an ironic reflection of the poet Tiutchev himself. Irina's friend and former lover Vitasik Merzlyakov has the same last name as the friend who encouraged Tiutchev in his early career.

Meanwhile, Pushkin is developed in two ways in the novel—through the "Skazka o rybake i rybke" (1833) (Tale of the Fisherman and the Fish) (of which more, later) and through the poem "K A. P. Kern" ("To A. P. Kern"). In this latter poem, Pushkin writes of the "genii chistoi krasoty" (genius of pure beauty): "Ia pomniu chudoe mgnoven'e: / Peredo mnoi iavilas' ty, / Kak mimoletnoe viden'e, / Kak genii chistoi krasoty" (1–4) (I remember the wondrous moment: / You appeared before me, / Like a fleeting apparition, / Like a genius of pure beauty).[7] When the beauty reappears years later, the poet has the same response (virtually the same lines in the first stanza), with this addition: "I serdtse b'etsia v upoen'e, / I dlia nego voskresli vnov' / I bozhestvo, i vdokhnoven'e, / I zhizn', i slezy, i liubov'" (21–24) (And my heart resounds in rapture, / And for it once again are resurrected / Awe and inspiration / And life, and tears, and love). Porter explains that "genii chistoi krasoty"

> was first used by Zhukovsky in a poem of 1821 addressed to the young wife of Nicholas I. Pushkin's subject was ostensibly Anna Kern, whom he first met in 1819. At their meeting in 1825 he wrote the poem and presented it to her in a copy of the published first chapter of *Evgeny Onegin*. However, in his correspondence Pushkin refers to her in somewhat vulgar terms ("The whore of Babylon"). (156)

Pushkin's conception of beauty combines the extremes of poetic purity and a male fantasy of female sexuality (the unruly desire and capacity of a famed prostitute, the whore of Babylon, who is also associated with the apocalypse). This genius-beauty's fresh return at the end of the poem, after the poet's lonely years have gone by ("shli gody"), shows her mastery over time, suggesting sublime eternal possibilities (as opposed to conventional

---

7. The translation of this poem is mine.

beauty's temporal limitations).

This conception of beauty is creatively and ironically revisited in *Russkaia krasavitsa* from a subversive woman's perspective. In a variation of Pushkin, Irina and Leonardik name her a "genius of love" (e.g., "ot tvoei krasoty baldeli i blekli muzhchiny" [18] [men went mad from your beauty] [15]; "i nedarom Leonardik nazyval menia geniem liubvi" [18] [not without good reason did Leonardik call me the "genius of love"] [16]; "Ia sdelaiu chudo. Ne skroiu: ia genii liubvi . . . NO ZA ETO VY NA MNE ZHENITES'!" [45] [I'll bring about a miracle. I won't deny it: I'm a genius of love. *But for this you will marry me!*] [50]). Irina nonetheless meets an apocalyptic end. The postmodern reflection of "genii chistoi krasoty" implies a hope to resurrect that ideal in the late Soviet period and a hopelessness at such a task. While Pushkin holds the status of Russia's Shakespeare, he is also associated with writing that tests state power. Throughout his writing career, Pushkin experienced notable censorship, the tsar eventually serving as Pushkin's personal censor, and at one point banishing Pushkin to his estate.

Irina's beauty contains a kind of genius which relates to both art and love, to life and destruction. Her beauty mirrors that of Dostoevsky's Nastasya Filippovna's extraordinary splendor in *The Idiot*. In this novel, Prince Myshkin is captivated by this fallen woman's beauty that suggests suffering.[8] A bystander, Adelaida, adds that such beauty has "power" (sila), the kind of power to "turn the world upside down." Idealized feminine Russian beauty contains Christ-like and apocalyptic elements; it does not belong to a sphere of serene purity. Irina's commensurability with Nastasya Filippovna and Dostoevsky's creative vision is highlighted in her photography session for the foreign magazine. She poses as the alluring, young "widowed" other woman. The presentation of her sexual beauty is framed by the tabloid-style statement to readers: "vy budete seichas imet' vozmozhnost' sami ubeditsia, chto KRASOTA POBEZHDAET SMERT'! (eto krasivo!)" (139) (now you can discover for yourself that *beauty conquers death!* [Magnificently put!]) (170). The phrase "Krasota pobezhdaet smert'!" reconfigures Dostoevsky's "Krasota spasiot mir" (Beauty will save the world) and variations of this phrase.[9]

In *The Idiot,* the phrase differs, in that Nastasya Filippovna's beauty can be seen as both Christ-like and apocalyptic. Prince Myshkin sees her photographic portrait and is struck by her beauty. The narrator expands on his impression:

8. Porter considers Irina as a female Myshkin for her supposed ability to suck up evil forces (157).

9. I am indebted to Christopher Barnes for pointing out that Dostoevsky is implied in "Krasota pobezhdaet smert'!"

Na portrete byla izobrazhena deistvitel'no neobyknovennoi krasoty zhenshchina. Ona byla sfotografirovana v chernom shelkovom plat'e, chrezvychaino prostogo i iziashchnogo fasona; volosy, po-vidimomu temnorusye, byli ubrany prosto, po-domashnemu; glaza temnye, glubokie, lob zadumchivyi; vyrazhenie litsa strastnoe i kak by vysokomernoe. Ona byla neskol'ko khuda litsom, mozhet byt', i bledna . . . (51)

The portrait showed a woman of extraordinary beauty indeed. She had been photographed in a black silk dress of a very simple and graceful cut; her hair, apparently dark blond, was done simply, informally; her eyes were dark and deep, her forehead pensive; the expression of her face was passionate and as if haughty. Her face was somewhat thin, perhaps also pale . . . (31)

Myshkin puzzles over the enigmatic portrait: "Eto neobyknovennoe po svoei krasote i eshche po chemu-to litso sil'nee eshche porazilo ego teper'. Kak bydto neob'iatnaia gordost' i prezrenie, pochti nenavist', byli v etom litse, i v to zhe samoe vremia chto-to doverchivoe, chto-to udivitel'no prostodushnoe; eti dva kontrasta vozbuzhdali kak budto dazhe kakoe-to sostradanie pri vzgliade na eti cherti. Eta oslepliaiushchaia krasota byla dazhe nevynosima [. . .]" (105) (That face, extraordinary for its beauty and for something else, now struck him still more. There seemed to be a boundless pride and contempt, almost hatred, in that face, and at the same time something trusting, something surprisingly simple-hearted; the contrast even seemed to awaken some sort of compassion as one looked at those features. The dazzling beauty was even unbearable [. . .]) (79). This kind of beauty contains internal forms of censoring, through its mystery, its antithetical contrasts of mortal flaws and innocence, and its brilliance, which prevents analysis, understanding, or epistemological knowledge; it seems structured by negation.

For Myshkin, beauty in general poses a problem of judgment: "'Krasoty trudno sudit' [. . .]. Krasota—zagadka" (102) (Beauty is difficult to judge [. . .]. Beauty is a riddle) (77); the face hides something ("chto-to skryvavsheesia v etom litse" [105]). In the case of Nastasya Filippovna, he claims to see "V etom litse stradania mnogo" (106) (so much suffering in that face) (80), while by contrast Adelaida suggests, "'Takaia krasota—sila . . . s etakoiu krasotoi mozhno mir perevernut'!'" (106) ('Such beauty has power [. . .]. You can overturn the world with such beauty') (80). Nastasya was seduced by an older man; she moves between despair and manipulative relationships with men.

Erofeev's intertextual reference strengthens the connection between Irina's officially inappropriate qualities as a Soviet Russian writer, woman, and national (or world) heroine, while also providing a subtext for her sudden conviction that her mission is to save Russia and her people. Meanwhile, like Nastasya Filippovna, Irina may have a powerful beauty that could "turn the world upside down," as opposed to saving it. Her beauty is strongly judged, both in positive and negative terms, by various characters. The upsetting or revolutionary quality of Irina's beauty suggests danger, sedition, and a prioritization of sexuality and eroticism in beauty, in opposition to the dogmatic master narratives that would excise sex. Erofeev's narrative aligns with Dostoevsky's in that such powerful beauty is not capable of saving the world, nor upturning it, although it makes forays in both directions.

Dostoevsky's alleged phrase ("Krasota spasiot mir" [Beauty will save the world])[10] has further dissenting political purchase in that Solzhenitsyn used it to model much of his 1970 Nobel Lecture.[11] He offers the following meditation on beauty as art:

> One day Dostoevsky threw out the enigmatic remark: "Beauty will save the world." What sort of a statement is that? For a long time I considered it mere words. How could that be possible? When in bloodthirsty history did beauty ever save anyone from anything? Ennobled, uplifted, yes—but whom has it saved? There is, however, a certain peculiarity in the essence of beauty, a peculiarity in the status of art: namely, the convincingness of a true work of art is completely irrefutable and it forces even an opposing heart to surrender.[12]

---

10. Pevear states that although these words have regularly been attributed to Dostoevsky "in fact he never said them" (xix). I agree with Pevear that this phrase is not found in *The Idiot*, although one could paraphrase certain passages to connote the idea. Myshkin states that her face is "veseloe" (gay) and "gordoe" (proud), and he ponders, "i vot ne znaiu, dobra li ona? Akh, kaby dobra! Vse bylo by spaseno!" (57) (and I don't know whether she is kind or not. Ah, if only she were kind! Everyone would be saved!) (36). With Nastasya Filippovna's tragic death and the disarray it engenders at the end of the novel, it would be hard to argue that her beauty saves the world.

11. This lecture would have especially resonated with Erofeev who, in the early 1970s, was completing a dissertation entitled "Dostoevskii i frantsuzskii ekzistentsializm" (Dostoevsky and French existentialism) (1975). He later published a version of this work, *Naiti v cheloveke cheloveka: Dostoevskii i ekzistentsializm* [*Finding Man in Man: Dostoevsky and Existentialism*].

12. Joseph Brodsky, in his Nobel Lecture (1987), offered a new variation on Dostoevsky's phrase:

> It is precisely in this applied, rather than Platonic, sense that we should understand Dostoevsky's remark that beauty will save the world, or Matthew Arnold's belief that we shall be saved by poetry. It is probably too late for the world, but for the individual man there always remains a chance. An aesthetic instinct develops in man rather rapidly, for, even without fully realizing who he is and what he actually requires, a person instinctively knows what he doesn't like and what doesn't suit him.

Several more allusions to the fallen woman modify our perception of Irina, the Russian beauty. Fallen women embody tragically beauty and impossible love, love judged harshly by social rules: we can list as prime examples Chernyshevskii's Vera Pavlovna in *Chto delat'?* (*What Is to Be Done?*), Tolstoi's Anna Karenina, Dostoevsky's Sonia of *Prestuplenie i nakazanie* (*Crime and Punishment*), and Pasternak's Lara in *Doktor Zhivago* (*Doctor Zhivago*).[13] For a sense of the contrast these fallen women make with the traditional pure Russian heroine of the nineteenth and early twentieth centuries, we could consider Andrei Siniavskii's (Abram Tertz) meditation in his *On Socialist Realism*. He explains that the idealized pure woman assumes a "passive and waiting position"; further, her vague, mysterious, ethereal qualities allow her to be blank space for a higher ideal or "absent and desired Purpose" (63–64). He argues,

> This was the woman that the nineteenth century found most to its liking. She impressed it by her vagueness, her mysteriousness, and her tenderness. Pushkin's dreamy Tatiana opened up an age; the "Beautiful Lady" to whom Blok dedicated his first collected poems closed it. Tatiana was indispensable for Onegin to suffer through the absence of somebody. And, concluding a love story that lasted for a century, Blok took the Beautiful Lady as his Bride, only to betray Her and to lose Her and to torment himself all his life by the purposelessness of his existence.

Poet Alexander Blok brings to a close this trend in ethereal idealized women. We can note that Irina takes up reading Blok, in addition to Tiutchev, during the course of her relationship with V. S.

As the female protagonist and the reader of Blok, Irina assumes an unusual position. She may read of herself in his work, but she is also writing about herself. In place of writing of herself as a "prekrasnaia dama" (beautiful lady) in poetry, she adopts a hybrid form of memoir and novel, riddled with digressions and anecdotes, and structured in swirling tracks that each time report some different aspects of the past while repeating others in rephrased terms. Blok's first collection of poems was dedicated to the "Beautiful Lady," and was inspired by Tiutchev's poems of difficult and passionate love with a beautiful woman.

Irina both embodies and cancels out the poetic beautiful lady motif,

---

13. Porter points out how Irina likens herself and Zinaida, V. S.'s wife, to *Anna Karenina*'s Karenin and Captain Vronsky at the grave of Anna; Porter notices Irina's lack of readerly precision when recalling the Russian classic (157). I would add that her playful interpretation repositions V. S. as the fallen woman and Irina as the dashing Vronsky (who will end up dying). Ironically, Vronsky as a man is far more powerful than the "other woman" in an adulterous relationship.

for, while she is a "genius of love," her confessional prose, framed by satire and realism, exposes the earlier century's poetic idealization of woman for postmodern reconsideration. As Hutcheon writes of postmodern uses of modernist or late-romantic poetry: "there is an opening up of poetry to material once excluded from the genre as impure: things political, ethical, historical, philosophical. This kind of verse can also work to contest representation and the traditional notion of the transparent referentiality of language [. . .]" (61). In a similar way, Erofeev opens up the earlier lyrical poetry of Pushkin, Blok, and Tiutchev to a narrative messiness and a heteroglot novelistic discourse (ranging from the Russian slang of *mat* and *chastushki* [dirty ditties] to Soviet-speak and mock-intellectual interludes, anecdotal digressions that dwell on everyday matters and bodily functions, and rambling confessional language). On the level of characterization, we might say that in Pushkin's poem he dwells on the woman as "genius of pure beauty" and censors out his epistolary comment "whore of Babylon." Meanwhile, *Russkaia krasavitsa* includes a range of feminine characterization for Irina, from pure beauty to whore, as well as lesbian, girlfriend, free spirit, worker, divorcée, savior, messiah, martyr, and bride.

Unlike western European concepts of beauty, which often connect it to aesthetic aims and temporal limits and oppose it to the sublime (e.g., Burke, Kant), Russian literary concepts of beauty can expand to include sublime features. Notably, the Russian nineteenth-century writers were able to explore the sublime features of Russian beauty in their interpretations of the British gothic novel. Russian gothic heroines resemble Irina in many ways: they are bright social climbers, sexually abused in childhood, intelligent but recognized primarily for their extraordinary beauty which has a pronounced sexual appeal; they have supernatural eroticized encounters with the demonic, which turn out to have human dimensions; they confront the dead, the fantastic, the grotesque, and the sexually unwholesome; they seek unsuccessfully for a safe haven to love and be loved. Simpson explains the gothic heroine: "Usually her terrifying experiences taught her neither self-reliance nor personal fortitude, because she always sought to subordinate herself, in the end, to yet another man. Subordination to men often led to rape and abuse. She was capable of great, often innocent, love" (13).[14]

14. Several Russian gothic heroines can be compared favorably to Irina: Lila in Nikolai Karamzim's *Ostrov Borngol'm* (*Bornholm Island*) (1794), a gothic tale of incest; Rogneda, of Kamenev's *Gromval;* Eda of Evgenii Baratynskii's lyric poem *Eda* (1820); Felicia and Liza in Alexander Bestuzhev-Marlinskii's *Kirasir* (*The Cuirassier*) (1832), a tale of obsession with freedom; Varvara Mikhailova in Pavel Ivanovich Mel'nikov-Pecherskii's *Starye gody* (*Bygone Days*) (1857); Katerina, the young kept mistress of an old man with demonic capacities in Dostoevsky's novella

This complex characterization coincides with Irina, for she is heralded as a "genius of love." She repeatedly seeks love in an innocent way, while passing from manipulative, dominating male partners and counterparts, starting with her father, then to two husbands from her town, then several Moscow lovers whose inability to commit to her indicates their abuse of her beauty, to Vladimir Sergeyevich who prefers her as a mistress, and to a group of fairly misogynistic intellectuals, who arrange for her to be hit by a car, and two shady pornographers. During these relationships, she is subject at times to violence and abuse. Irina's relationships with men plays out an allegory of the struggle for freedom, similar to the nineteenth-century British and Russian gothic novel's "post-revolutionary obsession" with freedom. Simpson explains the series of struggles of the Gothic novel:

> [T]hat well-documented struggle is against life's many unfair fetters: imprisonment, perhaps, or an unkind husband, a drunken, vicious father, a cruel priest, an unwanted pregnancy, an unsolicited passion, ridiculous social laws or small-minded judges. [. . .] The struggle for freedom is epitomised by male and female characters of stock composition, the Gothic hero's struggle is intellectual and complex, for he struggles to be free of both the burdens of genius and desire and of the shackles which prevent his realisation of potential and power. [. . .] The Gothic heroine's struggle is physical, material and emotional. She must be free of the worst aspects of male tyranny, she must prevent herself from being sexually misused and must seek that quiet place where she might love without fear. (90)

In a hybrid of the gothic genre, Irina's struggles pertain to both those of the gothic heroine and hero: her feminine struggle, from the outset, is a very special kind of unwanted pregnancy, a supernatural one, along with weighty social condemnation and internal exile; meanwhile, like the case of the male gothic hero, her genius and desire are prevented from realization. Erofeev excludes any true gothic hero from his story, instead prioritizing Irina's perspective and framing critically men's misogyny.

Irina's gothic quality is developed through the motif of rape: she has been the victim of rape, as a child and later as an adult by the ghost; her recurrent dream is that of being stalked by a rapist, an allusion to Soviet expression of sexuality (for example, Ermolaev explains how the rape

---

Khoziaika (*The Landlady*) (1847); Tamara of Lermontov's *Demon* (*The Demon*) (1842). Like Immalee in Charles Maturin's *Melmoth the Wanderer* (1820), Tamara dies because of the impossibility of her love with the demon figure. Simpson explains the conflict: "Both Melmoth and the demon seek to arouse love, possibly physical lust, within their proposed lovers, and it is precisely the intimated sexual contact [. . .] which destroys Tamara and Immalee" (76).

scenes in novels like Gladkov's *Tsement* [*Cement*] and Sholokhov's *Tikhii Don* [*Quiet Don*] have been read by some Soviet readers as scenes of erotica rather than brutality). Naiman explores instances of early Soviet literature's incorporation of the gothic ("NEP Gothic"): "Rape—or, at least, the threat of rape—is a quintessential moment in the Gothic; the collapse of borders between the self and an other, an event potentially present in any act of sexual intercourse, is bound up in rape with the themes of crime, humiliation, unwanted penetration, and the defeat of one's will, an especially horrifying event for members of the Bolshevik political vanguard" (178).

Irina's beauty is politicized as pre-Revolutionary and noble. Her last name, Tarakanova (literally "of the cockroaches"), alludes to the female imposter Princess Tarakanova during Catherine the Great's reign (1762–1796).[15] This "princess," or "notorious woman," claimed to be the daughter of Elizabeth, and was interviewed and imprisoned, and died in captivity on December 4, 1775. She was also reputed to have given birth to a child during her imprisonment.[16] Her story became the stuff of legends and early historical novels, and perhaps most famously, she became the subject of Konstantin Flavitskii's 1864 painting *Princess Tarakanova*.[17] The ironic allusion between the historical Tarakanova and Erofeev's Tarakanova is strengthened by the naming of Irina's gynecologist Flavitsky. The painter Flavitskii depicts in gothic romantic style a beautiful woman imprisoned in the Peter and Paul Fortress; by contrast the gynecologist Flavitsky serves Irina by tending to her venereal diseases, abortions, and her strange pregnancy.

Irina Tarakanova's role is akin to that of the imposter Princess Tarakanova in that Irina is the other woman, not the wife of Vladimir Sergeyevich.

15. Irina even names herself once "kniazhna Tarakanova" (249) (Princess Tarakanova) (310) when she begs Vitasik to stay with her until dawn.

16. My historical information is drawn from historian Alexander (esp. 180–82). He discusses this unusual historical figure:

> Nobody has yet determined who the "notorious woman" was. Her obscurity and notoriety were subsequently overshadowed by a romantic legend of martyrdom, expressed most poignantly by K. D. Flavitskii's famous painting of 1864 depicting "Princess Tarakanova" in her death throes in a flooded rat-infested casemate. Other tales insisted that she had given birth to a son before her own death, which had allegedly stunned a conscience-stricken Aleksei Orlov. Numerous novels were written about her exotic career. Posterity compounded the mystery by awarding the impostor the strange name of Tarakanova, literally "of the cockroaches," evidently a corruption of Daraganova (Sof'ia Daraganova had served as a maid of honor at court in 1763 before her marriage to Colonel Prince Khavanskii, but she had no known connection to any impostor). (181–82)

17. Flavitskii's painting *Princess Tarakanova in the Petropavlovsk Fortress at the Time of the Flood* (1864) can be seen in Moscow's Tretyakov Gallery and online at http://www.artrussia.ru/artists/ and http://www.russianartgallery.org/famous/tarakanova.htm.

Irina is the imposter in the marriage, claiming true love. After V. S.'s death, Irina's martyrdom is heavily politicized. She is pregnant with V. S.'s child, implying that she is pregnant with the next generation's Soviet Russian artistic genius, for V. S. is considered a literary lion by the State and Irina is recognized for her extraordinary beauty. Both Tarakanovas end tragically in death and are misunderstood; both aim to save or lead Russia in some way. That Irina is a Tarakanova implies that, although she may seem authentic to some, she may be a copy and a pretender. The name "Tarakanova" suggests comic baseness rather than serious elevation.[18]

The concept of the unreliable copy extends to Irina's commensurability with Pushkin's "genius of love," the beauty of the fallen woman and the suffering woman, and the apocalyptic protagonist. Irina's imitations both confirm and deny identifications, creating a kind of mirroring of images and allusions, all signifying frustrated or censored meaning. The genius of Irina's beauty, through censorious social, political, and literary forces, will not ultimately bloom and benefit Russia, unless it would sinisterly prevail from beyond the grave. As a final collapse of the Russian beauty motif, Erofeev ironically poeticizes Irina's sex, which she bequeaths to the public. If she cannot save the world with her beauty, perhaps her sex (the possible secret of her beauty) can be left to give the world pleasure (and possibly life).

3. APOCALYPTIC BEAUTY AND LOVE: TSENZURA AND PARODY

Russkaia krasavitsa intertwines in symbolic plot and character forms the Soviet censorship and apocalypse. The modern novel often focuses on beginnings or endings,[19] with the modern Russian novel tending more

---

18. Dark reminds us that another intertextual reference for Irina Tarakanova is the Greek Eirene of Aristophanes's play *Eirene (Peace)* (181). Dark further notes the similar satirical modes of Aristophanes and Erofeev. I would add that Aristophanes was known for ushering women's sexuality strongly and comically into his plays, often making women's sexual power a revolutionary force; we could consider Erofeev's similar portraiture of femininity and Aristophanic humor (e.g., the farting phallic god).

In the play *Peace*, Eirene or Peace is not an active character, but rather is a statue that has been buried by the gods of War and must be dug out. Humorously, the "hero" of the play mounts his giant dung beetle or cockroach (like a Pegasus) to undo this wrong and restore Peace. Thus, we discover in Aristophanes a kind of Irina of the Cockroach (Tarakanova). The parallel is operative in that Peace is resurrected, just as would be the mock messiah or savior Irina (provided she would succeed in her mission). Eirene is also a goddess of fertility and the harvest; ironically, Irina upturns the role of Eirene, for Irina has long been considered sterile, and, after miraculously conceiving, she will not gather her harvest (fulfill her pregnancy).

19. See Kermode's *The Sense of an Ending*, as it considers time and apocalypse in the theory

strongly toward endings, particularly apocalyptic ones. This trend can be noticed across genres of the Russian novel, from Gogol's *Mertvye dushi* (*Dead Souls*) (1842 and 1852) and Dostoevsky's psychological and social novel *Idiot* (*The Idiot*) (1868), to the utopian-dystopian novels *My* (*We*) (1922) by Zamiatin and *Chevengur* (1929) by Platonov, the modernist metropolitan novel *Peterburg* (*Petersburg*) (1916) by Bely, and the lyrical and political novel *Doktor Zhivago* (*Doctor Zhivago*) (1957) by Pasternak.[20] *Russkaia krasavitsa* incorporates an apocalyptic narrative by placing Irina both as a potential savior or messiah (as genius of beauty and love) and as the one who experiences harsh judgment and joins the dead.[21]

The Gospel parody is developed through negated twists in characterization and plot: Irina is a sexually active woman, not a chaste male Jesus; she is made pregnant by supernatural means, not by the Holy Ghost, but by her former lover (the immaculate conception parody is strengthened by the fact that Irina has had many lovers); her Christ-like features are compared comically with martyrs and saint Joan of Arc. While there are many permutations of the apocalypse, the basic apocalyptic narrative might be summarized in the following way: "'Apocalypse' is a genre of revelatory literature with a narrative framework, in which a revelation is mediated by an otherworldly being to a human recipient, disclosing a transcendent reality which is both temporal, insofar as it envisages eschatological salvation, and spatial, insofar as it involves another, supernatural world" (John Collins qtd. in Bethea, 7–8).

Christ's and other martyrs' stories contain apocalyptic elements because they experience harsh judgment, physical torture, and their deaths are both tumultuous awful ends as well as supernatural transformations. In the case of *Russkaia krasavitsa,* Irina experiences revelations of the phallic spirit on the famed battlefield of Kulikovo,[22] the ghost of Vladimir Sergeyevich, and revealing signs from the witch. Irina's salvation through belated marriage to her dead lover is ironically framed: what kind of wedded afterlife will these two share? If V. S. represents the sanctioned Soviet canon of Russian literature and aesthetics and Irina embodies the Russian beauty and love as combined in sexuality that is generally censored in Soviet literature and

---

of fiction.

20. Bethea's *The Shape of Apocalypse in Modern Russian Fiction* offers one of the best studies of this theme.

21. See Rylkova's "The Apocalypse Revisited: Viktor Erofeev's *Russian Beauty*" for a more extensive discussion of the novel's various parodies of the Gospel and Apocalypse.

22. In that battle of 1380, Dmitrii Donskoi's army defeated the Tatars for the first time. While the battle is glorified in Russian military mythology, the victory was not decisive, and Russians and Tatars continued feuding.

culture, then what could their supernatural marriage signify? Does their mutual end in death also signal the end of Soviet Russian culture? Does this ending actually celebrate, in some ironic way, the apocalyptic traditions of the pre-Soviet Russian literature?

Notably, Erofeev draws on a variety of apocalyptic Russian texts as well as the Book of Revelation for much of his parody. He strongly values late pre-Revolutionary writers and thinkers of the Silver Age, particularly V. V. Rozanov. Rylkova explains how, in early twentieth-century Russia, "Apocalypse was a welcome concept among intellectuals and artists" (327), and it offered a "way to foster ideas of spiritual rebirth," as seen in the works of philosophers Vladimir Soloviev, Nikolai Berdiaev, the poet Blok, and culminating in Rozanov's *Apokalipsis nashego vremeni* (*The Apocalypse of Our Time*) (1918–19). We can notice the irony that apocalypse as "spiritual rebirth" is a positive and modernist interpretation of what is traditionally an earth-shattering, destructive event to end all human existence.

On the negative side of apocalyptic interpretations, we might group writers like Gogol, Dostoevsky, Zamiatin, and Pasternak. For these writers, apocalypse comes in the form of a defeat, negation, or repression of collective and individual artistic and sexual liberty, and apocalyptic forces are strongly related *both* to social and political institutions and practices and to sexuality and beauty. The artistic censoring of sexuality (sexuality embodied in beauty, love, and sex) is connoted by the corrosive pairing of these forces. Erofeev winds these apocalyptic narrative traditions together, resulting in a tragicomic ending, the grotesquely celebratory wedding of Irina. The narrative resists giving us access to some other transcendent synthesizing view that would reconcile V. S. and Irina or save Russia. Erofeev uses the positive connotations of apocalypse to court the promise of new beginnings, but ultimately does not offer any. Further, the narratives of mystic redemption and rebirth are ludically insinuated, but not fulfilled.

The novel develops the tragic connotations of apocalypse in a celebratory way. The Soviet culture as formed by censorship should come to an end, dying in its secret erotic embrace with sexuality (as allegorized in the living V. S.'s last intercourse with Irina). What has been understood as "Russian beauty" (the amalgam of Russian and Soviet allusions that form the collage of Irina) is offered a grotesque union in the afterlife, suggestive of a failure of Russian beauty to save Russia (and Erofeev's laying to rest this compelling but illusory hope). Alternatively, we can interpret the novel's ending as an ironic apocalypse: only Irina and V. S. die in an attempt to overcome the censorious forces of society and politics, while the rest of the Soviet Union carries on living in these repressive conditions.

The novel's partially fulfilled promise of the pornographic fantasy of discovering a sexually desiring woman's voice further complicates and enriches the sense of artistic censoring of sexuality and the subject's foundation in lack. In Soviet censorship and mainstream Soviet literary criticism, many readers esteemed an ideal text as one exhibiting total control and totalized meaning, a kind of wholeness, completeness (*tselostnost'*), whose integrity (*tsel'nost'*)[23] would be blemished or disturbed by critical inquiry.[24] I suggest that *Russkaia krasavitsa* subverts those functions and aims of Soviet censorship and literary quality. On the one hand, there is an encyclopedic quality to the allusions that appeals to a sense of plenitude with integrity. On the other hand, the novel's twenty-four chapters are highly digressive and nonchronological; the ending and the skeletal story are established by chapter 2. In this way, Erofeev eschews Soviet stylistic standards, avoiding a teleologically oriented or totalizing work, while subversively implying a kind of destructive teleology and accumulative inclusiveness of literary analogies or intertextual counterparts.

Two of the novel's most pronounced narrative features are the unreliable first-person female narrator and her fragmented representation of herself, others, and social contexts. The protagonist and her text are negatively defined by their lack of adherence to Soviet literary and censorship ideals. The text and its writer exhibit multiple meanings and a lack of control. Although Irina may aspire to achieve a utopian ideal of *tselostnost'* (wholeness, completeness), her writing and her body are presented in fragments which do not add up to a coherent wholeness. Like Nastasya Filippovna, Irina is a study of contrasts that would seem to cancel each other out. Her beauty and genius of love promise salvation, but ultimately cannot fulfill it.

The theme of apocalypse is channeled through the personal experience of the character-narrator Irina. The apocalypse is a story of revelations, judgment, and destructive endings. At the same time, Irina's apocalyptic trajectory includes strong Christ-like and martyrdom features.[25] The collision of the two master narratives indicates simultaneously a kind of inclusiveness or aim for completeness (*tselostnost'*) and a lack of coherence. It would be hard for Irina as a character or narrator to resolve or synthesize the positions of John and the whore of Babylon from the Book of Revelation on the one hand, and, on the other, the position of Christ or Mary from

---

23. For discussions of the important significance of the concepts "tselostnost'" and "tsel'nost'" in relation to various streams of Russian thought, see Epshtein, *After the Future*.

24. Dark sees the novel working toward an ironized totalizing effect, an "encyclopedia of Russian life" (178), and as an antimemoir and a fable (among other things).

25. Rylkova has also noted how Erofeev cleverly combines the Gospels and Revelation ("Apocalypse Revisited," 329).

234 • Chapter 5

the Gospel books. It is useful to recall that the Book of Revelation makes references to Christ and his symbols (e.g., the Lamb) and, after the "Final Judgment," John ends the Book with the "Coming of Jesus." Therefore, the two biblical narratives are not entirely discrete, the latter Revelation drawing from the former (and of course both the Gospels and the Book of Revelation belong to the New Testament).

In Erofeev's Christ narrative, Irina is situated as a potential female Christ. She offers to suffer for Russia, for she has noticed that she has the unusual capacity to absorb evil ("zamechaiu v sebe odnu tainstvennuiu osobennost'. Mogu vsiu nechist' v sebia vsosat'" [167]; [I possess a mysterious quality. I can absorb all the evil forces] [206]). Ironically, as a woman, she becomes pregnant, not a Christ-like experience. The parallel between the Annunciation of Gabriel to Mary and the pregnancy announcement of the "chudo" (miracle) by the gynecologist Flavitsky to the nonvirginal, sterile Irina further subverts comparisons of Irina to Christ. The Christ theme of martyrdom and saintliness extends to the subnarrative of Joan of Arc. This legendary figure was welcomed into feminist symbolism, as is explored, for example, by Elaine Showalter's study of literature and culture around the fin de siècle in western Europe and the United States (*Sexual Anarchy*, 29).

Part of St. Joan's compelling power is her ability to represent femininity while transcending it. Irina, despite being treated as an outcast after Leonardik's death, aspires to save Russia by becoming its revitalizing womanly symbol and sacrificing her body to a mysterious phallic spirit. Her patriotic, ideological aim is played out in multilayered parodies of Joan of Arc and Mother Russia. Irina's overblown attempts to model herself into a Russian Joan of Arc comically (and pornographically) are deflated by her failures. For example, in her Dionysian encounter with a laconic higher power, he cannot maintain an erection and, on Irina's third try, he makes a loud, insulting fart (210; 261).

Irina's recounting of her attempt to become a surrealistic Russian Joan of Arc highlights her crisis of self-perception, of distinguishing between herself and her writing self, and her religious conviction that she should be praying. Irina's involvement in writing, prayer, prohibition combine in her account of the naked running on the battle field:

A Iurochka govorit:—Neuzheli vtoroi raz pobezhish'?—A Egor: Ty na vse pole orala!—A ia sizhu pered nimi, kak na kartine zavtrak na trave [...]—rvus' ia, ne poverite, nazad, v pole, to est' na polnuiu svoiu propazhu, kak khotite, tak i ob'iasniaite, i dazhe ne radi chego-to tam vozvyshennogo, eto kak by samo soboi, a manit, manit menia pogibel', ia kak by v drugoi razriad pereshla i ne zhilets na etom svete. He potomu, odnako, skazhu, chto smerti ne boialas', net, ia boialas', no ia rassloilas', ia i ne ia, odnu oznob b'et, drugaia krylyshkami mashet. I, konechno, tak zhit' nel'zia, ia zhe sama luchshe vsekh ponimaiu, pishu i ponimaiu, chto nel'zia, i pisat' ob etom nel'zia, ZAPRESHCHENO, tol'ko etot zapret uzhe ne Ivanovichi na menia nalozhat, eto tochno! Zdes' zapret inoi, bolee tonkoi organizatsii, mne ne pisat', a molit'sia, molit'sia polagaetsia, a ia pishu, mashu krylyshkami, i manit, manit menia eta pisanina, raspisalas', durekha, i sama kak budto snova po poliu begu, takoi zhe oznob i zhar, i ditia rokovoe v utrobe voet, iz utroby vzyvaet ne pisat', ugrozhaet vykidyshem, a ne skazat'—tozhe nel'zia, da mne i tak vse ravno propadat', takaia uzh moia planida, Ksiushechka. Tak chto pishu. Pishu, kak begala, i begala, kak pishu . . . (206)

But Yurochka says, Surely you're not going to go running again? And Yegor, You shouted so loud that the whole countryside could hear you! But I sit down beside them, like that painting Luncheon on the Grass [. . .]—I pull myself away, you won't believe it, rush back to the field, bargaining myself away, explain it how you like, and not even for the sake of something grand, this was already understood, but perdition beckons me, beckons me, I had moved into a new state of being and was no longer a dweller on this earth. I will tell you frankly, it's not that I wasn't afraid of death, no, I was afraid, but I had split into layers—I and not I, one is shivering, the other flaps its little wings. And of course, no one can live like that, I myself know this better than anyone, I write and I know this, and one must not write about these things, it is *forbidden*, except that this isn't the prohibition the Ivanoviches will afterward place on me, that's for sure! This is a different type of prohibition, of a more subtle force, I shouldn't be writing, I should be praying, praying, but I write, I flap my little wings, and this writing summons me, summons, I can't stop writing, fool, and it is as though I am again running through the field, the same shivers and fever, and the fateful child howls in my womb, orders me from the womb not to write, threatens a miscarriage, but I can't not tell, and indeed in any event I'm done for, such now is my fate, Ksyushechka. And so I write. I write how I ran, and I ran as I write. . . . (255–56)[26]

26. The non-Russian reader can note that "forbidden" is italicized in English whereas in the original it is presented in upper case letters: ZAPRESHCHENO. This typographical effect alludes to the way in which many documents were classified by various Soviet authorities in the legal field and elsewhere: "PROHIBITED." Irina thus typographically classifies her own writing.
  Conversely, in the Russian text, the *Luncheon on the Grass* title is presented modestly in lower-case letters ("zavtrak na trave") and without any other punctuation, allowing the subversive allusion to blend in with the rest of the text. Irina's self-reference to the *Déjeuner* joins in the subversion of Manet's painting; as the narrating protagonist, the writer Irina centers herself in art. See Peter

The frantic drive to write her life assumes a will to judgment. The prohibition allows her to envision two selves, her "not I," with a course into the Imaginary register of fantasy, and an "I" in the Symbolic register of signification and writing. The experience on the field and the subsequent writing of that experience result in apocalyptic moments of crisis for Irina. After the events on the field, she avoids the intellectuals Yegor and Yurochka, and takes the train home to Moscow.

The interlude on the train is conveyed in a semirealist, semisurrealist narrative that explores an alternative (nostalgic and imaginary?) life for Irina, with some of her girlfriends, and especially with an idealized relationship to a gay man Andriusha ("chudik" [a queer fellow]; "takoi elegantnyi" [so elegant]). In this nostalgic relationship of coffee and skiing, sex is not so important as a spiritual and poetic understanding, as he says, "—Davai ne stanem my oskverniat' nashu druzhbu zhadnymi gubami! Ty vidish' v fortku: na derev'iakh sneg. On–belyi, Ira . . ." (217) (Let's agree not to profane our friendship with all that sort of thing [greedy lips, i.e., kisses]! Look through the *fortochka*: snow on the trees. It's white, Ira . . .) (270). Irina responds to him with these thoughts: "Nu, pochemu na svete tak malo chistykh muzhchin, kak Andriusha! Bud' ikh bol'she, kakoi by gruz upal s uzkikh zhenskikh plech! Kak slavno by vse razriadilos'!" (Oh, why are there so few pure men like Andryusha in the world! If there were more of them, then what a burden would fall from fragile female shoulders! How gloriously everything would resolve itself!). Irina relates in her writing the idea of salvation for women, to be unburdened of the sexual desire of selfish heterosexual men. This miniature story is a tributary of the Joan of Arc one; in the larger story, Irina seeks to be the savior by sacrificing her sex to a petulant god, while in the smaller one, the pure Andriusha offers possible salvation by unburdening women of sex.

The Joan of Arc episodes especially emphasize Erofeev's tendency to use French cultural and historical references to complement and add ironic accents to Irina's experiences and trajectory.[27] Of course, Jeanne d'Arc is a

---

Brooks's discussion of this and other nineteenth-century French paintings that prioritize in critical and revolutionary ways the female body (*Body Work*).

27. As an academic, Erofeev specialized in nineteenth- and twentieth-century French literature and wrote his thesis on French existentialism. In much of his essay and editorial work, especially since the success of *Russkaia krasavitsa,* he has focused on French writers, philosophy, and art and has used comparative approaches to various literary and cultural questions. See, for example, his *V labirinte prokliatykh voprosov: Esse* (In the labyrinth of accursed problems: Essays), as well as "Russia's *Fleurs du mal.*"

Erofeev's French interests dovetail with those of one of his favorite writers, Nabokov. *Russkaia krasavitsa*'s title may have been inspired by Nabokov's short story "Krasavitsa" (Beauty) which was translated into English as "A Russian Beauty." At the end of both stories, the beautiful, pregnant heroine dies.

French icon. Porter explains that Soviet borrowing of this foreign icon was permissible, for Joan of Arc had a "special appeal to the Soviet establishment, which was happy to overlook her religious fanaticism, her canonisation in 1920, and the fact that she was a transvestite and a Sunday pacifist. She represents the very best example of the person of common stock who comes to save the nation from foreign aggression and imperialism, who acquires a special rapport with the ruler of her nation, who is chaste, commonsensical in discussion, yet who clings tenaciously to her principles and mission [. . .]" (160).

Meanwhile, Erofeev stretches the uses of this icon, partly mocking the Soviet iconic integration of Joan of Arc (indeed, Irina's emulation of "Zhanna d'Ark" prompts the phallic spirit's visit to her). As a potential Zhanna d'Ark, Irina offers a ritual sexual sacrifice of herself on the symbolically significant fields of the Battle of Kulikovo. The modern Russian bisexual diva manquée does share attributes with the medieval French teenage virgin-saint. Both have had a humble rural childhood; both claim to hear voices which call them to a greater destiny to restore a sense of national identity and self-confidence; both inspire men; both suffer cruel interrogations. But Irina fails to become another Donskoi ("of the Don") or d'Arc: the fame she acquires is of a luridly tasteful photo-op kind (a sort of American *Paris Match*), and the degrees of martyrdom leading to her suicide are supplemented by her fragmentation into madness and her decision to undo the church's blessing by resorting to witchcraft.

In addition to these references to historically symbolic heroism, Irina's seemingly casual mention of Édouard Manet's *Le déjeuner sur l'herbe* (1863) signals the scandalous, prohibited side of art which elicits censorship reactions from both the authorities and the public.[28] The reference to the *Déjeuner* mockingly reemphasizes the erotic and unequal juxtaposition of the clothed men and the beautiful, naked women, and in general the parodied muse-like aspect of Irina's character (she is more a writer than a muse). The nude body acts as a point of illumination and difference, an apparition

---

When Erofeev finally found his way back into publishing by the late 1980s, he was one of the major writers to [re-]introduce Nabokov's banned oeuvre to Soviet readers through essays and forewords. A detailed comparative study of these two authors would reap rich interpretations. Rylkova has pioneered such investigations.

28. The painting's exclusion by the Salon's jury in 1863 (and its subsequent debut in the Salon des Refusés) informs Irina's vulnerable and censored subjectivity. Brooks reports how Zola, in his analysis of the *Déjeuner*, did not find its revolutionary quality in the juxtaposition of clothed people and nudes, counting many examples across periods in the Louvre. Zola felt the *Déjeuner* was Manet's greatest painting because it realizes "the dream of every painter—to put life-size figures in a landscape," and it presents a "vast ensemble, full of air [*plein d'air*], this corner of nature rendered with such perfect simplicity" (Brooks, *Body Work*, 133).

of knowledge and sexuality. This and other French references juxtapose *Russkaia krasavitsa* with the daring aspects of France's mid-nineteenth-century artistic scene that looks for the obscene (what is usually kept out of the frame): the scandals of literature, especially Baudelaire's *Fleurs du mal* and Flaubert's *Madame Bovary*[29] (both works suffered from French censorship).[30]

Meanwhile, the Soviet reader of *Russkaia krasavitsa* who would recognize this intertextuality would be reminded that the Soviet literary and art establishment and its censorship did not consider those French works revolutionary, nor appropriately socialist realist. In this way, Erofeev heightens the effect of contrasting censorship values in political and artistic terms. We could further note how the theme of judgment is slyly embedded in the actual composition of the *Déjeuner*. Manet borrowed the layout for his painting from Raphael's *Judgment of Paris*.

The Joan of Arc theme parodies a Russian narrative of political agitation. Prior to Irina's run on Kulikovo Field, she and her mates visit a village marketplace. She decides to address the common people so that they know of her service to them, not unlike Jeanne d'Arc. The French people were galvanized by Jeanne's speeches. By contrast, the Russian villagers scurry away from Irina, afraid of the modern Muscovite and the trouble she might stir up. The episode comically harks back to a similar moment in Russian history, "going to the people movement of 1873–1874," "when thousands of Populist-minded young idealists went into the Russian countryside to convert the peasantry to their radical ideas, only to meet with apathy, incomprehension and, often, outright hostility. As the urbanite trio [Irina, Yegor, and Iurii] start disagreeing among themselves about the peasantry, it is significant that the 'THEY' to which they refer appears in block capitals and emphasises the social rift" (Porter, 155).

---

29. Flaubert's novel surfaces lightly in *Russkaia krasavitsa*. Ksyusha develops a Madame Bovary complex, and Irina stresses over Rouen shortly before her suicide-marriage ("A chto mne im skazat'? My ne v Ruane" [272] [What am I to say to them? We're not in Rouen] [340]). Rouen is the place of Emma Bovary's adulterous affair with Léon and the site of the burning at the stake of Joan of Arc. Dostoevsky similarly dangles *Madame Bovary* without completing the analogy: in his search to save his bride, Myshkin finds a copy of *Madame Bovary* in Nastasya Filippovna's room, a clue suggesting her suicide; but when he finally finds her dead, she has not committed suicide, but rather has been murdered by Rogozhin (although ostensibly she has decided to die by running off with him).

30. These two works and their censorship cases in 1857 constitute central precursors to twentieth-century literary censorship of sexuality; they mark a shift in censorship and artistic aims and interests. See especially Née, "1857: Le double procès de *Madame Bovary* et des *Fleurs du mal*"; Harrison, *Circles of Censorship;* Dury, "Du droit à la métaphore"; and LaCapra. In *The Trials of Modernism*, Parkes stresses the consequences of *Madame Bovary* for modern Anglo-American censorship; I would add that these consequences were felt by other writers and censorship practices in other cultures, such as the Russian and Spanish.

Irina's foray into the countryside to serve as a modern Joan of Arc arouses disbelief and the suppression by the local censoring force, the town's policeman. Once a product of the countryside, Irina has become a Muscovite, distanced from the people, "derzhateli tverdi, khraniteli tselogo, kapitalisty vechnosti. Oni zhili, my–sushchestvovali. [...] Raznitsa mezhdu nami okazalas' na udivlenie prosta: ikh zhizn' polna neosmyslennogo smysla, nasha–osmyslennaia bessmyslitsa" (189) (the possessors of the earth, the preservers of the whole, the capitalists of eternity. They lived, we existed. [...] The difference between us turned out to be amazingly simple: their life is full of uncomprehended sense and meaninglessness. It appears that consciousness is acquired in exchange for the loss of meaning) (233–34). In this set of relations, Irina appears to the people as a form of consciousness, while they possess meaning, without the conscious factor. The policeman prevents the interaction between the two parties, thus preventing the people from attaining a consciousness of their state. Implicit in this meditation is a criticism of both urban intellectuals and their separation from real, everyday life, and of the rural dwellers' separation from broader social and political life. More specifically, the sublime Russian beauty's cause is prevented from being communicated to the people. The people's ignorance might parody the ignorance of Christ's sacrifices.

In general, martyrs operate amongst those unable to appreciate immediately their value. In Irina's rural episodes, her political significance and potential are comically developed as subversive political elements. Although the "going to the people movement" of the 1870s initially failed, some surviving young radicals of the movement became members of the revolutionary organization Narodnaia Volia (People's Will) and what would become the Bolshevik Party (initially, Plekhanov's Social Democratic Movement), each of which became ironically "successful" in its own way: the one group producing those who would assassinate Alexander II in 1881 and the other party, the party of Lenin, responsible for the Revolution and the subsequent history of the Soviet Union.[31]

In the analogy of Irina as a new radical of the "going to the people movement" and Joan of Arc, Irina will not be understood by the people, but she may nonetheless aim to benefit them. Her project is deconstructed by her retrospective narration, in which she signals a kind of failure. Instead of saving Russia, her course might parallel that of Russia: "Itak, pole. Tragediia moei nelepoi zhizni. [...]. Cherez neskol'ko chasov (vecherom, v

---

31. For more historical details and analysis of these nineteenth-century movements, see Franco Venturi's *Roots of Revolution: A History of the Populist and Socialist Movements in Nineteenth Century Russia.*

sumerkakh) dolzhny byli reshit'sia dve sud'by: syd'ba Rossii i moia sud'ba" (183–84) (And so the field. The tragedy of my absurd life. [. . .] In a few hours [in the evening, at twilight] two fates were to be decided: Russia's and mine) (226–27). The Russian "sud'ba" (fate) resonates heavily with "sud" (court, trial, justice).

Irina's writing and actions script her as a postmodern Russian Joan of Arc whose beautiful sex or sexual beauty is censored in a series of episodes in which the character is rejected, silenced, or denied. Her writing seeks to patch together her story of fragmented digressions in search of completeness (*tselostnost'*). The narrative, both Irina's telling and living of it, revisits exemplary historical events in an attempt to solve matters idealistically. Her involvement with the Moscow intellectuals shows up these people's own ideological investment in apocalyptic narratives. While at first they scorn Irina (one calls her a "vrag kultury" [56] [enemy of culture] [63]), they later use her body (the car crash; the sacrifice on the field) to provoke a revolutionary apocalypse.

Irina's writing signals apocalypse brought on by her "beauty" in many ways: the whirling diachronic narrative structure, in which the conclusion in death echoes through the novel's beginning, middle, and end; the accumulation of comparable genres, types, story lines in history, philosophy, religion, and literature that tends toward a breakdown of categories, as opposed to a coherent reinforcement; the character-narrator's retrospective positions transpire in the short time preceding death and in the time just after death. The martyrdom narrative, with its predictable ending—indeed validation—in death, coincides with the broader apocalyptic theme.

4. RUSSIAN SUBLIME AND ROGUE NARRATOR: IRINA'S PORNO-GRAPHED VOICE AND IMAGE: NARRATIVE AND TSEL'NOST'

Irina's special beauty, given its extraordinary qualities, suggests the category of the sublime, rather than the beautiful. Irina's sublimity is related also to her terrifying experiences with the supernatural: her beauty brings her into contact with sublime forces. In Edmund Burke's influential eighteenth-century study of the beautiful and the sublime, the beautiful is typified by the small, smooth, and delicate. Beauty's qualities are measurable and harmonious. By contrast, the sublime is beauty in excess, to the point that there is no longer beauty: it defies full apprehension by the senses; it can involve terror and privation and be powerful, difficult, magnificent, vast, infinite; it involves sensations such as pain and the "emotion of distress" (79). Burke finds examples of the sublime in nature and in stunning, extreme creations, such as Stonehenge ("those huge rude masses of stone, set on end, and piled on each other" [71]) or a "cup of bitterness" (78). In the *Critique of Judgment,* Kant elaborates on Burke's study: for Kant, "the sublime is defined as a pleasure in the way that nature's capacity to overwhelm our powers of perception and imagination is contained by and serves to vivify our powers of rational comprehension. It is a distinctive aesthetic experience" (Crowther). In a more recent interpretation of the sublime and the beautiful, Slavoj Žižek suggests that, in terms of logical order,

> Sublimity should *follow* Beauty because it is the point of its breakdown, of its mediation, or its self-referential negativity. [. . .] [In Kant,] Beauty and Sublimity are opposed along the semantic axes quality-quantity, shaped-shapeless, bounded-boundless: Beauty calms and comforts; Sublimity excites and agitates. "Beauty" is the sentiment provoked when the suprasensible Idea appears in the material, sensuous medium, in its harmonious formation—a sentiment of immediate harmony between Idea and the sensuous material of its expression; while the sentiment of Sublimity is attached to chaotic, terrifying limitless phenomena [. . .]. Above all, however, Beauty and Sublimity are opposed along the axis of pleasure-displeasure: a view of Beauty offers us pleasure, while "the object is received as sublime with a pleasure that is only possible through the mediation of displeasure." (Žižek, *Sublime Object,* 202; emphasis in original)[32]

The beautiful and sublime are complicated in *Russkaia krasavitsa;* they still operate partially as oppositions. Irina, the beautiful, attracts sublime forces. But what makes her extraordinarily beautiful also seems to make her sublime. For example, she recognizes that she has the power to absorb evil forces. Her interactions with the supernatural powers of the phallic god and the ghost of Vladimir Sergeyevich, and her resulting sense of terror and being overwhelmed, situate her as a beholder of the sublime. If we refer to the Kantian opposition of beauty's pleasure—sublimity's displeasure—, then in Irina's case, her sexual affairs generally obtain pleasure while her sexualized contact with the supernatural forces result in a pleasure obtained through displeasure.

This more radical version of pleasure, that opens onto the abyss of power and eternity, would explain her terrible decision to hang herself and join V. S. in the afterlife. Irina's sexual relations in the realms of beauty and sublimity involve pleasure that is often censored or forbidden in Soviet

---

32. At the end of the quotation, Žižek cites Kant's *Critique of Judgment.* The line can be found in Kant, 151.

Russian discourse and society. The sublime relations involve a further negating twist in that they engulf Irina in a larger symbolic space of an eternally doomed, apocalyptic Russia, whose pregnancy or potential renaissance will be subsumed into the timeless space of death and comparisons with the dead past.

In sum, one of Erofeev's innovations in the artistic censoring of sexuality is the apocalyptic structure of the plot to combine the oppositions of beauty and sublimity through the personification of Russian beauty in Irina.

Kant determines judgment as a point of difference between beauty and sublimity. Beauty represents qualities in the object making it intelligible, while the sublime does not have to make the object intelligible. Kant explains how pleasure is involved in aesthetic judgment:

> That is beautiful which pleases in the mere judging (thus not by means of the sensation of sense in accordance with a concept of the understanding). From this it follows of itself that it must please without any interest. That is sublime which pleases immediately through its resistance to the interest of the senses. [. . .] The beautiful prepares us to love something, even nature, without interest; the sublime, to esteem it, even contrary to our (sensible) interest. (*Critique* 150–51)

Irina as Russian beauty does provide pleasure, but her beauty is extraordinary and goes unappreciated (e.g., her lovers do not commit). Further, Irina is a "genius of love," and like many geniuses she is misunderstood; "love" is meant both as love and sex, her "art." Kant points out that genius does not copy, but rather is original and exemplary (186–87). Erofeev offers us a postmodern version of the "genius," in that Irina is a partial copy of Pushkin's "genius of pure beauty" and of other Russian beauties and Russian lovers.

What makes her original and exemplary in the text *Russkaia krasavitsa* is her centralized role as character-narrator (rather than the male poet/lover's apprehended object of desire). She approximates picaresque character-narrators, from Lazarillo to Moll Flanders. Irina's upstart status, her rambling episodes, her servitude and apprenticeship under a variety of "masters," and her sufferings—all characterize her as a rogue or *pícara* narrator. Thus she approximates Moll's role in that both beautiful women provide a kind of confessional that promises to reveal secrets of feminine sexuality and that aims at redemption.

Irina's voice and beautiful image extend a promise to fulfill a reader's wish to encounter the desiring woman's voice. Her sexuality is embedded in her writing, and her writing methods contain elements of pornographic literature ("writing of harlots" from the Greek *porne* [harlot, courtesan] + *graphos* [writing]). As a writer, she sometimes "porno-graphs" herself, that is, inscribing herself as promised sexual pleasure and as source of sexual knowledge. Her writing apprehends her as sexual subject. But her narrative does not provide an uncomplicated, escapist pornographic image. For example, the text provides few concrete details measuring her physical beauty. Instead, her sexuality, beauty, and body become inscribed in an interconnected series of significant ideological and social relations, particularly with narratives of suffering, resurrection, and messianism, as well as forbidden love and desire. These inscriptions of sexuality thus become weighted with ethical value because they confront and demand subjective judgment (by other diegetic characters and by us the readers). As a censored person (i.e., the "other woman" or woman who does not cohere to Soviet values), Irina presents herself as an outcast Thing and as a martyr. She tries to inscribe herself into Soviet and Russian discourses and is either unsuccessful (e.g., her reading of Tiutchev and Blok) or is met with negatively judgmental reactions (e.g., the trial at the collective). Her increasing loss of reason and emerging alcoholism might be seen as effects of a crisis of self-censoring; her counterpart, Ksyusha, has taken refuge as a self-exile, another form of (self-)censoring.

Russkaia krasavitsa's privileging of the woman's confessional voice invites readers to anticipate a pornographic text in several ways. Traditionally, pornography as "writing of harlots" can be seen from two perspectives: pornography can be an observer's (a man's) writing about harlots or it can be the harlot's writing about herself and others. *Russkaia krasavitsa* ironically uses both perspectives: the novel presents the adventures and end of a romantic courtesan (a kind of exposé); the novel consists of a diegetic narration, that woman's narrating her life and self (an exposé of the exposé). The novel ironically relies on a presupposition about pornography: a pornographic text promises the illusion of an uncomplicated expression of the desiring woman and pleasure without a further exploration or grounding in ethics and judgment. When the pornographic diegetic narrator is a woman, she should reveal her desire for sex (the same basic premise functions in pornographic photography: she really wants it and enjoys it). By contrast, Irina's writing reconfigures this pornographic formula (e.g., she does not always want it, and men are not always desirable), while retaining erotic suggestions of it at times.

Russkaia krasavitsa's pornographic moments are designed as signifying acts with serious consequences and reflective uses. Just as Irina and her body are beautiful, her writing is an aesthetic object, presenting at times beautiful, lyrical passages rich in imagery and employing intertextual references to other artistic works. Irina's writing thus incorporates pornographic, ethical, and aesthetic features and signification. The act of her writing in an existential crisis just before death by suicide adds pathos, gravity, and urgency to the comic elements of her narrative mode.

Irina's role as narrator, as well as her self-portrait, presents a fragmented, complex portrait of her character. Is she a prostitute? Her sexual role is not defined along fixed categories, which partially reflects her own nondidactic yet critical, perspicacious approach to sexual relations. Bisexual, divorced, and still young, with several abortions and love affairs behind her, Irina presents herself as a worldly metropolitan woman. Her beauty and sexuality dazzle others as she makes her way through the Muscovite social circuit of intellectuals, foreign diplomats, and others. For example, at a foreign-currency shop, Irina runs into the well-known writer Bella Akhmadulina, who tells her that, "vy, ditia, neskazanno soboi khoroshi" (24) (you, child, are unspeakably good-looking) (24). This real contemporary Soviet Russian writer's point of view helps to authorize the transgressive and excessive quality of Irina's beauty, a beauty which should be censored. It appears that many men and women characters, and scholars, also take her for a prostitute, in professional and casual senses. Meanwhile, Erofeev's characterization of Irina's status remains ambiguous. As the mistress of V. S., Irina is somewhere in between a courtesan and a secret girlfriend, and his eventual marriage to her in death raises her to the status of bride.

The symbolic or actual prostitute in literature serves as a sign of alternative and transgressive womanhood. Irina's character draws from this tradition. In Aristophanes' and his contemporaries' plays, the hetaira-comedy provided audiences with insights into a usually hidden world. The hetairae or courtesans operate on a level closer to men than that occupied by married women; the hetaira-comedy is satirical and discusses diverse sexual practices from masturbation to lesbianism. In the nineteenth and twentieth centuries, the resurgence of the prostitute or fallen woman in literature is a sign of real social conditions (e.g., *Nana* by Zola; Sonia in Dostoevsky's *Crime and Punishment*), a sign of independence and power, and a sign of degradation of ethical values.[33]

---

33. See Peter Gay's discussion of the prostitute in literature and culture in nineteenth-century Europe; subjects like Nana are part of a revolutionary movement in the arts while also serving as sources of erotic pleasure and a sign of bourgeois sexual repression ("The Price of Repression" in *The Tender Passion*, volume II of *The Bourgeois Experience*). Irina and Nana share a special personal perfume which lures both men and women; Nana's terrible death at the end of the novel signals the idea of a "raw, overpowering, destructive sexual power" (Gay, 370). Gay also notes how "Russian writers from Gogol to Dostoevsky, Chernishevsky to Chekhov, portrayed the prostitute as a

The postmodern ambiguity of Irina's identity is important. While some readers might deem her a prostitute because of her adventures, it might be prudent to assume that Irina occupies a grey zone in between that of a kept woman and a party girl who accepts some gifts such as perfume bottles displayed on her dresser. Her claim of expensive tastes is shown to be somewhat inflated. For all her glamorous bravado, she does share an apartment with her grandfather and work at a nondescript collective. Erofeev's allusions to Irina as possible prostitute challenge Soviet values; officially, prostitution was illegal. This sexual character, who describes her experiences with humor, lyricism, fantasy, and at times in creatively graphic detail, acts like the Thing that the Soviet censor would wish never to appear on the pages of a book entitled dreamily *Russkaia krasavitsa*.

While sex often disrupts idealizations of love and femininity in most world literature, in Russia, its shock value is particularly strong. Many scholars have examined its powerfully dichotomizing force in Russia. For example, Igor Kon explains how Russians, unlike Western Europeans, did not integrate a love of the human body in artwork, including religious artwork. He gives examples of the luxuriant Renaissance revelry in the whole living human body in paintings of religious themes in contrast to the Russian minimization and desiccation of the body and exaggeration of the face and head in religious iconography ("Sexuality," 199). Kon notes an intense "gender stratification" in Russian tradition and society. In addition to the familiar dichotomy of madonna-whore, in Russia, the meek housewife who can be beaten by her husband contrasts with the "powerful woman" as illustrated in Russian fairy tales.[34] The Russian soul and identity are associated with the feminine domain, while the body and soul are strongly differentiated. Kon explains:

> On one hand Russian character, lifestyle, and mentality are often presented and represented as a realm of predominant spirituality (*dukhovnost*), in sharp contrast to western materialism, pragmatism and body-boundedness (*telesnost*). This ideology of disembodied spirituality, with the corresponding underestimation and denigration of the body and its physiological functions, is most clearly implemented in Russian Orthodox religious art. (198)

Meanwhile, there is a strong folk tradition of integrating sex into story-

---

human being," thus indicating that old complacent attitudes toward prostitution were under pressure. Brooks also explores the critical phenomenon of the prostitute, including Nana, in literature and art (*Body Work*).

34. The character Vasilissa Premudraya; her counterpart in *Russkaia krasavitsa* would be the powerful Veronika, the "witch" who does not need a man.

telling and using frank everyday language (*mat*); we see this tradition carried out in much of Irina's own storytelling and use of *mat* and *chastushki*. In addition to noting the Soviet period's lack of sex education, Kon points out that, "Even the extravagant Soviet prudery, with its bans and ideological campaigns against any kind of body display and nudity in art and everyday life, was historically rooted in this traditional religious mentality" (199).

Some of the prudery and silence of the Soviet years result in a severe lack of knowledge of sexuality, as acknowledged in *Russkaia krasavitsa*. For example, Irina mentions how she has had to explain to an ignorant co-worker Nina Chizh where women urinate from (58; 66). After the public denunciation of Irina, her grandfather asks what "lesbian" means: "[...] ia otstal ot sovremennogo vremeni i khotia vse ponial, kogda tebia razoblachali, odnogo ne ponial: lesbiianka . . . Eto chto eshche za novyi iarlyk na liudei stali veshat'?" (125) (I've lost touch with modern ways, and although I understood everything when they accused you, there was one thing I didn't get: lesbian. What sort of new label is this they're sticking on people?) (153). Irina's adult savvy does not save her from childhood sexual abuse from her father. She explains that she did not know that the incest was wrong, indicating a complicit silence of the society and family around the child.

It is important to stress for the non-Soviet reader the shocking impact of a novel which explores a Soviet woman's sexual identity, especially if prostitution is suggested as well. Prostitution was a taboo subject in public discourse until the final years of *glasnost'*; as we have seen, 1988 marked a dramatic shift toward openness. Officially, Soviet society did not have prostitutes; they were a sign of decadent, bourgeois capitalism.[35] Irina's affair with a married man, and her allusions to an earlier affair with her boss at the work collective, Viktor Kharitonych, are further signs of disruption of codified, censored Soviet life. The final years of *glasnost'*, with its easing of censorship, resulted in a flood of interest in all manner of publications and films involving sexuality at all social levels.[36] Erofeev's 1990 novel emerges

---

35. See especially Ermolaev for a fine account of the last years of Soviet censorship and publishing and the late emergence of the prostitution theme in literature. See Voronina, Mamonova, and Goscilo for various feminist reactions to the emergence of pornography and prostitution in the late Soviet and early post-Soviet cultural scene. For the rise in sex markets in the Russian Federation, see Hughes's "Supplying Women for the Sex Industry: Trafficking from the Russian Federation" and Khodyreva's "Sexuality for Whom? Paid Sex and Patriarchy in Russia."

36. This new openness did not mean an automatic change from the deeply engrained prudery and lack of knowledge. Stulhofer and Sandfort report that, in data collected between 1995 and 1997, "In comparison with the EU countries, the countries of Central, Southeastern, and Eastern Europe score lower on indicators of sexual permissiveness" (14), with Russians the most likely to insist that sexual freedom must be limited, for example, with regards to homosexuality (15). In the Soviet setting of the late 1970s and early 1980s, Irina Tarakanova's lesbianism would be very

not far apart from two late Soviet works focusing on the young Russian woman as primarily sexual being, Vladimir Kunin's novella *Interdevochka* (*Intergirl*) (1988) and the film *Malenkaia Vera* (*Little Vera*) (1988) by director Vasilii Pichul.[37]

The emphatic, puritanical traits of Soviet morality became part of Soviet literary censoring criteria (just as was the corresponding case of a prudish brand of Catholic morality operating in Francoist censorship).[38] This puritanism meant that Soviet literature generally lacked literary treatments of sexuality. If a sexual relationship did take place in a fictional work, it was usually implied through indirection and understatement. Of course, naturalistic descriptions of sexual acts or organs and obscene language (sexual or excremental terms) were strictly censored. This general set of expectations regarding sex became operative in Soviet censorship especially from the 1930s onward (but could already be detected from the outset of the Soviet era). As censorship conditioned the reading material for the public, a strongly defined taste in literary themes and style could be maintained.

---

underground; female homosexuality was so off the chart for Soviet lawmakers that only male homosexuality was outlawed. See Moss's article "The Underground Closet" for an exploration of how homosexual references (like oppositional political ones) were coded in Aesopian language or masked in Soviet texts. For example, in general, Russian can be crafted to provide elisions and empty spaces through use of the passive voice, indefinite pronouns, pronouns without established referents, indefinite personal constructions, and subjectless constructions (Moss, 232–33). By excluding the naming of actual subjects, actions, or objects the reader is prompted to determine the likely name. Moss draws on examples in Bulgakov's *The Master and Margarita* to show how these locutions function to avoid naming the "authorities" or NKVD in Moscow. We can note that likewise *Russkaia krasavitsa* frequently empties the logical subject nodes; the effect is more subtle as Irina is not in a position to know how to identify actants (whereas the wily omniscient narrator of *The Master and Margarita* is in control of that information).

37. See Azhgikhina and Goscilo's "Getting under Their Skin: The Beauty Salon in Russian Women's Lives," as well as Porter, for commentary on *Interdevochka* and *Malenkaia Vera*. Azhgikhina and Goscilo point out how Kunin's painstaking detailed mention of beauty procedures and name-brand products is knowledge acquired through his interviews with some two hundred prostitutes. They further note that another "reason for readers' sympathy and understanding is that in Soviet and post-Soviet Russia the attitude to one's appearance—to one's hairstyle, makeup, and contour of eyebrows—has never been merely a woman's personal affair, but has always revealed something larger: a worldview, a relationship to one's environment and to the prevailing ideology as a whole" (95).

In this perspective, we can note that Irina's beauty, as is indeed explored in Erofeev's novel, takes her beyond "body-boundedness" (*telesnost'*) to considerations of spirituality (*dukhovnost'*). Irina's unusual or extraordinary natural beauty sometimes separates her from other women, while her interest in fashion and perfume makes her commensurable with other women. But she is also presented at times as less than beautiful, such as after her car accident, during her bout of tonsillitis, and in her final decay before death.

38. For a fine, detailed overview of the whole Soviet period of literary censorship, with attention throughout to political and puritanical criteria, see Ermolaev. See Goldschmidt for a discussion of pornography in Russia beyond the literary realm.

This Soviet puritanism does not mean that there was no erotic quality to Soviet Russian literature at times. In *Men without Women*, Borenstein makes an excellent argument for the prevalence of masculinity and the minimization of feminine sexuality and women protagonists. Borenstein explains how the early Soviet literary cult of machines and scorn for women and a pronounced father worship also played out ideologically through Stalin as father figure. For Borenstein, in dialogue with Mosse, the pre-Revolutionary prostitute and the marriage plot decline drastically in the Soviet era, replaced by a celebration of men:

> . . . both comradeship and a "cult of masculinity" were an integral part of early-twentieth-century modernist discourse. George Mosse's groundbreaking *Nationalism and Sexuality* (1985) argues that an idealized "manliness" is at the heart of what he terms "the most powerful ideology of modern times, nationalism." [. . .] Of particular relevance to modernism is Mosse's assertion that by the early twentieth century "[m]asculinity was expected to stand both for unchanging values in a changing age and for the dynamic but orderly process of change itself, guided by an appropriate purpose." (31–32)

Counteracting this modernist promotion of masculinity, *Russkaia krasavitsa* reasserts a woman's world and perspective by installing a female character-narrator and a postmodern marriage plot. With V. S., Irina is working on her third marriage. Prior to meeting him, this Russian beauty has been ironically passed over by a collection of eligible suitors, indicative of their appreciation of her sex rather than for some ethereal feminine ideal. None of the novel's men exemplify an idealized Soviet masculinity, and they exhibit various degrees of powerlessness, inadequacy, and superfluity, including Vladimir Sergeyevich, whose literal impotence is made a central part of his sexual and romantic relationship with Irina. As a reader of Blok, the "beautiful lady" Irina reintegrates subversively Blok's dichotomized concept of the feminine. Borenstein explains that, for Blok, his

> approach to the Symbolist topos of the Eternal Feminine, while explicitly chivalric, relies heavily on the tension between madonna and whore. As early as his 1901 collection of verses about the "beautiful lady" (*Stikhi o prekrasnoi dame*), Blok expresses the fear that his feminine ideal could reveal herself to be something altogether different: "I'm afraid you will change your guise" (No strashno mne: izmenish' oblik ty); "What you will become—I do not know" (No vo chto obratish'sia—ne vedaiu). (52)

Borenstein suggests that Blok perceives a possible Antichrist or anti-

Sophia behind vision of heavenly beauty.

Irina offers similar antithetical qualities: men, including the supposedly powerful writer V. S., seem both attracted to her and fearful of her potential. It is as though her feminine sublimity could threaten to negate or wipe out men. Erofeev's nostalgic subversion of Blok can be seen in Irina's central perspective—she does not desire to ruin men, and in fact she decides to save Russia. She has a power to absorb evil, which positions her closer to the status of a saint. Despite her good intentions, she ultimately coincides with neo-Blokian fears in her apocalyptic ending.

Erofeev's novel contests ironically some Russian philosophers' metaphysics of sexuality, which tend to favor certain forms of masculinity and downplay dangerous femininity. For example, Hutchings explains how philosopher Soloviev traces a triumph in which "matter will become 'impregnated' by spirit and betrays a male drive to appropriate femininity's difference, thus removing the threat it poses to masculine sexuality" (142). Hutchings quotes Naiman's interpretation of this idea: "What can the spiritualization of matter [. . .] mean, but the molding of the essence of femininity to remove all traces of the feminine." Yet, masculinity is not always useful to such philosophers, as Hutchings explains: "On the one hand, then, philosophers like Berdiaev and Solov'ev suppress the influence of the masculine body with its possessive, violative impulses in their explication of the activity of spirit. On the other hand, though, they are accused of presupposing fixed values for those feminine and masculine categories—such as body and spirit—that they *do* care to specify" (emphasis in original).

Sameness and difference are central to discussing femininity and masculinity, and for Russian philosophers, gender could be used metaphorically to theorize metaphysics. The legacy of this trend in philosophy can be witnessed in Russian literature like Erofeev's that seeks to theorize sex similarly. Erofeev prioritizes the radical other Irina and her sexual relations with men and women, bringing her into a fatal collision course with social, political, and spiritual forces. She attempts to solve her pregnancy by first having her sex blessed with holy water, and then, undoing this act by performing witch Katerina Maksimovna's folk spell with an egg (chapter 22). Thus, Irina attempts to follow two distinct "Russian" paths, the Russian Orthodox one (in which women are subservient) and the Russian folk way (in which women turn to each other for power, and are at times their own source of power). Ironically, neither option resolves her pregnancy. She ends up becoming Vladimir Sergeyevich's bride in death, marrying herself to the Russian Soviet cultural past for the sake of love and marriage, and perhaps as a last act of martyrdom for Russia.

The narrative creates a series of Russian story lines which lead to a thematic cul-de-sac: the comic-tragic premature death of the Russian beauty and genius of love and sexuality. Irina is the negative reflection of Soloviev's Sophia. Rylkova describes Sophia as a "twofold unity," on the one hand a "unity of the divinely originated word" (logos) and on the other hand, the "created," a unity realized in the body (333). While Sophia ennobles creation (eros + logos), Irina attempts but ultimately fails in achieving this positive synthesis. Irina's combination of eros and logos results in destruction and endings of the self and writing.

Given these cultural contexts, Irina as a protagonist and her use of language represent censored Soviet Russian topics. These are ideologically incorrect, as well as morally offensive to the censor-reader. A provocative, beautiful woman who is possibly a whore[39] does not correspond to dominant fictions about Soviet womanhood or heroine (of course, as we have seen she does correspond to various literary fallen women who are sometimes viewed as whores, such as Dostoevsky's Nastasya Filippovna and Pasternak's Lara). Indeed, in Soviet dominant fiction, as explored by Naiman and Borenstein, the Soviet heroine becomes diminished altogether, serving as man's helper or as maternal figure. Irina's maternity is made ironically patriotic: she is pregnant with the dead V. S.'s child, but she conceived from a ghost, not a man, hardly a wholesome pregnancy for the future of Soviet culture. Irina's ambiguous sexual qualities are an affront to the didactic demands of Soviet ideology. The Soviet censor desires a transparency and explicitness that Irina as a narrator, despite her own aim toward disclosure, cannot provide. For example, in chapter 2, Irina tries to define herself:

Ne raz sadilas' ia v luzhu v vechernikh nariadakh, ne raz obrekala sebia na pozor, i menia vyvodili, no ved' ne iz kakogo-nibud' kabaka, kak privokzal'nuiu kurvu, a iz zala konservatorii, gde na prem'ere ia zabrosala apel'sinami britanskii orkestr iz-za polnoi bezvykhodnosti moego polozheniia! Net, Ira, ty byla ne posledniaia zhenshchina [. . .] (18)

More than once I had sat down in a puddle wearing an evening dress, more than once I had covered myself with shame and had been led away, but not from some dive, like a tart who works the railway station, but from the hall of the Conservatory, where during a premiere I bombarded a British orchestra with oranges as a result of the hopeless position I found myself in. No, Ira

---

39. The Russian word for "whore," *bliad'*, was and remains a taboo expression (unlike the word "whore" in English). For many Russian readers, *bliad'* is especially obscene in print.

Apocalyptic Beauty, Russian Sublimity ▪ 251

[Irina], you were not the least of women [. . .]. (15)

This passage complicates our perception of Irina in several ways. First, she distinguishes herself from a "privokzal'nuiu kurvu" (tart who works the railway station), an acknowledgment of the lowest-paid rank of Soviet prostitutes recognizable by their typical place of work. Indirectly, then, she seems to suggest that she is some other kind of "tart," only a classier one. When V. S. finally takes Irina to a Benjamin Britten concert by a visiting British orchestra at the Conservatory, he experiments with showing Irina in a hyperpublic sphere, but he then behaves as if embarrassed, as though he has brought along a prostitute. In response, Irina misbehaves, resulting in her expulsion from the Conservatory. This cultural center is not a place typically associated with prostitution; Irina is expelled for throwing oranges at the foreign orchestra, but by acting out she ensures that everyone sees that V. S. is accompanied by a beautiful young woman in a low-cut dress. Her expulsion signifies a censoring of the unwanted sign.

Only later will the reader discover that her "hopeless position" (a more literal translation of "iz-za polnoi bezvykhodnosti moego polozhenia" would be "the utter exitlessness of my position") has been that of a mistress to a married man, Vladimir Sergeyevich. A mistress is a dubious position to occupy, a bridge between the respectable, regulated position of a wife and the censured position of a prostitute. The disparity between V. S.'s position of power and respectability and Irina's humble position as upstart is stark. Their erotic relationship remains necessarily ambiguous and embedded in class disparity. The final line of the cited passage indicates early in the text the degree to which Irina shifts into the mode of addressing herself in the second person, as well as her need to rank herself in comparison with other women ("Net, Ira, ty byla ne posledniaia zhenshchina" [No, Ira (Irina), you were not the least of women]). This sense of separation from one's self, this self-observation, will be discussed in depth later.

Russian prostitution, adultery, and love are further complicated by the intertextual use of Pushkin's "Tale of the Fisherman and the Fish," a cautionary tale about greed and vanity.[40] The old fisherman in the story asks the golden fish for too many things for his greedy wife so that finally the

---

40. The Russian fairy tale transcribed by Pushkin, "Skazka o rybake i rybke" ("Fairy Tale of the Fisherman and the Fish"), contrasts with the Grimm fairy tale, "Von dem Fischer und Seiner Frau" ("The Fisherman and His Wife"). In the Russian tale, the fish is a golden fish, is featured in the title, and is the ultimate wish of the insatiable wife before the fish returns the couple to their original hut. The wife asks that the fish serve her. By contrast, in the German version (and English translation), the fish is a large flounder (*Bütt*) and is not mentioned in the title. When the wife asks to become like God, the fish returns the couple to their pigsty.

golden fish returns the peasants to their former poverty. When the fisherman first encounters the golden fish in his net, he kindly sets her free and does not initially wish for anything, despite the fish's offer. When Vladimir Sergeyevich refers to this tale in his first meeting alone with Irina, he uses it as a proposition: would Irina like to be the golden fish? (chapter 5).

He completely subverts the story and its power dynamics. While in the original tale, the golden fish has the power to grant wishes, to give and take away, the golden-fish role proposed to Irina is really that of a lover who will grant wishes, but who is under the power of the fisherman. Further, the fisherman of the tale is kind to the fish and meekly follows his shrewish wife's orders. By contrast, Vladimir Sergeyevich is selfish with Irina; he evades his wife and her possible orders by involving himself with Irina. Irina is duped by the story. It is flattering that she appeals to a great Soviet Russian writer who in turn uses Pushkin as a mode of enchantment and authentification, and it is tempting to be offered a golden-fish role. She tries to assert her power by including the condition that she must have love, that he must agree to marry her. While he is alive, he does not intend to fulfill that condition. Yet, Irina's dubious power as a golden fish is belatedly and apocalyptically confirmed when the dead Vladimir Sergeyevich claims Irina as his bride.

Irina discloses herself as the Thing ("unspeakably beautiful") that is usually a censored subject in Soviet literature and society. As a counterpart to her identity, her writing also represents a text which would normally be censored or banned by Soviet literary censors. Her writing possesses an erotic edge as the style moves between the high and low, the lyrical and the pornographic, the fantastic and the realistic, the cynical and the naïve, the sophisticated and the obscene. The expectations of a mainstream Soviet readership (and the censorship that produces it) are broken in the following ways: the clashes of style, their ironic effects, and the restless, shifting focus and associative strategies (which can appear as a lack of aesthetic taste and skill); the plot is presented in a nonchronological retrospective; the ending lacks a clear ideological resolution or moral judgment; the story as a whole cannot be taken as a prescriptive guide for living; the candid descriptions of unseemly or vulgar aspects of Soviet life, normally excluded from literary fiction, would be an affront to good taste or even anti-Soviet.[41]

---

41. Over the course of the Soviet period, literary standards do vary. For example, Vera Dunham has chronicled the rise of middle-class values in post–World War II Soviet literature (e.g., the mention of material goods, private property such as real estate and cars); such literature introduces a marked class aspiration that in pre–World War II literature would have been unthinkable or, if attempted, censored. Erofeev's novel playfully acknowledges some of these trends in middle-brow Soviet literature; for example, Irina is a Soviet commoner compared to the privileged V. S., who

First-person narrations present problems for the reader (as we have also seen in *Lolita*). There is more than a hint of the manic quality of Dostoevsky's Underground Man in Irina's rambling effusion of words and her sense of persecution.[42] First-person narration promises the presentation of some (illusory) unmediated view on the person's inner thoughts. In this way, *Russkaia krasavitsa*'s confessional mode emphasizes disclosure of some truth or reality. Further, the mise-en-abyme text, her photo-exposé for the Western magazine, discloses her beautiful body as well as her once secret relationship with V. S.

Irina's disclosures have a strong realist effect of the authentic. Even her contradictions lend to a growing awareness of her character, how it contrasts with her ideal image of herself, and how her beauty fails to save Russia or the world. As a personal memoir, Irina's tumbling narrative gives the impression of a text not edited or controlled by an official censor or even editor. Irina as rogue narrator is modified by additional practices of the Russian first-person narrator, such as memoirists, whose narratives in the Soviet period had dissident facets, literary (as opposed to historical-biographical) inclinations in terms of style and structure, and martyrdom themes.[43] As *pícara* narrator and Soviet memoirist, Irina and her discourse find themselves located in the margins of Soviet literature and society.

5. INCORPORATING WRITING: IRINA'S BODY AND BEAUTY AS SUBLIME CENSORED THING IN SOVIET RUSSIAN LITERATURE

Irina repeatedly defines herself by her sexuality and her beauty. These combined qualities constitute censored subjects in Soviet Russian writing. But as they are constitutive features of herself and her life, so they become the necessary focus in her confession. This protagonist's life is largely defined

---

has a private house, servants, a car, and who gives Irina gifts such as sand-colored jeans and boots from the West. The acknowledgment of these items shows up V. S.'s and the Soviet elite's lack of communist values. Consumer materialism, especially in terms of beauty products, becomes an aspect of some literature directed toward women; see Azhgikhina and Goscilo's "Getting under Their Skin: The Beauty Salon in Russian Women's Lives."

42. Dostoevsky's work was grudgingly accepted into the Soviet Russian literary canon. The intertextuality lends Irina a status as a writer and subject who does not conform to approved official standards. Dostoevsky in this way can serve as a sign of nonconformity (and consequently as an ironic recognition that official standards and judgment are not necessarily the most appropriate measures of outstanding artistic quality). Bulgakov's *Master i Margarita* (*The Master and Margarita*) makes such ironic intertextual use of Dostoevsky as a prominent Russian writer whose works were at times censored or limited in access in the Soviet era.

43. For discussions of the Soviet memoir, see, for example, Holmgren; Prokhorov.

by her body; so, too, is her death. By removing her body from the stage of life, she commits an ultimate act of censoring in a confessional mode of writing by removing herself as the subject from the stream of the text.[44]

As we learn about her life, we see that almost everything that Irina does or that happens to her is predicated upon her extraordinary beauty and sex. Her best friend and lover Ksyusha, who comes from a privileged family, introduces Irina to various select and intellectual circles in Moscow. Irina's dramatic adulterous affair with Vladimir Sergeyevich is prompted by her beauty and sexual flair: "nazyval menia geniem liubvi" (18); Sergeyevich calls her a "genius of love" (16). Their Moscow affair ends in a sexual embrace with death, as he dies during a rough session of sadomasochistic intercourse.

The subsequent episodes of Irina's life are also based on her body and beauty: her inspired, surreal goal to become a symbolic Russian Joan of Arc by running on a famous battlefield and offering her naked body for penetration by a higher force; her Soviet-style show trial and exercise in self-criticism staged by her coworkers who condemn her work ethic (e.g., wearing beads) and sexual immorality (lesbianism); her encounters with her gynecologist, Stanislav Albertovich Flavitsky; her attempt to purify her pregnant body by way of a baptism conducted by Father Veniamin and then by a witch; her photo-interview for the foreign magazine; the New York super models' support for her; her negotiations with the twin journalists, Sergei and Nikolai Ivanovich, to correct her unseemly, counterideological image in Soviet publicity. Her body presents the foundation for the novel's exploration of beauty and sublimity, martyrdom, love, freedom, transgression, and the problem of the body's opposition to spirituality.

Just as in her writing Irina inscribes accounts of her "unspeakable" beauty and body, so in her life's events is her body the signifying entity in its encounters with characters who represent the Symbolic Other. Her attempts to incorporate herself into the Soviet and Russian Symbolic are especially illustrated in her relation with Vladimir Sergeyevich. Their sexual and romantic relation is overlaid by their oppositional roles as writers. Leonardik, as a composite character of prestigious Soviet male literati, represents the approved intersection of culture and ideology in dominant Soviet discourse.[45] He has been so canonized that Irina as a child in school

---

44. This situation leaves the character-narrator in a paradoxical position at the end of the text: how can she still be writing her confession while she is hanging herself? The final chapter's present tense suggests simultaneous action and speech/writing. Has the writing been taken over by phantom forces? Or does she complete her text from the afterlife?

45. Dark, Porter, and Rylkova discuss Vladimir Sergeyevich as Soviet literary lion.

has learned his name and works. His achievements and longevity have earned him public and political respect and advantages.

This status implies that he has been a wily veteran of Soviet censorship, a cunning negotiator of Soviet ideology and shifting trends in the political interpretation of it. His sense of self-preservation has probably come at the cost of creativity. While Irina mentions that he "pro menia sobiralsia povest' pisat' i uzhe zagotovil libretto dlia opery" (154–55) (was planning to write a novella about me and had already prepared a libretto for the opera) (191), she also explains that he fears it will be banned (117). V. S.'s novel "beretsia opisat' rokovuiu liubov' ne khoreem, a v prozaicheskoi allegorii" (96) (is going to portray a fatal love not in trochees but in the trenches, in a trenchant prose allegory) (116). He is planning to "uvekovechit'" (immortalize) Irina, casting her as a "sanitarka bedovaia, vliubchivaia, a on, pozhiloi kontuzhenyi polkovnik [...] vliubliaetsia" (mischievous nurse, open to love, while he, a middle-aged wounded colonel, falls in love with her).

Irina's sublime beauty attracts Vladimir Sergeyevich with its exciting, transgressive promise of Soviet-censored value and consequently creative inspiration and sexual reinvigoration. But he must negotiate a contract with a woman demanding love in return for a sexual relationship. Irina's guiding fantasy vis-à-vis Vladimir Sergeyevich is that he might be the agent to hail her into a comforting dominant fiction of Soviet life: marriage, children, and a home. Yet their one public appearance at the Britten concert illustrates how Irina, as Soviet-censored sexuality, is thwarted in her aim to insert herself into the mainstream fiction of Soviet life. In public, Vladimir Sergeyevich is generally ashamed to be noticed with her. She only momentarily breaks through the barriers of Soviet censorship to appear transgressively on the inside of the collective dominant fiction. In this and other instances, Irina's active presence as character parallels what in writing is the censored object's crossing the lines of censorship and appearing in language. Her behavior mirrors her writing. Her agency as an individual reflects her agency as a writer and subject of that writing.

Vladimir Sergeyevich's phantasmal visit from the dead to Irina's bedside—his resurrection—presents another aspect of Irina as censored sexual subject and writing subject. In an ironic variation of his first promise to the golden fish Irina, and his second proposal in their last live encounter, the ghost appears to her as the desiring prospective bridegroom. The scene and its macabre results of pregnancy reverse comically the basic structure of necrophilia. Erich Fromm explains how necrophilia is "the passionate attraction to all that is dead, decayed, putrid, sickly" (325) and is almost exclusively a masculine passion. For Fromm, "[Necrophilia] is the passion to transform that which is alive into something unalive; to destroy for the sake of destruction; the exclusive interest in all that is purely mechanical. It is the passion to tear apart living structures" (332). Borenstein notes how necrophilia operates in Soviet Russian novels like *Chevengur*. In his overview of highly masculinized cultures and relationships in Soviet Russian literature, Borenstein considers Fromm's account of necrophilia: "Fromm firmly grounds necrophilia in the traditionally male world: necrophiles love not only corpses, but war, destruction, commerce, and machines. If Fromm's definition of necrophilia is reevaluated in terms of gender and taken to its logical extremes, necrophilia becomes the apotheosis of an exclusive, self-absorbed masculinity that denies both women and the family" (254).

Erofeev's inversion of literary Russian necrophilia positions Irina with the living and V. S. with the dead. Irina is reluctant to become involved with the dead V. S.; his passion and insistence lock her into a kind of necrophilic relationship. Powerful femininity, in the form of the sublimely beautiful Irina, becomes subsumed or negated in V. S.'s deathly, terrifying embrace.

His visit functions on the level of forbidden fantasy. The fantasy of his visit and the couple's comic-erotic intercourse demonstrate Irina's continuing desire to find a desiring other in a prestigious, respected man, even if he is deceased. On an allegorical level, that desire can be perceived as the censored Soviet writer-subject's desire to have Soviet discourse's approval, love, and incorporation. Dramatized here is the censored subject's desire to be named, interpellated, called into the Symbolic register where it might acquire wholeness through the solidifying effects of language.

The ghost's insemination of Irina offers several more possibilities to expand on the drama of censoring relations. First, the couple's intercourse, described in semipornographic, semitragic style, and resulting in insemination and conception, parodies the immaculate conception of the Virgin and her subsequent conception of Christ. The illustrious dead representative of Soviet literature, a Soviet holy ghost of sorts, sows his seed in a plainly nonvirginal woman, whose worthiness is found not in her purity, but in her beauty, her sexuality, and her desire to become a Russian heroine or savior (her Joan of Arc project). The miraculous nature of her pregnancy is emphasized by the pleased astonishment of her gynecologist Flavitsky, who has imagined her to be sterile. Chapter 1 in fact serves as a kind of humorous parody of the Annunciation, with Flavitsky as Gabriel.

The parodies replace fulfillment with negation. The pregnancy develops into a terrifying condition which will have no joyous end in the birth of a savior, but rather in a grotesque double death of sublime mother and changeling-fetus. Irina first senses a change in her body by the vile, corpse-like odor that replaces her bergamot scent, an aromatic signature of her intrinsically lyrical, sexualized beauty. As she recognizes who the father must be, she is faced with a doubly negative dilemma. She cannot give birth to such a changeling, and she cannot decide to abort it. As the pregnancy progresses, she advances into an increasingly deep psychosis.

On an allegorical level, Irina's conflict might be seen in the following way. If she would remain alive as the vessel that would gestate Soviet literature, she would produce Death (as boded in the hideous smell coming from her). If she would join Vladimir Sergeyevich as his bride in death, as he urges her to do, she, as the censored sexual object in Soviet life and literature, could overcome the rules and barriers of worldly censorship and be symbolically reunited with the reformed lover-writer in the afterlife. By choosing the latter option, Irina acts as her own censor in life and in writing by removing herself from the text of signification (self-erasure). But paradoxically also through this censoring act, she produces one resounding judgment. She condemns the existing Soviet system and the society it produces through removing herself and her fetus (that system's potential rotting future anti-Christ) from the chain of signification of her writing of her life and the life of her writing.[46]

The Mother Russia association, implicit in Irina's status as a pregnant Russian protagonist and her patriotic drive, is ironically negated by her diverse nonconformity to the Soviet heroine. Work and politics do not feature prominently and positively in her life.[47] Her fertility and reproduction are determined by death and the supernatural. She fails to overcome the hurdles in her life. In addition, she demonstrates all manner of traits that are normally kept out of Soviet literature, owing to an ideologically prescriptive censorship: she smokes and drinks, at times to excess; she has sex frequently and with different partners of both sexes; she has had numerous abortions; she lives semilegally at her grandfather's apartment; she is a vain materialist (her perfume bottles and clothes); she has suffered from incest and beatings as a child; her ex-husband has beaten and disfigured her savagely for an adulterous affair; her rural education has been rude

---

46. Irina's act of joining the canonized Soviet writer in the afterlife parodically mirrors the beautiful muse Margarita's decision to join her dead lover and banned Russian writer, the Master, in a harmonious, romantic marriage in the afterlife in Bulgakov's *The Master and Margarita*.

47. Irina subverts the ideal Soviet worker's paradigm by having an affair with her boss Kharitonych, by gaining from him a degree of patronage that allows her to slack off, and, finally, by being held to account by a people's court at work (in which she is criticized not for how she works but instead for her personal preferences). In contrast, her grandfather has been a model worker, an actual Stakhanovite, who once hospitalized himself because of overexertion in overfilling quotas. Despite this worker heritage, Irina and her parents do not carry out the zealous tradition, an ironic signal of the mindless overvaluation of certain types of work in the Stalinist era and the decay of work in the late Soviet era.

and brief; she reads foreign literature; she associates with foreigners (as well as with Soviet Jews, Georgians, Armenians, and Caucasians); she candidly discusses various hypocritical or paradoxical qualities of Soviet life (racism, anti-Semitism, alcoholism, lingering Stalinism, and so on); and she displays naïveté and lapses of logic.

Taken as a whole, her qualities do not produce an ideologically correct Soviet literary protagonist, but they do reflect the reality of many different Soviet Russian women. Furthermore, despite her flaws and impediments, Irina insistently uses her rogue body to inscribe herself as a Soviet Russian heroine.

6. SPLIT SUBJECTHOOD: ALIENATION AND THE PRODUCTION OF FANTASY

Irina's whirling, digressive writing modes of confession and self-portrayal emphasize her split subjecthood: her growing alienation from others and from herself. This exercise in self-observation is akin to self-analysis. In order to analyze herself, she looks upon herself from a different standpoint, using the first- and second-person singular to create a dialogue and self-observation.

The novel's apocalyptic conclusion—foreshadowed since the earliest chapters of the novel—dramatically stages Irina's split subjectivity. Shortly before she hangs herself, she addresses her readers as though they were her hallucinated wedding guests and self-inventions, for they all play roles in the narrative: "Ia vas sochinila, chtoby sochinit' sebia, no rassochiniv vas, ia samoraspuskaius' kak persona . . ." (273) (I composed you in order to compose myself, but when I discompose you I shall dissolve myself as a person . . .) (342).

This conceptualist gesture—a self-awareness of Irina's manipulation of (and intervention with) her interlocutors—underlines writing's interdependence between the writer and reader, the doing and undoing of writing, the writing and the censoring of writing. The paraliterary elements of the text—the comic list of dramatis personae at the novel's outset and the penultimate chapter's wedding announcement and suicide note from Irina—augment the constructed quality of the confessional novel with Irina in her dual perspectives as character-narrator and as character.

Early on in the novel, Irina articulates her concerns about achieving wholeness and accuracy through her writing, ingeniously revealing the limitations of the Soviet literary scene and practices:

Napisat', konechno, ia mogu, no nevol'noe bespokoistvo vyzyvaet u menia to, chto ia ne znaiu kak, to est' k literature ne imeiu nikakogo otnosheniia. Bylo by kuda luchshe, esli by moiu istoriiu vzialsia opisat', naprimer, Sholokhov. Predstavliaiu, on by ee tak opisal, chto u vsekh by rty otvalilis' [. . .]. Ostal'nye iz zhivushchikh pisatelei ne vyzyvaiut vo mne doveria, potomu chto pishut skuchno i vse vrut, norovia ili priukrasit' fakty narodnoi zhizni, ili, naoborot, polnost'iu oskvernit', kak Solzhenitsyn [. . .], nedarom potom i sbelenilsia, v otlichie ot togo zhe Sholokhova, kotoryi pisal chestno i kak bylo i potomu zasluzhil vseobshchee uvazhenie i dazhe imeet sobstvennyi samolet. Bolee interesno i po-chelovecheski pishut inostrannye avtory [. . .], kotorye zachastuiu pechataiutsia na stranitsakh zhurnala «Inostrannaia literatura» [. . .]. Oni udachnee, chem nashi, umeiut peredat' psikhologiiu [. . .], no oni tozhe inogda chego-nibud' takoe zavernut i zaum' napustiat', ne poimesh', gde konets, gde nachalo, spoloshnoi modernizm, kotoryi oslabliaet khudozhestvennuiu silu, i neiasno, zachem publikuiut. (16–17)

I can of course write, but I can't help worrying about the fact that I don't know how; that is, I have no connection whatsoever with literature. It would be so much better if, for example, Sholokhov were to take up the writing of my story. I can just imagine how he would describe it, in a way that would make everyone's jaw drop [. . .]. No other living writers inspire my confidence, because what they write is boring and they all lie, either painting a pretty picture of the facts of our national life or, on the contrary, putting it down completely, like the gulag dissidents [like Solzhenitsyn] [. . .]. It was not surprising that they went mad afterward, in contrast to Sholokhov, who wrote honestly about everything just as it was and therefore earned universal respect and even a private plane. More interesting and compassionate are the writings of foreign authors [. . .], which are published frequently in the journal *Foreign Literature* [. . .]. They are more successful than our writers in conveying psychology [. . .]; but their writers sometimes rant on and on and produce such "transense" that you can't tell the end from the beginning, pure modernism, which weakens artistry, and it's unclear why they publish it. (13–14)[48]

One of the many ironies expressed in this passage is that Irina herself

---

48. The translator Reynolds makes "transense" out of the Russian "zaum'" (or "zaumnyi iazyk"); he might have chosen a more down-to-earth term for Irina, such as "mumbo jumbo," but I suggest that his is a strategic choice. "Zaum'" means unintelligible language, and especially suggests a kind of futuristic language, based on what might seem to be arbitrary usage; experimental language or "zaum'" was an element in the Oberiuty of Russian futurism. Irina seems to use the term to criticize what she sees as nonsense language usage in modernist works (and has me thinking of a not uncommon reader's reaction to *Finnegans Wake*).

produces a work endowed with a sort of postmodern "transense," the sort that never would have passed censorship. Meanwhile, in her comments, she reads the foreigners' works (published in what was traditionally a carefully censored literary journal) in a manner common to Soviet literary criticism. Here the contradiction enacted in her initial praise ("Bolee interesno i po-chelovecheski" [More interesting and compassionate], "udachnee" [successful]) and then abrupt dismissal of the foreigners' literature are demonstrations of how a Soviet critic, in working against the censor, might try to disguise a fragment of nonconformist opinion amidst a negating mass of criticism. "Transense" itself is a qualified term of aesthetic value in Erofeev's own critical lexicon, but to uphold the irony he makes it an object of Irina's disdain, in the same way that he ensures that Irina heaps insults on the dissident writers and kudos on Sholokhov.[49] Her readerly qualities position her in an ambiguous zone between Soviet aesthetics and subversive or alternative Russian aesthetics.

As a censored, sexual Thing of beautiful sublimity, Irina is not supposed to try to insert herself into Russian discourse, but she is nevertheless compelled to do so. Why? I suggest that, in her roles as fallen woman, genius of love and pure beauty, and writer, she desires the desire of the other, the Soviet Russian Symbolic, in three stages. First, she wants to encounter a desiring other in the person of Vladimir Sergeyevich. Second, after his death, she seeks to fulfill the desire of the big other: a patriotic, selfless sacrifice for one's country implied in Soviet ideology and martyrdom narratives, including that of Joan of Arc. Finally, her extraordinary beauty is related to the sublime. Her decision to plunge into a marriage in death with her grotesque ghost-groom signals a desire for the sublime experience and for escape from an impossible life. Her approach to death is apocalyptic, yet oriented toward a future.

Plagued by the psychosis that this fantastic pregnancy has brought about, Irina displays signs of a split subjecthood in her writing throughout the text. While all subjectivity is basically barred or split, in *Russkaia krasavitsa,* that barred subjecthood, the porno-graphed self in fragments, is dramatically emphasized in order to signify a crisis in Soviet literature and society owing to the weighty, judgmental demands of its ruling ideology. While others perceive Irina as an obscenely sublime presence in the Soviet world, always in excess, she insistently tries to assert herself into collective visions:

---

49. See "Russia's *Fleurs du mal*" for a concise yet detailed assessment of the changing landscape of twentieth-century Russian literature. In Erofeev's explanation of late and post–Soviet literature, he describes *alternative literature* as drawing inspiration from diverse sources: "It adores the 'transense' of the *Oberiuty* and Hollywood blockbusters, pop-art and guitar poetry, Stalinist skyscrapers and Western post-modernism" (xiii).

by making a scene at the Conservatory; by posing seductively for a foreign magazine photo-spread; by traveling into the countryside, appealing to a crowd of villagers, and running on the battlefield as a parodic Russian Joan of Arc; by agreeing to cooperate with the two Soviet journalists who will smooth her image over. Irina's bodily and textual crises of coherence occur because she is not apprehended by others in the way she aims to be apprehended. In Burkean and Kantian terms, her sublimity cannot be fully apprehended. To others, even admiring others, her body is excessively beautiful. Her attempt to use it as a discursive image or symbol, especially with the art of love and sex, is met with censorious reaction.

Irina's crisis as subject can be related to Lacan's explanation of the ego's role in subjectivity and its core relation with death. In his view, the subject needs the ego in order to have access to the "symbolic reality" (*The Ego*, 210). The ego intimately links to the subject's "primitive gap" and thus to death. He further explains,

> The relation of the ego to death is an extremely close one, for the ego is a point of intersection between the common discourse, in which the subject finds himself caught, alienated, and his psychological reality. In man, the imaginary relation has deviated, in so far as that is where the gap is produced whereby death makes itself felt. The world of the symbol, the very foundation of which is the phenomenon of repetitive insistence, is alienating for the subject, or more exactly it causes the subject to always realise himself elsewhere, and causes his truth to be always in some part veiled from him.

This basic account of the alienated subject can be seen as dramatically exaggerated in Irina's case in *Russkaia krasavitsa*. As an apocalyptic anatomy of her life and self, Irina's narrative shows how the subject-narrator searches for meaning for herself in her relations with others. Part of that drive is to derive meaning from, or creatively contribute meaning to, the Soviet symbolic. But her attempts do not lead her to a stronger, more defined sense of self.

As we have noted, Irina's originality as beauty is complicated in its reflection or echo in numerous literary, historic and spiritual predecessors, from Nastasya Filippovna and Anna Karenina, Pushkin's "genius of pure beauty," Tiutchev's "murderous" love, and Blok's beautiful lady, to Joan of Arc and Mother Russia. Many of these women's narratives are based on suffering, love, and beauty. Irina's narrative incorporates the larger trend in Russian literature and memoirs to live and present one's life in terms of creative martyrdom. However, the more Irina tries to analyze and describe herself and the events from different angles, the more she moves toward madness, despair, and death. It is as though writing brings her perilously close to an actual encounter with death.

The portrayal of a subject trying to inscribe herself into a highly regimented, judgmental symbolic has had many variations in literature, some of which include an overt or underlying presupposition of a porno-graphic dynamics. For example, eighteenth-century literature abounds in such texts (e.g., *Clarissa; Moll Flanders*). For female protagonists' representations of the self, the conflict often lies in their written (confessed) version of sexuality versus versions held by others (family, society).[50] Irina's deep conflict is between life and death; her bisexuality and her embracing of the role of "genius of love" signal a lack of typical neurotic repression.

Unlike the other novels discussed in this book (*Ulysses; Lolita; Tiempo de silencio*), which involve men's drive to know and find value in sex (what I called earlier epistemic and ethical drives), the woman's narrative of *Russkaia krasavitsa* works from a feminine core of knowledge. Irina, therefore, does not share the variations of the male fantasy of coming to know the desiring female other. So what is Irina's fantasy? Her writing and actions reveal a desire to become incorporated into the Soviet dominant fiction. She despairs because her fabulous sexual beauty, her genius of love, should have earned her love from her lovers and others, not abandonment, rejection, or censure. The man's and woman's approaches to the porno-graphic self complement each other in that they are demonstrations of the will to judgment. That judgment promises to supply meaning and love.

The pornographic premise contained in confessional women's writing about themselves is that the reader might learn about her intimate, sexual secrets and encounter the desiring woman's voice. The confessional mode implies that the subject has committed some kind of transgression and is called to judgment. Such writing, if it would be pornographic, should promise fullness (explicit, naturalistic detail), pleasure (sensual and narrative detail), and a revelation of the desiring woman (she really wants sex). *Russkaia krasavitsa* takes these premises of the pornographic genre and turns them to postmodern use as ironic modes of producing a meaningful text about the taboo woman in Soviet society. Irina's discursive art involves censoring stratagems to present a multifaceted, intertextual image of her ideal self, her heroic life, and her romantic love relationships.

Although the confession shows a will to be judged, it also functions as

---

50. See Steven Marcus's *Other Victorians* for a discussion of the intersection of novels and pornography. In *Sexual Anarchy*, Elaine Showalter explores how Victorian, fin-de-siècle, and twentieth-century female protagonists are conflicted by inner oppositional desires and deconstructs some masculine narratives of repressed or conflicted sexuality by applying these to female subjects (e.g., a woman as Dr. Jekyll and Mr. Hyde).

a *defense* against harsh judgment (ideological and social censure) and shows that the woman's desire consists of censored fantasy and a will to be loved. In Irina's case, that fantasy involves the subject's desire to be interpellated by the big Other (Soviet ideology personified in Leonardik). The usually censored sexual obscenity is thus related to, and derives meaning from, the Symbolic as represented in Soviet law, literature, and other discourses.

Irina's narrative is characterized by its splitting of point of view (selfhood as "I" and "you"), its apparently incoherent sequencing of events, and its frequent associative and critical comparisons and commentaries. Her text works toward disclosure (thus toward an openness or explicitness), but many of her discursive moments and strategies complicate that disclosure by disavowal, contradiction, delay, embellishment, and lack of control. These very censoring strategies in narrative help to produce the complex image and signification of the desiring subject.

Irina's writing partially fulfills the pornographic desire to read the desiring woman's enjoyment of sex (especially men's sex). While she uses some explicit language and expressions, she is not always a sexually desiring or willing subject. For example, at times, she admits to feeling like the awkward schoolgirl in pigtails when speaking of her early years in the countryside, a time when her father began his incestuous abuse of her "nakatilo na menia neposredstvennym obrazom" (53) (in a brutally direct way) (60), causing schoolmates to tease her since first grade. This ridicule crushed a girl who had yet to show signs of sublime beauty: "a byla ia na redkost' krupnaia maloletka, s glupeishei rozhei, dvumia kosichkami i robkoi kosobokoi ukhmylochkoi. Ochen' byla zastenchivaia, do dikosti, v zhenskoi bane stesnialas' razdet'sia, i v dushe ostalas' takoi navsegda" (54) (I was an unusually big girl for my age, with a foolish expression, two pigtails and a bashful, lopsided smirk. I was very shy, timid as a deer, I was embarrassed about undressing in the girls' bathhouse, and in my soul I have remained the same) (61).

Irina's writing and speech shift readily from the poetic to the candid in discussing delicate sexual issues in her adulthood: "Vpervye ia chustvovala otvrashchenie k proslavlennomu korniu zhizni. Dato nedoumeval. Ia sama vialo nedoumevala. Tvoi miasistyi otrostok mne vovse ne interesen!" (158–59). (For the first time I felt an aversion to the sublime root. Dato [an occasional lover] was perplexed. I was a bit perplexed too. "Your dick doesn't interest me at all!") (196).[51]

Our final point of examination of Irina's split subjectivity takes us to

---

51. Note that the novel's English translator chose a different word to convey the flattening effect of Irina's remark to Dato; instead of "dick," she actually uses a comically porno-poetic term, "meaty shoot." Her words, nevertheless, offend the macho Georgian Dato.

two examples of postmodern pictorial representation. By this I mean the writing of paintings and photographs in literature. Hutcheon notes how

> [p]ostmodernism's relation to late capitalism, patriarchy, and the other forms of those (now suspect) master narratives is paradoxical: the postmodern does not deny its inevitable implication in them, but it also wants to use that "insider" position to "de-doxify" the "givens" that "go without saying" in those grand systems. Thus, it is neither neoconservatively nostalgic nor radically revolutionary; it is unavoidably compromised—and it knows it. (115)

As beauty and sublimity are often strongly related to the visual,[52] it seems no mistake that Erofeev would include some pictorial representation in his narrative to document Russian beauty (as we noted earlier with the intertext of Manet's *Déjeuner*). The two pictures, done at very different points in time, frame Irina ideologically as a Russian product. The first is the picture of her great-grandmother, a portrait in oils that Irina keeps pinned above her bed and later to her mirror to better compare faces (19; 16). The image of this woman from the pre-Revolutionary past, whom Irina resembles, connects her to something unspoken and unknown, to an image that can be seen in one direction, from the present to the past. Irina knows that she has inherited her pride from this great-grandmother. Instead of an icon or crucifix, the worldly female ancestor's portrait watches over Irina. Irina's photo-graph narrative of this image explores a diachronic facet of her subjectivity, the pre-Revolutionary remnant that will not be dismissed.

Irina's prized picture indicates her pre-Soviet values of class, property, family, and respected femininity: "Von, posmotrite, u menia prababushka—stolbovaia dvorianka iz Kalinina! Von portret, pisannyi maslom! Sovershenno shikarnaia zhenshchina, bezdna obaianiia, dekol'te, nadmennyi vzor, dragotsennosti. Ia vse prodam, poidu po miru pobirat'sia, no portret ne prodam [. . .]. A probabushky ne prodam! Eto pamiat'" (66) (Look, there, my grandmother—she's a member of a long-established family of Russian gentry from Kalinin! There's her portrait, painted in oils! A supremely elegant woman, masses of charm, décolleté, a haughty mien, jewels. I'll sell everything, I'll go around the world begging, but I won't sell the portrait. [. . .] But I shan't sell my great-grandmother! It's a memento) (77). The picture and the woman are considered one and the same. Irina insists that the resemblance between her and this woman is "nesomnennoe" (indubi-

---

52. While Burke explores sublimity and beauty in various forms, the visual form tends to dominate. See Lyotard's appreciation for Burke over Kant in terms of laying out an aesthetics for future avant-garde artists ("The Sublime and the Avant-Garde").

table). It is possible that the woman Anastasiia Petrovna addressed in the novel's penultimate chapter's suicide note is this great-grandmother.[53]

The second photo-graph combines the magazine photo-shoot and Irina's narrative of this event. Her descriptions of the photographic images provide a kind of fantasy narrative to explain the concept. The photographer X compares his art with Renoir's; but Irina prefers to leave the overly fleshy Renoir women in the past, stressing her Russianness: "a vy podberite drugoi kliuch, i voobshche uchtite: moia krasota ochen' russkaia!" (134) (You take another approach and remember: my beauty is Russian!) (165).

Often literary pornographic moments are characterized by comic, lyrical, and fantastic descriptive style and gaps which leave the rest to the reader's imagination. Weeks points out how "pornotopia" suspends time and place, offering instead "the kind of boundless, featureless freedom that most pornographic fantasies require for their action" (269). Weeks explains how the "essential imagination of nature in pornotopia [. . .] is this immense, supine, female form" (272). Irina's lyrical-melodramatic recounting of her photo-shoot demonstrates the paradoxical combination of verbal outpouring (ecstatic, pornographic woman's voice) and the withholding of explicit detail (censoring to create fantasy):

[Fotograf] ozaril iarkim svetom moiu zreluiu krasotu i velikolepie, i akhnula Ksiusha v ladoshku, divias' potaennoi roskoshi, i prishel v izumlenie besstrastnyi professional, povestvuia ob odinochestve istinnoi vdovy, [. . .] i otkrylas' ia, i chernye tonen'kie chulki podnialis' v vozdukh, i oglianulas' ia v polusumrake, privetstvuia radostnogo chitatelia, i plachu, [. . .] vspominaia bezvremenno minuvshego supruga, no vot uzhe raskrasnelas' ot odinokoi muki shcheka, i uchastilos' nerovnoe dykhanie, i prikrylis' vospalennye, otumanennye slezami i dumami glazki [. . .]. (134–35)

[The photographer's lights] illuminated my mature beauty and magnificence, and Ksyusha covered her gasps with her hand, amazed at the secret splendor, and the dispassionate professional is dumbfounded, as he composed the story of the true widow's loneliness, [. . .] and I open up, and my black stockings rise sheer in the air, and I glance back in the half twilight, greeting the joyous reader, and I weep, [. . .] remembering my spouse, who passed on before his time, but look, my cheek has already blushed red from solitary torment, and my uneven breathing is getting faster and faster, and my inflamed eyes have half closed, eyes dimmed with tears and perfume [. . .]. (165–66)

---

53. The name may refer to the Princess Golitsyna (Anastasia Petrovna).

Irina's breathlessly pastiched, erotic, photo-graphed narrative of her image expresses a fantasy of woman's desire: to be desired by admiring others and *not* to attain full explicitness. Artistic censoring here functions to produce desire, to eliminate aspects of harsh judgment or crude reality from the moment, to suggest the illusion of securing a romantic self or a romantic lover. As opposed to the notion of the passive pornographic model, Irina actively constructs and delivers her photo-graphed pornotopia in modeling and writing. The passage also ironically anticipates a Russian readership's poetic-romantic (and at times clichéd) taste, including mystical predilections for sentimental essentialism and soulful transformations.

The results of the photo-shoot are equally significant: her naked image and scandalous identity (a leading Soviet figure's "widowed" mistress) on the covers of foreign magazines and tabloids create a political stir. Despite the authorities' efforts to suppress the issue, some copies of Irina's sexual image reach regular readers. The porno-photographic image of her body (and subsequently the photo-graphed version of it in her writing) crosses the lines of Soviet censorship and enters public discourse, "de-doxifying," in Hutcheon's terms, master narratives of coherent, whole Soviet ideology.

Irina's eventual fate in death is also forecasted in these events. In her photo-graphed account of the photo-shoot, she points out that, "chernye tonkie, bezo vsiakikh kruzhev, chulki stoiat budto ramki nekrologa, i skvoz' tkan' traurnogo rubishcha svetitsia zakatnym svetom izgib" (135) (the black and sheer stockings, without lace trimming, stand like the black frame of an obituary notice, and through the fabric of the mourning rags shines a meandering light, a dusty and winding road, with the light of sunset [. . .]) (166).[54]

The image of a death notice around her textualized sex is ironically counterbalanced by Irina's recounting of the accompanying tabloid-style invitation to readers: "vy budete seichas imet' vozmozhnost' sami ubeditsia, chto KRASOTA POBEZHDAET SMERT'! (eto krasivo!)" (139) (now you can discover for yourself that *beauty conquers death!* [Magnificently put!]) (170).[55] Her posing in black parodies Nastasya Filippovna's portrait in a simple black silk dress. The caption parodies in promotional jargon ("vy budete seichas" [now you . . .]) the Dostoevskian phrase "Beauty will save the world," replacing the messianic idea with that of conquest (a more

---

54. As Christopher Barnes has pointed out to me, the translation lacks the suggestion of the curve of Irina's thigh or body which is "shining through the fabric of her mourning rags with a sunset glow."

55. Her textualized sex frames the whole novel with birth and death imagery: the novel opens with her gynecologist's fantastic vaginal journey to survey her impregnated womb; as she closes her narrative, Irina bequeaths her sex to the people (327–79).

erotically loaded phrase) and connecting beauty to the apocalyptic theme. Just as beauty alone cannot save the world, beauty cannot conquer death. The suffering widow Irina echoes the inspirational suffering glimpsed by the desiring Myshkin in Nastasya Filippovna's photo-graph.

The two pictures of Irina, apocalyptic Russian beauty and genius of love, provide visual frames for her narrative and split subjectivity. The first picture, the treasured portrait of her great-grandmother whom Irina resembles in beauty and pride, places Irina in a pre–Soviet Russian category. The second, the erotic photo-essay, projects a Russian Irina of death and of the future in the no-place of pleasure and desire. These images each signal woman as a potential source of fantastic beauty, love, power, freedom, and pleasure outside the Soviet censorship. Yet, paradoxically, as we have seen, Irina's postmodern position of dispersal and lack also shows her artistic incorporation of censorship values.

Conclusion

COMPARATIVE REFLECTIONS

When we started our investigation, these four novels may have seemed strange bedfellows. This investigation has established how these texts, representing four distinct instances of barrier-breaking publishing at four different points in the twentieth century, share an investment in critical explorations of sexuality, and through these, the artistic censoring of sexuality.

Sexuality and the act of writing are centralized in these works as potential transgressions and as mediations between the individual and society. The narrative techniques and themes highlight the symbiosis of writing and censoring practices. In *Ulysses*'s "Circe," with the adaptation of the dramatic format to the narrative, the dialogue and stage directions expose the human subject's inward confrontation with his fantasies; these fantasies are predicated on narratives of judgment. The dialogue and directions largely pertain to the mental worlds of Bloom and Stephen. In this way, Joyce makes exterior and actually stages the inner conflicts of the desiring men in Nighttown. Joyce's emphasis on characterization in "Circe" makes dramatic discourse perform like a narrative of dreaming and inner monologue. While the writing tends toward revelation and openness, on the one hand, the men's inner conflicts are depicted as negating, masochistic, and nostalgic. Stephen's and Bloom's experience of sexuality derives from unpleasurable judgments and trials of the self. In this way, while superficially a chapter about two men's midnight trip to a prostitution district, a trip suggesting release and access to unruly sexual freedom, it turns out that the men enter a realm as heavily regulated as the rest of Dublin, both by others and themselves.

Bloom's masochistic transformations into a suffering novice female prostitute and savior of Dublin, martyred for his sexuality, show a desire to be judged harshly and to enjoy erotically such judgment. For Stephen, sexuality is assigned a forbidden space of freedom in which art and desire can be practiced. His fantasies involve pleasure in punishment of the self and martyrdom, as well as negating fantasies of achieving a hypermasculine ideal in paternal figures like Shakespeare. Stephen's insistent idealization of Yeats's "Who Goes with Fergus" draws him toward a nostalgic, retrogressive place in an idyllic but ambiguous Irish past. Altogether, the two men's voyeurism, exhibitionism, postponement, narcissism, and masochistic posturing are indicative of complex performative, solitary masculinity, in which the traditional phallic man and dominant discursive sexual arrangement are marginalized.

With *Lolita* and *Russkaia krasavitsa,* the character-narrator in both instances is an unusual hybrid of the *pícaro* (or *pícara*) or rogue who provides a confessional text. In Humbert's case, his writing both reveals and disavows alternately his sexual abuse of the girl Dolores Haze. Meanwhile, Irina tells her story in a whirling series of returns and digressions to moments in the plot of her life: as a postmodern mimetic version of the Russian beauty and martyr characters in literature, Irina's beauty is censored for its sexual transgressiveness and lack of coherence with Soviet ideology. In both novels, the character-narrators' writing and lives are interwoven. Their sexuality is reencountered and artistically censored in their writing. Whereas Humbert is framed as a criminal monster, camouflaged in postwar middle-class America, Irina's narrative depicts her as an impossible martyr, whose extraordinary sexual beauty is not sufficient to save Russia.

In *Tiempo de silencio,* the two main narrative voices, those of the omniscient narrator and the protagonist Pedro, develop through Pedro's thoughts and acts; through this character, the novel configures sexuality as potentially liberating pleasure, a source of scientific knowledge, and a site of pain and damage. Pedro's interpellation into Spanish master narratives of triumphant defeat and isolation criticizes Franco's regime, a complicit society, and a complacent or cynical middle class and body of intellectuals.

In each of the novels, the style and forms of writing impose specific conditions on the writing of sexuality. With these modernist and postmodernist works, one aim of writing is to relate the inner workings of the mind, to transcribe thoughts, fantasies, and perceptions. This psychological emphasis on character and writing in the twentieth-century novel brings together the social- and publication-censorship concerns on the one hand, and, on the other, the psychic, mental censorship of the human subject. The authors in this study prioritize this collision of inner and outer worlds in the form of the protagonists, who each offers, to some degree, cases of neurosis or pathology, exaggerated examples of human subjectivity and of problematic symptoms. The most pathological of the characters studied is Humbert. This pedophile attempts to seduce the reader by explaining how the girl Dolores Haze is mimetic of his former love Annabel; then his fantasy nymphet and lover "Lolita" partially screens Dolores. His narrative often aims to conceal or camouflage (censor) his abuse of a child by overlaying it with the narratives of the fairy tale, the frontier bride, the fallen woman or seductress, and the beautiful woman as revered, loved object.

Irina's state of mind approximates psychosis by the end of her text. Her split subjectivity is presented in her writing in self-observation ("I" and "you") and in her experiences as harshly judged woman. Moreover, in the novel's fantastic context, she is both of this world and called to a world beyond her Soviet Russian reality, to her former lover Vladimir Sergeyevich. Her necrophilic union with this Soviet ghost removes Irina from the text and from her place in the Soviet world. Her attempts to fulfill a martyr's narrative as a Russian Joan of Arc, as a new Russian beauty, do not succeed; her fantastic potential to absorb the world's evils remains unappreciated by Soviet Russians.

Bloom and Stephen are also subject to fantastic visions or hallucinations. Although these visions express their inner fantasies, they appear as though real and able to interact with the protagonists. In what could be seen as a dramatic version of a series of long sessions, each man revisits his desires, fears and memories, largely in the form of fantasies. Both men demonstrate forms of masochism; the elements of judgment and suffering in both cases are crucial for developing a sense of censored sexuality. Bloom's masochism is luxuriously and often comically explored in numerous wild scenarios in which he becomes victimized, often by women. Meanwhile, Stephen's masochism is largely moral, deriving from the weighty institutions of the Irish family, the Catholic Church, and the British Empire, as well as the awesome influences of literary precursors (notably Yeats and Shakespeare).

Perhaps paralleling Stephen, we find in Pedro another moral masochist. Pedro is at once attracted to and repulsed by sexuality, and his fantasies of sexual pleasure, investigation, and pain in the woman's body are imbricated in his cancer research. Pedro's series of misadventures lead him to a sort of triumphant failure, or victory of the fatalist. For he condemns himself to a pleasurable but complacent life in the provinces as a doctor, while fulfilling a Spanish master narrative of defeat in assimilation and isolation, symbolic castration, and martyrdom, as shown in his comparisons between himself and the martyred San Lorenzo (St. Lawrence) who was toasted on both sides. While in a heroic novel, a doctor takes the role of healer or therapist, in this satirical novel, Pedro the doctor moves toward a masochistically pleasurable existence.

While the novels suggest sexuality as a potential realm of freedom and pleasure, they tend to deny a fulfillment of such a view by insisting on political and social problems and concerns that condition sexuality and sexual pleasure. In this way, the works transcend pornography (pornography in the sense of literature designed almost exclusively with the aim to arouse sexually), because they complicate and question the basis of men's pleasure in pornography and, on a broader level, sexuality. In this way, the novels fulfill Bakhtin's principles of the modern dialogic and heteroglot novel. Sexuality is made dialogic, referring to two or more narrative perspectives, and opening interpretation to critical review by the reader. The novelists also involve many societal strands in their works, using heteroglossia to represent conflicting or contrasting social perspectives. In "Circe," Stephen parodies a French presentation of a brothel act ("Vive le vampire!"); the Continental brothel collides with the provincial Dublin brothel ("Parley-voo!"). Bloom's hallucinations rearrange Jewish, legal, colonial British, Irish, and feminine discourses. *Lolita*'s teacher Miss Pratt spouts supposedly enlightened psychological jargon at a masked pedophile (Humbert). In *Tiempo de silencio*, Pedro's mind alternates between the medical discourses of his study and his prurient interests in the female (and male) body. Irina's voice in *Russkaia krasavitsa* brings together the discourses of pornographic fantasy in photography with Dostoevskian hope that beauty will save the world.

Fantasy offers a space for artistic exploration of sexuality and censoring of it. The many fantasies of "Circe" integrate both sexuality and the protoganists' concerns related to the family or society. In *Lolita,* Humbert's fantasies dangerously mediate and collide with his acts in reality. In contrast to the devious plotter Humbert, Pedro passively allows himself to be manipulated, in part enticed by his own fantasies of sexuality and ambition. In all of these cases, men's desires, when acted upon, affect others negatively, especially women. Their desires in fantasy form reflect back on the masculine subject in negating and judgmental ways. *Russkaia krasavitsa* turns the narrative tables by considering a woman's point of view. As a Russian beauty, Irina is mimetic of certain former literary and historic Russian beauties, who meet a tragic and early end.

If censoring helps to create the fantasy that is the sexual relationship, then sexuality also helps us to understand the dynamics of censoring. The protagonists of all four novels come to define themselves in relation to, or in contrast with, their countries' ideologies and dominant fictions. This commonality shows that sex does not take the individual further away into some private, unregulated realm. Sexuality, despite the illusion of its private, personal pleasures, is a regulated domain; sexual pleasures are a product of regulation and signifying structure. The novelists highlight their protagonists' concomitant social isolation and integration in order to meditate on the relationship between the modern human subject and society: how do we live in the world with others? In each case, the political, social, and cultural specificities are emphasized and cannot be divorced from consideration of their respective protagonists and crises: *Ulysses* is a novel about 1904 colonial Ireland, *Lolita* about postwar America, *Tiempo de silencio* about Francoist Spain, and *Russkaia krasavitsa* about Soviet Russia.

The differences between the novels' settings in liberal democracies and repressive regimes are not stark. *Tiempo de silencio* and *Russkaia krasavitsa* stress the alienated individual's position in a strongly regimented society that pretends to have a homogeneous unity. Similarly, *Lolita* and *Ulysses* show how alienated individuals' erotics are derived from confrontations with the dominant fictions of their societies. The individual does this not so much through analysis, but through erecting his or her own fantasies and crises. Those fantasies and crises, when focused on sex, are produced through a creative filter of censorship and with the rules and prohibitions of society in mind.

■

Applying censoring and judgment entails eroticism; the will to Law involves an erotic drive to be loved in the form of judgment. The conflict of choosing between love and sexuality (or finding a reconciliation or compromise) is at stake in the censoring of sexuality. Censoring itself is an eroticized function, in its play of affirmational and negating techniques.

Censoring's role in determining ethical meaning and value is dramatically emphasized when it comes to sexual references because at stake is the subject's potential loss (i.e., of love, parental love, of meaningful structure). These novels tend to reconfigure love in the form of lack and mourning, suggesting a crisis or negation of love. In "Circe," Stephen and Bloom both mourn loved ones: Stephen mourns a dead mother whose Catholic version of the Law stifled him; Bloom mourns an infant son, the fantasy of an unfulfilled love of purity and promise. Both men mourn, in effect, a filial loss of self, an authentic self: themselves as once dearly loved sons. Humbert frames his narrative with mourning and regret; he has stipulated that his text be read only once Dolores has died. His supposed "love," not shown to her in her lifetime, is expressed in part as mourning. Pedro has experienced keen erotic interest in both Florita and Dorita; when he remembers their deaths, particularly Florita's, he is implicated in guilt. Although he is not an actual murderer, he has been involved contiguously in their deaths; moreover, as Dorita's fiancé, he mourns in a way that replaces her with new concerns, the life as provincial doctor he is traveling toward. Irina's love for Vladimir Sergeyevich, made difficult and unfulfilled during his lifetime, is transformed into an erotic mourning, as explored in several episodes: her running on the field as a Russian Joan of Arc; her sexual intercourse with him as a ghost lover-groom; her erotic photo-shoot in which she seduces the viewer as the mourning widow; her pregnancy and eventual submission to her groom's wishes to join him in the afterlife. None of these novels present love as a successful, life-affirming element; love is made impossible in each narrative, in part through censoring mediations with sexuality.

Mourning can be seen as a developmental stage in human subjectivity, on a symbolic level, and not just as an actual mourning of a deceased loved one. Lacan explains how the function of the superego (which administers the subject's collection of sources of the Law) is constructed on the foundation of mourning: "Oedipus's mourning is at the origin of the superego, the double limit—from the real death risked to the preferred or the assumed death, to the being-for-death—only appears as veiled. [. . .] [A]ny alert author locates the final term of the psychic reality we deal with in the ambivalence between love and hate" (*Ethics,* 309).

For Lacan, mourning may mask or conceal not only love but hate; mourning is an ambiguous response, involving a kind of domination or mastery. Oedipus's mourning of his father involves a recognition that Oedipus has taken the father's place; the son can occupy the place of the Law. Also in mourning, the mourner can regret the loss of powerlessness and innocence. The superego is closely related to the psychic censor; both oversee and regulate the subject's thoughts and actions. In *Lolita,* Humbert constructs a confessional narrative predicated on death. His mourning of "Lolita" attempts to renegotiate his transgression of the Law. Stephen's and Bloom's mourning involves reconsideration of their roles as (symbolic) fathers, who would occupy the place of the Law, rather than their more familiar roles as sons, in which they can act pleasurably, erotically dreading parental censorship. Pedro arguably resists mourning altogether in order to remain in the position of masochistic son in his paternalistic society. *Russkaia krasavitsa,* another confessional narrative predicated on death, presents the protagonist's attempt to become the Soviet heroine and enter the dominant fiction by using her sexuality, her unspeakable beauty or sublimity.

Her erotic mourning of Vladimir Sergeyevich, the canonized Soviet writer (her "Leonardik," "a legend in his lifetime"), positions her as potentially empowered to negotiate a Russian renaissance; ultimately, however, her beauty and writing lead her to death, not to new life.

All four texts filter instances of sexuality through the context of the individual and the body. This mode of presentation emphasizes how sexuality determines the outwardly desiring aims of our subjectivity and a misapprehended belief that the physical body will yield meaning, value, love, or truth. In "Circe," the body is most pleasurable as fantasy and in various masks and disguises. Bloom's own body is transformed, dressed up in various costumes, and dies several times in his eroticized encounters with the judgment of the Other (family, Jewishness, Irish society) and others (desiring women). Both Bloom and Stephen reenact masochistic fantasies of identifications with Christ's martyrdom; Christ's mutilated, revered body erotically presents a version of the loved child. The imaginary bodies of dead loved ones haunt Bloom's and Stephen's fantasies of negating or censorious desire, provoking unpleasure (the awful cancerous specter of May Dedalus) and pleasure (the fairy image of Rudy). Humbert cloaks the childish body of Dolores Haze with the womanly and fantastic guises of "Lolita" as nymphet, Carmen, fallen woman, and eternal love object. In his confession, he seeks to render his pleasure in the girl's body sensible by veiling it with his various aesthetic discourses and his narrative maneuvers that partially reveal and conceal the obscenely abused body of the prostituted child. Pedro's contact with Florita and Dorita, along with his confrontations with himself in the brothel and the prison, signals his belief that one can find a certain truth in the body; his dedication to scientific research and medicine emphasize his fixation on the body and the possible knowledge it can reveal. Finally, Irina's extraordinarily beautiful or sublime body is the actual site and framing context of her narrative; she writes the textual story of her body, beginning and ending with her negated sex, in an effort to make it speak, and therefore to produce some kind of truth. In all of these novels, the body of the other is at once the site of desire, sexuality, and knowledge. The novelists problematize critically the body of the desired other by making it a conflicting site of pleasure and transgression in the terms of the respective social and political contexts.

By extension of the sexual human body, the novels explore the twin issues of pornography and prostitution. On an uncritical level, these resources serve men's sexual pleasure; the novels reconfigure critically pornography and prostitution so that the characters' involvement in these realms, and society's participation, are highlighted and offered for judgment. Given the twentieth century's dramatic change in the status of women in Europe and North America, the social contexts of pornography and prostitution become more apparent. The novels' prostitution theme dramatizes modern man's troubled negotiation with women's changing status. Joyce and Martín-Santos show women's economic dependence on prostitution in harsh economic times. Although these authors recognize that men may approach the brothel with their fantasies, and that part of the "profession" encourages those fantasies in order to conduct business, they also dramatize women's perspectives, including the local political and legal authorities' hypocritical accommodation of prostitution. Nabokov shows how the prostitute can emerge from the figure of the child (e.g., in the case of the French adolescent prostitute Monique); further, Humbert's fantasy of a sexual-love relation with his "Lolita" is debunked by the fact that he is compelled to bribe and pay her for sexual cooperation. In all of these novels, prostitution does not provide access to love, although it can provide the site for fantasized desire. In *Russkaia krasavitsa,* Irina's status is left ambiguous: while not a prostitute, her love for Vladimir Sergeyevich is brought into question by his maintaining her partially as a secret mistress. Like other fallen women (e.g., Moll Flanders), Irina believes that she has negotiated marriage and love in exchange for sex. Erofeev thus returns to the critical question, already posed by Chernyshevskii in the nineteenth century (*Chto delat'?; What Is to Be Done?*), of the status of women in their relationship with men: marriage and prostitution are not oppositional, but rather tangential in that both institutions place the woman in a situation of economic dependence on man. *Ulysses, Lolita,* and *Tiempo de silencio* visit this intersection of prostitution and marriage in critical ways as well. For example, Bloom's fantasies of his wife (and of himself) deploy prostitution motifs; Humbert's marriages, and his relation with Dolores, bleed into the sphere of prostitution; *la vieja* ensnares Pedro in an engagement to her granddaughter (that would benefit her family economically) by essentially pimping the young Dorita.

Pornography, or the writing of prostitutes (writing about them or by them), is integrated critically in all of these texts. While the novelists make use of certain narrative techniques related to pornographic writing (e.g., confession; fantasy), they embed these in modernist and postmodernist styles in order to create ironic, self-reflective texts that problematize potential pornography and aestheticize erotic language. Their artistic censoring produces critical and aesthetic versions of the sexual self. By endowing literary sexual contexts with ethical meaning (i.e., indicating the subject's responsibility for the other, or lack thereof), the authors of these texts make the often taboo subject of sexuality an ethical domain of human relations and conduct to be explored and questioned. In framing sexuality in dramatic, ironic, nondidactic ways, they leave much of the judgmental activity to an implied reader.

The judgment that the novels' protagonists bring to weigh upon themselves functions as an evaluation or census taking, as a form of censoring (in that original dual sense of *censura* as moral evaluation and property taxation). These novels' underlying prostitution motif blurs the border between our potential, modern sexual liberation and a possible devaluation of ourselves and others. These novels reprioritize sexuality as meaningful to their societies and as a vitally important theme in art, not just to be celebrated or deplored, but to be questioned and judged. They present sexuality in a manner particularly reflective of our problematic interpersonal relations, especially power relations between men and women and between the society and the individual. The personal inner world of sexual desire and artistic censoring—what constitutes fantasy—is integrated into these narratives, so that the distinctions between society and the individual are questioned, and an interpersonal and dialogic perspective is prioritized.

Appendix

SUMMARIES OF NOVELS' HISTORICAL CENSORSHIP

Ulysses

1. While early chapters of *Ulysses* were published in serialized form in the *Little Review*, the U.S. Postal Authorities confiscated two issues, the January 1920 issue (second half of "Cyclops") and the July–August 1920 issue (second half of "Nausicaa"). The New York Society for the Suppression of Vice lodged a complaint, citing "Nausicaa." The final serialized chapter (the first part of "Oxen of the Sun") was published in the September–December 1920 issue.
2. With the court proceedings of February 1921, editors of the *Little Review* were convicted of publishing obscenity and publication ceases.
3. Sylvia Beach published *Ulysses* in 1922 in book form under imprint of her Paris bookstore, Shakespeare and Company.
4. U.S., English, Canadian, Irish, and other Customs authorities regularly from 1922 to 1933 seized and confiscated copies of *Ulysses*. The U.S. ban's strictness extended to the post office.
5. From 1925 to 1927, Samuel Roth, a well-known publisher of pornography and erotica, without Joyce's permission, attempted to publish an expurgated version of the novel in serialized form; Roth then attempted publishing bootlegged editions of the whole novel. His efforts were often curtailed by local authorities.
6. In December 1933, in the case *The United States v. Ulysses*, Judge John Woolsey, U.S. District Court, ruled that *Ulysses* was not obscene and could be published in the United States. The end of the ban resulted in its gradual removal, such as in Great Britain in 1936.

Lolita

1. In 1955, the novel was published by Olympia Press in Paris. Owing to market censorship, especially publishers' concerns for possible court actions after publication, Nabokov could not find a willing U.S. publisher.
2. In 1956, the British Home Office influenced censorship in France. Great Britain's Customs were seizing *Lolita* along with other Olympia publications. The Home Office asked the French authorities to ban *Lolita,* along with other books from Olympia Press.
3. In 1957, *Lolita* was signed to be published in the United States by G. P. Putnam's Sons; Nabokov cut his ties with Girodias. In August 1958, the novel was published successfully in the United States. The United States did not ban the novel, despite the ongoing censorship activity in Great Britain and France.
4. From 1956 to 1958, British Customs seized copies of the novel.
5. In January 1958, the French ban was ruled illegal. At the end of that same year, France's Conseil d'état found favor on the part of the Ministère de l'Intérieur for taking action on *Lolita* and the French ban was renewed.
6. In 1958, the British used the novel as a case study for the formulation of a new obscenity bill to update and revise the old nineteenth-century law for obscenity that had used the *Hicklin* rule. After the new Obscene Publications Bill (1958), *Lolita* was published in Great Britain by the then fledgling publishers Weidenfeld and Nicolson (1959).

Tiempo de silencio

1. First edition with one of Spain's leading literary publishers Seix y Barral was published in late 1961 with some passages and episodes heavily censored. Until 1965, the various print runs maintained this censorship.
2. In the 1966 edition, most of the censored passages were restored.
3. Subsequent editions maintained the state of restored 1966 edition.
4. In 1980, Seix y Barral published an "edición definitiva" (definitive edition), reprinted in 1993. This edition actually appears identical to the 1966 and subsequent editions. The "definitive edition" of 1980 (and subsequent reprints) is longer in pagination, but does not seem to restore any previously censored passages according to my comparison of segments and the overall text. It does not include additions from a manuscript or notes that were never submitted to the censor.

Russkaia krasavitsa

1. The first edition of *Russkaia krasavitsa* (Moscow: Moskovskii rabochi, 1990) was lightly censored; several sexual or other offensive words were replaced by dashes or ellipses (words such as "blow job" or "whore").
2. With the collapse of the Soviet Union in 1991, Erofeev sought to republish the uncensored novel. In 1994, Molodaia gvardiia published it without any suppressions (*Russkaia krasavitsa: Roman, rasskazy*).

Works Cited

Abella, Rafael. *La vida cotidiana bajo el régimen de Franco.* Madrid: Temas de hoy, 1996.
Abellán, Manuel L. *Censura y creación literaria en España (1939–1976).* Barcelona: Península, 1980.
———, ed. *Censura y literaturas peninsulares.* Amsterdam: Rodopi, 1987.
Aizlewood, Robin. "Berdiaev and Chaadaev, Russia and Feminine Passivity." *Gender and Sexuality in Russian Civilization.* Ed. Peter I. Barta. London and New York: Routledge, 2001. 121–39.
Aksenov, Vasilii Pavlovich, comp. *Metropol': Literaturnyi al'manakh.* Ann Arbor, MI: Ardis, 1979.
Alexander, John T. *Catherine the Great: Life and Legend.* New York and Oxford: Oxford University Press, 1989.
Alexandrov, Vladimir E., ed. *The Garland Companion to Vladimir Nabokov.* New York: Garland, 1995.
———. "*Lolita.*" *Lolita.* Ed. Harold Bloom. New York: Chelsea House, 1993. 169–93.
———. *Nabokov's Otherworld.* Princeton, NJ: Princeton University Press, 1991.
"Alienation." *Dictionary of Philosophy.* Ed. Thomas Mautner. London: Penguin, 1997. 13–14.
Althusser, Louis. "Ideology and Ideological State Apparatuses (Notes towards an Investigation)." *Essays on Ideology.* London: Verso, 1984. 1–60.
Amber, Effie. *Russian Journalism and Politics: The Career of Aleksei S. Suvorin, 1861–1881.* Detroit: Wayne State University Press, 1972.
Amezúa, Efigenio. *La erótica española en sus comienzos: Apuntes para una hermenéutica de la sexualidad española.* Barcelona: Fontanella, 1974.
Andrews, David. *Aestheticism, Nabokov, and Lolita.* Lewiston, NY: Edwin Mellen, 1999.

———. "Varieties of Determinism: Nabokov among Rorty, Freud, and Sartre." *Nabokov Studies* 6 (2000–2001): 1–33.
Appel, Alfred, Jr., ed. *The Annotated* Lolita. By Vladimir Nabokov. New York: Vintage, 1991.
———. "Backgrounds of *Lolita.*" *Triquarterly* 17 (Winter 1970): 17–40.
Aristophanes. "Peace." *"The Birds" and Other Plays.* Trans. Alan H. Sommerstein. New York: Penguin, 2003. 91–146.
Arte del franquismo. Ed. Antonio Bonet Correa. Madrid: Cátedra, 1981.
Attwood, Lynne. *The New Soviet Man and Woman: Sex-Role Socialization in the USSR.* Basingstoke: Macmillan, 1990.
Azhgikhina, Nadezhda, and Helena Goscilo. "Getting under Their Skin: The Beauty Salon in Russian Women's Lives." *Russia. Women. Culture.* Ed. Helena Goscilo and Beth Holmgren. Bloomington: Indiana University Press, 1996. 94–121.
Baker, George Pierce. *Dramatic Technique.* Cambridge, MA: Houghton Mifflin, 1947.
Bakhtin, M. M. *The Dialogic Imagination: Four Essays by M. M. Bakhtin.* Trans. Caryl Emerson and Michael Holquist. Austin: University of Texas Press, 1981.
———. "Discourse in the Novel." *The Dialogic Imagination: Four Essays by M. M. Bakhtin.* Trans. Caryl Emerson and Michael Holquist. Austin: University of Texas Press, 1981. 259–422.
———. "Forms of Time and Chronotope in the Novel: Notes toward a Historical Poetics." *The Dialogic Imagination: Four Essays by M. M. Bakhtin.* Trans. Caryl Emerson and Michael Holquist. Austin: University of Texas Press, 1981. 84–258.
Barger, Jorn. "Advanced Notes for *Ulysses* ch3 (Proteus)." *The Internet Ulysses by James Joyce,* October 1999 (updated February 2001. http://www.robotwisdom.com/jaj/ulysses/index.html#proteus) (accessed May 15, 2004).
Baroja, Pío. *El árbol de la ciencia.* Ed. Pío Caro Baroja. Madrid: Cátedra, 1999.
Barrie, J. M. *The Adventures of Peter Pan.* Literature.org. http://www.literature.org/authors/barrie-james-matthew/the-adventures of-peter-pan(accessed October 11, 2007).
———. *The Little White Bird.* New York: C. Scribner's Sons, 1902.
———. *Peter Pan.* [*Peter and Wendy; Peter in Kensington Park.*] 1911. Ed. Jack Zipes. New York: Penguin, 2004.
Barron, John. *KGB: The Secret Work of Soviet Secret Agents.* London: Hodder and Stoughton, 1974.
Barthes, Roland. *A Lover's Discourse: Fragments.* Trans. Richard Howard. New York: Hill and Wang, 1983.
———. "Reflections on a Manual." [1969] Trans. Sandy Petrey. *PMLA* 112.1 (1997): 69–75.
———. *S/Z.* Trans. Richard Miller. New York: Hill and Wang, 1974.
Bauman, Zygmunt. *Life in Fragments: Essays in Postmodern Morality.* Oxford, UK: Blackwell, 1995.
Beardsmore, R. W. "The Censorship of Works of Art." *Philosophy and Fiction: Essays in Literary Aesthetics.* Ed. Peter Lamarque. Aberdeen, Great Britain: Aberdeen University Press, 1983. 93–107.
Beauvoir, Simone de. *Brigitte Bardot and the Lolita Syndrome.* 1959. Trans. Bernard Fretchman. New York: Arno, 1972.
Bécourt, Daniel. *Livres condamnés, livres interdits: Régime juridique du livre, outrage aux bonnes mœurs, arrêtés d'interdiction.* Paris: Cercle de la Librairie, 1961.
Bely, Andrei. *Peterburg.* Ed. L. K. Dolgopolov. Moscow: Nauka, 1981.
———. *Petersburg.* Trans. Robert A. Maguire and John E. Malmstad. Bloomington: Indiana

University Press, 1978.

Beneyto, Antonio. *Censura y política en los escritores españoles.* Barcelona: Euros, 1975.

Benstock, Bernard. "Redhoising JJ: USSR/11." *James Joyce Quarterly* 6.2 (1968): 177–80.

Berdiaev, Nikolai. *Eros i lichnost': Filosofiia pola i liubvi.* Moscow: Prometi, 1989.

———. *Sud'ba Rossii.* Moscow: Filosofskoe ob-vo SSSr, 1990.

Berman, Jeffrey. "Nabokov and the Viennese Witch Doctor." Lolita. Ed. Harold Bloom. New York: Chelsea House, 1993. 105–19.

Bersani, Leo. *The Freudian Body: Psychoanalysis and Art.* New York: Columbia University Press, 1986.

Bethea, David M. *The Shape of Apocalypse in Modern Russian Fiction.* Princeton, NJ: Princeton University Press, 1989.

Beti Sáez, Iñaki, ed. *Luis Martín-Santos.* Actas de las IV Jornadas internacionales de literatura. Mundaiz: Cuadernos universitarios departamento de literatura 8 (1990). San Sebastián: Universidad de Deusto, 1990.

Birrell, Augustine. *Seven Lectures on the Law and History of Copyright in Books.* 1899. New York: Augustus M. Kelley, 1971.

Black, Martha Fodaski. "S/He-Male Voices in *Ulysses:* Counterpointing the 'New Womanly Man.'" *Gender in Joyce.* Ed. Jolanta W. Wawrzycka and Marlena G. Corcoran. Gainesville: University Press of Florida, 1997. 62–81.

Blackwell, Stephen H. "Nabokov's Wiener-schnitzel Dreams: *Despair* and Anti-Freudian Poetics." *Nabokov Studies* 7 (2002–2003): 129–50.

Blanchard, Edward Litt Leman. "Aladdin." *Pantomimes, Extravaganzas and Burlesques.* Vol. 5 of *English Plays of the Nineteenth Century.* Oxford: Clarendon, 1976. 337–77.

Blium, Arlen Viktorovich. "Early Soviet Censorship Directives." Trans. Donna M. Farina. *Book History.* Ed. Ezra Greenspan and Jonathan Rose. Vol. 1. Philadelphia: Pennsylvania State University Press, 1998. 268–82.

———. *Evreiskii vopros pod sovetskoi tsenzuroi, 1917–1991.* St. Petersburg: Peterburgskii evreiskii universitet, 1996.

———. *Sovetskaia tsenzura v epokhu totalitarnogo terrora, 1929–1953.* St. Petersburg: Akademicheskii proekt, 2000.

Bloom, Harold. Introduction. *Lolita.* New York: Chelsea House, 1993. 1–3.

———. Introduction. *Vladimir Nabokov's* Lolita. New York: Chelsea House, 1987. 1–4.

Boheemen-Saaf, Christine van. "Joyce, Derrida, and the Discourse of 'the Other.'" *James Joyce: The Augmented Ninth.* Ed. Bernard Benstock. Syracuse, NY: Syracuse University Press, 1988. 88–102.

———. *Joyce, Derrida, Lacan, and the Trauma of History: Reading, Narrative and Postcolonialism.* Cambridge: Cambridge University Press, 1999.

Booker, M. Keith, and Dubravka Juraga. *Bakhtin, Stalin, and Modern Russian Fiction: Carnival, Dialogism, and History.* Westport, CT: Greenwood, 1995.

Boone, Joseph Allen. "A New Approach to Bloom as 'Womanly Man': The Mixed Middling's Progress in *Ulysses.*" *James Joyce Quarterly* 20.1 (1982): 67–85.

———. "Representing Interiority: Spaces of Sexuality in *Ulysses.*" *The Languages of Joyce: Selected Papers from the 11th International James Joyce Symposium, Venice, 12–18 June 1988.* Ed. Rose Maria Bollettieri Bosinelli, Vaglio C. Marengo, and Christine van Boheemen. Philadelphia: Benjamins, 1992. 69–84.

———. "Staging Sexuality: Repression, Representation, and 'Interior' States in *Ulysses.*" *Joyce: The Return of the Repressed.* Ed. Susan Stanford Friedman. Ithaca, NY: Cornell University Press, 1993. 190–221.

Booth, Michael R. Introduction. *Pantomimes, Extravaganzas and Burlesques.* Vol. 5 of *English Plays of the Nineteenth Century.* Oxford: Clarendon, 1976. 1–63.

Booth, Wayne C. *The Company We Keep: An Ethics of Fiction.* Berkeley: University of California Press, 1988.

———. *The Rhetoric of Fiction.* Chicago: University of Chicago Press, 1968.

Bordo, Susan. "The Moral Content of Nabokov's *Lolita.*" *Aesthetic Subjects.* Ed. Pamela R. Matthews and David McWhirter. Minneapolis: University of Minnesota Press, 2003. 125–52.

Borenstein, Eliot. *Men without Women: Masculinity and Revolution in Russian Fiction, 1917–1929.* Durham, NC: Duke University Press, 2000.

Bornstein, George. Introduction. *Representing Modernist Texts: Editing as Interpretation.* Ann Arbor: University of Michigan Press, 1991. 1–16.

———, ed. *Representing Modernist Texts: Editing as Interpretation.* Ann Arbor: University of Michigan Press, 1991.

Bourdieu, Pierre. "Censorship and the Imposition of Form." *Language and Symbolic Power.* Trans. Gino Raymond and Matthew Adamson. Ed. John B. Thompson. Cambridge: Polity Press, 1991. 137–59.

Bowen, Zack. *Musical Allusions in the Works of James Joyce: Early Poetry through* Ulysses. Albany: State University of New York Press, 1974.

———. Ulysses *as a Comic Novel.* Syracuse, NY: Syracuse University Press, 1989.

Boyd, Brian. *Vladimir Nabokov: The American Years.* Princeton, NJ: Princeton University Press, 1991.

———. *Vladimir Nabokov: The Russian Years.* London: Chatto & Windus, 1991.

Bozal, V., et al. *España: Vanguardia artística y realidad social, 1936–1976.* Barcelona: Gustavo Gili, 1976.

Bozonnet, Jean-Jacques. "Censors Who Strive to Curb Net Access." *Guardian Weekly,* August 19–25, 1999, 26.

Bracher, Mark. *Lacan, Discourse, and Social Change: A Psychoanalytic Cultural Criticism.* Ithaca, NY: Cornell University Press, 1993.

Brea, José Luis. *Before and after the Enthusiasm (Antes y después del entusiasmo).* The Hague: SDU, 1989.

Brivic, Sheldon. "Dialogic Monologue, or Divided Discourse in *Ulysses* and *Othello.*" *Pedagogy, Praxis,* Ulysses: *Using Joyce's Text to Transform the Classroom.* Ed. Robert Newman. Ann Arbor: University of Michigan Press, 1996. 167–78.

———. *The Veil of Signs: Joyce, Lacan, and Perception.* Urbana and Chicago: University of Illinois Press, 1991.

Brockman, William S. "American Librarians and Early Censorship of *Ulysses:* 'Aiding the Cause of Free Expression'?" *Joyce Studies Annual* 5 (1994): 56–74.

Brodsky, Joseph. "Nobel Lecture." 1987. http://nobelprize.org/literature/laureates/1987/brodsky-lecture-e.html (accessed April 29, 2006).

———. "Nobel Prize Speech." Trans. Barry Rubin. *Index on Censorship* 17.2 (1988): 12–15.

Brooks, Peter. *Body Work: Objects of Desire in Modern Narrative.* Cambridge, MA: Harvard University Press, 1993.

———. *Reading for the Plot: Design and Intention in Narrative.* Cambridge, MA: Harvard University Press, 1992.

Brown, Deming. *The Last Years of Soviet Russian Literature: Prose Fiction 1975–1991.* Cambridge and New York: Cambridge University Press, 1993.

Brown, Richard. *James Joyce and Sexuality.* Cambridge: Cambridge University Press, 1985.
———. "Joyce, Postculture and Censorship." *Writing and Censorship in Britain.* Ed. Paul Hyland and Neil Sammells. London: Routledge, 1992. 243–58.
Brown, Susan Sutliff. "The Joyce Brothers in Drag: Fraternal Incest in *Ulysses.*" *Gender in Joyce.* Ed. Jolanta W. Wawrzycka and Marlena G. Corcoran. Gainesville: University of Florida Press, 1997. 8–28.
Brownlow, Jeanne P., and John W. Kronik. "The Death and Life of Intertextuality: An Introduction." *Intertextual Pursuits: Literary Mediations in Modern Spanish Narrative.* Lewisburg, PA: Bucknell University Press, 1998. 11–25.
Bruns, Gerald L. "The Otherness of Words: Joyce, Bakhtin, Heidegger." *Postmodernism–Philosophy and the Arts.* Ed. Hugh J. Silverman. New York: Routledge, 1990. 120–36, 277–80.
Bryer, Jackson R. "Joyce, *Ulysses,* and the *Little Review.*" *South Atlantic Quarterly* 66.2 (Spring 1967): 148–64.
Budgen, Frank. *James Joyce and the Making of* Ulysses. New York: Harrison Smith and Robert Haas, 1934.
Buñuel, Luis, dir. *Las Hurdes.* Ramón Acín, 1932.
Burke, Edmund. *A Philosophical Inquiry into the Origin of Our Ideas of the Sublime and Beautiful.* Ed. Adam Phillips. Oxford and New York: Oxford University Press, 1990.
Burt, E. S. "'An Immoderate Taste for Truth': Censoring History in Baudelaire's 'Les bijoux.'" *Diacritics* 27.2 (1997): 19–43.
Burt, Richard, ed. Introduction. *The Administration of Aesthetics: Censorship, Political Criticism, and the Public Sphere.* Minneapolis: University of Minnesota Press, 1994. xi–xxix.
———. "(Un)Censoring in Detail: The Fetish of Censorship in the Early Modern Past and the Postmodern Present." *Censorship and Silencing: Practices of Cultural Regulation.* Ed. Robert C. Post. Santa Monica, CA: Getty Foundation and Oxford University Press, 1998. 17–41.
Butler, Judith. "Ruled Out: Vocabularies of the Censor." *Censorship and Silencing: Practices of Cultural Regulation.* Ed. Robert C. Post. Santa Monica, CA: Getty Foundation and Oxford University Press, 1998. 247–59.
Byrd, Charles L. "Freud's Influence on Bakhtin: Traces of Psychoanalytic Theory in *Rabelais and His World.*" *Germano-Slavica* 5.5–6 (1987): 223–30.
Caballero, Oscar. *El sexo del franquismo.* Madrid: Cambio 16, 1977.
Cadalso, José. *Cartas marruecas; Noches lúgubres.* Ed. Russell P. Sebold. Madrid: Cátedra, 1999.
Califa, Pat. Introduction. *Forbidden Passages: Writings Banned in Canada.* Pittsburgh, PA: Cleis, 1995. 9–24.
Carr, Raymond, and Juan Pablo Fusi Aizpurua. *Spain: Dictatorship to Democracy.* London and New York: Routledge, 1993.
Carroll, Lewis. *Ania v strane chudes.* Trans. V. Sirin [i.e., V. V. Nabokov]. Berlin: Gamaion, 1923.
———. *More Annotated Alice:* Alice's Adventures in Wonderland *and* Through the Looking Glass and What Alice Found There. Illustrated by Peter Newey. Ed. Martin Gardner. New York: Random House, 1990.
Caviglia, John. "A Simple Question of Symmetry: Psyche as Structure in *Tiempo de silencio.*" *Hispania* 60.3 (1977): 452–60.
Censorship and Freedom of Expression: Essays on Obscenity and the Law. Ed. Harry M. Clor. Chicago: Rand McNally, 1971.

Censorship and Obscenity. Ed. Rajeev Dhavan and Christie Davies. London: Martin Robertson, 1978.

Censorship and Political Communication in Eastern Europe. Ed. George Schöpflin. New York: St. Martin's Press, 1983.

Censorship and Silencing: Practices of Cultural Regulation. Ed. Robert C. Post. Santa Monica, CA: Getty Foundation and Oxford University Press, 1998.

Censorship and the Control of Print in England and France, 1600–1910. Ed. Robin Myers and Michael Harris. Winchester, UK: St Paul's Bibliographies, 1992.

The Censorship of Books. Ed. Walter M. Daniels. New York: Wilson, 1954.

La censure en France à l'ère démocratique (1848– . . .): Histoire culturelle. Ed. Pascal Ory. Bruxelles: Complexe, 1997.

Censures: De la Bible aux larmes d'Éros; Le livre et la censure en France. Paris: Centre Georges Pompidou, Bibliothèque publique d'information, 1987.

Chalidze, Valerii. *To Defend These Rights: Human Rights and the Soviet Union.* Trans. Guy Daniels. New York: Random House, 1974.

Cheng, Vincent J. "'Goddinpotty': James Joyce and the Language of Excrement." *The Languages of Joyce: Selected Papers from the 11th International James Joyce Symposium, Venice, 12–18 June 1988.* Ed. Rose Maria Bollettieri Bosinelli, C. Marengo Vaglio, and Christine van Boheemen. Philadelphia: Benjamins, 1992. 85–99.

———. *Joyce, Race and Empire.* Cambridge and New York: Cambridge University Press, 1995.

Choldin, Marianna Tax. *A Fence around the Empire: Russian Censorship of Western Ideas under the Tsars.* Durham, NC: Duke University Press, 1985.

Cirici, Alexandre. *La estética del franquismo.* Barcelona: Gustavo Gili, 1977.

Cisquella, Georgina. *Diez años de represión cultural: La censura de libros durante la Ley de prensa, 1966–1976.* Barcelona: Anagrama, 1977.

Cixous, Hélène. "At Circe's, or the Self-Opener." Trans. Carol Bové. *boundary 2* 3.2 (1975): 387–97.

Cleland, John. *Fanny Hill: Or Memoirs of a Woman of Pleasure.* Ed. Peter Wagner. Harmondsworth, UK: Penguin, 1986.

Clifton, Gladys M. "Humbert Humbert and the Limits of Artistic License." *Nabokov's Fifth Arc: Nabokov and Others on His Life's Work.* Ed. J. E. Rivers and Charles Nicol. Austin: University of Texas Press, 1982. 153–70.

Coetzee, J. M. *Giving Offense: Essays on Censorship.* Chicago: University of Chicago Press, 1996.

Communications Control: Readings in the Motives and Structures of Censorship. Ed. John Phelan. New York: Sheed & Ward, 1969.

Couturier, Maurice. "Nabokov and Flaubert." *The Garland Companion to Vladimir Nabokov.* Ed. Vladimir Alexandrov. New York: Garland, 1995. 405–12.

———. *Roman et censure: Ou la mauvaise foi d'Éros.* Seyssel: Champ Vallon, 1996.

Cowan, James. "Lawrence, Joyce, and the Epiphanies of *Lady Chatterley's Lover.*" *D. H. Lawrence's "Lady": A New Look at* Lady Chatterley's Lover. Ed. Michael Squires and Dennis Jackson. Athens: University of Georgia Press, 1985.

Craig, Alec. *The Banned Books of England and Other Countries: A Study of the Conception of Literary Obscenity.* London: George Allen & Unwin, 1962.

———. "Censorship of Sexual Literature." *The Encyclopedia of Sexual Behavior.* Vol. 1. New York: Hawthorne, 1961. 235–46.

———. *Suppressed Books: A History of the Conception of Literary Obscenity.* Cleveland, OH: World Publishing Company, 1963.
Critical Ethics: Text, Theory and Responsibility. Ed. Dominic Rainsford and Tim Woods. Houndmills, Basingstoke, UK: Macmillan, 1999.
Crowther, Paul. "The Sublime." *Routledge Encyclopedia of Philosophy.* Ed. E. Craig. London: Routledge. http://www.rep.routledge.com/article/M040SECT1 (accessed May 8, 2006).
Culler, Jonathan. *Framing the Sign: Criticism and Its Institutions.* Norman and London: University of Oklahoma Press, 1988.
———. "Textual Self-Consciousness and the Textual Unconscious." *Style* 18.3 (1984): 369–76.
Culleton, Claire. "Joyce and the G-Men." *James Joyce Quarterly* 32.3–4 (1995): 748–54.
Cummins, George M. "Nabokov's Russian *Lolita.*" *Slavic and East European Journal* 21 (1977): 354–65.
Daily, Jay E. *The Anatomy of Censorship.* New York: Marcel Dekker, 1973.
Dark, Oleg. "Chernovoe pis'mo." *Strelets* 1.68 (1992): 177–87.
Davies, Norman. *Europe: A History.* Oxford: Oxford University Press, 1996.
Day, Gary. "Looking at Women: Notes toward a Theory of Porn." *Perspectives on Pornography: Sexuality in Film and Literature.* Ed. Gary Day and Clive Bloom. New York: St. Martin's Press, 1988. 83–100.
De Grazia, Edward. *Girls Lean Back Everywhere: The Law of Obscenity and the Assault on Genius.* New York: Vintage, 1993.
Dean, Carolyn. *The Self and Its Pleasures: Bataille, Lacan, and the History of the Decentered Subject.* Ithaca, NY: Cornell University Press, 1992.
Deleuze, Gilles. *Masochism: Coldness and Cruelty.* Trans. Jean McNeill. New York: Zone Books, 1989.
Delibes, Miguel. "La censura de prensa en los años 40." *La censura de prensa en los años 40 (y otros ensayos).* Valladolid: Ambito, 1985. 5–30.
Dennison, Sally. *[Alternative] Literary Publishing: Five Modern Histories.* Iowa City: University of Iowa Press, 1984.
Derrida, Jacques. *Acts of Literature.* Ed. Derek Attridge. New York: Routledge, 1992.
———. "Before the Law." *Acts of Literature.* Ed. Derek Attridge. New York: Routledge, 1992. 181–220.
———. "Freud and the Scene of Writing." *Writing and Difference.* Trans. Alan Bass. Chicago: University of Chicago Press, 1978.
Devlin, Kimberly J. "Castration and Its Discontents: A Lacanian Approach to *Ulysses.*" *James Joyce Quarterly* 29.1 (Fall 1991): 116–44.
———. "Pretending in 'Penelope': Masquerade, Mimicry, and Molly Bloom." *Novel* 25 (Fall 1991): 71–89.
———. *Wandering and Return in* Finnegans Wake*: An Integrative Approach to Joyce's Fictions.* Princeton, NJ: Princeton University Press, 1991.
The Distinctiveness of Soviet Law. Ed. F. J. M. Feldbrugge. Dordrecht, The Netherlands: Kluwer, 1987.
Dollimore, Jonathan. *Sex, Literature, and Censorship.* Cambridge: Polity Press; Malden, MA: Blackwell, 2001.
———. *Sexual Dissidence: Augustine to Wilde, Freud to Foucault.* Oxford: Clarendon Press; New York: Oxford University Press, 1991.

Dostoevsky, Fyodor. *Idiot.* 1868. Moscow: Khudozhestvennaia literatura, 1960.

———. *The Idiot.* 1868. Trans. Richard Pevear and Larissa Volokhonsky. New York: Knopf, 2002.

———. *Notes from Underground.* New York: Norton, 1989.

Drugovskaia, A. Iu. "Iz istorii tsenzurnykh presledovanii proizvedenii N. G. Chernyshevskogo: Po novym materialam." *Russkaia literatura* 1 (1988): 191–95.

Dujardin, Édouard. *Les lauriers sont coupés.* Paris: Albert Messein, 1925.

Dunham, Vera. *In Stalin's Time: Middleclass Values in Soviet Fiction.* Durham, NC: Duke University Press, 1990.

Dury, Maxime. *La censure: La prédication silencieuse.* Paris: Publisud, 1995.

———. "Du droit à la métaphore: Sur l'intérêt de la définition juridique de la censure." *La censure en France à l'ère démocratique (1848– . . .): Histoire culturelle.* Ed. Pascal Ory. Bruxelles: Complexe, 1997. 13–24.

Eaglestone, Robert. *Ethical Criticism: Reading after Levinas.* Edinburgh: Edinburgh University Press, 1997.

Eberly, Rosa A. *Citizen Critics: Literary Public Spheres.* Urbana and Chicago: University of Illinois Press, 2000.

Edwards, T. R. N. *Three Russian Writers and the Irrational: Zamyatin, Pil'nyak, and Bulgakov.* Cambridge: Cambridge University Press, 1982.

Ehrenreich, Barbara, Elizabeth Hess, and Gloria Jacobs. *Re-making Love: The Feminization of Sex.* New York: Anchor-Doubleday, 1986.

Elias, Norbert. *The History of Manners: The Civilizing Process.* Vol. 1. Trans. Edmund Jephcott. New York: Pantheon, 1978.

———. *Power and Civility: The Civilizing Process.* Vol. 2. Trans. Edmund Jephcott. New York: Pantheon, 1982.

Ellis, Havelock. "The Function of Taboos." *More Essays of Love and Virtue.* Garden City, NY: Doubleday, 1931. 74–98.

———. "The Revaluation of Obscenity." *More Essays of Love and Virtue.* Garden City, NY: Doubleday, 1931. 99–136.

Ellman, Richard. Ulysses *on the Liffey.* New York: Oxford University Press, 1972.

Elms, Alan C. "Cloud, Castle, Claustrum: Nabokov as a Freudian in Spite of Himself." *Russian Literature and Psychoanalysis.* Ed. Daniel Rancour-Laferrière. Amsterdam: John Benjamins, 1989. 353–68.

The Emancipation of Soviet Law. Ed. F. J. M. Feldbrugge. Dordrecht, The Netherlands: Kluwer, 1992.

Engelstein, Laura. *The Keys to Happiness: Sex and the Search for Modernity in Fin-de-Siècle Russia.* Ithaca, NY: Cornell University Press, 1992.

Epshtein, Mikhail. *After the Future: The Paradoxes of Postmodernism and Contemporary Russian Culture.* Trans. Anesa Miller-Pogacar. Amherst: University of Massachusetts Press, 1995.

———. "How Society Censors Its Writers." *Index on Censorship* 19.6 (1990): 8.

Ermolaev, Herman. *Censorship in Soviet Literature, 1917–1991.* Lanham, MD, and Boulder, CO: Rowman & Littlefield, 1997.

Ernst, Morris L. "Reflections on the *Ulysses* Trial and Censorship." *James Joyce Quarterly* 3 (1965): 3–11.

———, and Alan U. Schwartz. *Censorship: The Search for the Obscene.* New York: Macmillan, 1964.

Erofeev, Viktor. "Anna's Body, or The End of the Russian Avant Garde." *Glasnost: An Anthology of Russian Literature under Gorbachev.* Ed. Helena Goscilo and Byron Lindsey.

Ann Arbor, MI: Ardis, 1990. 379–82.

———. "*Lolita*, ili zapovednyi oazis liubvi." Foreword. *Lolita*. By Vladimir Nabokov. Moscow: Izvestiia, 1989. 5–15.

———. *Naiti v cheloveke cheloveka: Dostoevskii i ekzistentsializm*. Benson, VT: Chalidze, 1991.

———. "Russia's *Fleurs du mal*." Introduction. *The Penguin Book of New Russian Writing*. Harmondsworth, UK: Penguin, 1995. ix–xxx.

———. *Russian Beauty*. Trans. Andrew Reynolds. London: Hamish Hamilton, 1992.

———. *Russkaia krasavitsa*. Moscow: Moskovskii rabochi, 1990.

———. *Russkaia krasavitsa: Roman, rasskazy*. Moscow: Molodaia gvardiia, 1994.

———. "Russkii metaroman V. Nabokova, ili v poiskakh poteriannogo raia." *Voprosy literatury* 10 (1988): 125–60.

———. *V labirinte prokliatykh voprosov: Esse*. Moscow: Soiuz fotokhudozhnikov Rossii, 1996.

Erzgräber-Freiburg, Willi. "Polyphony and the Carnivalesque in Shakespeare and Joyce." *Erzählen und Erzältheorie im 20.Jahrhundert: Festschrift für Wilhelm Füger*. Heidelberg: Winter, 2001. 269–82.

Etkind, Aleksandr. *Eros of the Impossible: The History of Psychoanalysis in Russia*. Trans. Noah Rubins and Maria Rubins. Boulder, CO: Westview, 1997.

———. "Psychological Culture." *Russian Culture at the Crossroads: Paradoxes of Postcommunist Consciousness*. Ed. Dmitri N. Shalin. Boulder, CO: Westview, 1996. 99–125.

Evans, Bergen. "*Lady Chatterley's Lover*." *Coronet* 12.2 (1959): 144–51.

Feal Deibe, Carlos. "Consideraciones sicoanalíticas sobre *Tiempo de silencio* de Luis Martín-Santos." *Revista hispánica moderna* 36.3 (1970–1971): 117–27.

Fernández, Enrique. "La fractura del espacio urbano: El Madrid galdosiano en *Tiempo de silencio*." *Anales galdosianos* 35 (2000): 53–64.

Ferrer, Daniel. "Characters in *Ulysses*: 'The Featureful Perfection of Imperfection.'" *James Joyce: The Augmented Ninth*. Ed. Bernard Benstock. Syracuse, NY: Syracuse University Press, 1988. 148–51.

Fiedler, Leslie A. *Love and Death in the American Novel*. New York: Stein, 1966.

———. "To Whom Does Joyce Belong? *Ulysses* as Parody, Pop and Porn." *Light Rays: James Joyce and Modernism*. Ed. Heyward Ehrlich. New York: New Horizon, 1984. 26–37.

Field, Andrew. *Nabokov: His Life in Art*. Boston: Little, Brown, 1967.

———. *VN: The Life and Art of Vladimir Nabokov*. New York: Crown, 1986.

Filosofía y sexualidad. Ed. Fernando Savater. Barcelona: Anagrama, 1988.

Fitzpatrick, Samuel A. Ossory. "Dublin Theatres." *Dublin: A Historical and Topographical Account of the City*. 1907. http://www.chapters.eiretek.org/books/ossory/ossory8.htm (accessed January 11, 2006).

Fjågesund, Peter. "Joyce's 'The Dead': Carnival, Eucharist and Medieval Visions." *English Studies* 2 (1997): 139–48.

Flavitskii, Konstantin. *Princess Tarakanova in the Petropavlovsk Fortress at the Time of the Flood*. 1864. Tretyakov Gallery, Moscow.

———. *Princess Tarakanova in the Petropavlovsk Fortress at the Time of the Flood*. 1864. Tretyakov Gallery, Moscow. http://www.russianartgallery.org/famous/tarakanova.htm (accessed April 20, 2006).

Flieder, Laurent. "Petite rhétorique du contournement." *La censure en France à l'ère démocratique (1848– . . .): Histoire culturelle*. Ed. Pascal Ory. Bruxelles: Complexe, 1997. 177–87.

Ford, Jane M. *Patriarchy and Incest from Shakespeare to Joyce.* Gainesville: University Press of Florida, 1998.

Foster, David William. "Cela and Spanish Marginal Culture." *Review of Contemporary Fiction* 4.3 (1984): 55–59.

Foucault, Michel. *The History of Sexuality: An Introduction.* Vol. 1. Trans. Robert Hurley. New York: Vintage, 1990.

———. *The History of Sexuality: The Use of Pleasure.* Vol. 2. Trans. Robert Hurley. New York: Vintage, 1986.

———. "What Is Enlightenment?" Trans. Catherine Porter. *The Foucault Reader.* Ed. Paul Rabinow. New York: Pantheon, 1984. 32–50.

Franklin, Benjamin Fisher, IV. "Sensation Fiction in a Minor Key: *The Ordeal of Richard Feverel.*" *Nineteenth-Century Literary Perspectives: Essays in Honor of Lionel Stevenson.* Durham, NC: Duke University Press, 1974. 283–94.

Franz, Thomas R. "Baroja's 'Science' in Martín-Santos' 'Time.'" *Hispania* 66.3 (1983): 324–32.

Freccero, Carla. "Historical Violence, Censorship, and the Serial Killer: The Case of *American Psycho.*" *Diacritics* 27.2 (1997): 44–58.

Freeman, Elizabeth. "Honeymoon with a Stranger: Pedophiliac Picaresques from Poe to Nabokov." *American Literature: A Journal of Literary History, Criticism, and Bibliography* 70.4 (December 1998): 863–97.

French, Marilyn. *The Book as World: James Joyce's* Ulysses. New York: Paragon House, 1993.

Freud, Sigmund. *Beyond the Pleasure Principle.* Trans. James Strachey. New York: Bantam, 1967.

———. "The Censorship of Dreams." *Introductory Lectures on Psychoanalysis.* Trans. James Strachey. Harmondsworth, UK: Penguin, 1987.

———. "Civilization and Its Discontents." *The Standard Edition of the Complete Psychological Works of Sigmund Freud.* Vol. 21. Trans. James Strachey. London: Hogarth, 1978. 59–145.

———. "The Economic Problem of Masochism." *The Standard Edition of the Complete Psychological Works of Sigmund Freud.* Vol. 19. Trans. James Strachey. London: Hogarth, 1961. 157–70.

———. *The Interpretation of Dreams.* Trans. James Strachey. New York: Avon, 1965.

———. *Jokes and Their Relation to the Unconscious. The Standard Edition.* Vol. 8. Trans. James Strachey. London: Hogarth, 1971.

———. "Leonardo da Vinci and a Memory of His Childhood." *Art and Literature: Jensen's* Gradiva, *Leonardo da Vinci and Other Works.* Ed. Albert Dickson. Trans. James Strachey. Harmondsworth, UK: Penguin, 1990. 143–231.

———. "A Note upon the 'Mystic Writing-Pad.'" *The Standard Edition.* Vol. 19. Trans. James Strachey. London: Hogarth, 1973. 227–32.

———. "Repression." *The Standard Edition.* Vol 14. Trans. James Strachey. London: Hogarth, 1978. 143–58.

———. "Three Essays on the Theory of Sexuality." *The Standard Edition.* Vol. 7. Trans. James Strachey. London: Hogarth, 1971. 135–245.

Friedman, Susan Stanford. "The Return of the Repressed in Joyce: (Self) Censorship and the Making of a Modernist." *The Languages of Joyce.* Ed. R. M. Bollettieri, C. Marengo Vaglio, and Christine van Boheemen. Philadelphia and Amsterdam: John Benjamins, 1992. 55–68.

Fromm, Erich. *Escape from Freedom.* New York: Avon, 1971.

———. *Man for Himself: An Inquiry into the Psychology of Ethics.* New York: Fawcett, 1967.

Frosch, Thomas R. "Parody and Authenticity in *Lolita*." *Nabokov's Fifth Arc: Nabokov and Others on His Life's Work*. Ed. J. E. Rivers and Charles Nicol. Austin: University of Texas Press, 1982. 171–87.
Galán Font, Eduardo. *Claves para la lectura de* Tiempo de silencio. Madrid: Punto Clave, 1986.
García Lorca, Federico. *La casa de Bernarda Alba*. Ed. Allen Josephs. Madrid: Cátedra, 1999.
García Ronda, Angel. "El sexo en *Tiempo de silencio*." *Journal of Basque Studies* 8.1–2 (1987): 36–38.
Garrard, John Gordon. *Inside the Soviet Writers' Union*. New York: Free Press, 1990.
Gaskins, Richard H. *Burdens of Proof in Modern Discourse*. New Haven, CT: Yale University Press, 1992.
Gay, Peter. *The Bourgeois Experience: Victoria to Freud*. 5 vols. New York: Oxford University Press, 1984–1995.
Geller, Evelyn. *Forbidden Books in American Public Libraries, 1876–1939: A Study in Cultural Change*. Westport, CT: Greenwood, 1984.
Gender and Sexuality in Russian Civilization. Ed. Peter I. Barta. London and New York: Routledge, 2001.
Gender in Joyce. Ed. Jolanta W. Wawrzycka and Marlena G. Corcoran. Gainesville: University Press of Florida, 1997.
Geng, J. M. *Traité des censures: À l'usage des éditeurs, informateurs, professeurs, éducateurs, libérateurs et autres censeurs*. Paris: Epi, 1975.
Giddens, Anthony. *The Transformation of Intimacy: Sexuality, Love and Eroticism in Modern Societies*. Stanford, CA: Stanford University Press, 1992.
Gifford, Don, with Robert J. Seidman. Ulysses *Annotated: Notes for James Joyce's* Ulysses. Rev. ed. Berkeley: University of California Press, 1988.
Gilbert, Stuart. *James Joyce's* Ulysses. Harmondsworth, UK: Penguin, 1963.
Giles, Paul. "Virtual Eden: *Lolita*, Pornography, and the Perversions of American Studies." *Journal of American Studies* 34.1 (2000): 41–66.
Gillespie, David C. *The Twentieth-Century Russian Novel: An Introduction*. Oxford and Washington: Berg, 1996.
Girodias, Maurice, ed. *L'affaire* Lolita: *Défense de l'écrivain*. Paris: Olympia, 1957.
Glasnost: An Anthology of Russian Literature under Gorbachev. Ed. Helena Goscilo and Byron Lindsey. Ann Arbor, MI: Ardis, 1990.
Godzich, Wlad, and Nicholas Spadaccini. Introduction. *The Institutionalization of Literature in Spain*. Ed. Wlad Godzich and Nicholas Spadaccini. Minneapolis: Prisma Institute, 1987. 9–38.
Gogol, Nikolai Vasil'evich. *Dead Souls: A Poem*. Trans. Robert A. Maguire. London; New York: Penguin, 2004.
———. *Mertvye dushi: Poema*. Moscow: Gos izd-vo det. lit.-ry, 1953.
Goldman, Eric. "'Knowing' Lolita: Sexual Deviance and Normality in Nabokov's *Lolita*." *Nabokov Studies* 8 (2004): 87–104.
Goldschmidt, Paul W. *Pornography and Democratization: Legislating Obscenity in Post-Communist Russia*. Boulder, CO: Westview, 1999.
Goldstein, Robert Justin. *Political Censorship of the Arts and the Press in Nineteenth-Century Europe*. Houndmills, Basingstoke, UK: Macmillan, 1989.
Gontarski, S. E. *Modernism, Censorship, and the Politics of Publishing: The Grove Press Legacy*. Chapel Hill: Hanes Foundation, University of North Carolina at Chapel Hill, 2000.

Goodheart, Eugene. "Censorship and Self-Censorship in the Fiction of D. H. Lawrence." *Representing Modernist Texts: Editing as Interpretation.* Ed. George Bornstein. Ann Arbor: University of Michigan Press, 1991. 223–40.

———. *Desire and Its Discontents.* New York: Columbia University Press, 1991.

———. *The Reign of Ideology.* New York: Columbia University Press, 1997.

Goodrich, Peter. *Languages of Law: From Logics of Memory to Nomadic Masks.* London: Weidenfeld and Nicolson, 1990.

———. *Legal Discourse: Studies in Linguistics, Rhetoric and Legal Analysis.* Houndmills, Basingstoke, UK: Macmillan, 1987.

Gordon, George N. *Erotic Communications: Studies in Sex, Sin and Censorship.* New York: Hastings House, 1980.

Goriaeva, T. M., ed. *Istoriia sovetskoi politicheskoi tsenzury: Dokumenty i kommentarii.* Moscow: Rossiiskaia politicheskaia entsiklopediia, 1997.

Goscilo, Helena. *Dehexing Sex: Russian Womanhood during and after Glasnost.* Ann Arbor: University of Michigan Press, 1996.

Grant, Damian. "D. H. Lawrence: A Suitable Case for Censorship." *Writing and Censorship in Britain.* Ed. Paul Hyland and Neil Sammells. London: Routledge, 1992. 200–18.

Green, Geoffrey. *Freud and Nabokov.* Lincoln: University of Nebraska Press, 1988.

Green, Jonathon. *The Encyclopedia of Censorship.* New York: Facts on File, 1990.

Green, Leslie. "Pornographizing, Subordinating, and Silencing." *Censorship and Silencing: Practices of Cultural Regulation.* Ed. Robert C. Post. Santa Monica, CA: Getty Foundation and Oxford University Press, 1998. 285–311.

Greene, Graham. "Books of the Year-I." [London] *Sunday Times,* December 25, 1955, 4.

Gregg, Richard A. *Fedor Tiutchev: The Evolution of a Poet.* New York and London: Columbia University Press, 1965.

Groden, Michael. *Ulysses in Progress.* Princeton, NJ: Princeton University Press, 1977.

Gubern, Román. *La censura: Función política y ordenamiento jurídico bajo el franquismo (1936–1975).* Barcelona: Península, 1981.

Gumbrecht, Hans Ulrich. "Censorship and the Creation of Heroes in the Discourses of Literary History." *The Institutionalization of Literature in Spain.* Ed. Wlad Godzich and Nicholas Spadaccini. Minneapolis, MN: Prisma Institute, 1987. 229–43.

Harder, Benjamin. "Stephen's Prop: Aspects of the Ashplant in *Portrait* and *Ulysses.*" *Joycean Cultures / Culturing Joyces.* Ed. Vincent J. Cheng, Kimberly J. Devlin, and Margot Norris. Newark: University of Delaware Press, 1998. 241–52.

Harrison, Nicholas. *Circles of Censorship: Censorship and Its Metaphors in French History, Literature, and Theory.* Oxford: Clarendon Press, 1995.

Hart, Stephen M. *The Other Scene: Psychoanalytic Readings in Modern Spanish and Latin-American Literature.* Boulder, CO: Society of Spanish and Spanish-American Studies, 1992.

Henke, Suzette A. *James Joyce and the Politics of Desire.* London and New York: Routledge, 1990.

Herbold, Sarah. "'(I Have Camouflaged Everything, My Love)': *Lolita* and the Woman Reader." *Nabokov Studies* 5 (1998–1999): 71–98.

———. "Reflections on Modernism: *Lolita* and Political Engagement; Or, How the Left and the Right Both Have It Wrong." *Nabokov Studies* 3 (1996): 145–50.

Herr, Cheryl. "Irish Censorship and 'The Pleasure of the Text': The 'Aeolus' Episode of Joyce's *Ulysses.*" *Irish Renaissance Annual* 3 (1982): 141–79.

———. *Joyce's Anatomy of Culture.* Urbana: University of Illinois Press, 1986.

Herzberger, David K. *Narrating the Past: Fiction and Historiography in Postwar Spain.* Durham, NC: Duke University Press, 1995.

———. "Splitting the Reference: Postmodern Fiction and the Idea of History in Francoist Spain." *Intertextual Pursuits: Literary Mediations in Modern Spanish Narrative.* Lewisburg, PA: Bucknell University Press, 1998. 126–42.

Hiatt, L. R. "Nabokov's *Lolita*: A 'Freudian' Cryptic Crossword." *American Imago* 24.4 (Winter 1967): 360–70.

Hiley, Nicholas. "'Can't You Find Me Something Nasty?': Circulating Libraries and Literary Censorship in Britain from the 1890s to the 1910s." *Censorship and the Control of Print in England and France, 1600–1910.* Ed. Robin Myers and Michael Harris. Winchester, UK: St. Paul's Bibliographies, 1992. 123–47.

Hitchcock, Peter. "Answering as Authoring: or, Marxism's Joyce." *Mosaic* 32.1 (March 1999): 55–69.

Holman, C. Hugh. *A Handbook to Literature.* Indianapolis, IN: Bobbs-Merrill, 1972.

Holmgren, Beth, ed. *The Russian Memoir: History and Literature.* Evanston, IL: Northwestern University Press, 2003.

Holquist, Michael. "Answering as Authoring: Mikhail Bakhtin's Trans-Linguistics." *Critical Inquiry* 10 (December 1983): 307–19.

———. "Corrupt Originals: The Paradox of Censorship." *PMLA* 109 (1994): 14–25.

Horkheimer, Max, and Theodor W. Adorno. *Dialectic of Enlightenment.* Trans. John Cumming. New York: Herder and Herder, 1972.

Hosking, Geoffrey. *Beyond Socialist Realism: Soviet Fiction since* Ivan Denisovich. New York: Holmes & Meier, 1980.

———. "The Institutionalization of Soviet Literature." *Perspectives on Literature and Society in Eastern and Western Europe.* Ed. Geoffrey A. Hosking and George F. Cushing. Basingstoke, UK, and London: Macmillan, 1989. 55–75.

Hubbs, Joanna. *Mother Russia: The Feminine Myth in Russian Culture.* Bloomington and Indianapolis: Indiana University Press, 1988.

Hudon, Edward G. "Anglo-Saxon Law against Seditious Libel." *Communications Control: Readings in the Motives and Structures of Censorship.* Ed. John Phelan. New York: Sheed & Ward, 1969. 171–89.

Hughes, Donna M. "Supplying Women for the Sex Industry: Trafficking from the Russian Federation." *Sexuality and Gender in Postcommunist Eastern Europe and Russia.* New York: Haworth, 2005. 209–30.

Hunter, Ian, David Saunders, and Dugald Williamson. *On Pornography: Literature, Sexuality and Obscenity Law.* New York: St. Martin's Press, 1993.

Hutcheon, Linda. *The Politics of Postmodernism.* 2nd ed. London and New York: Routledge, 2003.

Hutchings, Stephen. "Gender Theory and the Metaphysics of Losev and Florenskii: Flashpoint as Fleshpoint." *Gender and Sexuality in Russian Civilization.* Ed. Peter I. Barta. London and New York: Routledge, 2001. 141–60.

Huyssen, Andreas. "Introduction to Adorno." *New German Critique* 6 (Fall 1975): 3–11.

Hyde, G. M. *Vladimir Nabokov: America's Russian Novelist.* London: Marion Boyars, 1977.

Hyde, H. Montgomery. Introduction. *The* Lady Chatterley's Lover *Trial (Regina v. Penguin Books Limited).* London: Bodley Head, 1990.

Ibsen, Henrik. *Ghosts: A Family Drama in Three Acts.* Trans. Lanford Wilson. New York: Dramatists Play Service, 2003.

———. *Rosmersholm.* London: Nick Hern, 2003.

———. "When We Dead Awaken." *The Complete Major Prose Plays*. New York: New American Library, 1978.

Imperial Russia: A Source Book, 1700–1917. 3rd ed. Ed. Basil Dmytryshyn. Fort Worth, TX: Holt, Rinehart and Winston, 1990.

"Interview with Chief Censor." *Index on Censorship* 18.3 (1989): 22–23.

The Invention of Pornography: Obscenity and the Origins of Modernity, 1500–1800. Ed. Lynn Hunt. New York: Zone Books, 1993.

Iser, Wolfgang. *The Implied Reader: Patterns of Communication in Prose Fiction from Bunyan to Beckett*. Baltimore: Johns Hopkins University Press, 1974.

Istoriia sovetskoi politicheskoi tsenzury: Dokumenty i kommentarii. Ed. T. M. Goriaeva. Moscow: Rossiiskaia politicheskaia entsiklopediia, 1997.

Jambet, Christian, and Guy Lardreau. *L'ange: Pour une cynégétique du semblant*. Paris: Grasset, 1976.

James, Vaughan C. *Soviet Socialist Realism: Origins and Theory*. London and Basingstoke, UK: Macmillan, 1973.

Jameson, Fredric. *The Political Unconscious: Narrative as a Socially Symbolic Act*. Ithaca, NY: Cornell University Press, 1981.

Jansen, Sue Curry. *Censorship: The Knot That Binds Power and Knowledge*. New York and Oxford: Oxford University Press, 1988.

Jerez-Farrán, Carlos. "'Ansiedad de influencia' versus intertextualidad autoconsciente en *Tiempo de silencio* de Martín-Santos." *Symposium* 42.2 (1988): 119–32.

Jiménez Losantos, Federico. *La dictadura silenciosa: Mecanismos totalitarios en nuestra democracia*. Madrid: Temas de hoy, 1993.

Johnson, D. Barton. *Worlds in Regression: Some Novels of Vladimir Nabokov*. Ann Arbor, MI: Ardis, 1985.

———, and Sheila Golburgh Johnson. "The Return of 'Our' Nabokov." *Index on Censorship* 16.4 (1987): 11–12.

Johnson, Jeri, ed. *Ulysses*. By James Joyce. Oxford: Oxford University Press, 1993.

Jones, Frances M. *Defusing Censorship: The Librarian's Guide to Handling Censorship Conflicts*. Phoenix, AZ: Oryx, 1983.

Jones, Margaret E. W. *The Contemporary Spanish Novel, 1939–1975*. Boston: Twayne, 1985.

Jordan, Barry. *Writing and Politics in Franco's Spain*. London and New York: Routledge, 1990.

Joyce, James. "The Dead." *Dubliners: Authoritative Text, Contexts, Criticisms*. Ed. Margot Norris, Hans Walter Gabler with Walter Hettche. New York: W. W. Norton, 2006. 151–92.

———. *Dubliners: Authoritative Text, Contexts, Criticism*. Ed. Margot Norris and Hans Walter Gabler with Walter Hettche. New York: W. W. Norton, 2006.

———. *Exiles*. Harmondsworth, UK: Penguin, 1979.

———. *A Portrait of the Artist as a Young Man*. Ed. Seamus Deane. London: Penguin, 1992.

———. *Stephen Hero*. Ed. Theodore Spencer. New York: New Directions, 1963.

———. *Ulysses*. Ed. Hans Walter Gabler. New York: Random House, 1986.

———. *Ulysses*. Ed. Jeri Johnson. Oxford: Oxford University Press, 1993.

Judging Lyotard. Ed. Andrew Benjamin. London: Routledge, 1992.

Juliar, Michael. *Vladimir Nabokov: A Descriptive Bibliography*. New York: Garland, 1986.

Kaite, Berkeley. *Pornography and Difference*. Bloomington and Indianapolis: Indiana University Press, 1995.

Kant, Immanuel. *Critique of the Power of Judgment*. Trans. Paul Guyer and Eric Matthews. Cambridge: Cambridge University Press, 2000.

———. "What Is Enlightenment?" *Foundations of the Metaphysics of Morals and "What Is Enlightenment?"* Trans. Lewis White Beck. Indianapolis, IN: Bobbs-Merrill, 1959. 85–92.
Kaplan, Abraham. "Obscenity as an Esthetic Category." *Communications Control: Readings in the Motives and Structures of Censorship.* Ed. John Phelan. New York: Sheed & Ward, 1969. 127–52.
Karlinsky, Simon, ed. *The Nabokov-Wilson Letters: Correspondence between Vladimir Nabokov and Edmund Wilson, 1940–1971.* New York: Harper & Row, 1979.
Kauffman, Linda S. "Framing *Lolita:* Is There a Woman in the Text?" *Special Delivery: Epistolary Modes in Modern Fiction.* Chicago and London: University of Chicago Press, 1992. 53–79.
Kazin, Alfred. "*Lady Chatterley* in America." *Atlantic* 204 (1959): 33–36.
Kendrick, Walter. "The Corruption of Gerty MacDowell." *James Joyce Quarterly* 37.3–4 (Spring–Summer 2000): 413–23.
Kenner, Hugh. *Ulysses.* London: George Allen & Unwin, 1980.
Kermode, Frank. *The Sense of an Ending: Studies in the Theory of Fiction: With a New Epilogue.* Oxford and New York: Oxford University Press, 2000.
Kershner, R. Brandon. *Joyce, Bakhtin, and Popular Literature: Chronicles of Disorder.* Chapel Hill: University of North Carolina Press, 1989.
———. "Teaching *Howards End* through *Ulysses* through Bakhtin." *Pedagogy, Praxis,* Ulysses*: Using Joyce's Text to Transform the Classroom.* Ed. Robert Newman. Ann Arbor: University of Michigan Press, 1996. 153–65.
Kevelson, Roberta. *The Law as a System of Signs.* New York: Plenum, 1988.
Khodyreva, Natalia. "Sexuality for Whom? Paid Sex and Patriarchy in Russia." *Sexuality and Gender in Postcommunist Eastern Europe and Russia.* New York: Haworth, 2005. 243–62.
Kincaid, James R. *Child-Loving: The Erotic Child and Victorian Culture.* New York and London: Routledge, 1992.
Kinsey, Alfred C. *Sexual Behavior in the Human Female.* Philadelphia: W. B. Saunders, 1953.
———. *Sexual Behavior in the Human Male.* Philadelphia: W. B. Saunders, 1948.
Kipnis, Laura. *Bound and Gagged: Pornography and the Politics of Fantasy in America.* New York: Grove, 1996.
Knickerbocker, Dale F. "*Tiempo de silencio* and the Narration of the Abject." *Anales de la literatura española contemporánea* 19.1–2 (1994): 11–31.
Kon, Igor S. *The Sexual Revolution in Russia: From the Age of the Czars to Today.* Trans. James Riordan. New York: Free Press, 1995.
———. "Sexuality and Politics in Russia, 1700–2000." *Sexual Cultures in Europe: National Histories.* Ed. Franz X. Eder, Lesley A. Hall, and Gert Hekma. Manchester and New York: Manchester University Press, 1999. 197–218.
Krafft-Ebing, Richard von. *Psychopathia sexualis: With Especial Reference to Contrary Sexual Instinct: A Medico-Legal Study.* New York: Classics of Medicine Library, 1993.
Krasnogorov, Valentin. "'Glasnost'' i bezglasnost'': Zametki po istorii otechestvennoi tsenzury." *Neva* 3 (1990): 146–65.
Kristeva, Julia. *Powers of Horror: An Essay on Abjection.* Trans. L. S. Roudiez. New York: Columbia University Press, 1982.
Kunin, Vladimir. *Interdevochka.* Moscow: Moladaia gvardiia, 1988.
———. *Intergirl: A Hard Currency Hooker.* Trans. Antonina W. Bouis. New York: Bergh, 1991.
Labanyi, Jo. *Ironía e historia en* Tiempo de silencio. Madrid: Taurus, 1985.

Lacan, Jacques. "La censure n'est pas la résistance." *Le séminaire de Jacques Lacan: Le moi dans la théorie de Freud et dans la technique de la psychanalyse, 1954–55*. Vol. 2. Paris: Seuil, 1978. 151–62.

———. *Écrits: A Selection*. Trans. Alan Sheridan. London: Tavistock, 1977.

———. *The Ego in Freud's Theory and in the Technique of Psychoanalysis, 1954–1955*. Ed. Jacques-Alain Miller. Trans. Sylvana Tomaselli. New York: Norton, 1991.

———. *The Ethics of Psychoanalysis, 1959–1960*. Ed. Jacques-Alain Miller. Trans. Dennis Porter. New York: Norton, 1992.

———. *The Four Fundamental Concepts of Psycho-analysis*. Ed. Jacques-Alain Miller. Trans. Alan Sheridan. London: Hogarth, 1977.

———. *Le séminaire de Jacques Lacan: Le moi dans la théorie de Freud et dans la technique de la psychanalyse, 1954–55*. Vol. 2. Paris: Seuil, 1978.

———. *Le séminaire de Jacques Lacan: Encore, 1972–1973*. Vol. 20. Paris: Seuil, 1975.

LaCapra, Dominick. *Madame Bovary on Trial*. Ithaca, NY: Cornell University Press, 1982.

Ladenson, Elisabeth. *Dirt for Art's Sake: Books on Trial from Madame Bovary to Lolita*. Ithaca, NY: Cornell University Press, 2007.

The Lady Chatterley's Lover Trial (Regina v. Penguin Books Limited). London: Bodley Head, 1990.

Lamos, Colleen. "Signatures of the Invisible: Homosexual Secrecy and Knowledge in *Ulysses*." *James Joyce Quarterly* 31.3 (Spring 1994): 337–55.

Langton, Rae. "Subordination, Silence, and Pornography's Authority." *Censorship and Silencing: Practices of Cultural Regulation*. Ed. Robert C. Post. Santa Monica, CA: Getty Foundation and Oxford University Press, 1998. 261–83.

Lanser, Susan Sniader. *The Narrative Act: Point of View in Prose Fiction*. Princeton, NJ: Princeton University Press, 1981.

Laplanche, Jean. "Aggressiveness and Sadomasochism." *Life and Death in Psychoanalysis*. Trans. Jeffrey Mehlman. Baltimore, MD: Johns Hopkins University Press, 1976. 85–102.

———. *Essays on Otherness*. Ed. John Fletcher. London: Routledge, 1999.

———. *Life and Death in Psychoanalysis*. Trans. Jeffrey Mehlman. Baltimore, MD: Johns Hopkins University Press, 1976.

———, and J.-B. Pontalis. *The Language of Psychoanalysis*. Trans. Donald Nicholson-Smith. New York: Norton, 1973.

Laqueur, Thomas. *Making Sex: Body and Gender from the Greeks to Freud*. Cambridge, MA: Harvard University Press, 1990.

Larra, Mariano José de. *Artículos*. Madrid: Cátedra, 1999.

Law, Jules David. "'Pity They Can't See Themselves': Assessing the 'Subject' of Pornography in 'Nausicaa.'" *James Joyce Quarterly* 27 (Winter 1990): 219–39.

Lázaro, Alberto. "James Joyce's Encounters with Spanish Censorship, 1939–1966." *Joyce Studies Annual* 12 (Summer 2001): 38–54.

Leckie, Barbara. *Culture and Adultery: The Novel, the Newspaper, and the Law, 1857–1914*. Philadelphia: University of Pennsylvania Press, 1999.

———. "Reading Bodies, Reading Nerves: 'Nausicaa' and the Discourse of Censorship." *James Joyce Quarterly* 34.1–2 (Fall 1996–Winter 1997): 65–85.

Legendre, Pierre. *L'amour du censeur: Essai sur l'ordre dogmatique*. Paris: Seuil, 1974.

Lenin, V. I. "Party Organization and Party Literature." *Soviet Socialist Realism: Origins and Theory*. By Vaughan C. James. London and Basingstoke, UK: Macmillan, 1973. 103–6.

Leonard, Garry M. "The Masquerade of Gender: Mrs. Kearney and the 'Moral Umbrella' of Mr. O'Madden Burke." *Gender in Joyce*. Ed. Jolanta W. Wawrzycka and Marlena G.

Corcoran. Gainesville: University Press of Florida, 1997. 133–49.
Leonardo de Argensola, Lupercio. "Al sueño." *Rimas.* Madrid: Espasa-Calpe, 1972.
Lévi-Straus, Claude. *The Elementary Structures of Kinship.* Ed. Rodney Needham. Trans. James Harle Bell, John Richard von Sturmer, and Rodney Needham. London: Eyre & Spottiswoode, 1969.
———. *Structural Anthropology.* Trans. Monique Layton. Chicago: University of Chicago Press, 1983.
Levine, Michael G. *Writing through Repression: Literature, Censorship, Psychoanalysis.* Baltimore, MD, and London: Johns Hopkins University Press, 1994.
Levine, Peter. "*Lolita* and Aristotle's Ethics." *Philosophy and Literature* 19.1 (April 1995): 32–47.
Lewis, Felice Flanery. *Literature, Obscenity, and Law.* Carbondale: Southern Illinois University Press, 1976.
Linetski, Vadim. "The Mechanism of the Production of Ambiguity: Freud's *Dora* and Nabokov's *Lolita.*" *Canadian Review of Comparative Literature* 23.2 (June 1996): 531–46.
Linz, Juan J. "An Authoritarian Regime: Spain." *Politics and Society in Twentieth-Century Spain.* Ed. Stanley G. Payne. New York: Franklin Watts, 1976.
Litz, A. Walton. *The Art of James Joyce: Method and Design in* Ulysses *and* Finnegans Wake. London: Oxford University Press, 1964.
Llorens Castillo, Vicente. *Aspectos sociales de la literatura española.* Madrid: Castalia, 1974.
Losev, Lev. *On the Beneficence of Censorship: Aesopian Language in Modern Russian Literature.* Munich: Otto Sagner, 1984.
Loss, Archie. "The Censor Swings: Joyce's Work and the New Censorship." *James Joyce Quarterly* 33.3 (1996): 369–76.
Luna, Norman. "Parallel, Parody and Satire in *Tiempo de silencio.*" *Revista de Estudios Hispánicos* 18.2 (May 1984): 241–57.
Lyotard, Jean François. "Going Back to the Return." *The Languages of Joyce: Selected Papers from the 11th International James Joyce Symposium, Venice, 12–18 June 1988.* Ed. Rose Maria Bollettieri Bosinelli, C. Marengo Vaglio, and Christine van Boheemen. Philadelphia: Benjamins, 1992. 193–210.
———. "The Sublime and the Avant-Garde." *The Continental Aesthetics Reader.* Ed. Clive Cazeaux. London and New York: Routledge, 2000. 453–64.
MacCabe, Colin. *James Joyce and the Revolution of the Word.* Houndsmills: Palgrave, 2003.
MacKinnon, Catharine. *Only Words.* Cambridge, MA: Harvard University Press, 1993.
Mahaffey, Vicki. "Intentional Error: The Paradox of Editing Joyce's *Ulysses.*" *Representing Modernist Texts: Editing as Interpretation.* Ed. George Bornstein. Ann Arbor: University of Michigan Press, 1991. 171–91.
Malenkaia Vera [*Little Vera*]. Dir. Vasilii Pichul. Gorkii Film, 1988.
Malo de Molina, Carlos A. *Los españoles y la sexualidad.* Madrid: Temas de hoy, 1992.
Mamonova, Tatiana. *Women's Glasnost vs. Naglost: Stopping Russian Backlash.* Westport, CT: Bergin and Garvey, 1994.
Manet, Édouard. *Le déjeuner sur l'herbe.* 1863. Musée D'Orsay, Paris.
Marcus, Steven. *Freud and the Culture of Psychoanalysis: Studies in the Transition from Victorian Humanism to Modernity.* New York: Norton, 1984.
———. *The Other Victorians: A Study of Sexuality and Pornography in Mid-Nineteenth-Century England.* New York: Basic Books, 1966.
Marcuse, Herbert. *Eros and Civilization: A Philosophical Inquiry into Freud.* Boston: Beacon, 1966.

———. "Repressive Tolerance." *A Critique of Pure Tolerance*. By Robert Paul Wolff, Barrington Moore, Jr., and Herbert Marcuse. Boston: Beacon, 1969. 81–123.

Markstein, Elisabeth. "Censorship, Samizdat, and New Trends." *Twentieth-Century Russian Literature: A Critical Study*. Ed. Johannes Holthusen. New York: Frederick Ungar, 1972.

Marsh, Joss. *Soviet Marxism: A Critical Analysis*. New York: Columbia University Press, 1969.

———. *Word Crimes: Blasphemy, Culture, and Literature in Nineteenth-Century England*. Chicago: University of Chicago Press, 1998.

Marsh, Rosalind J. *Soviet Fiction since Stalin: Science, Politics and Literature*. London & Sydney: Croom Helm, 1986.

Martin, Wallace. *Recent Theories of Narrative*. Ithaca, NY: Cornell University Press, 1986.

Martín-Santos, Luis. *El análisis existencial: Ensayos*. Ed. José Lázaro. Madrid: Triacastela, 2004.

———. *Apólogos y otras prosas inéditas*. Ed. Salvador Clotas. Barcelona: Seix Barral, 1970.

———. *Grana gris*. Ed. José Francisco Ruiz Casanova. Madrid: Biblioteca Nueva, 2002.

———. *Libertad, temporalidad y transferencia en el psicoanálisis existencial: Para una fenomenología de la cura psicoanalítica*. Barcelona: Seix Barral, 1964 and 1975.

———. *Teoría marxista de la revolución*. Madrid: Akal, 1977.

———. *Tiempo de destrucción*. Ed. José-Carlos Mainer. Barcelona: Seix Barral, 1975.

———. *Tiempo de silencio*. 1961. Barcelona: Seix Barral, 1962. (First or second edition—censored)

———. *Tiempo de silencio*. Barcelona: Seix Barral, 1966. (Virtually uncensored)

———. *Tiempo de silencio*. Barcelona: Seix Barral, 1971. (Eighth edition—virtually uncensored)

———. *Tiempo de silencio*. Barcelona: Seix Barral, 1980–1993. ("Complete and definitive edition")

———. *Time of Silence*. Trans. George Leeson. New York: Columbia University Press, 1989. (Leeson's translation of 1964, with copyright from Spanish 1962—but includes most of the censored material [with some notable exceptions, see Rapin]; sometimes the translation is poor.)

Maryniak, Irena. "Meeting Erofeev." *Index on Censorship* 21.7 (1992): 31.

———. "Whither the Writers' Union?" *Index on Censorship* 21.2 (1992): 8–9.

Masters, William H., and Virginia Johnson. *Human Sexual Inadequacy*. Boston: Little, Brown, 1970.

———. *Human Sexual Response*. Boston: Little, Brown, 1966.

Materer, Timothy. "Make It Sell! Ezra Pound Advertises Modernism." *Marketing Modernisms: Self-Promotion, Canonization, Rereading*. Ed. Kevin J. H. Dettmar and Stephen Watt. Ann Arbor: University of Michigan Press, 1996. 17–36.

McCleery, Alistair. "A Curious History: United Kingdom Government Reaction to *Ulysses*." *James Joyce Quarterly* 32.3–4 (1995): 631–40.

McDonald, Michael Bruce. "'Circe' and the Uncanny, or Joyce from Freud to Marx." *James Joyce Quarterly* 33.1 (Fall 1995): 49–68.

McGee, Patrick. "*Ulysses* as 'Profane Illumination.'" *Joyce beyond Marx: History and Desire in* Ulysses *and* Finnegans Wake. Gainesville: University Press of Florida, 2001. 111–30.

McKee, Richard E. "Censorship Research: Its Strengths, Weaknesses, Uses, and Misuses." *An Intellectual Freedom Primer*. Ed. Charles H. Busha. Littleton, CO: Libraries Unlimited, 1977. 192–220.

McNeely, Trevor. "'Lo' and Behold: Solving the *Lolita* Riddle." Lolita. Ed. Harold Bloom.

New York: Chelsea House, 1993. 134–48.
Mead, Margaret. *Male and Female*. Harmondsworth, UK: Penguin, 1975.
Medina Casado, Carmelo. "Sifting through Censorship: The British Home Office *Ulysses* Files (1922–1936)." *James Joyce Quarterly* 37.3–4 (Spring–Summer 2000): 479–508.
Medvedev, Roy. "M. A. Suslov: 'Ideologist-in-Chief.'" *All Stalin's Men: Six Who Carried Out the Bloody Policies*. Trans. Harold Shukman. Garden City, NY: Anchor Books, 1985. 61–81.
Melberg, Arne. *Theories of Mimesis*. Cambridge: Cambridge University Press, 1995.
Meredith, George. *The Ordeal of Richard Feverel*. London: Dent, 1954.
Merimée, Prosper. "Carmen." *Romans et nouvelles de Merimée*. Paris: Gallimard, 1951. 609–66, 819–25.
Middleton, Peter. *The Inward Gaze: Masculinity and Subjectivity in Modern Culture*. London: Routledge, 1992.
Milesi, Laurent, ed. *James Joyce and the Difference of Language*. Cambridge: Cambridge University Press, 2003.
Miller, Arthur. "On Censorship." *Censored Books: Critical Viewpoints*. Ed. Nicholas J. Karolides, Lee Burress, and John M. Kean. Metuchen, NJ: Scarecrow Press, 1993. 3–10.
Minois, Georges. *Censure et culture sous l'Ancien régime*. N.p.: Fayard, 1995.
Molina, Tirso de. *El burlador de Sevilla y Convidado de piedra*. Ed. Luis Vázquez. Madrid: Razón Social, 1989.
Molinero, César. *La intervención del Estado en la prensa*. Barcelona: Dopesa, 1971.
Monas, Sidney. "Censorship as a Way of Life." *Perspectives on Literature and Society in Eastern and Western Europe*. Ed. Geoffrey A. Hosking and George F. Cushing. Basingstoke and London: Macmillan, 1989. 7–22.
Mooney, Susan. "Bronze by Gold by Bloom: The Aurteur of 'Sirens.'" *Bronze by Gold: The Music of Joyce*. Ed. Sebastian D. G. Knowles. New York and London: Garland, 1999. 229–44.
Moore, Anthony R. "How Unreliable Is Humbert in *Lolita*?" *Journal of Modern Literature* 25.1 (Fall 2001): 71–80.
Moore, Tony. "Seeing through Humbert: Focussing on the Feminist Sympathy in *Lolita*." *Discourse and Ideology in Nabokov's Prose*. Studies in Russian and European Literature 7. Ed. David H. J. Larmour. London: Routledge, 2002. 91–110, 167–68.
Moret, Xavier. *Tiempo de editores: Historia de la edición en España, 1939–1975*. Barcelona: Destino, 2002.
Moss, Kevin. "The Underground Closet: Political and Sexual Dissidence in East European Culture." *Postcommunism and the Body Politic*. Ed. Ellen E. Berry. New York: New York University Press, 1995. 229–52.
Moynahan, Julian. "Nabokov and Joyce." *The Garland Companion to Vladimir Nabokov*. Ed. Vladimir Alexandrov. New York: Garland, 1995. 433–44.
Mozart, Wolfgang Amadeus. *Don Giovanni*. Libretto by Lorenzo da Ponte. English and Italian. Ed. Burton D. Fisher. Coral Gables, FL: Opera Journeys, 2002.
Mullin, Katherine. *James Joyce, Sexuality and Social Purity*. Cambridge: Cambridge University Press, 2003.
Murphy, Sean P. *James Joyce and Victims: Reading the Logic of Exclusion*. Madison, NJ: Fairleagh Dickinson University Press, 2003.
Nabokov, Vladimir. *The Annotated Lolita*. Ed. Alfred Appel, Jr. New York: Vintage, 1991.
———. *The Enchanter*. Trans. Dmitri Nabokov. New York: Putnam's, 1986.
———. *Lectures on Literature*. Ed. Fredson Bowers. New York: Harbrace Jonanovich, 1980.

———. *Lectures on Russian Literature*. Ed. Fredson Bowers. New York: Harcourt Brace Jonanovich, 1981.

———. *Lolita*. New York: Vintage, 1997.

———. "On a Book Entitled *Lolita*." *The Annotated Lolita*. Ed. Alfred Appel, Jr. New York: Vintage, 1991. 311–17, 453–57.

———. "A Russian Beauty." *"A Russian Beauty" and Other Stories*. Trans. Dmitri Nabokov and Simon Karlinsky with Vladimir Nabokov. New York: McGraw-Hill, 1973. 1–8. ("Krasavitsa," first published in émigré daily *Poslednaia novosti*, Paris, August 18, 1934; and then in collection *Sogliadatai*, Paris: Russkaia zapiski, 1938.)

———. "Russian Writers, Censors, and Readers." *Lectures on Russian Literature*. Ed. Fredson Bowers. New York: Harcourt, 1981. 1–12.

———. *Speak, Memory: An Autobiography Revisited*. New York: Putnam, 1966.

———. "The Strange Case of Dr. Jekyll and Mr. Hyde." *Dr. Jekyll and Mr. Hyde* by Robert Louis Stevenson. New York: Signet, 1980. 7–34.

———. *Strong Opinions*. New York: McGraw-Hill, 1973.

———. *Vladimir Nabokov: Selected Letters, 1940–1977*. Ed. Dmitri Nabokov and Matthew J. Bruccoli. San Diego: Harcourt, 1989.

Nadel, Ira B. *Joyce and the Jews: Culture and Texts*. Iowa City: University of Iowa Press, 1989.

Naiman, Eric. *Sex in Public: The Incarnation of Early Soviet Ideology*. Princeton, NJ: Princeton University Press, 1997.

Née, Patrick. "1857: Le double procès de *Madame Bovary* et des *Fleurs du mal*." *La censure en France à l'ère démocratique (1848– . . .): Histoire culturelle*. Ed. Pascal Ory. Bruxelles: Complexe, 1997. 119–43.

Negroni, Barbara de. *Lectures interdites: Le travail des censeurs au XVIIIe siècle, 1723–1774*. Paris: Albin, 1995.

Neuschäfer, Hans-Jörg. *Adiós a la España eterna: La dialéctica de la censura: Novela, teatro y cine bajo el franquismo*. Trans. Rosa Pilar Blanco. Barcelona: Anthropos, 1994.

Nicolson, Nigel. *Long Life: Memoirs*. London: Weidenfeld & Nicolson, 1997.

Nietzsche, Friedrich Wilhelm. *On the Genealogy of Morals: A Polemic: By way of clarification and supplement to my last book, Beyond Good and Evil*. Trans. Douglas Smith. Oxford and New York: Oxford University Press, 1996.

Norris, Margot. "Disenchanting Enchantment: The Theatrical Brothel of 'Circe.'" *Ulysses—En-Gendered Perspectives: Eighteen New Essays on the Episodes*. Ed. Kimberly J. Devlin and Marilyn Reizbaum. Columbia: University of South Carolina Press, 1999. 229–41, 316–17.

———. "Theater of the Mind: 'Circe' and Avant-Garde Form." *Pedagogy, Praxis, Ulysses: Using Joyce's Text to Transform the Classroom*. Ed. Robert Newman. Ann Arbor: University of Michigan Press, 1996. 79–95.

Oboler, Eli M. *The Fear of the Word: Censorship and Sex*. Metuchen, NJ: Scarecrow Press, 1974.

Ohi, Kevin. *Innocence and Rapture: The Erotic Child in Pater, Wilde, James, and Nabokov*. New York and Houndsmills: Palgrave Macmillan, 2005.

———. "Sentimentality, Desire, and Aestheticism in *Lolita*." *Innocence and Rapture: The Erotic Child in Pater, Wilde, James, and Nabokov*. New York and Houndsmills: Palgrave Macmillan, 2005. 155–90, 203–6.

Ost, François. "The Law as Mirrored in Literature." Trans. Roxanne Lapidus. *SubStance* 35.1 (2006): 1–19.

Osteen, Mark. "A High Grade Ha: The 'Politicoecomedy' of Headwear in *Ulysses.*" *Joycean Cultures/Culturing Joyces.* Ed. Vincent J. Cheng, Kimberly J. Devlin, and Margot Norris. Newark: University of Delaware Press, 1998. 253–83.

Overton, Bill. *The Novel of Female Adultery: Love and Gender in Contintental European Fiction, 1830–1900.* New York: St. Martin's Press, 1996.

Pagnattaro, Marisa Anne. "Carving a Literary Exception: The Obscenity Standard and *Ulysses.*" *Twentieth Century Literature* 47.2 (Summer 2001): 217–40.

Palley, Julian. "The Periplus of Don Pedro: *Tiempo de silencio.*" *Bulletin of Hispanic Studies* 48 (1971): 239–54.

Pardo Bazán, Emilia. *Los Pazos de Ulloa.* 2nd ed. Ed. María Ángeles Ayala. Madrid: Cátedra, 1999.

Parker, David. *Ethics, Theory and the Novel.* Cambridge: Cambridge University Press, 1994.

Parkes, Adam. *Modernism and the Theater of Censorship.* New York: Oxford University Press, 1996.

Pasternak, Boris. *Doktor Zhivago: Roman.* Tom 4. *Polnoe sobranie sochinenii s prolozheniiami.* Moscow: Slovo, 2004.

Patnoe, Elizabeth. "Discourse, Ideology, and Hegemony: The Double Dramas in and around *Lolita.*" *Discourse and Ideology in Nabokov's Prose.* Studies in Russian and European Literature 7. Ed. David H. J. Larmour. London: Routledge, 2002. 111–36, 168–70.

Patterns of Censorship around the World. Ed. Ilan Peleg. Boulder, CO: Westview, 1993.

Patterson, Annabel. "Censorship." *The Encyclopedia of Literature and Criticism.* Ed. Matthew Coyle et al. London: Routledge, 1990. 901–14.

———. *Censorship and Interpretation: The Conditions of Writing and Reading in Early Modern England.* Madison: University of Wisconsin Press, 1984.

Patterson, Lyman Ray. *Copyright in Historical Perspective.* Nashville, TN: Vanderbilt University Press, 1968.

Paulhan, Jean. Foreword. *Histoire d'O.* By Pauline Réage. N.p.: Jean-Jacques Pauvert, 1972.

Pauvert, Jean-Jacques. *Nouveaux (et moins nouveaux) visages de la censure; suivi de "L'affaire Sade."* Paris: Les Belles Lettres, 1994.

Pease, Allison. *Modernism, Mass Culture, and the Aesthetics of Obscenity.* Cambridge: Cambridge University Press, 2000.

Pérez, Janet. "The Game of the Possible: Francoist Censorship and Techniques of Dissent." *Review of Contemporary Fiction* 4.3 (1984): 22–30.

Pérez Firmat, Gustavo. "Repetition and Excess in *Tiempo de silencio.*" *PMLA* 66.2 (March 1981): 194–209.

Pérez Galdós, Benito. *Fortunata y Jacinta.* Barcelona: Planeta, 1993.

———. *Tristana.* Edición de Pilar Torralba Álvarez. Madrid: Akal, 2003.

Pérez-Magallón, Jesús. "El proyecto acosado: El fracaso en *Tiempo de silencio* de Luis Martín-Santos." *Revista hispánica moderna* 47.1 (1994): 134–45.

Pérez Rojas, Javier, and Manuel García Castellón. *El siglo XX: Persistencias y rupturas.* Madrid: Sílex, 1994.

Perrin, Noel. *Dr. Bowdler's Legacy: A History of Expurgated Books in England and America.* New York: Atheneum, 1969.

Perspectives on Literature and Society in Eastern and Western Europe. Ed. Geoffrey A. Hosking and George F. Cushing. Basingstoke and London: Macmillan, 1989.

Perspectives on Pornography: Sexuality in Film and Literature. Ed. Gary Day and Clive Bloom. New York: St. Martin's Press, 1988.

Pevear, Richard. Introduction. *The Idiot.* By Fyodor Dostoevsky. Trans. Richard and Larissa Volokhonsky. New York: Knopf, 2002. xi–xxiii.
Phelan, James. "Double Focalization, Discourse as Story, and Ethics: *Lolita.*" *Living to Tell about It: A Rhetoric and Ethics of Character Narration.* Ithaca, NY and London: Cornell University Press, 2005. 98–131.
———. *Living to Tell about It: A Rhetoric and Ethics of Character Narration.* Ithaca, NY, and London: Cornell University Press, 2005.
Pifer, Ellen. "De la Russie à *Lolita:* La découverte de l'Amérique par Nabokov." Trans. Hélène Fiamma. *Europe* 791 (March 1995): 64–70.
———. "*Lolita.*" *The Garland Companion to Vladimir Nabokov.* Ed. Vladimir Alexandrov. New York: Garland, 1995. 305–21.
———. *Nabokov and the Novel.* Cambridge, MA: Harvard University Press, 1980.
———. "Nabokov's Novel Offspring: Lolita and Her Kin." *Vladimir Nabokov's* Lolita: *A Casebook.* Ed. Ellen Pifer. Oxford and New York: Oxford University Press, 2003. 83–109.
Platonov, Andrei. *Chevengur.* Trans. Anthony Olcott. Ann Arbor, MI: Ardis, 1978.
———. *Chevengur: Roman.* Moscow: Khudozhestvennaia literatura, 1988.
A Plot of Her Own: The Female Protagonist in Russian Literature. Ed. Sona Stephan Hoisington. Evanston, IL: Northwestern University Press, 1995.
Popovskii, Mark. *Tretii lishnii: On, ona i sovetskii rezhim* (*The Superfluous Third: He, She and the Soviet Regime*). London: Overseas Publications Interchange, 1985.
Pornography and Censorship. Ed. David Copp and Susan Wendell. Buffalo, NY: Prometheus Books, 1983.
Porter, Robert. *Russia's Alternative Prose.* Oxford and Providence, RI: Berg, 1994.
Post, Robert C. "Censorship and Silencing." *Censorship and Silencing: Practices of Cultural Regulation.* Ed. Robert C. Post. Santa Monica, CA: Getty Foundation and Oxford University Press, 1998. 1–12.
Power, Mary. "The Discovery of Ruby." *James Joyce Quarterly* 18.2 (1981): 115–21.
Pratt, Dale J. *Signs of Science: Literature, Science, and Spanish Modernity since 1968.* West Lafayette, IA: Purdue University Press, 2001.
Press and Speech Freedoms in the World, from Antiquity until 1998: A Chronology. Comp. Louis Edward Ingelhart. Westport, CT: Greenwood Press, 1998.
Preston, Paul. *Franco: A Biography.* New York: Basic Books, 1994.
Proctor, Robert N. *Cancer Wars: How Politics Shapes What We Know and Don't Know about Cancer.* New York: HarperCollins, 1996.
Proffer, Carl R. *Keys to* Lolita. Bloomington: Indiana University Press, 1968.
Prokhorov, Alexander. "Accommodating Consumers' Desires: El'dar Riazanov's Memoirs in Soviet and Post-Soviet Russia." *The Russian Memoir.* Evanston, IL: Northwestern University Press, 2003. 70–89.
Pushkin, Alexander S. "K A. P. Kern." *Sochineniia.* Moscow: Khudozhestvennaia literatura, 1949. 119.
———. "Skazka o rybake i rybke." *Sochineniia.* Moscow: Khudozhestvennaia literatura, 1949. 393–95.
Racevskis, Karlis. *Michel Foucault and the Subversion of the Intellect.* Ithaca, NY: Cornell University Press, 1983.
Radley, Philippe D. "Censorship as a Creative Stimulus: The Russian Experience." *World Literature Today* 53 (1979): 201–5.
Raguet-Bouvart, Christine. Lolita: *Un royaume au-delà des mers.* Talence: Presses universi-

taires de Bordeaux, 1996.

Ramos Gascón, Antonio, ed. *Spain Today: In Search of Modernity*. Madrid: Cátedra, 1991.

Ramsey, Harly. "Mourning, Melancholia, and the Maternal Body: Cultural Constructions of Bereavement in *Ulysses.*" *Joycean Cultures/Culturing Joyces*. Ed. Vincent J. Cheng, Kimberly J. Devlin, and Margot Norris. Newark: University of Delaware Press, 1998. 59–77.

Rancour-Laferrière, Daniel. Introduction. *Russian Literature and Psychoanalysis*. Amsterdam: John Benjamins, 1989. 1–38.

———, ed. *Russian Literature and Psychoanalysis*. Amsterdam: John Benjamins, 1989.

Randall, Richard S. *Freedom and Taboo: Pornography and the Politics of a Self Divided*. Berkeley: University of California Press, 1989.

Rapin, Ronald F. "The Phantom Pages of Luis Martín Santos' *Tiempo de silencio*." *Neophilologus* 71.2 (April 1987): 235–43.

Reck, Vera T. *Boris Pil'niak: A Soviet Writer in Conflict with the State*. Montreal: McGill-Queen's University Press, 1975.

The Red Pencil: Artists, Scholars, and Censors in the USSR. Ed. Marianna Tax Choldin and Maurice Friedberg. Boston: Unwin Hyman, 1989.

Reich, Wilhelm. *The Mass Psychology of Fascism*. Trans. Vincent R. Carfagno. New York: Farrar, Straus & Giroux, 1970.

Reig Tapia, Alberto. *Ideología e historia: Sobre la represión franquista y la guerra civil*. Madrid: Akal, 1984.

Renegotiating Ethics in Literature, Philosophy, and Theory. Ed. Jane Adamson, Richard Freadman, and David Parker. Cambridge: Cambridge University Press, 1998.

Restuccia, Frances L. "From Typology to Typography." *Joyce and the Law of the Father*. New Haven, CT: Yale University Press, 1989. 20–72.

———. "From Whip to Reed." *Joyce and the Law of the Father*. New Haven, CT: Yale University Press, 1989. 1–19.

———. *Joyce and the Law of the Father*. New Haven, CT: Yale University Press, 1989.

Rey, Alfonso. *Construcción y sentido de* Tiempo de silencio. Madrid: Porrúa, 1977.

Rickard, John S. *Joyce's Book of Memory: The Mnemotechnic of* Ulysses. Durham, NC, and London: Duke University Press, 1999.

Riezu, Jorge. *Análisis sociológico de la novela* Tiempo de silencio. Salamanca: San Esteban, 1993.

Riffaterre, Michael. "The Intertextual Unconscious." *Critical Inquiry* 13.2 (Winter 1987): 371–85.

Rigby, Brian. "L'affaire *Lolita*." *La censure en France à l'ère démocratique (1848– . . .): Histoire culturelle*. Ed. Pascal Ory. Bruxelles: Complexe, 1997. 305–12.

Rippon, Maria R. *Judgment and Justification in the Nineteenth-Century Novel of Adultery*. Westport, CT: Greenwood, 2002.

Riquelme, John Paul. *Teller and Tale in Joyce's Fiction: Oscillating Perspectives*. Baltimore, MD, and London: Johns Hopkins University Press, 1983.

Riviere, Joan. "Womanliness as a Masquerade." 1929. *Psychoanalysis and Female Sexuality*. New Haven, CT: College & University Press, 1966. 209–20.

Robbins, Louise S. *Censorship and the American Library: The American Library Association's Response to Threats to Intellectual Freedom, 1939–1969*. Westport, CT: Greenwood, 1996.

Roberts, Gemma. *Temas existenciales en la novela española de postguerra*. Madrid: Gredos, 1973.

Robins, Natalie. *Alien Ink: The FBI's War on Freedom of Expression.* New York: William Morrow and Company, 1992.
Robinson, Paul. *The Freudian Left: Wilhelm Reich, Geze Roheim, Herbert Marcuse.* New York: Harper & Row, 1969.
———. *The Modernization of Sex: Havelock Ellis, Alfred Kinsey, William Masters and Virginia Johnson.* New York: Harper & Row, 1976.
Rodríguez García, José María. "Determinismo, destino y fatalidad en *Tiempo de silencio* (a propósito de dos nuevos subtextos ingleses)." *Anales de la literatura española contemporánea* 27.2 (2002): 261–78.
Rorty, Richard. "The Barber of Kasbeam: Nabokov on Cruelty." *Contingency, Irony, and Solidarity.* Cambridge: Cambridge University Press, 1989. 141–68.
———. *Contingency, Irony, and Solidarity.* Cambridge: Cambridge University Press, 1989.
Rose, Jacqueline. *The Case of Peter Pan or the Impossibility of Children's Fiction.* London: Macmillan, 1984.
Rothstein, Eric. "'Lolita': Nymphet at Normal School." *Contemporary Literature* 41.1 (Spring 2000): 22–55.
Rozanov, Vasilii Vasil'evich. *Liudi lunnogo sveta: Metafizika khristianstva.* Moscow: Druzhba narodov, 1990.
———. *V mire neiasnogo i nereshennogo; Iz vostochnykh motivov.* Moscow: Respublika, 1995.
Russian Culture at the Crossroads: Paradoxes of Postcommunist Consciousness. Ed. Dmitri N. Shalin. Boulder, CO: Westview, 1996.
Ruud, Charles A. *Fighting Words: Imperial Censorship and the Russian Press, 1804–1906.* Toronto: University of Toronto Press, 1982.
Rylkova, Galina. "The Apocalypse Revisited: Viktor Erofeev's *Russian Beauty.*" *Gender and Sexuality in Russian Civilization.* Ed. Peter I. Barta. London and New York: Routledge, 2001. 325–43.
———. "Silver Spoons in Their Mouths: The Legacy of the Russian Silver Age in the Works of Nabokov, Pasternak and Viktor Erofeev." Diss., University of Toronto, 1998.
Sacher-Masoch, Leopold, Ritter von. "Venus in Furs." *Masochism: Coldness and Cruelty.* By Gilles Deleuze. New York: Zone Books, 1989. 143–271.
Sade, D. A. F. de. *La philosophie dans le boudoir.* Œuvres complètes. Vol. 25. Paris: Jean-Jacques Pauvert, 1970.
Said, Edward W. "Identity, Negation and Violence." *New Left Review* 171 (September–October 1988): 46–60.
Sammells, Neil. "Writing and Censorship: An Introduction." *Writing and Censorship in Britain.* Ed. Paul Hyland and Neil Sammells. London: Routledge, 1992. 1–14.
Sánchez Reboredo, José. *Palabras tachadas: Retórica contra censura.* Alicante: Instituto de estudios «Juan Gil-Albert», 1988.
Saunders, David. "Victorian Obscenity Law: Negative Censorship or Positive Administration?" *Writing and Censorship in Britain.* Ed. Paul Hyland and Neil Sammells. London: Routledge, 1992. 154–70.
Schacht, Richard. "Alienation." *Encyclopedia of Ethics.* Vol. 1. Ed. Lawrence C. Becker. Chicago and London: St. James, 1992. 33–35.
Schauer, Frederick. "The Ontology of Censorship." *Censorship and Silencing: Practices of Cultural Regulation.* Ed. Robert C. Post. Santa Monica, CA: Getty Foundation and Oxford University Press, 1998. 147–68.
Schiller, Friedrich von. "On the Sublime." *"Naïve and Sentimental Poetry" and "On the Sublime": Two Essays.* Trans. Julius A. Elias. New York: Ungar, 1966. 193–212, 220.

Schneiderman, Leo. "Nabokov: Aestheticism with a Human Face, Half-Averted." *Psychoanalysis and Contemporary Thought* 8 (1985): 105–30.

Scholes, Robert. *Protocols of Reading*. New Haven, CT: Yale University Press, 1989.

Schwaber, Paul. *The Cast of Characters: A Reading of Ulysses*. New Haven, CT: Yale University Press, 1999.

Schweighauser, Philipp. "Metafiction, Transcendence, and Death in Nabokov's *Lolita*." *Nabokov Studies* 5 (1998–1999): 99–116.

Scotto, Peter. "Censorship, Reading, and Interpretation: A Case Study from the Soviet Union." *PMLA* 109 (1994): 61–70.

Sexuality and the Body in Russian Culture. Ed. Jane T. Costlow, Stephanie Sandler, and Judith Vowles. Stanford, CA: Stanford University Press, 1993.

Shackleton, Robert. *Censure and Censorship: Impediments to Free Publication in the Age of Enlightenment*. Austin, TX: Humanities Research Center, 1975.

Shaffer, Brian W. "Negotiating Self and Culture: Narcissism, Competing Discourses, and Ideological Becoming in 'Penelope.'" *Molly Blooms: A Polylogue on "Penelope" and Cultural Studies*. Madison: University of Wisconsin Press, 1994. 139–51.

Shakespeare, William. "Hamlet." *The Complete Works*. Ed. Charles Jasper Sisson. New York and Evanston, IL: Harper & Row, 1953. 997–1042.

———. "The Merchant of Venice." *The Complete Works*. Ed. Charles Jasper Sisson. New York and Evanston, IL: Harper & Row, 1953. 231–59.

———. "Othello." *The Complete Works*. Ed. Charles Jasper Sisson. New York and Evanston, IL: Harper & Row, 1953. 1083–1123.

Shanor, Donald R. *Behind the Lines: The Private War against Soviet Censorship*. New York: St. Martin's Press, 1985.

Shechner, Mark. *Joyce in Nighttown: A Psychoanalytic Inquiry into Ulysses*. Berkeley: University of California Press, 1974.

Shelton, Jen. "'The Word Is Incest': Sexual and Linguistic Coercion in *Lolita*." *Textual Practice* 13.2 (Summer 1999): 273–94.

Shneidman, N. N. *Russian Literature, 1988–1994: The End of an Era*. Toronto: University of Toronto Press, 1995.

———. *Russian Literature, 1995–2002: On the Threshold of the New Millennium*. Toronto: University of Toronto Press, 2004.

———. *Soviet Literature in the 1970s: Artistic Diversity and Ideological Conformity*. Toronto: University of Toronto Press, 1979.

———. *Soviet Literature in the 1980s: Decade of Transition*. Toronto: University of Toronto Press, 1989.

Showalter, Elaine. *Sexual Anarchy: Gender and Culture at the Fin de Siècle*. New York: Viking, 1990.

Shute, Jenefer. "Nabokov and Freud." *The Garland Companion to Vladimir Nabokov*. Ed. Vladimir Alexandrov. New York: Garland, 1995. 412–20.

———. "'So Nakedly Dressed': The Text of the Female Body in Nabokov's Novels." *Vladimir Nabokov's* Lolita: *A Casebook*. Ed. Ellen Pifer. Oxford and New York: Oxford University Press, 2003. 111–20.

Sieburth, Stephanie. *Inventing High and Low: Literature, Mass Culture, and Uneven Modernity in Spain*. Durham, NC, and London: Duke University Press, 1994.

Silverman, Kaja. *The Acoustic Mirror: The Female Voice in Psychoanalysis and Cinema*. Bloomington: Indiana University Press, 1988.

———. *Male Subjectivity at the Margins*. New York: Routledge, 1992.

Simpson, Mark S. *The Russian Gothic Novel and Its British Antecedents.* Columbus: Slavica, 1986.
Siniavskii, Andrei. *On Socialist Realism.* New York: Pantheon, 1960.
Sinova, Justino. *La censura de prensa durante el franquismo (1936–1951).* Madrid: Espasa Calpe, 1989.
Škulj, Jola. "The Modern Novel: The Concept of Spatialization (Frank) and the Dialogic Principle (Bakhtin)." *Proceedings of the XIIth Congress of the International Comparative Literature Association: Space and Boundaries in Literary Theory and Criticism.* Vol. 5. Munich: iudicium, 1990. 43–50.
Slonim, Marc. *Soviet Russian Literature: Writers and Problems, 1917–1977.* New York: Oxford University Press, 1977.
Sloterdijk, Peter. *Critique of Cynical Reason.* Trans. Michael Eldred. Theory and History of Literature. Vol. 40. Minneapolis: University of Minnesota Press, 1987.
Smirnoff, Victor. "The Masochistic Contract." *Essential Papers on Masochism.* Ed. M. A. F. Hanly. New York: New York University Press, 1995. 62–73.
Smith, Eric D. "'I Have Been a Perfect Pig': A Semiosis of Swine in 'Circe.'" *Joyce Annual Studies* 13 (Summer 2002): 129–46.
Smith, Peter Alderson. "*The Countess Cathleen* and the Otherworld." *Eire-Ireland: A Journal of Irish Studies* 17.2 (Summer 1982): 141–46.
Smith, S. Stephenson, and Andrei Isotoff. "The Abnormal from Within: Dostoevsky." *The Psychoanalytic Review* 22 (October 1935): 361–91.
Solomon, Robert. "Existentialism." *Dictionary of Philosophy.* Ed. Thomas Mautner. London: Penguin, 1997. 186–88.
Solzhenitsyn, Alexander. Nobel Lecture. http://nobelprize.org/literature/laureates/1970/index.html (accessed April 29, 2006).
Southworth, Herbert Rutledge. "The Falange: An Analysis of Spain's Fascist Heritage." *Spain in Crisis: The Evolution and Decline of the Franco Régime.* Ed. Paul Preston. Hassocks, Sussex, UK: Harvester, 1976.
The Soviet Censorship. Ed. Martin Dewhirst and Robert Farrell. Metuchen, NJ: Scarecrow Press, 1973.
"Spain: *Indice:* Twenty Years of Censorship." *Index on Censorship* 1.3 (1972): 197–210.
Spires, Robert C. *Beyond the Metafictional Mode: Directions in the Modern Spanish Novel.* Lexington: University Press of Kentucky, 1984.
———. "The Discursive Field of *Tiempo de silencio.*" *Intertextual Pursuits: Literary Mediations in Modern Spanish Narrative.* Ed. Jeanne P. Brownlow and John W. Kronik. Lewisburg, PA: Bucknell University Press, 1998. 161–78.
———. *La novela española de posguerra: Creación artística y experiencia personal.* Madrid: Cupsa, 1978.
———. *Post-Totalitarian Spanish Fiction.* Columbia and London: University of Missouri Press, 1996.
Spoo, Robert. "Uncanny Returns in 'The Dead': Ibsenian Intertexts and the Estranged Infant." *Joyce: The Return of the Repressed.* Ed. Susan Stanford Friedman. Ithaca, NY: Cornell University Press, 1993. 89–113.
Staten, Henry. *Eros in Mourning: Homer to Lacan.* Baltimore, MD: Johns Hopkins University Press, 1995.
Stegner, Page. *Escape into Aesthetics: The Art of Vladimir Nabokov.* London: Eyre and Spottiswoode, 1967.
Steuer, Daniel. "A Book That Won't Go Away: Otto Weininger's *Sex and Character.*" Intro-

duction. *Sex and Character: An Investigation of Fundamental Principles.* By Otto Weininger. Ed. Daniel Steuer with Laura Marcus. Trans. Ladislaus Löb. Bloomington and Indianapolis: Indiana University Press, 2005. xi–xlvi.

Stevenson, Robert Louis. *Dr. Jekyll and Mr. Hyde.* New York: Signet, 1980.

———. *Treasure Island.* Ed. Wendy R. Katz. Edinburgh: Edinburgh University Press, 1998.

Stewart, Suzanne R. *Sublime Surrender: Male Masochism at the Fin-de-siècle.* Ithaca, NY, and London: Cornell University Press, 1998.

Stoljar, Samuel. *Moral and Legal Reasoning.* London and Basingstoke: Macmillan, 1980.

Stoltzfus, Ben. Introduction. *Lacan and Literature: Purloined Pretexts.* Albany: State University of New York Press, 1996. 1–17.

Strauss, Leo. *Persecution and the Art of Writing.* Westport, CT: Greenwood, 1973.

Streliani, Anatoli. "Signs of Life." *Index on Censorship* 18.3 (1989): 21–25.

Štulhofer, Aleksandar, and Theo Sandfort. "Sexuality and Gender in Times of Transition." Introduction. *Sexuality and Gender in Postcommunist Eastern Europe and Russia.* New York and London: Haworth, 2005. 1–25.

Suagee, Stephen. "An Artist's Memory Beats All Other Kinds: An Essay on *Despair.*" *A Book of Things about Vladimir Nabokov.* Ed. Carl R. Proffer. Ann Arbor, MI: Ardis, 1974. 54–62.

Swayze, Harold. *Political Control of Literature in the USSR, 1946–1959.* Cambridge, MA: Harvard University Press, 1962.

Tamir-Ghez, Nomi. "The Art of Persuasion in Nabokov's *Lolita.*" *Poetics Today* 1.1–2 (1979): 65–83.

Tanner, Tony. *Adultery in the Novel: Contract and Transgression.* Baltimore, MD: Johns Hopkins University Press, 1979.

Téna, Jean, ed. *Luis Martín Santos:* Tiempo de silencio: *Une écriture de silence.* Co-textes CERS (November 1980).

Terrón Montero, Javier. *La prensa en España durante el régimen de Franco: Un intento de análisis político.* Madrid: Centro de investigaciones sociológicas, 1981.

Thody, P. M. W. *Four Cases of Literary Censorship.* Leeds: Leeds University Press, 1968.

Thomas, Brook. "*Ulysses* on Trial: Some Supplementary Reading." *The Administration of Aesthetics: Censorship, Political Criticism, and the Public Sphere.* Ed. Richard Burt. Minneapolis: University of Minnesota Press, 1994. 125–48.

Thomières, Daniel. "Cherchez la femme: Who Really Was Annabel Leigh?" *Journal of Modern Literature* 23.1 (Summer 1999): 165–71.

Tiutchev, Fedor Ivanovich. "How murderously we love." Trans. Richard A. Gregg. *Fedor Tiutchev: The Evolution of a Poet* by Richard A. Gregg. New York and London: Columbia University Press, 1965. 163.

———. "I sit pensive and alone." *Poems and Political Letters of F. I. Tyutchev.* Trans. Jesse Zeldin. Knoxville: University of Tennessee Press, 1973.

———. "O, kak ubiistvenno my liubim." *Polnoe sobranie stikhotvorenii.* Leningrad: Sovetskii pisatel', 1957. 188–89.

———. *Poems and Political Letters.* Trans. Jesse Zeldin. Knoxville: University of Tennessee Press, 1973.

———. "Sizhu zadumchiv i odin." *Polnoe sobranie stikhotvorenii.* Leningrad: Sovetskii pisatel,' 1957. 146–47.

"*To Deprave and Corrupt . . .*": *Original Studies in the Nature and Definition of "Obscenity."* Ed. John Chandos. New York: Association Press, 1962.

Toker, Leona. "L'éthique du camouflage narratif." Trans. Hélène Fiamma. *Europe* 791 (March 1995): 71–80.

Tribe, David. *Questions of Censorship.* London: George Allen & Unwin, 1973.

Trilling, Lionel. "The Last Lover: Vladimir Nabokov's *Lolita.*" *Vladimir Nabokov's* Lolita. Ed. Harold Bloom. New York: Chelsea House, 1987. 5–11.

Tsenzura v tsarskoi Rossii i Sovetskom Soiuze: Materialy konferentsii 24–27 maia 1993 r. Ed. T. V. Gromova. Moscow: Rudomino, 1995.

Tsymbal, Evgenii. "Damming the Tide of Glasnost." *Index on Censorship* 20.3 (1991): 21–22.

Twarog, Leon I. "Literary Censorship in Russia and the Soviet Union." *Essays on Russian Intellectual History.* Ed. Leon Borden Blair. Austin: University of Texas Press, 1971. 98–123.

Ugarte, Michael. "*Tiempo de silencio* and the Language of Displacement." *MLN* 96.2 (1981): 340–57.

Ungar, Andras P. "Among the Hapsburgs: Arthur Griffith, Stephen Dedalus, and the Myth of Bloom." *Twentieth Century Literature* 35.4 (Winter 1989): 480–51.

The United States of America v. One Book Entitled Ulysses *by James Joyce: Documents and Commentary; a 50-Year Retrospective.* Ed. Michael Moscato and Leslie LeBlanc. Frederick, MD: University Publications of America, 1984.

Valente, Joseph. "The Perils of Masculinity in 'Scylla and Charybdis.'" Ulysses—*En-Gendered Perspectives: Eighteen New Essays on the Episodes.* Ed. Kimberly J. Devlin and Marilyn Reizbaum. Columbia: University of South Carolina Press, 1999. 111–35, 296–98.

Vanderham, Paul. "Ezra Pound's Censorship of *Ulysses.*" *James Joyce Quarterly* 32.3–4 (1995): 583–95.

———. *James Joyce and Censorship: The Trials of Ulysses.* New York: New York University Press, 1998.

Venturi, Franco. *Roots of Revolution: A History of the Populist and Socialist Movements in Nineteenth Century Russia.* Trans. Francis Haskell. New York: Universal Library, 1966.

Versions of Censorship. Ed. John McCormick and Mairi MacInnes. Chicago: Aldine, 1962.

Vice, Sue. "The Construction of Femininity in *Ulysses* and *Under the Volcano*: A Bakhtinian Analysis of the Late Draft Versions." *Joyce/Lowry: Critical Perspectives.* Ed. Patrick A. McCarthy and Paul Tiessen. Lexington: University Press of Kentucky, 1997. 96–108.

———. *Introducing Bakhtin.* Manchester and New York: Manchester University Press, 1997.

Vladimir Nabokov's Lolita: *A Casebook.* Ed. Ellen Pifer. Oxford and New York: Oxford University Press, 2003.

Vladimirov, Leonid. "Glavlit: How the Soviet Censor Works." *Index on Censorship* 1.3–4 (1972): 31–43.

Voronina, Olga. "Virgin Mary or Mary Magdalene? The Construction and Reconstruction of Sex during the Perestroika Period." *Women in Russia: A New Era in Russian Feminism.* Ed. Anastasia Posadskaya et al. Trans. Kate Clark. London: Verso, 1994. 135–45.

Vries, Gerard de. "'Perplex'd in the Extreme': Moral Facets of Vladimir Nabokov's Work." *Nabokov Studies* 2 (1995): 135–52.

Wagner, Peter. Introduction. *Fanny Hill: Or Memoirs of a Woman of Pleasure.* By John Cleland. Harmondsworth, UK: Penguin, 1986. 7–30.

Wagner, Richard. *Der Ring des Nibelungen.* Deutsche Grammophon, 1998.

Walsh, Michael J. "Church Censorship in the 19th Century: The Index of Leo XIII." *Censorship and the Control of Print in England and France, 1600–1910.* Ed. Robin Myers and

Michael Harris. Winchester, UK: St Paul's Bibliographies, 1992. 111–22.

Walter, Brian D. "Romantic Parody and the Ironic Muse in *Lolita.*" *Essays in Literature* 22.1 (Spring 1995): 123–43.

Ward, Ian. *Kantianism, Postmodernism and Critical Legal Thought*. Dordrecht: Kluwer, 1997.

Wasserman, Carol. "A Stylist, an Institution, a Book: Cela, Censorship, and *Mazurca para dos muertos.*" *Review of Contemporary Fiction* 4.3 (1984): 44–49.

Weeks, Jeffrey. *Sex, Politics and Society: The Regulation of Sexuality since 1800*. London: Longman, 1981.

———. *Sexuality*. Chichester, West Sussex, UK: E. Horwood; London and New York: Tavistock, 1986.

———. *Sexuality and Its Discontents: Meanings, Myths and Modern Sexualities*. London: Routledge, 1985.

Weininger, Otto. *Sex and Character: An Investigation of Fundamental Principles*. Ed. Daniel Steuer with Laura Marcus. Trans. Ladislaus Löb. Bloomington and Indianapolis: Indiana University Press, 2005.

Weir, David. "What Did He Know, and When Did He Know It: The *Little Review*, Joyce, and *Ulysses.*" *James Joyce Quarterly* 37.3–4 (Spring–Summer 2000): 389–412.

Welsen, Peter. "Charles Kinbote's Psychosis—A Key to Vladimir Nabokov's *Pale Fire.*" *Russian Literature and Psychoanalysis*. Ed. Daniel Rancour-Laferrière. Amsterdam: John Benjamins, 1989. 381–400.

Wexler, Joyce. "Selling Sex as Art." *Marketing Modernisms: Self-Promotion, Canonization, Rereading*. Ed. Kevin J. H. Dettmar and Stephen Watt. Ann Arbor: University of Michigan Press, 1996. 91–108.

Whiting, Frederick. "'The Strange Particularity of the Lover's Preference': Pedophilia, Pornography, and the Anatomy on Montrosity in *Lolita.*" *American Literature: A Journal of Literary History, Criticism, and Bibliography* 70.4 (December 1998): 833–62.

Whitman, Walt. *Leaves of Grass and Selected Prose*. New York: Modern Library, 1950.

Women in Russia. Ed. Dorothy Atkinson, Alexander Dallin, and Gail Warshofsky Lapidus. Stanford, CA: Stanford University Press, 1977.

Women in Russia and Ukraine. Ed. and trans. Rosalind Marsh. Cambridge: Cambridge University Press, 1996.

Wood, Michael. *The Magician's Doubts: Nabokov and the Risks of Fiction*. London: Chatto & Windus, 1994.

Woolsey, John M., Jr. "Judge John M. Woolsey." *James Joyce Quarterly* 37.3–4 (Spring–Summer 2000): 367–69.

Wozniuk, Vladimir. "Soviet Censorship's 'True Colors': A Chameleon Adapting to Glasnost." *Patterns of Censorship around the World*. Ed. Ilan Peleg. Boulder, CO: Westview, 1993. 35–48.

Writing and Censorship in Britain. Ed. Paul Hyland and Neil Sammells. London: Routledge, 1992.

Wylie, Kathryn. *Satyric and Heroic Mimes: Attitude as the Way of the Mime in Ritual and Beyond*. Jefferson, NC, and London: McFarland, 1994.

Yeats, W. B. *The Countess Cathleen: Manuscript Materials*. Ed. Michael J. Sidnell and Wayne K. Chapman. Ithaca, NY and London: Cornell University Press, 1999.

———. "Who Goes with Fergus?" *Major British Writers*. Vol. 2. Ed. George Bagshawe Harrison. New York: Harcourt, Brace, 1959. 790.

Zaczek, Barbara Maria. *Censored Sentiments: Letters and Censorship in Epistolary Novels and Conduct Material*. Newark: University of Delaware Press, 1997.

Zamiatin, Evgenii Ivanovich. *My.* Moscow: Molodaia gvardiia, 1990.
———. *We.* Trans. Clarence Brown. New York: Penguin, 1993.
Zavala, Iris. "Bakhtin and the Third: Communication as Response." *Critical Studies* 1.2 (1989): 43–63.
Ziarek, Ewa Plonowska. "'Circe': Joyce's *Argumentum ad Feminam.*" *Gender in Joyce.* Ed. Jolanta W. Wawrzycka and Marlena G. Corcoran. Gainesville: University of Florida Press, 1997. 150–69.
Zichy, Francis. "Readerly/Writerly Text." *Encyclopedia of Contemporary Literary Theory: Approaches, Scholars, Terms.* Ed. Irena Makaryk. Toronto: University of Toronto Press, 1995. 616–17.
Žižek, Slavoj. *Metastases of Enjoyment: Six Essays on Woman and Causality.* London: Verso, 1994.
———. *The Sublime Object of Ideology.* London: Verso, 1995.
———. *Tarrying with the Negative: Kant, Hegel, and the Critique of Ideology.* Durham, NC: Duke University Press, 1993.
Zlosnik, Sue. "Meredith, George." *The Literary Encyclopedia.* September 20, 2002. The Literary Dictionary Company. http://www.litencyc.com/ (accessed on January 6, 2006).
Zorrilla, José. *Don Juan Tenorio.* Ed. Aniano Peña. Madrid: Cátedra, 1999.
Zverev, Aleksei. "Literary Return to Russia." Trans. Anna K. Primrose. *The Garland Companion to Vladimir Nabokov.* Ed. Vladimir Alexandrov. New York: Garland, 1995. 291–305.

Index

abortion, 34, 162, 164, 165, 170, 171, 180, 187n31, 189, 190, 201n40, 202, 203, 205, 210, 211, 229, 244, 257. *See also* birth; pregnancy
adultery, xiv, xv, 12, 17, 26, 43, 57, 58, 60, 69, 75, 77, 84–87, 97, 102, 107, 218, 226, 238, 251, 254, 259
Alice in Wonderland. *See* Carroll.
alienation: 36, 272; and *Lolita*, 123, 139; and *Russkaia krasavitsa*, 258–67, 261; and *Tiempo de silencio*, 161, 164, 165–72, 167n9, 168, 174, 176, 180, 189, 193, 195, 196, 200; and *Ulysses*, 60, 68n40, 90, 91, 96, 105
Althusser, Louis, 35n14
Anna Karenina (Tolstoi), 57n22, 215, 226, 226n13, 261
Anderson, Hans Christian, 150
apocalypse, 15, 35, 58, 63n33, 98n68, 100, 104, 105, 188, 215–17, 219, 221n6, 222, 223, 230–40, 230n19, 231nn20–21, 242, 249, 252, 258, 260, 261, 266, 268
El árbol de la ciencia (*The Tree of Science*) (Baroja), 175
Aristophanes, 230n18, 244

Bakhtin, M. M., 41n4, 43, 44n9, 46, 49n12, 56n18, 61n29, 64n35, 141, 142, 151, 217, 271. *See also* character zones; dialogism; heteroglossia; narrative; narrators
Baroja, Pío, 175
Barrie, J. M., 114n3, 125, 125n14, 126, 150
Barthes, Roland, xii, 13, 46, 64, 64n34, 151
beautiful, the, ix, xi, xiv, 36, 37, 76, 84, 94, 96, 119, 125, 135, 140, 145, 149, 150, 156, 159, 164, 186, 192, 193, 213, 215, 215n1, 216–18, 219–30, 225n10 and n12, 230–40, 236n27, 240–44, 247n37, 248–58, 257n46, 260–67, 264n52, 269–74. *See also* beautiful woman; *blason du corps feminin*; Blok; Burke; Dostoevsky; heroine; Kant; Tiutchev
beautiful woman (*prekrasnaia dama*), 226, 229, 248, 250, 270. *See also* beautiful; *blason du corps feminin*; Blok; Dostoevsky; femininity; femme fatale; heroine; Tiutchev
Beauvoir, Simone de, 129n17
Berdiaev, Nikolai, 32n9, 232, 249
birth, 70n42, 76n47, 78n50, 88–89n57,

116, 136, 141, 159, 173, 207, 208, 229, 229n16, 232, 256, 266n55. *See also* abortion; pregnancy
blason du corps feminin, 119, 121n9, 139
Blok, Aleksander, 219, 222, 226, 227, 232, 243, 248, 249, 261
Boheemen-Saaf, Christine van, 63n33, 97, 97n67
Boone, Joseph Allen, 51n13
Borenstein, Eliot, 248, 250, 256
Bourdieu, Pierre, xii, 5, 80
Bowen, Zack, 91n60, 109n76, 110
Boyd, Brian, 28n4, 125n15, 129n17, 131n19
bride. *See* marriage
Brivic, Sheldon, 60, 90n60
Brodsky, Joseph, 31n7, 225n12
Brooks, Peter, 17n19, 62n32, 64, 235n26, 237n28, 245n33
brothel, and *Tiempo de silencio,* 162–64, 164n4, 165, 167, 172, 177, 178n21, 200–208, 203n41, 209, 274, 275; and *Ulysses,* 42, 43n7, 51, 51n15, 56, 58, 64, 65, 73, 84, 91n11, 93, 95, 98, 103, 271, 275. *See also* prostitution
Brown, Richard, 41n4, 62n32
bullfight (*corrida; lidia*), 183, 183n27, 186, 192, 193
Burke, Edmund, 227, 240, 241, 261, 264n52
El burlador de Sevilla (Tirso de Molina), 175n16, 187n31. *See also* Law; theater

cancer, 30, 37, 93, 93n61, 96, 109, 164, 166, 167–75, 170nn11–12, 179, 182n26, 189, 190, 196–200, 199n38, 203, 208–12, 212n46, 213, 270, 274
Carmen, 122n10, 131, 131n19, 133, 274
Carroll, Lewis, 125, 125n15, 126, 150, 150n32
castration, 36n15, 49, 50, 53, 58n24, 89n59, 161, 170, 174, 176, 176n18, 178, 189, 193, 213, 214, 271
Catholicism, xii, 5, 7, 27, 33, 34, 39, 41, 50, 53, 58, 60, 66n36, 77, 79, 81, 92, 93, 93n61, 95, 96, 101, 107–9, 138, 139, 163, 168, 172, 176, 185, 208, 247, 270, 272
censoring (artistic), x, xii, xiv, 2, 8, 14, 15–21, 24, 26, 27, 38, 268, 271–76; in *Lolita,* 26, 119, 124, 129n17, 131, 132, 135, 144, 145–52, 154, 155, 157–60; in *Russkaia krasavitsa,* 217, 224, 232, 239, 242, 243, 247, 251, 254–58, 262–65; in *Tiempo de silencio,* 161, 162, 165, 166, 172–78, 179, 181–85, 188–95, 197, 200–202, 206, 208, 209, 211–14; in *Ulysses,* 26, 39–41, 52, 53, 55, 56, 59–63, 67, 69, 71, 72–74, 77–93, 96–101, 105, 107, 109–111. *See also* narrative; negation
censorship, etymology of, 3–8; political, 1–8, 8–11, 14–15, 19–21, 23–38, 39, 40, 40–41nn1–2, 42nn3–4, 52, 60, 68, 68n40, 72, 80, 107, 161, 162, 162–63n3, 176, 177, 184, 184n28, 194, 194n35, 200, 203, 205, 205n43, 215, 216, 216n2, 217, 217n3, 223, 230–33, 238, 238n30, 239, 240, 246, 247, 246–47n36, 247n38, 250, 253n42, 255–57, 260, 266, 267, 277–78; post-publication, 3–8, 11–15, 20–21, 23–31; pre-publication (prior), 3–8, 11–15, 31–38, 20–21 23–24, 31–38; psychoanalytic, 2, 8–11, 8n10, 16, 23, 103n72; religious, xi n1, 3–8, 10–13, 26–27, 31, 31n7, 32, 33, 33n10, 82, 86, 101, 247
Cervantes, Miguel de, 174, 175n16, 193, 197
character zones (*zony geroev*), 35, 61, 61n29, 67, 72, 103, 105, 106, 114, 132, 136, 149, 160, 162, 184. *See also* Bakhtin
child, 4, 16, 37, 70, 76, 89n57, 95, 104, 105, 110, 112, 114n3, 115, 117, 119, 120–25, 125nn14–15, 126–28, 128n19, 132, 132nn20–21, 133–60, 137nn24–25, 152n33, 227–29, 235, 237, 246, 250, 254, 257, 270, 274, 275. *See also* girl; sons
Christ, Jesus, 77, 83, 84, 94, 95n64, 97n67, 105, 109, 215, 222, 231, 233, 234, 239, 256, 274. *See also* apocalypse; birth; Christianity; Easter; martyrs; sons
Christianity, 10, 12, 71n44, 77, 83, 84, 94, 95n64, 97n67, 102n71, 105, 109, 215, 223, 231, 233, 234, 239, 248, 256, 257, 274. *See also* apocalypse; birth; Catholicism; Christ; confession; Easter; martyrs
Cleland, John, 44–45n10, 144, 216
clothes, 12, 51n14, 63, 84, 89–91, 237,

237n28, 257
commedia dell'arte, 43, 99. See also irony; pantomime; theater
confession, x, xiii, 15, 18, 20, 26 35, 269, 273, 274–75; in *Lolita*, 26, 112, 114–18, 121, 127–30, 135–38, 137n25, 139–45, 152, 154–60, 269, 273, 274; in *Russkaia krasavitsa*, 35, 216, 218, 226, 227, 242, 243, 253, 254, 254n44, 258, 262, 269, 273; in *Tiempo de silencio,* 168; in *Ulysses,* 101. See also Catholicism; discourse; Foucault; masochism; narrators; narrative; *pícaro/pícara;* rogue narrators
copy, 112, 119, 122, 122n10, 155, 218, 219, 230, 242, 266. See also double; fantasy; masochism; mimesis; repetition
copyright, 4, 13
Countess Cathleen, The (Yeats), 97–98n67, 103, 107–9, 107n75. See also "Who Goes with Fergus?"; Yeats
cuckold, 60, 69, 85, 86, 89n59, 95n64. See also adultery; marriage; masochism
cutting, 36n15, 63, 165–72, 176, 183, 186, 188–90, 192, 193, 213. See also abortion; castration, histology; martyrs; masochism; medicine; science; vivisection

Dark, Oleg, 34n13, 220n5, 230n18, 233n24, 254n45
De Grazia, Edward, xi nn1–2, 4n2, 11n13, 12n16, 25n1, 28n4, 40n1
death, xi, xiv, 17, 36, 37, 272–74; in *Lolita,* 115–20, 135, 136, 143, 145, 146, 148, 151, 158, 159; in *Russkaia krasavitsa,* 215, 219, 221n6, 223, 225n10, 227, 229, 229n16, 230, 231, 234, 235, 238n29, 240, 242, 244, 244n33, 247n37, 249, 250, 254–57, 260–62, 266, 266n55, 267; in *Tiempo de silencio,* 161, 164, 165, 166n6, 169, 171, 178, 180, 183n27, 186, 187, 187n31, 189, 190, 193, 209–11, 214; in *Ulysses,* 42, 43, 43n5, 45, 58n25, 65, 66, 69, 73, 76n47, 77, 78, 78nn49–50, 80, 83, 85–87, 90–91n60, 93n61, 94, 95n64, 96, 97–98n67, 98n68, 100, 102n71, 104, 104n73, 105, 106, 109, 110. See also apocalypse; cancer; femme fatale; negation; martyrs
Defoe, Daniel, 216, 242, 262, 275
Le déjeuner sur l'herbe (Manet), See Manet; painting
Deleuze, Gilles, 48, 88n56, 89n58, 172
Devlin, Kimberly J., 49, 49n12, 50, 58n24, 96n60
dialogism, 41, 44, 44n9, 56n18, 57, 57n21, 60, 65, 69, 70–72, 70n43, 71n44, 87, 93, 100, 103, 105, 110, 114, 124, 142, 143, 150, 185, 217, 271, 276. See also Bakhtin
discourse, x–xiii, 2, 13, 20, 25, 26, 27, 30, 36, 39, 44, 49n9, 46, 47, 52, 61n31, 62, 63, 71n44, 88, 98, 101, 105, 127, 129n16, 138–47, 151, 152, 163, 172, 187, 193, 194, 200, 212, 241, 243, 246, 254, 256, 260, 261, 263, 266, 271; literary (artistic, dramatic; narrative, novelistic), ix, xii, 20, 26, 39, 40n2, 41, 41n4, 43n7, 44, 44n9, 45–47, 47n14, 52, 55, 56, 56n19, 56n20, 57, 59, 60–62, 65, 67–70, 70n43, 71n44, 72, 76, 78, 78n49, 79, 80, 83–86, 88, 89, 89n58, 91, 92, 98, 105, 106, 112, 114, 127, 129n17, 130–33, 132n21, 136–38, 141–52, 157, 160, 162, 163, 167, 176, 179, 194, 214, 227, 243, 248, 253, 260–63, 266, 268, 269, 274. See also narrative
Don Giovanni (Mozart), 76, 76n47
Don Juan, 175n16, 187n31. See also Law; masculinity
Don Quijote (Cervantes), 174, 175n16, 193, 197
Dostoevsky, Fyodor, 141, 142, 215, 215n1, 219, 223, 223n9, 225, 225nn11–12, 226, 227n14, 231, 232, 238n29, 244, 244n33, 250, 253, 253n42, 266, 271. See also *The Idiot; Notes from Underground*
double, 122, 136–38, 159, 169n10, 191n32, 211. See also copy; fantasy; masochism; mimesis; repetition
Dr. Jekyll and Mr. Hyde (Stevenson), 114, 114n3, 142, 143, 143n27, 262n50. See also Stevenson
Dubliners (Joyce), 68n40. See also Joyce

Easter, 70, 94, 96n65. See also birth; Catholicism; Christ; Christianity; confession;

martyrs
Enchanted Hunters, 121n8, 122, 123n11, 124n13, 125n14, 131, 146, 149–51, 154. *See also* fairy tale; mimesis; theater
engagement (compromiso), 35, 161, 184n28. *See also* Sartre
Epshtein, Mikhail, 31n7, 32n9, 34n12, 233n23
Ermolaev, Herman, 31n7, 32n9, 33n10, 216n2, 228, 246n35, 247n38
Erofeev, Viktor, ix, xiv, 1, 8, 18, 20, 34, 37, 38, 215–67, 215n1, 216n2, 217, 219, 225n11, 230n18, 231n21, 236n27, 260n49, 278–79. See also *Russkaia krasavitsa*
Exiles (Joyce), 45, 68n40, 73–74n45. *See also* Joyce

fairy tale, 102, 104, 108, 109, 109n77, 110, 114, 120, 123–27, 131, 139, 142, 145, 146, 149–51, 154, 159, 222, 245, 251, 251n40, 252, 255, 270, 274. *See also* Anderson; Barrie; Carroll; child; fantasy; girl; Grimm Brothers; nymph; Pushkin; sons
fantasy, xi, xi, 2, 8, 10, 15–18, 23–27, 36–38, 268–76; in *Lolita,* 112, 118–39, 122n10, 125n15, 140, 143, 143n28, 144, 150, 151, 155–60; in *Russkaia krasavitsa,* 216, 218, 222, 227, 232, 236, 245, 252, 255, 256, 258–67, 266n55; in *Tiempo de silencio,* 161, 162, 166, 167, 170–82, 182n26, 185, 186, 188–90, 191–201, 204, 207–14; in *Ulysses,* 39, 42, 45, 48, 51, 51n15, 52–54, 60, 61–67, 62–62n33, 70, 72–81, 76n47, 79n51, 82–96, 88–89n57, 101–106, 110
fathers, xiv n4, 4, 6n5, 7, 31, 269, 273; in *Lolita,* 115, 128, 131, 133, 134, 138, 140, 141, 146–51, 154, 159; in *Russkaia krasavitsa,* 34, 228, 245–48, 254–57, 257n7, 263; in *Tiempo de silencio,* 34, 171, 201n40, 209–11; in *Ulysses,* 42, 43, 48, 49, 51n14, 53–55, 57n21, 57–60, 60n28, 62–63n33, 64, 72–81, 83, 84, 87, 89n58, 92–94, 94n63, 97n67, 102–3n71, 104–6, 109–11, 109n76. *See also* castration; Law; patriarchal; sons
femininity, x, 30, 271, 274; in *Lolita,* 112, 119, 133, 146, 147; in *Russkaia krasavitsa,* 216, 223, 227, 228, 230n18, 234, 242, 245, 248, 249, 256, 262, 264; in *Tiempo de silencio,* 163, 172, 187, 208; in *Ulysses,* 39, 49, 49n12, 50–52, 51n13, 59n26, 65, 65–66n36, 77–79, 83, 86–89, 89n59, 97–98n67. *See also* beautiful woman; *blason du corps feminin;* femme fatale; girl; heroine; mothers; *pícaro/pícara;* pregnancy
femme fatale, 95n64, 112, 122n10, 124, 141
film, 6n5, 12n15, 47, 121, 124, 146, 147, 151, 172, 210n45, 246, 247
Finnegans Wake (Joyce), 73–74n45, 259n48
Flaubert, Gustave, xiv, xv, 5, 6n5, 57n22, 238, 238n9. See also *Madame Bovary*
Flavitskii, Konstantin, 229, 229n17. See also *Princess Tarakanova*
focalization, 44, 46, 52, 56n19, 57, 66, 68, 113n2, 118, 125, 136, 143, 160, 168, 180n24, 193, 203, 212. *See also* narratives; narrators
Foucault, Michel, x, xiii, 15, 20, 139, 143
France, x, xi n2, xii, xv, 1, 7, 11, 11n3, 13, 29, 30, 40n1, 62n32, 65, 75, 124, 129n17, 225n11, 235n26, 236–38, 236n27, 271, 275, 278
Franco, Francisco, x, xii, 2, 6, 7, 7n8, 8, 20, 24, 31, 31n8, 32, 31–32n8, 33, 33n10, 34–37, 162, 163, 162–63n3, 171, 176, 179, 194, 195, 200, 203n42, 205, 205n43, 206, 209, 210, 214, 247, 269, 272
Freud, Sigmund, xiii, xiii n3, 8, 8n10, 9, 12n16, 17n19, 36n15, 48, 79, 89n58, 90–91n60, 103n72, 137, 137n25, 172, 176n18, 214. *See also* Lacan; psychoanalysis
Fromm, Erich, 255, 256. *See also* necrophilia

Gay, Peter, 57n23, 244n33
gaze, 36n15, 48, 58, 63, 87, 121, 122, 135, 140, 150, 194, 207, 221. *See also* fantasy; film; mimesis; mirror; painting; photography; voyeurism
ghosts, 42, 45, 46, 49, 57, 58n25, 65, 78n49, 102n71, 102–3n71, 108–10, 121n9, 151,

187n31, 218, 228, 231, 241, 250, 255, 256, 260, 270, 273. *See also* fantasy; gothic; vampires

girl, 40n1, 43, 47, 51nn14–15, 52, 52n16, 84, 96, 112, 113n2, 115–25, 120n7, 121nn8–9, 122n10, 128–38, 129nn16–17, 137n24, 139n26, 142, 143, 145, 146, 148, 151, 154–56, 159–60, 165, 169, 174–78, 182, 182n26, 195, 198, 199, 211, 218, 263, 269, 270, 274, 275. *See also* child

Girodias, Maurice, 28, 28n4, 29, 129n17, 278. *See also* France; Nabokov; Olympia Press

Goodheart, Eugene, xi n2, 25n1, 29n5

Goodrich, Peter, xi n1, 26n2, 134n22

Goriaeva, T. M., 33n10

Goscilo, Helena, 32n9, 246n35, 247n37, 252–53n41

gothic, 51n15, 66, 102–3n71, 114, 138, 146, 149, 227–29, 227–28n14. *See also* fantasy; ghosts; heroic; heroine; love; Russian gothic; vampires

Goya, Francisco, 165, 165n5, 188. *See also* painting

Great Britain, x, 1, 4n2, 6n5, 7, 11, 11n13, 12, 27, 28n3, 29, 30, 40nn1–2, 41, 45, 53, 74, 75n46, 88, 95n64, 98, 99nn69–70, 100, 102, 102–3n71, 250, 251, 270, 271, 277, 278

Greene, Graham, 29, 113n1, 129n17

Grimm brothers, 150, 251n40. *See also* fairy tale

Gubern, Román, 31–32nn7–8, 184n28, 194n35

gynecology, 229, 234, 254, 256, 266n55. *See also* abortion; birth; medicine; mothers; pregnancy

hallucination, 43, 44n10, 56n19, 61, 75, 77, 79, 83, 84, 87, 88–89n57, 92, 93n61, 94, 96, 97, 98n68, 100–106, 201, 218, 258, 270, 271

Hamlet (Shakespeare), 42, 56n19, 57, 58, 69. *See also* Shakespeare

Hathaway, Anne, 58, 69, 95. *See also* Shakespeare

Henke, Suzette A., 87n56

Herbold, Sarah, 113n2, 117

heroic, x, xiii, 32, 34, 40, 57, 57n21, 64, 90–91n60, 101, 102n71, 102–3n71, 105, 114, 141, 146, 162, 163, 172, 176, 194, 200, 212, 213, 216, 228, 237, 262, 271. *See also* heroine; *pícaro/pícara*; rogue narrators

heroine, 57, 76, 124n12, 136, 141, 217–20, 225–27, 227n14, 228, 230n18, 236n27, 237, 250, 256–58, 262, 273. *See also* heroic; *pícaro/pícara*; rogue narrators

Herr, Cheryl, 25n1, 41n2, 43, 44n9

Herzberger, David K., 31n7, 194n35

heteroglossia, 39, 44n9, 45, 51, 52, 56n18, 61, 65, 71n44, 83, 84, 98, 114, 139, 151, 191, 217, 227, 271. *See also* Bakhtin

histology, 170, 183, 189. *See also* cutting; Ramón y Cajal; science; vivisection

Hitchcock, Peter, 41n4

homoeroticism, 66, 73, 95, 100

homosexual, 6n5, 30, 49, 50n14, 59, 59n26, 73, 173, 227, 236, 244, 246–47n36, 254

husband. *See* marriage

Hutcheon, Linda, 219, 227, 263, 266

Ibsen, Henrik, 42–43, 43n5, 45, 46, 108

Idiot (*The Idiot*) (Dostoevsky), 36, 215, 223–25, 223n8, 225n10, 231, 233, 238n29, 250, 261, 266. *See also* Dostoevsky

Imaginary, the, xiv n4, 88, 236. *See also* Lacan; Real; Symbolic

incest, xiii, 15, 30, 34, 43, 43n5, 73–74n45, 76n47, 85, 117, 134, 136, 159, 162, 167, 171, 182, 183, 205, 208–10, 227n14, 246, 257, 263. *See also* child; fathers; mothers; pregnancy

interpellation, 34, 35n14, 175, 269

Ireland, x, 1, 7, 20, 39, 40–41n2, 41n4, 43, 49, 50, 53, 57n21, 58, 60, 65–66n36, 74–77, 75n46, 82–85, 92, 93n61, 94, 94n62, 95n64, 96–102, 98n68, 99n70, 104n73, 107–9, 107n75, 269–72, 272, 274, 277

irony, xi, 19, 27, 35, 275, 276; in *Lolita*, 113, 113n1, 116, 117, 117n4, 124–29, 124n12, 129n17, 134, 137, 139–41, 144, 146–48, 150, 153, 154, 156, 159, 160; in *Russkaia krasavitsa*, 216–19, 222, 223, 226n13,

229–36, 230n18, 239, 243, 248–52, 253n42, 255, 257, 257n47, 262, 266; in *Tiempo de silencio,* 161, 163, 165, 166, 168, 171, 172, 175, 175n16, 180n24, 185, 188, 193–97, 199n38, 200–202, 205, 210; in *Ulysses,* 46, 49n12, 51n13, 61, 62n32, 68n39, 77n48, 88, 93n61, 96, 100, 104. See also Hutcheon; parody

Jewishness, in *Ulysses,* 39, 51n13, 79, 79n51, 81–86, 82n53, 89n59, 271, 274; in *Tiempo de silencio,* 164, 184, 186; in *Russkaia krasavitsa,* 257
Joan of Arc, 218, 231, 234–40, 238n29, 254, 256, 260, 261, 270, 273
Jordan, Barry, 31n7, 212n47
Joyce, James, ix, xiv, 1, 7, 18, 20, 24–28, 25n1, 32, 38, 40, 40nn1–2, 41nn3–4, 43, 43n5, n6, and n7, 44n9, 45–47, 49n12, 50, 51n32, 64, 68, 68n40, 70, 71, 71n44, 73–74n45, 79n51, 84, 89n58, 90–91n60, 99, 107, 109, 120n7, 201, 201n39, 268, 275, 277. See also *Dubliners; Exiles; Finnegans Wake; Portrait; Stephen Hero; Ulysses*
judgment, x–xii, xiv, 2, 3, 10, 13, 15–20, 23–32, 28n4, 34, 36, 271, 272, 274, 276; in *Lolita,* 27, 113, 115–19, 122n10, 127–29, 137, 142, 144, 145, 152–60; in *Russkaia krasavitsa,* 34, 215, 217, 224–28, 231, 233–36, 238, 241–43, 241n32, 252, 253n42, 257, 260, 262, 265, 270; in *Tiempo de silencio,* 34, 162, 163, 185, 187n31, 188, 191, 193, 196, 205; in *Ulysses,* 24, 26, 28, 39, 41n3, 45, 47–54, 56, 57, 57n3, 58, 60, 63, 67–73, 77, 78, 80, 81–87, 88, 91–103, 105, 106, 111, 268–70, 274. See also castration; fathers; Law; trials
Justine. See Sade

Kaite, Berkeley, 12n16, 36n15, 61n31, 143n28
Kant, Immanuel, xi, 62–63n33, 227, 241, 241n32, 242, 261, 264n52
Kenner, Hugh, 42, 51n14, 78n50, 102, 102–3n71

Kermode, Frank, 230n19
knowledge, x–xii, xiv n4, 5, 8, 17, 17n19, 19, 23, 28, 30, 35, 37, 38, 274; in *Lolita,* 116–23, 128, 128–29n16, 129n17, 135, 138–43, 151, 159, 160; in *Russkaia krasavitsa,* 224, 235, 237, 243, 246, 246n36, 259, 262, 264, 269; in *Tiempo de silencio,* 163, 166–68, 172, 179, 190–93, 200, 206, 211, 212, 274; in *Ulysses,* 39, 52, 56n18, 58n24, 64, 65, 65–66n36, 68, 72, 75, 77–79, 78n49, 79n51, 82, 86, 88, 91, 97, 97–98n66, 105, 106. See also medicine; science
Kon, Igor S., 32n9, 245, 246

Labanyi, Jo, 32n9, 168n9, 180n23, 183, 183n27, 191n32, 193n34, 214
Lacan, Jacques, xiii, xiv n4, 8n10, 10, 10n11, 16, 18, 36n15, 49–50, 62–63n33, 76, 90–92, 96, 97, 106 110, 134, 168, 261, 273. See also fantasy; Freud; Imaginary; Real; Symbolic
Lady Chatterley's Lover (Lawrence), 25, 25n1, 29, 29n5. See also Lawrence, D. H.
Lawrence, D. H., xi, 28n4, 29, 29n5. See also *Lady Chatterley's Lover*
Law, xii, xiv, xiv n4, 7, 9, 14–18, 15n18, 23, 27, 31, 31n8, 35, 272, 273; and *Lolita,* 124, 125, 131, 134, 134n22, 137, 137n24, 139, 143n28, 157, 174; and *Russkaia krasavitsa,* 223, 246–47n36, 263; and *Tiempo de silencio,* 179, 187n31, 191, 201–9; and *Ulysses,* 62–63n33, 72–87, 78n49, 89n58, 92–95, 98, 101–6, 109
Legendre, Pierre, 11nn13–14, 26n2, 134n22
Leonard, Garry, 29n12
Lévi-Strauss, Claude, 10n11
Little Review, 7, 27, 40–41nn1–2, 68, 277
Lolita (Nabokov), x, 1, 1n1, 7, 17, 18, 20, 24, 26–30, 35, 36, 40n1, 112–60, 253, 262, 269, 270–75, 278; characters in: Annabel, 115, 119–21, 120nn6–7, 121n8, 132n20, 140, 144n29, 158, 270; Gustave Godin, 114, 124n13; Charlotte Haze, 114, 115, 128, 130, 131, 144n29, 147, 148, 155, 156, 156n37, 158; Dolores Haze, 112–60, 120n6, 122n10, 124n12, 125n15,

128–29n16, 129n17, 131n19, 136n23, 137n24, 139n26, 152n33, 269–75; Gustave Godin, 114, 124n13; Humbert Humbert, 18, 27, 29, 112–60, 178n21, 269–75; Monique, 115, 275; Miss Pratt, 114, 149, 271; Clare Quilty, 114–16, 124, 124nn12–13, 125n14, 131, 147–54, 158, 159; John Ray, Jr., 114, 116, 131, 158; Richard Schiller, 116, 124n13, 128–29n16, 136, 136n23, 147, 150, 151, 152n33, 159

love, 9, 11, 13, 19, 35–37, 272–74; in Lolita, 112, 115–24, 120n6, 121n9, 127, 129n17, 131–41, 132n20, 145, 148–52, 156, 159, 270, 273–75; in Ulysses, 50, 57, 58, 62–63n33, 65n36, 69–70n42, 75, 78–83, 78n49, 79n51, 86, 89, 92, 93n61, 94n63, 96–98, 97n66, 97–98n67, 100, 102, 104–9, 109n76, 270, 274. See also blason; fantasy; femme fatale; gothic; marriage

MacKinnon, Catharine, xi n1, 26n2, 143n28

Madame Bovary (Flaubert), xiv, xv, 6n5, 57, 57n22, 68, 141, 238, 238nn29–30. See also adultery; Flaubert; heroine

Manet, Édouard, 235, 235n26, 237, 237n28, 238, 264

marriage, ix, xi, 275; in Lolita, 112, 115–17, 128–29n16, 136, 139, 140, 144, 146, 147, 152n33, 155–57, 159, 270; in Russkaia krasavitsa, 35, 218–20, 223, 226–29, 226n13, 231, 232, 238n29, 244–52, 251n40, 255, 257, 257n46, 258, 260, 265, 266, 273, 275; in Tiempo de silencio, 164, 165, 202, 203, 210, 213, 273; in Ulysses, 39, 57–60, 58n25, 75, 76, 76n47, 83–87, 95n64, 102–3n71, 275. See also adultery; cuckold; love

Martin, Wallace, 46, 47

Martín-Santos, Luis, ix, xiv, 1, 8, 18, 20, 34, 37, 38, 161, 163, 162–63n3, 167–68n9, 172, 175, 175n16, 183, 191n32, 193n34, 201, 201n39, 203nn41–42, 214, 275

martyrs, 15, 48, 77, 83, 102, 172–76, 195, 200, 215, 217, 227, 229, 229n16, 231, 233, 234, 237–40, 243, 249, 253, 254, 260, 261, 269–71, 274. See also Christ; masochism; negation

masculinity, x, 17, 269, 271; and Lolita, 113n1, 129n17, 140, 155; and Russkaia krasavitsa, 217, 248, 249, 255, 256, 262n50; and Tiempo de silencio, 174, 187, 195, 197; and Ulysses, 39, 41n3, 47–53, 49n12, 51n15, 57, 59n26, 60–64, 61n31, 66, 73–76, 78, 83, 85–89, 92, 93, 95, 97n67, 102, 102n71, 105, 111. See also castration; fathers; heroic; homosexual; Law; masquerade; patriarchy; sons

masks, 43, 49, 49n12, 50, 99, 125, 133, 153, 188, 246–47n36, 271, 273, 274

masochism, 18; and Lolita, 122, 124; and Russkaia krasavitsa, 254; and Tiempo de silencio, 161, 162, 172–78, 179, 186, 189, 195, 200, 213, 214, 271, 273; and Ulysses, 40, 47–55, 56, 62, 75, 77, 78, 84–89, 87–88n56, 89n58, 92, 97n67, 102, 110, 268–70, 274. See also judgment; Law; martyrs; Sacher-Masoch; sadism; sadomasochism; trials; Venus in Furs; vivisection

masquerade, 44, 44n9, 47, 49, 49n12, 50–53, 57, 77–78n48. See also Lacan; masks; Riviere

masturbation, 17, 40n1, 41n3, 59, 68, 76, 120, 185, 186, 187n31, 197, 201n40, 208, 244, 277

maternal. See mothers

medicine, xii, xiii, 19, 32n9, 48, 77, 162–65, 168, 173–80, 173n15, 182, 188, 190, 200, 202, 203n42, 209, 212nn46–47, 213, 270–74. See also abortion; cancer; gynecology; pregnancy; science; vivisection

Memoirs of a Woman of Pleasure (Fanny Hill) (Cleland), 44–45n10, 144, 216. See also memory; narrative; prostitution

memory, 35; and Lolita, 115, 116, 119–21, 121n9, 134, 135, 138, 141, 144, 149, 158, 159, 190; and Russkaia krasavitsa, 34n13, 216, 219, 221, 222, 226, 233n24, 253, 253n43, 261, 265; and Tiempo de silencio, 166, 273; and Ulysses, 59, 61, 63, 67, 70, 71, 74, 77–80, 78n50, 85, 86, 91–103, 97–98n67, 102–3n71, 110, 270. See also

confession; narrators
Merchant of Venice (Shakespeare), 83. See also Shakespeare
Meredith, George, 102–3n71, 107, 107n74
mimesis, xiv; and *Lolita,* 112–14, 119, 120, 127, 136, 145, 148, 150, 151, 153, 270; and *Russkaia krasavitsa,* 218, 230, 264, 267, 269, 271; and *Tiempo de silencio,* 191; and *Ulysses,* 43–46, 43n7, 44n9, 49n12, 55, 56n20, 61–67, 68, 70, 71n44, 72, 77, 78, 86, 92–94, 98, 100, 105, 111. *See also* copy; double; fantasy; mask; masquerade; mirror; repetition; theater
mirror, 55, 58–60, 58n24, 63, 67, 79, 113, 118, 126, 131, 132, 134, 135, 171, 190, 192, 205, 223, 230, 255, 257n46, 264. *See also* copy; double; fantasy; gaze; mimesis; repetition
mitosis, 169, 170, 170n11, 196. *See also* cancer
Moll Flanders (Defoe), 216, 242, 262, 275
Moss, Kevin, 246–47n36
mothers, 37, 272; and *Lolita,* 115, 117, 128, 137n24, 138, 140, 147, 148, 156, 156n37, 158, 159; and *Russkaia krasavitsa,* 234, 250, 256, 261, 264, 267; and *Tiempo de silencio,* 165, 169, 172, 173n14, 179, 180, 199, 202, 205–8, 213; and *Ulysses,* 42, 47, 51, 53, 58n25, 59, 60n28, 62–63n33, 65–66n36, 66, 69, 77–78n48, 78, 78n49, 80, 88–89n57, 92, 93n61, 94–98, 96n65, 97–98n67, 98n68, 100, 102, 102n71, 105, 107–11, 109n76, 272. *See also* abortion; child; fathers; girl; gynecology; pregnancy; sons
Mozart, Wolfgang Amadeus, 76, 76n47
Mullin, Katherine, 40n2, 51n15, 52

Nabokov, Vladimir, ix, xiv, 1, 7, 18, 20, 24, 26, 28, 28n4, 29, 32, 38, 40n1, 113n1, 114n3, 117, 118n5, 123, 124, 125n15, 129n17, 130, 131n19, 132, 132n20, 137n25, 135, 140–42, 142n27, 154n35, 236n27, 275, 278. *See also* Erofeev; Girodias; *Lolita;* Olympia Press
Nadel, Ira, 79n51, 82–85, 82n53
Naiman, Eric, 32n9, 36, 37, 229, 249, 250

narrative, x–xiii, 15, 18, 19, 26, 27, 32–37, 268–76; and *Lolita,* 112–25, 124n13, 125n14, 127–60, 128–29n16, 137n25; and *Russkaia krasavitsa,* 215–27, 231–36, 235n26, 238–54, 254n44, 258, 260–67, 262n50, 266n55; and *Tiempo de silencio,* 161, 162, 165–71, 174–78, 175n16, 180–83, 187n31, 188, 191–200, 191n32, 192n33, 204–8, 205n44, 212, 212n46, 213, 214; and *Ulysses,* 39, 40, 43, 44n9, 45–48, 54–60, 56n20, 57n23, 61–64, 61n29, 62n32, 66–70, 70n43, 86–89, 87–88n56, 91, 100–5, 111. *See also* Bakhtin; character zone; confession; dialogism; discourses; focalization; heteroglossia; narrators; *pícaro/pícara;* rogue narrators
narrators, 18, 35, 36, 269; and *Lolita,* 112–19, 121n9, 122, 125n15, 126, 128–29n16, 130, 132, 132nn20–21, 133–36, 139–45, 144n29, 152–54, 157–60, 269; and *Russkaia krasavitsa,* 36, 216–20, 223, 232, 240–53, 246–47n36, 254n44, 258, 261, 262, 265, 269, 271; and *Tiempo de silencio,* 161–63, 165–68, 175n16, 180n24, 181, 183, 188, 191–96, 199, 201–14, 269; and *Ulysses,* 39, 40, 44–47, 44n9, 44–45n10, 49n12, 56n18, 57n23, 60, 65–66n36, 66, 67. *See also* Bakhtin; character zone; confession; dialogism; discourses; focalization; heteroglossia; mask; masquerade; narrative; *pícaro/pícara;* rogue narrators
national discourses. *See* discourses
Nausicaa, 40n1, 41n3, 44–45n10, 46, 68, 70n43, 77–78n48, 201n40, 277
necrophilia, 17, 66, 255, 256, 270. *See also* death; fantasy; gothic; masculinity; vampire
negation, x, 2, 6n7, 9–12, 18, 19–21, 27, 28, 33, 35–37, 36n15, 271, 272, 274; and *Lolita,* 122, 153, 159, 271, 272; and *Russkaia krasavitsa,* 215–17, 221, 224, 225, 231–33, 241–43, 249, 250, 256–60, 271, 272, 274; and *Tiempo de silencio,* 161, 162, 168, 170, 174–78, 185, 186, 191, 194–97, 201, 203n42, 207–14, 271, 272; and *Ulysses,* 49, 52, 53, 62, 62–63n33, 66, 71, 73, 88, 93, 95, 98–101, 104–5n73, 106,

108, 268–72, 274. *See also* abortion; apocalypse; castration; censoring; cutting; death; fantasy; judgment; masochism; sadism; vivisection
Norris, Margot, 43, 43n7, 51n14
Notes from Underground (Dostoevsky) 139, 141, 142, 215, 253. *See also* Dostoevsky
nymph, 77, 87, 112–15, 113n2, 120, 121n8, 122, 122n10, 125, 125n15, 126, 132, 132n20, 133, 136, 137, 140, 143, 145, 147, 152, 152n33, 157–59, 270, 274. *See also* child; fairy tale; fantasy; femme fatale; girl

"O, kak ubiistvenno my liubim" ("How murderously we love") (Tiutchev), 220–222, 261
obscenity, xi n1, 5–8, 11–15, 12n15 and n16, 25–32, 28n3, 35; and *Lolita,* 121, 128, 131–33, 143, 145–48, 154, 157, 160, 274, 278; and *Russkaia krasavitsa,* 238, 247, 250n39, 252, 260, 263; and *Tiempo de silencio,* 177, 178, 206, 209, 216; and *Ulysses,* 40n2, 41, 41n3, 56n19, 61, 71, 83, 85, 100, 277
Olympia Press, 7, 28, 29, 278. *See also* Girodias; Nabokov
The Ordeal of Richard Feverel (Meredith), 102–3n71. *See also* Meredith
oscillation, 19, 27, 39, 54, 55–60, 55n17, 70, 75, 119, 135, 166, 172, 174, 200, 206. *See also* censoring; confession; knowledge; narrative; negation
Othello (Shakespeare), 42, 60. *See also* adultery; cuckold; Shakespeare

painting, 102–3n71, 147, 157, 164, 165, 165n5, 184–88, 184n28, 229, 229nn16–17, 235, 235n26, 237, 237n28, 238, 245, 263, 264, 265, 267. *See also* photography
pantomime, 43–45, 55, 57, 102, 109–11, 109n77. *See also* commedia dell'arte; fantasy; mimesis; theater
Parkes, Adam, 25n1, 40n2, 41n3, 238n30
parody, 19; in *Lolita,* 116, 117, 127, 134–39, 137n25, 154, 155, 159, 160; in *Russkaia*

krasavitsa, 216, 217, 219, 220n4, 230–40, 256, 257n46, 261; in *Tiempo de silencio,* 165, 175, 187n31, 201n40; in *Ulysses,* 49n12, 52, 52n16, 57, 68, 88, 96, 101. *See also* Hutcheon; irony
paternal. *See* fathers; Law; patriarchal
patriarchal, 41n3, 78n49, 209, 246n35, 264. *See also* fathers; Law
Peace (*Eirene*) (Aristophanes). *See* Aristophanes
Pease, Allison, 40n2, 52
pedophile, 15, 17, 26, 30, 114, 120, 127–29, 139, 159, 270, 271. *See also* child; girl
Pérez Firmat, Gustavo, 180, 186n30
Pérez Galdós, Benito, 175, 180n24, 203n41, 209
performance, 6n5, 268, 269; in *Lolita,* 112, 113, 118, 120, 124n12, 128, 146, 147, 151; in *Russkaia krasavitsa,* 249; in *Tiempo de silencio,* 162n2, 164, 170, 171, 174, 189, 202, 211, 214; in *Ulysses,* 47–55, 49n12, 51n14, 56, 62, 66, 74, 75, 83, 87, 88, 93, 107, 268, 269. *See also* mask; masquerade; mimesis; narrators; theater
Peter Pan, 114, 114n3, 125, 125n14, 126, 150n32. *See also* Barrie; child; fantasy; girl
phantasy. *See* fantasy
Phelan, James, 113n2, 117, 122
La philosophie dans le boudoir (Sade). *See* Sade
photography, 86, 147, 148, 218, 223, 224, 237, 243, 253, 254, 260, 263–67, 271, 273. *See also* fantasy; film; gaze; mimesis; mirror; painting; pornography
picaresque, the, 139–41, 242. *See also* narrative; *pícaro/pícara;* rogue narrators
pícaro/pícara, 139–41, 242, 253, 269. *See also* heroic; heroine; narrators; picaresque; rogue narrators
police, 41, 100, 104, 107n75, 116, 165, 167, 168, 183n27, 187n31, 191, 202, 206, 210, 211, 213, 239. *See also* fathers; judgment; Law; trials
porno-graph, 218, 240–53, 260, 262. *See also* narrative; narrators; photography; pornography; prostitution

pornography, ix, xi, xi n1, 8, 12, 12nn15–16, 13, 15, 17, 25, 27, 30, 32, 36, 36n15, 61n31, 62n32, 143n28, 246n35, 247n38, 262n50, 265, 271, 274–75; in *Lolita*, 30, 114, 123, 124, 124n13, 126, 127, 139, 143, 143n28, 144, 271, 274–75; in *Russkaia krasavitsa*, 36, 216, 218, 228, 232, 234, 240–53, 246n35, 247n38, 256, 260, 262, 262n50, 263, 263n51, 265, 266, 271, 274–75; in *Tiempo de silencio*, 173, 174, 184–88, 201, 271, 274–75; in *Ulysses*, 30, 41, 41n3, 43n7, 51n15, 52, 61, 61n31, 62, 62n32, 65, 66, 69–70n42, 71, 72, 79, 84, 271, 274–75, 277. *See also blason;* fantasy; film; Kaite; MacKinnon; photography; porno-graph; Randall

Porter, Robert, 217n3, 220nn4–5, 222, 223n8, 226n13, 237, 238, 247n37, 254n45

Portrait of the Artist as a Young Man (Joyce), 51n14, 62n32, 68n40, 69, 95, 96n65, 101, 107, 107n5, 108, 120n7. *See also* Joyce

pregnancy, 37; in *Lolita*, 128–29n16, 136; in *Russkaia krasavitsa*, 37, 219, 228–31, 230n18, 234, 236n27, 242, 249, 250, 254–57, 260, 273; in *Tiempo de silencio*, 37, 164, 167, 169, 171, 187, 199, 206–11; in *Ulysses*, 65–66n36, 100. *See also* abortion; birth; cancer; child; fathers; gynecology; incest; mothers

prekrasnaia dama, 226, 229, 248, 250, 270. *See also* beautiful; beautiful woman; Blok

Princess Tarakanova in the Petropavlovsk Fortress (Flavitskii), 229, 229nn16–17. *See also* Flavitskii; painting

Prodigal Son, 74, 93. *See also* sons

prostitution, ix, xi, 12, 15, 17, 26, 34, 269, 274–76; and *Lolita*, 26, 115, 122, 133, 142, 144, 148, 159, 162; and *Russkaia krasavitsa*, 34, 216, 216n2, 218, 222, 227, 233, 244, 244–45n33, 245, 246, 246n35, 247n37, 248, 250, 250n39, 251, 278; and *Tiempo de silencio*, 34, 163, 173, 199, 200–208, 203nn41–42, 213; and *Ulysses*, 26, 39, 41, 41n4, 42, 49, 50, 51n15, 52, 53, 62, 62n32, 64, 65, 66, 71, 72, 74, 75, 76n47, 77n48, 84–88, 93, 95–100, 95n64, 99n70, 101

psychoanalysis, xiii, xiv n4, 2, 8–11, 8n10, 16, 23, 30, 92, 134n22, 166n6; and *Lolita*, 137–39, 137n25, 166n6; and *Tiempo de silencio*, 193, 202, 214; and *Ulysses*, 77, 88, 89, 89n58, 92, 128, 134n22. *See also* Freud; Lacan; Silverman; Žižek

Pushkin, Alexander S., 219–23, 226, 227, 230, 242, 251, 251n40, 252, 261

Ramón y Cajal, Santiago, 170, 171, 171n13, 175, 189

Randall, Richard S., xi n1, 12, 12n16, 26n2, 28n3, 143n28, 155n36

rape, 66, 127, 135, 137, 154, 157, 171, 178, 227–29, 249. *See also* gothic; pedophile; vampire

Real, the, xiv n4, 10, 16, 74, 88, 168, 183, 194. *See also* Imaginary; Lacan; Law; Symbolic

realism, 19, 32, 34, 44, 56n19, 62, 64, 67, 71, 71n44, 78, 85, 90–91n60, 92, 100, 141, 184, 191, 211, 236, 252, 253. *See also* mimesis; socialist realism; surrealism

repetition, 27, 39, 43n5, 54–56, 59, 65–66n36, 69, 71, 72, 75–77, 79n51, 82, 85, 88, 91, 95, 103, 107, 108, 112, 114, 117, 119–24, 132, 135, 137n24, 155, 157, 168, 169, 174–77, 180, 187n31, 194, 199, 200, 202, 207, 208, 219, 229, 226, 228, 253, 261. *See also* copy; double; fantasy; masochism; mimesis

Restuccia, Frances L., 50, 71n44, 89n58, 97n67

Riquelme, John Paul, 55, 56, 56n20

Riviere, Joan, 49, 52, 53

rogue narrators, 139–45, 153, 160, 240–53, 258, 269. *See also* confession; heroic; heroine; narrators; narrative; picaresque; *pícaro/pícara*

Rozanov, V. V., 32n9, 219, 232

Russian Beauty (Erofeev). *See Russkaia krasavitsa*

Russian gothic, 227–29, 227n14. *See also* gothic

Russkaia krasavitsa (Erofeev), x, 1, 1n1, 8, 17, 18, 21, 24, 34–37, 34n13, 215–67, 269, 271–73, 275; characters in: Flavitsky, 229, 234, 254, 256; Irina Tarakanova, x, 18, 35–37, 215–67, 269–71, 273–75; Ksyusha, 238n29, 243, 254, 265;Vladimir Sergeyevich (Leonardik; V. S.), 218–23, 221n6, 226–31, 234, 241, 244, 248–57, 252–53n41, 260, 263, 270, 273–75; publication history, 278–79
Rylkova, Galina, 220n5, 231n21, 232, 233n25, 236–37n27, 250, 254n45

Sacher-Masoch, Leopold, Ritter von, 47, 48, 54, 87n56, 89n58, 172. See also *Venus in Furs*
Sade, D. A. F. de, 123, 124, 124n12, 147, 155n36. See also pornography; sadism; sadomasochism
sadism, 51–54, 97n67, 125, 142, 143n27, 178
sadomasochism, 54, 254. See also masochism; sadism
San Lorenzo (St. Lawrence), 174, 176, 177n20, 200, 213, 271. See also martyrs
Sartre, Jean-Paul, 35, 161, 167–68n9, 214
scalpel. See cutting; histology; vivisection
Schiller, Friedrich von, 136n23. See also *Lolita* (character Richard Schiller); sublime
Schwaber, Paul, 52n25, 60n28, 77n48, 95
science, 18, 19, 30, 128–29n16, 139n26, 143, 162–75, 169n10, 170n12, 171n13, 178, 180n24, 181–83, 182n26, 187–90, 187n31, 196–200, 199n38, 203, 206, 208–13, 212–13nn46–47, 269, 270, 274. See also cancer; cutting; gynecology; histology; knowledge; medicine; mitosis; Ramón y Cajal; virus; vivisection
scopophilia, 207. See also fantasy; gaze; masochism; mirror; voyeurism
sexual reproduction. See medicine; pregnancy
Shakespeare, William, 42, 46, 51n14, 56–60, 56n19, 58nn24–25, 59n27, 67, 69, 70n43, 83, 92, 107, 223, 269, 270. See also adultery; cuckold; fathers; *Hamlet*; Hathaway; marriage; *Merchant of Venice*; mimesis; *Othello*; theater
Shakespeare and Company, 7, 28, 277
Shechner, Mark, 41n4, 90n60
Showalter, Elaine, 234, 262n50
Silverman, Kaja, 36n15, 61n31, 87–88n56, 172
Sloterdijk, Peter, 45
Smirnoff, Victor, 54. See also masochism
socialist realism, 33, 34, 226, 227, 238. See also realism; Soviet Union
Soloviev, Vladimir, 219, 232, 249, 250
Solzhenitsyn, Alexander, 225, 259
sons, 42, 51n14, 53, 57, 57n21, 58, 69, 72–81, 78n49, 83, 92–94, 94n63, 96, 97n67, 102–3n71, 104–7, 110, 111, 272, 273. See also child; Christ; fathers; mothers
Soviet Union, x, 1–3, 6–8, 7n9, 11n13, 20, 24, 31–37, 31nn7–8, 32n9, 33n10, 216–19, 216n2, 217n3, 223, 230–33, 235n26, 236–37n27, 237–41, 243, 245–48, 246–47nn35–36, 247nn37–38, 250, 252–58, 252–53n41, 253n42, 257n47, 260–67, 269, 272–74, 278
Spain, x, 1, 2, 6–8, 7n8, 11, 20, 31, 31–32nn7–8, 32–35, 32n9, 33n10, 35n14, 37, 161–63, 167n8, 168, 170, 170n12, 172–79, 175–76n16, 182, 184, 185, 188, 191, 194, 195, 199, 199n38, 203, 203–4nn41–42, 206, 208, 209, 212–14, 269, 271, 272, 278
Stephen Hero (Joyce), 68n40, 73–74n45
Stevenson, Robert Louis, 114, 114n3, 142, 143, 143n27, 262n50, 147–48. See also *Dr. Jekyll and Mr. Hyde*; *Treasure Island*
Stewart, Suzanne R., 48, 53, 87–88n56, 172
sublime, the, ix, xi, 17, 36, 60, 136n23, 149, 215, 216, 222, 227, 239, 240–53, 253–58, 260, 263, 264, 264n52, 273, 274. See also beautiful; Burke; Kant; Schiller; Žižek
surrealism, 56n19, 84, 90–91n60, 147, 148, 184n28, 234, 236, 254
Symbolic, xiii, xiv n4, 9, 34, 36n15, 49, 66, 73, 77–80, 88, 89n59, 105, 106, 168, 176, 212, 236, 242, 254, 256, 260–63, 271. See also Imaginary; Lacan; Law; Real

theater, 6n5, 18, 26, 39–49, 43n7, n8, 44n9, 44–45n10, 51, 51n14, 54–61, 56nn18–20, 59n27, 63–74, 70n43, 77–81, 81n52, 84–94, 87–88n56, 89n59, 97–98n67, 99–109, 107n75, 109n77, 113, 115, 116, 123–25, 124nn12–13, 125n15, 128, 131, 138, 139, 145–49, 150, 151, 154, 187n31, 205n44, 220n4, 230n18. *See also* discourses; *Enchanted Hunters*; mask; masochism; masquerade; mimesis; pantomime; Shakespeare; Yeats

Tiempo de silencio (Martín-Santos), x, xii, 1, 1n1, 8, 17, 18, 21, 24, 34–37, 161–214, 262, 269, 271, 272, 275, 278; characters in: Amador, 164, 179–81, 181n25, 193, 197, 210; Cartucho, 163, 165, 171, 174, 191, 210; Dorita, 162n2, 164, 165, 167, 170, 171, 174, 179–81, 183, 186, 187, 187n31, 191–93, 200, 205, 207, 211, 213, 214, 273–75; Encarna/Ricarda, 164, 165, 167, 172; Florita, 164, 165, 170, 171, 174, 179–83, 180n24, 182n26, 186, 187n31, 190, 192n33, 200, 201n40, 207, 209–11, 214, 273, 274; doña Luisa, 163–65, 172, 174, 179, 181, 184n28, 185–87, 191, 201–2, 204–206, 209, 213; Matías, 164–65, 165n5, 172, 174, 179, 181, 184n28, 185–87, 191, 201–2, 204–206, 209, 213; Muecas, 164, 167, 168, 171, 179–83, 180n24, 181n25, 193, 199, 199n38, 201n40, 203, 209, 210; Pedro, 18, 35, 35n14, 37, 161–214, 269–71, 273–75; don Similiano, 191, 202, 206; *la vieja*, 163, 164, 167, 172, 191, 205, 206, 213, 275; publication history, 278

Time of Silence (Martín-Santos). See *Tiempo de silencio*

Tirso de Molina, 175n16, 187n31

Tiutchev, Fedor, 219–22, 220n5, 221n6, 226, 227, 243, 261

Tolstoi, Lev, 57n22, 215, 226, 226n13, 261

trials, xii, xiv, 1, 6n5, 7, 10, 15, 25–30, 29n5, 31–32n8, 40–41nn1–2, 42n3, 68, 73, 81–87, 103, 115, 116, 130, 141, 143, 158, 186, 240, 243, 254, 268. *See also* discourses; judgment; Law; police; theater

Treasure Island (Stevenson), 147–48. *See also* Stevenson

Turko the Terrible, 109, 109n77, 110. *See also* pantomime; theater

Ulysses (Joyce), x, 1, 1n1, 7, 17, 18, 20, 21, 24, 25, 25n1, 27–30, 35, 36, 39–111, 120n7, 164n4, 201, 201n40, 262, 268, 272, 275, 277, 278; characters in: Ellen (Higgins) Bloom, 77–78n48, 80; Leopold Bloom, 18, 27, 39–111, 201n40, 268–75; Molly (Marion) Bloom, 42, 44, 49, 49n12, 56–58, 60, 67, 74–78, 75n46, 76n47, 77–78n48, 78n50, 81, 83–85, 87, 89n58; Rudolph Bloom, 51n14, 80, 81; Rudy Bloom, 42, 49, 76n47, 78–80, 78n50, 88–89n57, 92, 104–106, 110, 111, 274; Blazes Boylan, 50, 57, 58, 69, 74, 75, 76–77n47, 81, 87; Bella/Bello Cohen, 42, 51, 51nn14–15, 52, 56n19, 62, 64, 73, 73–74n45, 76n47, 77, 77–78n48, 84, 85, 90–91n60, 92, 98; May Goulding Dedalus, 49, 58n25, 78n49, 92, 94, 96–98, 102, 102–3n71, 107–10, 272, 274; Simon Dedalus, 50, 51n14, 75, 93, 94, 109n76; Stephen Dedalus, 18, 27, 39–111, 120n7, 268–74; Zoe Higgins, 65, 77n48, 87, 95n64; Virag Lipoti, 77, 79, 80, 90n60; publication history, 278

United States of America, x, xi n2, xiii, 1, 2, 4n2, 7, 20, 24, 25n1, 27–29, 28nn3–4, 40–41nn1–2, 68, 114, 115, 123, 128, 128–29n16, 131n19, 135, 136, 139, 139n26, 140, 146, 151, 153, 156, 164, 169, 179, 234, 237, 238n30, 269, 272, 275, 277, 278

vampires, 65, 66, 65–66n36, 97, 97–98n67, 102, 102n71, 114, 146, 147, 271. *See also* fantasy; ghost; gothic; masculinity; Russian gothic

Vanderham, Paul, 25n1, 40–41n2, 41n3

Venus, 43n7, 48, 83, 89n58, 135, 147, 148, 172

Venus in Furs (Sacher-Masoch), 43n7, 47, 48, 54, 83, 87n56, 89n58, 172. *See also* femme fatale; martyrs; masochism; Sacher-Masoch; theater

virus, 170n12, 179, 182n26, 198, 211, 212n46. *See also* cancer; medicine; science
vivisection, 188–90. *See also* cancer; castration; cutting; histology; masochism; medicine; Ramón y Cajal; science
voyeurism, 17, 62, 76, 123, 178, 183, 207, 210, 269. *See also* fantasy; gaze; mirror

Wagner, Richard, 48, 98
wedding. *See* marriage
Weininger, Otto, 51n13
"Who Goes with Fergus?" (Yeats), 47, 97–98n67, 102, 107–9, 111, 269. *See also Countess Cathleen;* Yeats
whore. *See* prostitution
wife. *See* marriage

Yeats, William Butler, 47, 92, 97–98n67, 102, 103, 107–9, 269, 270. *See also Countess Cathleen;* "Who Goes with Fergus?"

Ziarek, Ewa Plonowska, 65–66n36
Žižek, Slavoj, 17, 23, 37, 62–63n33, 241, 241n32. *See also* Burke; fantasy; Freud; Kant; Lacan